For
Not to be taken
from the room.
reference

HISTORICAL DICTIONARIES OF
U.S. HISTORY AND POLITICS

Jon Woronoff, Series Editor

Historical Dictionary of United States Political Parties

Second Edition

Harold F. Bass Jr.

Historical Dictionaries of
U.S. History and Politics, No. 14

The Scarecrow Press, Inc.
Lanham • Toronto • Plymouth, UK
2009

Published by Scarecrow Press, Inc.
A wholly owned subsidiary of The Rowman & Littlefield Publishing Group, Inc.
4501 Forbes Boulevard, Suite 200, Lanham, Maryland 20706
http://www.scarecrowpress.com

Estover Road, Plymouth PL6 7PY, United Kingdom

British Library Cataloguing in Publication Information Available

Library of Congress Cataloging-in-Publication Data

Bass, Harold Franklin.
  Historical dictionary of United States political parties / Harold F. Bass Jr. —
2nd ed.
    p. cm. — (Historical dictionaries of U.S. history and politics)
  Includes bibliographical references.
  ISBN 978-0-8108-5599-1 (cloth : alk. paper) — ISBN 978-0-8108-6322-4
(ebook)
  1. Political parties—United States—History—Dictionaries. I. Title.
JK2261.B345 2010
324.27303—dc22

                                                              2009015578

Contents

Series Editor's Foreword

The system of political parties in the United States is more complex than it first appears. Unlike their counterparts in nations with multiparty systems, the two major U.S. parties, the Democrats and the Republicans, must represent within their ranks an amazingly varied spectrum of voters, from liberal to conservative, as well as an array of special interests. Yet they have done an uncommonly good job, as shown by the stability and durability of the system. They are also less rudimentary and more solid than they seem. Though they lack the institutional machinery of many foreign parties, they nonetheless manage to accomplish their main tasks of selecting candidates, getting them elected, adopting policies, and implementing those policies.

This system, sometimes decried but more often admired at home and abroad, is the subject of the *Historical Dictionary of United States Political Parties*. The book consists of concise entries on the parties — major and minor, past and present — and their leaders. It includes all presidents and vice presidents, everyone who has received presidential votes in the electoral college, congressional party leaders, and national party chairs. The workings of the parties and the jargon associated with the party system are explained. The dictionary is supplemented by an introduction that provides a broad study of the system, a chronology, and a list of acronyms. Also useful is a well-structured bibliography covering the party system, the parties, and their leadership.

This volume was written by Harold F. Bass Jr. He is a professor of political science at Ouachita Baptist University, where he has taught for over two decades. His major teaching and research interests are the American presidency, political parties and elections, and political thought — in short, the subject matter of this book. He has published numerous journal articles, book chapters, and reviews. In this *Historical Dictionary of United States Political Parties*, Professor Bass has brought the various strands of our party system together to produce a very thorough and detailed compendium that should quickly become an essential tool for those in the field.

Jon Woronoff
Series Editor

Acronyms and Abbreviations

BCRA	Bipartisan Campaign Reform Act
COS	Conservative Opportunity Society
CREEP	Committee to Reelect the President
DAC	Democratic Advisory Council
DCCC	Democratic Congressional Campaign Committee
DLC	Democratic Leadership Council
DNC	Democratic National Committee
DSCC	Democratic Senatorial Campaign Committee
DSG	Democratic Study Group
FEC	Federal Election Commission
FECA	Federal Election Campaign Act
FCC	Federal Communications Commission
GOP	Grand Old Party
PAC	Political Action Committee
RCCC	Republican Congressional Campaign Committee
RNC	Republican National Committee
RSCC	Republican Senatorial Campaign Committee

Chronology

1787   14 May–17 September: Constitutional Convention meets in Philadelphia to consider a new federal government for the United States. Their proposal makes no reference to political parties, which have yet to appear on the national scene.

1788   June 21: New Hampshire ratifies proposed constitution, the 9th state to do so, and the new federal government is authorized.

1789   February: Inaugural electoral college designates George Washington as the first president and John Adams as the vice president. **4 March:** First session of Congress scheduled, but quorum is lacking. **April:** With quorum finally present, Frederick Muhlenberg is chosen first Speaker of the House of Representatives and John Langdon the first president pro tempore of the Senate, with the provision that he serve in that capacity only until the arrival of the vice president. **30 April:** Washington inaugurated. Partisan divisions soon appear within the new government, separating the Federalists, led by Secretary of the Treasury Alexander Hamilton, and the Democratic-Republicans, the supporters of Secretary of State Thomas Jefferson. This pattern of party competition is later labeled the First Party System. President Washington deplores this development and refuses to identify with either group, but his policies generally tilt in favor of Hamilton, whose followers also constitute a majority in both houses of Congress.

1792   December: Electoral college reelects President Washington and Vice President Adams. Clear partisan divisions emerge within the government, assembling as caucuses, and partisan organizations develop to mobilize the citizenry to support party nominees. The Democratic-Republicans take control of the House of Representatives for the 3rd Congress.

1793   4 March: Washington and Adams inaugurated for second terms on congressionally prescribed date. 4 March will remain inauguration day until adoption of the 20th Amendment in 1933 shifts it to 20 January, beginning in 1937.

1794   Federalists return to congressional power in midterm elections.

1796   With Washington declining to seek a third term, the presidential election becomes the first to be contested on openly partisan terms. **December:** Electoral college chooses John Adams, the choice of the Federalist caucus, to be president. His chief rival, Thomas Jefferson, the standard-bearer of the Democratic-Republican caucus, is the runner-up and thus becomes vice president.

1800   May: Congressional party caucuses renominate Adams and Jefferson as standard-bearers, along with respective running mates C. C. Pinckney and Aaron Burr. **November:** The Democratic-Republicans win majorities in both houses of Congress, ushering in a quarter-century of electoral dominance of both the White House and the Capitol. **December:** Presidential electors cast their ballots.

1801   11 February: Results of electoral vote announced. Rematch in the electoral college clearly goes to the Democratic-Republicans. However, their victory is complicated by the balloting procedure, which requires each elector to cast a single ballot with two names on it. A majority of electors vote for both Thomas Jefferson and his running mate, Aaron Burr, producing a tie and invoking the contingency procedure for election of the president by the House of Representatives. **February 17:** The House of Representatives resolves the presidential election by choosing Jefferson to be the chief executive. Burr thus becomes vice president.

1804   25 February: The Democratic-Republican legislative caucus nominates Jefferson for a second term but drops Burr from the presidential ticket, replacing him with George Clinton. **25 September:** 12th Amendment ratified, altering balloting arrangements in electoral college. **5 December:** Jefferson is reelected president against weak Federalist opposition in the person of Charles C. Pinckney. In initial separate balloting for vice president, Clinton is also easily elected.

1808   23 January: Jefferson follows Washington's precedent and declines to seek a third term. The party caucus designates James Madison as its presidential nominee. **7 December:** Madison wins comfortably in the electoral college over Federalist nominee Charles C. Pinckney.

1811 November: Freshman representative Henry Clay named Speaker of the House; his leadership invigorates the constitutional office.

1812 18 May: Madison wins caucus renomination. **2 December:** Madison prevails in presidential election.

1816 16 March: Madison retires from public life, passing the party torch to James Monroe, endorsed by the legislative caucus. **4 December:** Monroe elected against nominal Federalist opposition. In the wake of yet another national repudiation, the Federalist Party disintegrates, signaling the end of the First Party System and ushering in the Era of Good Feelings, a unique period without interparty competition.

1820 6 December: Monroe is reelected without partisan opposition. A single presidential elector casts a ballot for John Quincy Adams, to keep intact Washington's singular status as a unanimous choice.

1824 9 February: Factional rivalries emerge within the dominant Democratic-Republican Party, marking the end of the Era of Good Feelings. The caucus nominates William Crawford for president. However, party rivals John Quincy Adams, Andrew Jackson, and Henry Clay also seek to win the support of presidential electors. This development erodes the legitimacy of the caucus as a presidential nominating institution. **1 December:** With most electors now being designated by popular vote, electors increasingly serve as surrogates for presidential contenders. Jackson leads in both the indirect popular vote and the electoral vote but falls short of a majority required in the latter case, again necessitating election by the House. Calhoun elected vice president.

1825 9 February: House elects John Quincy Adams, the son of John Adams, president. Jackson immediately begins campaign for election to the presidency in 1828.

1826 4 July: On 50th anniversary of signing of the Declaration of Independence, Thomas Jefferson and John Adams, codrafters and later partisan rivals, die.

1828 3 December: Dominant Democratic-Republican Party now splits into two clear factions. President Adams leads the National Republicans against Jackson and the Democrats. Jackson easily prevails in the presidential balloting.

1831 26 September: Anti-Masonic Party holds the first national nominating convention, putting forward William Wirt for president. **December:** The National Republican Party follows suit and meets in convention, unanimously proposing Henry Clay for president.

1832 21 May: The Democratic Party holds its inaugural national nominating convention, adopting a rule requiring extraordinary two-thirds majorities to nominate presidential ticket. Convention endorses President Jackson for a second term and replaces out-of-favor Vice President John C. Calhoun with Martin Van Buren for the second spot on the presidential ticket. **5 December:** In the fall contest, Jackson wins reelection over National Republican Henry Clay, signaling the onset of a new era of party competition, the Second Party System. In a strong minor-party showing, Wirt wins 7.8 percent of the popular vote and carries Vermont, with seven electoral votes. **28 December:** Vice President Calhoun resigns in wake of policy disputes with President Jackson.

1835 20 May: Democratic National Convention follows the lead of retiring President Jackson in nominating Vice President Martin Van Buren for president.

1836 A new political party, the Whigs, a coalition embracing the now defunct National Republicans and Anti-Masons, along with dissident Democrats, emerges as the primary alternative to the Democratic Party. The Whig leaders decline to hold a national convention, instead authorizing regional tickets nominated by state legislatures. **7 December:** Van Buren wins the presidency that fall. However, the electoral college is unable to arrive at a majority choice for vice president, as Van Buren's running mate, Richard M. Johnson, falls one vote short.

1837 7 February: The Senate chooses Johnson as vice president.

1839 4–7 December: Whigs hold their first national convention, designating William Henry Harrison and John Tyler as their presidential ticket.

1840 5 May: Democrats renominate President Van Buren. **2 December:** Carried forward by the popular slogan "Tippecanoe and Tyler

Too," Whigs sweep the fall elections, winning majorities in both houses of Congress and the ensuing electoral college tally.

1841   4 April: President Harrison dies a month after his inauguration, elevating Vice President Tyler to the presidency.

1842 Democrats reclaim the House of Representatives in the fall elections.

1844 President Tyler's claim for a term in his own right is rejected by both Democrats and Whigs, as both parties spurn his candidacy at their nominating conventions. **27 May:** At the Democratic National Convention, former president Van Buren's comeback bid produces a first-ballot majority, but Van Buren continues to fall short of the required two-thirds standard. On the 9th ballot, convention nominates dark horse James K. Polk for president. **4 December:** In fall elections, Democrats reestablish united party government, returning to majority status in the Senate and prevailing in the electoral college balloting.

1846 Whigs win control of the House in the fall midterm elections.

1848   22–26 May: Democratic National Convention nominates Lewis Cass and establishes Democratic National Committee. **7–9 June:** Whigs nominate Mexican War hero Zachary Taylor. **August:** Former president Van Buren mounts a minor party campaign on behalf of the Free Soil Party. **7 November:** In the first presidential election held on uniform election day, Taylor prevails in the popular vote, securing sufficient electors to guarantee election. However, the Democrats retain control of Congress; so for the first time since the beginning of party competition, divided party government prevails at the outset of a presidency. Van Buren receives an impressive 10.1 percent of the popular vote but carries no states. (Hereinafter presidential elections are noted as of the general election rather than the electoral college balloting.)

1850   9 July: President Taylor dies. Vice President Millard Fillmore becomes the second accidental president.

1852   1–6 June: Democrats nominate Franklin Pierce for president. **16–21 June:** Whigs counter with Winfield Scott. **2 November:** Pierce prevails, and Democrats reestablish unified party government.

1854   7 November: With the unstable Whig coalition disintegrating as the slavery issue heightens in intensity, the Second Party System begins to unravel, while a new party, the Republicans, emerges and wins control of the House.

1856   2–5 June: Democrats nominate James Buchanan for president. **17–19 June:** Inaugural Republican National Convention establishes Republican National Committee and nominates John C. Fremont for president. **4 November:** Democrats return to power, as Buchanan wins the presidency and the House is restored to Democratic control.

1858   2 November: Republicans retake the House, as the Democrats also experience increasing factional division over the slavery question.

1860 Party system is in disarray. **23 April–3 May:** Democratic National Convention is severely divided and unable to arrive at a consensus choice required by the two-thirds rule. **9 May:** Former Whigs from the border states reconstitute themselves as the Constitutional Union Party, nominating former House Speaker John Bell for president. **16–18 May:** Republicans convene in Chicago and nominate favorite son Abraham Lincoln. **18–23 June:** Northern faction of Democratic Party nominates Senator Stephen A. Douglas. **28 June:** Southern Democrats put forward Vice President John Breckinridge as their presidential standard-bearer. **6 November:** With opposition severely divided, Republicans sweep the fall elections, winning control of the presidency and majorities in both houses of Congress, indicating that a new era of party competition, the Third Party System, is under way.

1864   7 June: With the Civil War raging, President Lincoln seeks and wins renomination, abandoning the Republican label in favor of a Union Party nomination. Andrew Johnson, a pro-Union Southern Democrat, joins the ticket as the vice presidential nominee. **29 August:** Democratic Party, minus its Southern wing, nominates General George McClellan for president. **8 November:** In the fall elections, Lincoln wins reelection as the Union ticket prevails.

1865   15 April: Amid celebration over the end of the Civil War, Lincoln dies, the victim of an assassin. Johnson assumes the presidency and quickly becomes embroiled in conflict with Radical Republicans in Congress over Reconstruction policy.

Harrison for president. Republicans also win back the House, restoring unified party government.

1890 12 March: Senate passes rule providing that once elected, its president pro tempore will hold that office at the pleasure of the Senate, until a successor is chosen. This measure greatly enhances the stability of the office. **4 November:** Republicans experience a crushing defeat in the midterm House elections, surrendering control to the Democrats.

1891 19 May: Populist Party appears on national scene, nominating James B. Weaver for president.

1892 In rematch of 1888 presidential contest, Cleveland succeeds in his comeback bid, winning the Democratic presidential nomination and then ousting Harrison in the fall elections. Weaver mounts a formidable minor party challenge, winning 8.5 percent of the popular vote and receiving 22 electoral votes. **8 November:** Democrats also win back the Senate, giving them unified party control of the national government.

1894 6 November: Midterm elections shift power on Capitol Hill back to the Republicans.

1896 18 June: With currency issues dominating the policy agenda, Republicans take a hard-money position and nominate Ohio Governor William McKinley. **1 July:** Democrats, seeking to bring the Populists into their coalition, embrace William Jennings Bryan and an easy-money stance. **3 November:** In the fall elections, Republicans complete their takeover of national government with a resounding presidential victory for McKinley. The impressive scope of the Republican triumph terminates the Third Party System, which had typically featured narrow Republican wins in presidential contests and unstable partisan majorities in Congress. The ensuing Fourth Party System demonstrates more reliable Republican domination.

1899 In 56th Congress, political parties in the House of Representatives initiate practice of officially designating floor leaders and whips.

1900 21 June: McKinley renominated, with Theodore Roosevelt as his vice presidential running mate. **5 July:** Democrats again turn to Bryan. **6 November:** McKinley prevails in rematch.

1901   14 September: President McKinley dies from assassin's bullet. Roosevelt assumes the presidency.

1903   Wisconsin becomes the first state to mandate primary elections for party nominees.

1904   21 June: Roosevelt becomes the first accidental president to receive a major party presidential nomination. **6–9 July:** Democrats counter with a hard-money nominee, Alton B. Parker. **3 November:** Roosevelt wins unprecedented election in his own right in the fall.

1908   16–20 June: Roosevelt declines to seek a second full term, designating William Howard Taft as his heir apparent. Taft receives Republican nomination. **7–10 July:** Democrats turn once again to William Jennings Bryan as their presidential nominee. **3 November:** Taft triumphs in presidential election. **8 November:** In midterm elections, Democrats secure control of the House, reinstituting divided party government. First Socialist elected to Congress.

1911   In 62nd Congress, political parties in the Senate follow House's lead in officially designating floor leaders. **12 December:** Former President Roosevelt indicates his intention to contest President Taft for the 1912 Republican presidential nomination.

1912   18 June: At Republican National Convention, Taft defeats Roosevelt. **25 June–2 July:** At the Democratic National Convention, James B. "Champ" Clark attains majority support on the 9th presidential ballot, but like Martin Van Buren in 1844, he falls short of the two-thirds requirement, and his delegate support begins to decline. On the 49th ballot, the convention nominates Woodrow Wilson, known as a progressive. **5 August:** Roosevelt bolts Republican Party, mounting a third-party campaign as the nominee of the Progressive Party, more popularly known as the Bull Moose Party. **5 November:** In the fall elections, Wilson wins a plurality of the popular vote and a convincing majority of the electoral vote. Roosevelt runs second, leaving Taft a poor third in the worst showing ever by a major party nominee. Socialist Party reaches peak of its popular support, winning 6 percent of the popular vote. Democrats win control of the Senate and retain their majority in the House, reestablishing unified party government.

1913   31 May: Adoption of 17th Amendment, providing for popular election of senators.

1916   Senatorial campaign committees are established by both Republicans and Democrats, to complement congressional campaign committees. **10 June:** Reunited Republican Party rallies behind Charles Evans Hughes. **14–16 June:** Democrats renominate President Wilson. **7 November:** Wilson, campaigning with the slogan, "He's kept us out of war," wins narrow reelection victory.

1918   5 November: Midterm elections, conducted in the waning days of World War I, transfer control of both houses of Congress to the Republicans.

1920   8–12 June: Republican Party nominates Senator Warren G. Harding (Ohio) for president. **28 June–5 July:** Democrats nominate Governor James M. Cox (Ohio) for president. **26 August:** 19th Amendment adopted, prohibiting states from using gender as a suffrage requirement. **2 November:** Republican tide advances, as Harding prevails in the fall elections with the potent slogan "Return to Normalcy."

1923   2 August: President Harding dies suddenly, amid rising allegations of scandalous conduct in his administration. Vice President Calvin Coolidge assumes the presidency.

1924   12 June: President Coolidge secures Republican presidential nomination. **24 June–10 July:** Faction-ridden Democratic National Convention requires an unprecedented 104 ballots to designate its presidential nominee, John W. Davis. **4 July:** Progressive Party nominates Senator Robert La Follette (Wisconsin) as its standard-bearer. **4 November:** Coolidge elected for a presidential term in his own right. La Follette makes good minor-party showing, winning 16.6 percent of the popular vote and 13 electoral votes.

1927   2 August: President Coolidge announces intention not to run for a second full term.

1928   12 June: The Republican National Convention turns to Secretary of Commerce Herbert Hoover as its standard-bearer. **26–29 July:** Democrats nominate Governor Alfred E. Smith (New York), the first

Roman Catholic to head a major-party presidential ticket. **6 November:** In the fall elections, Hoover wins a comfortable victory, extending GOP domination.

1929 29 October: Stock market collapses, signifying onset of Great Depression and ensuing decline of Republican electoral fortunes.

1930 4 November: With the Great Depression well under way, in the midterm elections Democrats win a majority of seats in the House.

1932 14–16 June: Republicans renominate President Hoover. **27 June–2 July:** Democrats turn to Governor Franklin D. Roosevelt (New York) as their presidential choice. **8 November:** Roosevelt soundly defeats Hoover. Democrats retain the House and win the Senate. Democratic victories inaugurate a new era of party competition, the Fifth Party System, featuring sustained Democratic dominance.

1933 6 February: 20th Amendment adopted, eliminating traditional lame duck congressional session and realigning schedule of presidential and congressional terms, shifting date for presidential inauguration to 20 January.

1934 6 November: Ascendancy of Democrats is confirmed, as party occupying the White House picks up seats in the midterm House elections.

1936 9–12 June: Republicans nominate Governor Alfred M. Landon (Kansas) for president. **23–27 June:** Democratic National Convention renominates President Roosevelt and abandons its controversial two-thirds rule in favor of a simple majority requirement for nominations. **3 November:** In the fall elections, Roosevelt carries all but two states in a landslide victory.

1940 9–12 June: Republican National Convention turns to outsider Wendell Willkie, a private citizen without experience in public office, as its presidential nominee. **15–19 July:** With war raging in Europe and Asia, President Roosevelt accepts nomination of Democratic National Convention for an unprecedented third term. **5 November:** Roosevelt wins reelection, breaking two-term tradition established by Washington.

1944 26–28 June: Republican Party designates Governor Thomas E. Dewey (New York) as its presidential nominee. **19–21 July:** With U.S.

troops in the field in Europe and the Pacific, Roosevelt is renominated for a fourth term. **7 November:** Roosevelt again prevails, winning the presidency for the fourth time.

1945   12 April: President Roosevelt dies. Vice President Harry Truman becomes president.

1946   5 November: In the midterm congressional elections, Republicans ask, "Had Enough?" Voters respond affirmatively, giving the GOP control of both houses.

1948   24 June: Republicans, anticipating victory in the upcoming presidential election, renominate New York Governor Thomas E. Dewey. **15 July:** President Truman succeeds in quest for nomination for a full term. Truman's nomination splits the Democratic Party, with factions bolting to support the Progressive Party under Henry Wallace and the States' Rights Democratic Party under Strom Thurmond. **2 November:** Truman unexpectedly overcomes significant party defections to prevail, and the Democrats also win back control of both houses of Congress.

1951   26 February: 22nd Amendment adopted, limiting presidential tenure to two terms.

1952   11 July: The Republicans nominate World War II hero Dwight D. Eisenhower, whose nonpartisan campaign slogan is "I Like Ike." **26 July:** President Truman, his popularity falling, declines to seek another full term. The Democrats turn to Illinois Governor Adlai Stevenson. **4 November:** Eisenhower wins presidency, with coattails long enough to restore Republican control of both houses of Congress.

1954   2 November: Midterm congressional elections return the Democrats to majority status in both houses. They will sustain that majority in the Senate until 1980 and in the House until 1994.

1956 13–17 August: Presidential contest features rematch. Democrats renominate Stevenson. **20–24 August:** Republicans again designate Eisenhower as standard-bearer. **6 November:** Eisenhower is reelected, but Democrats retain congressional control.

1960   13 July: Democrats nominate Senator John F. Kennedy (Massachusetts) for president. **25 July:** Vice President Richard Nixon wins the

Republican presidential nomination, the first incumbent vice president to win the party nomination since Martin Van Buren in 1836. **8 November:** In the fall elections, Kennedy prevails in a close race, becoming the first, and to date the only, Roman Catholic to be elected president.

1961   29 March: 23rd Amendment adopted, authorizing minimal representation in the electoral college for the District of Columbia, enabling its voters to participate in the presidential election.

1963   22 November: President Kennedy assassinated; Vice President Lyndon B. Johnson becomes president.

1964   23 January: 24th Amendment adopted, prohibiting poll tax as a suffrage requirement for elections to federal office. **15 July:** Republicans nominate candidate of their right-wing faction, Arizona Senator Barry Goldwater. **26 August:** Johnson nominated for a presidential term in his own right. **3 November:** In the fall elections, Johnson wins a landslide victory, carrying sweeping majorities of Democrats into office with him.

1967   10 February: 25th Amendment adopted, providing mechanisms for filling vacancy in the vice presidency and addressing presidential disability.

1968   8 February: Former Alabama governor George Wallace announces his intention to mount a third-party presidential campaign. **3 March:** President Johnson, facing challenges to his anticipated Democratic Party renomination from Senators Eugene McCarthy (Minnesota) and Robert Kennedy (New York), withdraws from presidential contention. **27 April:** Vice President Hubert Humphrey announces his presidential candidacy. **4–5 June:** On primary election night in California, where he won an important victory over McCarthy, Kennedy is assassinated. **8 August:** Richard Nixon captures Republican presidential nomination. **26–29 August:** Humphrey prevails at tumultuous Democratic National Convention. **5 November:** In general election, Nixon wins a narrow plurality of the popular vote and a clear majority of the electoral vote, whereas Wallace, in an impressive showing, wins 13.5 percent of the popular vote and carries five Southern states.

1972   7 April: Federal Election Campaign Act (FECA) goes into effect, dramatically extending federal regulation of campaigns. **10–13 July:** In the aftermath of significant reform of the presidential nomination process within the Democratic Party, Senator George McGovern (South Dakota) wins the presidential nomination. McGovern designates Jean Westwood as the national party chair. She is the first woman to head a major party's national committee. **21–23 August:** President Nixon renominated. **7 November:** Nixon prevails with a landslide victory, amid allegations that Watergate scandals link leading members of his campaign organization and his administration to improper and illegal behavior.

1973 Watergate inquiries in media and Congress gain momentum, undermining Nixon's political base. **10 October:** Vice President Spiro Agnew, under criminal investigation for unrelated charges that he had been collecting illegal kickbacks from contractors in his native Maryland, resigns. **12 October:** Under provisions of 25th Amendment, Nixon nominates House Minority Leader Gerald Ford to be vice president. **6 December:** Majorities in both houses of Congress approve the Ford nomination, and he is sworn in as vice president.

1974 **9 August:** His political base in precipitous decline from ongoing revelations in Watergate scandals, and facing imminent impeachment by the House, President Nixon resigns, and Vice President Ford is elevated to the presidency. **20 August:** President Ford nominates New York Governor Nelson Rockefeller to fill vacancy in vice presidency. **16 September:** With a vacancy in the position of chair of the Republican National Committee (RNC), President Ford elevates Vice Chair Mary Louise Smith, making her the first woman to head the RNC. **10 October:** FECA modified to provide for public funding of presidential campaigns and restrictions on raising and expending campaign funds. **19 December:** Rockefeller's nomination is confirmed by Congress, and he is sworn in as vice president.

1976 **14 July:** Former Georgia governor Jimmy Carter wins Democratic presidential nomination. **19 August:** President Ford is nominated by Republican National Convention for a term in his own right, surmounting a formidable challenge from California Governor Ronald Reagan. **2 November:** Carter prevails in a close election, making Ford the first incumbent president since Hoover to suffer defeat at the polls.

1980 **14–17 July:** Former governor Reagan succeeds in quest for Republican presidential nomination. **11–14 August:** President Carter overcomes a strong challenge from Senator Edward Kennedy (Massachusetts) to win the Democratic nomination. **4 November:** The fall contest matches the major party nominees against Independent John Anderson. Reagan wins a convincing victory, and the Republicans win a majority in the Senate for the first time since 1954.

1984   16–19 July: Democrats nominate Walter Mondale, vice president under Jimmy Carter, for president. Mondale designates Representative Geraldine Ferraro (New York) as his running mate. She is the first woman to appear on the presidential ticket of a major political party. **11–14 August:** Republicans renominate President Reagan. **6 November:** Reagan wins a landslide popular and electoral vote victory.

1986   4 November: In the midterm congressional elections, the Republicans lose control of the Senate.

1988   15–18 July: Democrats select Governor Michael Dukakis (Massachusetts) as their presidential nominee. **15–18 August:** Vice President George Bush wins the Republican presidential nomination. Bush prevails in the fall elections, making him the first incumbent vice president to be elected president since Martin Van Buren in 1836.

1992   13–16 July: Democrats choose Arkansas Governor Bill Clinton as their presidential nominee. **17–20 August:** Republicans renominate President Bush. **3 November:** Clinton emerges victorious in the presidential race that features a strong third-party challenge from independent Ross Perot, who wins an impressive 19 percent of the popular vote.

1994   5 November: In the midterm congressional elections, Republicans sweep to victory in both chambers for the first time since 1954, reinstituting divided party government.

1996   12–15 August: Republicans nominate Robert Dole, who had recently resigned his Senate seat and his majority leadership position to devote full time to the presidential quest. **26–29 August:** President Clinton renominated. **5 November:** President Clinton wins comfortable reelection. Perot, now running under the label of the Reform Party, sees his popular vote percentage reduced by more than half. Republicans retain control of Congress, as divided party government persists.

1998   3 November: In midterm House elections, Democrats pick up five seats, the first time since 1934 that the president's party has improved its position in the House at midterm. Republicans maintain majority control of both chambers for the third straight election, for the first time since the decade of the 1920s. **19 December:** Republican House impeaches President Clinton, charging him with perjury and obstruction of justice.

1999   12 February: Senate trial acquits President Clinton of charges brought forward by House.

2000   25 June: Green Party gives presidential nomination to consumer advocate Ralph Nader. **31 July–3 August:** Republicans nominate Texas Governor George W. Bush for president. **14-17 August:** Democrats nominate Vice President Al Gore for president. **7 November:** Gore narrowly leads in popular vote for president, but election outcome uncertain, with the vote in Florida, whose 25 electoral votes will determine the winner, too close to call. Bush emerges with small lead that is sustained by a required voting machine recount. Gore requests manual recounts in four populous counties. Legal challenges in state and federal courts wind up in the Supreme Court. Congressional election outcomes leave GOP in control of the House, and the Senate is evenly divided, making the vote of the vice president the determining factor for party control. **12 December:** Supreme Court rules against Gore's request for further hand counts, leaving Bush's victory margin intact. **18 December:** Presidential electors, including Bush electors in Florida, meet and cast ballots, providing Bush with a bare majority of 271 electoral votes. The same majority of electoral votes for Republican vice presidential nominee Richard Cheney signifies that Republicans will again control the Senate in the 107th Congress

2001   3 January: 107th Congress convenes, with Democrats taking temporary control of the Senate, thanks to tie-breaking vote by outgoing vice president Al Gore. **20 January:** Inauguration of Bush and Cheney places Senate back under Republican leadership. **5 June:** Republican Senator James Jeffords (Vermont) declares himself an independent who will caucus with the Democrats, making them the majority party in the chamber. **11 September:** Terrorist attacks on New York City and Washington generate strong rallying effect, dramatically elevating public support for President Bush.

2002   **5 November:** In midterm congressional elections, Republicans regain control of Senate and extend House majority.

2004   **26–29 July:** Democratic National Convention nominates Senator John F. Kerry for president. **30 August–2 September:** Republican National Convention renominates President George W. Bush. **2 November:** President Bush reelected; Republicans increase majorities in both congressional chambers.

2006   **7 November:** With President Bush's popularity in decline, midterm elections provide Democrats with majorities in both chambers of Congress for the first time since 1995.

2007   **4 January:** 110th Congress convenes. House of Representatives elects Democrat Nancy Pelosi (California) Speaker, the first woman to hold that office.

2008   **25–28 August:** Democratic National Convention meets in Denver and nominates Senator Barack Obama (Illinois) for president. Obama is the first African American to receive a major party nomination. **1–4 September:** Republican National Convention meets in Minneapolis–St. Paul and nominates Senator John McCain (Arizona) for president. The vice presidential nominee, Sarah Palin, governor of Alaska, is the first woman nominated to run on a Republican presidential ticket. **7 November:** Obama elected president, and Democrats increase majorities in both houses of Congress.

2009   **20 January:** Obama inaugurated, reinstituting united Democratic Party government for the first time in 14 years.

In this attempt, Jefferson assembled and integrated for the first time all three distinct structural elements of a modern political party: a party-in-office, a party organization, and a party-in-the-electorate. *Party-in-office* pertains to those individuals who hold public office under the banner of the political party, along with those who aspire to do so. *Party organization* refers to the apparatus of the party, its machinery at the national, state, and local levels in the U.S. political order. Party organization activists now gather as committees, conventions, and headquarters staffs. The *party-in-the-electorate* consists of voters and potential voters, who, with varying degrees of commitment, support a party's nominees and its programs. In sum, then, a political party can be conceived of as an entity seeking electoral authorization for its specified representatives to occupy public offices and make public policies.

Jefferson's integrating initiative required a similar effort from Hamilton, who had to go beyond his own party-in-office to develop a party organization to mobilize voters on behalf of nominees committed to his agenda. Such an innovative response of course depended on the presence of an electorate authorized to fill public offices, a condition relatively rare on the international scene in the era of the constitutional framers.

HOW PARTIES TRANSFORMED U.S. POLITICS

Having quickly emerged on the national scene, political parties have maintained their central presence ever since. Their extraconstitutional origins notwithstanding, political parties in the United States have been profoundly shaped by the constitutional framework. In particular, the constitutional principles of separation of powers and federalism have guided and directed the course of party development. The separation of powers principle has generated conflict within the party-in-office, dividing the White House and the Congress even when the same party controls both chambers. Further, this principle makes possible divided party government, whereby different parties control different branches. The federal principle divides the party-in-office along vertical lines: national, state, and local. It similarly affects the party organization, which parallels governmental organization at any level. Thus, the constitutional order generally promotes fragmentation and decentralization within the political parties. Conversely, as will be shown below, parties can also build bridges to unify separated branches and levels of government, providing a foundation for coherence otherwise thwarted by the constitutional design.

Once established, political parties have profoundly affected the subsequent development of the constitutional order. Indeed, it is virtually impossible to describe and comprehend the organization and operation of the U.S. political system without repeated references to them. Their presence quickly necessitated a formal amendment to the Constitution, the 12th, which alters the balloting arrangement in the electoral college. Indeed, that institution's role and status have been substantially reshaped and reduced by the presence of parties.

Less formally, parties have effectively transformed the process of presidential selection into one that features far more popular participation than that envisioned and instituted by the constitutional framers. In doing so, the parties have elevated the status of the presidency in the constitutional order.

In nominating presidential tickets, political parties placed their presidential nominees atop the list of their nominees for lesser offices, conferring the status of party leader on each party's presidential nominee. After being elected president, that party leader then had a basis for claiming to be more than the constitutionally established chief executive. There was now a basis for claiming to be government leader as well, with the idea and organization of party uniting the constitutionally separated institutions under the leadership of the president.

Indeed, the president's claim to leadership could embrace the party-in-the-electorate as well as the party-in-office. Linking up with the public gave the president a base of national support unavailable to any other government official. This development both contributed to and was a product of the increasing democratization of the American political culture. Finally, the evolving presidential prerogative of naming the national party chair enabled the president to assert leadership over the party organization. In all these ways, then, the emergence of parties effectively empowered the presidency in the political order.

In a somewhat different fashion, parties transformed the organization and operation of Congress. Two parties soon supplanted 13 states as the chief organizing units aggregating individual members of Congress. Thus, the two-party pattern clearly made it easier to assemble majority coalitions of legislators. Moreover, selection of congressional leadership quickly became partisan. Congressional party caucuses came to designate occupants of the institution's constitutional offices, the emerging floor leadership positions, and committee assignments and leaders as well.

Moreover, within the executive and the judiciary, party identity and loyalty emerged as central foundations for claims to, and awards of, governmental positions. Parties provided criteria for filling vacancies, via executive appointments or nominations and legislative confirmations, again potentially serving as a unifying force in the political order.

Political parties thus positioned themselves at the very center of political life in the United States. They became key intermediary institutions, connecting masses with elites and fragmented elites with one another.

PARTY NOMINATIONS

Since their origins in the 1790s, at the heart of party activity in the United States has been the nomination of candidates for public office. This activity emerged informally and extraconstitutionally on the national level. At the state level, however, it has come under the authority of law.

Initially, the national parties nominated their presidential tickets through the legislative caucus. Like-minded partisans in the national legislature assembled and agreed on their nominees. By the 1820s, this institution was in precipitous decline, a victim of party factionalism and allegations of elitism in an increasingly democratic political culture. A new institution, the national party convention, soon supplanted the caucus, bringing together representatives from the party rank and file in the states to designate the presidential ticket. This shift from legislative caucus to convention empowered the party organization at the expense of the party-in-office. The convention quickly became the norm for party nominations at all levels of the federal system.

Ironically, toward the end of the 19th century, the convention came under attack for its alleged elitism. A new generation of reformers promoted the notion of a primary, or party election, to choose nominees.

This idea resonated with the ever-advancing democratic norms of the culture. Primaries empower the party-in-the-electorate within the party structure. States quickly embraced primary nominations, while the convention endured for presidential nominations. However, a century later, presidential primaries, which select delegates to the national party conventions, now effectively determine presidential nominations.

State party organizations nominate presidential electors, who are then elected by popular vote in their states. These slates of electors run as surrogates for the presidential nominees to whom they are committed. Thus, the popular selection of electors effectively determines the subsequent decision of the electors designated in the Constitution.

PARTIES AND GOVERNANCE

Complementing the pervasive electoral activities of U.S. political parties are programmatic endeavors. Although generally less focused than their European counterparts, American parties articulate and advocate distinctive ideological and issue positions. In the United States, this party function is often muted by the centripetal tendencies of the two-party system in a culture that values consensus.

Political parties seek control of the machinery of government. Winning elections is both an end in itself and a means to an end: the opportunity to enact public policies in keeping with the party's principles and programs. However, formidable structural and cultural barriers impede this governing aspiration.

A TWO-PARTY SYSTEM?

In studying political parties in a particular setting, or party system, a distinction must be made between major parties and minor parties. A major party is one that competes with a realistic prospect of winning political offices for its nominees and taking control of the government. An abiding feature of party competition in the United States has been its two-party character. That is not to say that only two parties occupy the political landscape; far from it. Typically, however, two major parties have competed for control of the government, with minor parties playing a peripheral role. The United States is thus characterized as a two-party system, one of a relative handful, as distinguished from single-party and multiparty counterparts elsewhere in the world.

The two major parties at any given point in time constitute coalitions of factional interests that are social, economic, ideological, and demographic in composition. These party coalitions are dynamic entities, featuring the embrace of emerging interests and shifts of established interests from one party to another.

The enduring presence of two major parties, and the difficulties minor parties face in challenging them, can be attributed primarily to prevailing electoral arrangements, particularly single-member electoral districts in which the winner takes all. In addition, distinctly historical and cultural factors contribute to the two-party pattern.

This reality should not diminish the significance of minor political parties in U.S. politics. Without realistic prospects of winning electoral offices, at least in sizable numbers, minor parties often elevate issues that the major parties initially decline to confront. Such initiatives often force a response from the major parties in an effort to bring outsiders into the party's electoral coalition and enhance its prospects of winning elections.

Eras of Party Competition

The major parties have competed for political power in the context of distinctive historical eras in which particular competitive patterns manifested themselves. Scholars surveying the history of U.S. political parties typically focus on these sequential party systems, distinct eras, and patterns of competition between the two major political parties. There have been five such systems in the past; we now appear to be in the sixth.

First Party System (1790s–1820s)

The pioneering Democratic-Republicans and Federalists maintained their adversarial relationship for over a quarter-century, from the 1790s to the 1820s, an era that has come to be labeled the First Party System. In subsequent decades, although the two-party pattern has typically persisted, the party labels and partisan coalitions of electoral forces they embraced have undergone substantial periodic transformations.

In the critical election of 1800, the Democratic-Republicans prevailed in dramatic fashion, winning the presidency for their standard-bearer, Jefferson, and gaining majorities in both houses of Congress. The Federalists, no longer dominant, steadily declined, and by the middle of the century's second decade, they were a spent force. They ceased to compete nationally after the 1816 presidential election, inaugurating the short-lived Era of Good Feelings, absent interparty competition, which left the Democratic-Republicans without organized opposition.

Second Party System (1820s–1850s)

By the mid-1820s, however, factional division within that party signaled an end to good feelings. In less than a decade, these factions transformed themselves into separate political parties, the Democrats and the Whigs, who battled for control of the national political arena for the next quarter-century. The Democrats championed the person and causes of Andrew Jackson; the Whigs assembled, in unstable fashion, diverse anti-Jackson forces in the body politic. The Democrats generally prevailed, but in the decade of the 1840s, the Whigs experienced noteworthy successes, winning two presidential elections. In addition, they once won both houses of Congress, and on two other occasions, a single chamber fell under their control.

The intensifying slavery controversy divided and undermined both major party coalitions. The Whigs essentially disintegrated after the 1852 presidential election, signaling the end of the Second Party System. By 1860, the Democrats were also in disarray, split into apparently irreconcilable Northern and Southern wings.

Third Party System (1850s–1896)

Meanwhile, a new party appeared on the scene to replace the Whigs. Taking advantage of the growing divisions in the Democratic camp, the Republican Party assembled a majority in the House in 1854 and again in 1858, and it won the presidency and the Senate as well in 1860, demonstrating that a Third Party System was now clearly under way. Ever since, Democrats and Republicans have remained the major combatants in partisan battle.

In the initial distinctive era of their party competition, which lasted until 1896, the Republicans generally prevailed, by relatively narrow margins, in the quadrennial presidential contests. The Democrats were able to win only two interrupted presidential terms for Grover Cleveland, in 1884 and 1892. During this period spanning over three decades, they similarly controlled the Senate in only two Congresses. However, the Democrats were somewhat more successful in the House races, winning majorities in 8 out of 18 elections. During this time of heated party competition, minor parties flourished. Notable among them were the Greenback Party, the Liberal Republican Party, the Prohibition Party, and the People's Party.

Fourth Party System (1896–1932)

With the critical election of 1896, yet another distinctive era of party competition emerged, the Fourth Party System. It featured clearer Republican dominance, centered in regional strongholds in the Northeast and Midwest. The minority Democrats remained solid in the South and competitive in the West. Republican ascendancy in Congress was interrupted when the Democrats took control of the House in the 1910 midterm elections. Two years later, with the Republicans severely divided, the Democrats retained the House and also won the Senate and the White House, with Woodrow Wilson as their standard-bearer for two presidential terms. The 1912 election featured the temporary collapse of the Republican coalition. Former president Theodore Roosevelt, rebuffed in his effort to regain the party's presidential nomination, mounted a formidable third-party campaign and ended up outpolling his one-time heir apparent, President William H. Taft.

Four years later, the Grand Old Party (GOP), as the Republicans were known, was reunited, but incumbency enabled Wilson to squeak through with a narrow reelection victory. Normalcy began to return with the Republican successes in the midterm 1918 elections and persisted with a presidential triumph for Warren G. Harding in 1920. The Republicans continued to dominate throughout the decade.

Fifth Party System (1932–?)

However, the onset of the Great Depression in 1929 anticipated the conclusion of this Republican era, as an electoral realignment, portended in the Democratic successes in the House in the midterm elections of

1930, again elevated the Democrats to majority party status. Franklin D. Roosevelt spearheaded the Democrats' return to sustained national dominance for the first time since the slavery controversy shattered the Democratic coalition on the eve of the Civil War. Roosevelt carried through on his campaign promises of a New Deal, and the heightened level of federal government activism had immediate and substantial political benefits for sizable elements of the electorate. The outbreak of World War II reinforced this development. Roosevelt's unprecedented election to four terms, while the Democrats maintained control of both houses of Congress, made clear the transformed character of party competition, now known as the Fifth Party System.

The Republicans rebounded temporarily in the midterm elections of 1946, when they won majorities in both houses of Congress. They looked forward with anticipation to the 1948 presidential election, with their longtime nemesis, Franklin Roosevelt, now dead and his successor, Harry Truman, appearing extremely vulnerable. However, Truman overcame substantial internal Democratic Party division to win an amazing upset victory in his bid for a presidential term in his own right, and his coattails carried the Democrats back into control of Congress as well.

Four years later, the Republicans swept back into power at the national level, behind the potent appeal of their presidential nominee, General Dwight D. Eisenhower, who had commanded the Allied forces in Europe during World War II. Despite the Democrats' victories in the 1954 midterm congressional elections, which they sustained for over a quarter-century, Eisenhower won reelection handily in 1956. These developments indicated the onset of a new norm of divided party government. Heretofore, this situation had been relatively rare, occurring typically as a temporary product of midterm elections. In the ensuing decades, it became commonplace.

This developing pattern of sustained divided government was interrupted by eight years of unified party government under Democratic control from 1961 until 1969. John F. Kennedy, by a nose, and Lyndon B. Johnson, by a landslide, led the party ticket to presidential victories complemented by congressional majorities in 1960 and 1964. However, the election of Republican Richard Nixon to the presidency in 1968, alongside a Democratic Congress, reinstated divided government for another eight years. This proved to be a time of extraordinary partisan and institutional conflict between the executive and legislative branches of government, featuring an unprecedented presidential resignation that short-circuited apparently imminent impeachment, conviction, and removal.

Jimmy Carter's election to the presidency in 1976 briefly reinstituted unified party government. Four years later, Carter lost his reelection bid to Republican Ronald Reagan, and the Democrats lost control of the Senate for the first time since 1954, while retaining their long-standing hold on the House. Divided government persisted throughout Reagan's two terms. Indeed, in the 1986 midterm congressional elections, the Democrats recaptured the Senate. Divided government also characterized the ensuing presidential term of George H. W. Bush.

Democrat Bill Clinton defeated Bush when the latter sought reelection in 1992, and there was a brief period of unified party government, but the Democrats lost control of the entire Congress in the midterm elections of 1994. This development, coupled with Clinton's reelection as president, reversed the customary pattern of divided government since the Eisenhower presidency, in which a Republican president confronted a Democratic Congress.

George W. Bush, son of the former president, won the hotly contested and bitterly disputed 2000 presidential election over the incumbent vice president, Al Gore. For most of the next six years, the Republicans enjoyed unified party government, their longest such tenure since the 1920s. Early on, the GOP benefited from the aftermath of terrorist attacks on September 11, 2001, which generated a rally in public support of the president. Having initiated a war in Iraq, the president won reelection in 2004. By 2006, public support for the war and the president was in steep decline. The Democrats won back control of both congressional chambers for the first time since 1995, reinstating the more common post–World War II pattern of divided party government.

In 2008, the electoral tides continued to favor the Democrats. They expanded their majorities on Capitol Hill. Moreover, they reclaimed the White House and reinstated unified party government under their banner for the first time since 1994. Their presidential nominee, Barack Obama, the first African American to be elected president, won convincing victories in both the popular vote and the electoral college.

Sixth Party System?

Moving beyond the heightened incidence of divided party government, the broader pattern of party competition since 1952 differs in significant respects from earlier patterns. In particular, the regular alternation of party control of the White House experienced since 1952, with no party winning more than three consecutive presidential elections, is abnormal. Further, evidence mounted during the 1970s that for voters, party identification lacked the intensity of commitment that apparently prevailed and structured voting behavior for previous generations, though this pattern ebbed in ensuing decades. The coalitional foundations of the two major parties realigned as well, most notably with the shift of white Southerners into the Republican ranks. These altered patterns indicate that the Fifth Party System, grounded in the New Deal era, has given way to a new, Sixth Party System. However, establishing a precise time frame for the transition has proven problematical.

ORGANIZATION OF THE DICTIONARY

Specific entries address these partisan developments and topics both historically and conceptually. The bulk of the entries are about party leaders, those individuals who meet the following criteria. All of the nominees on major party presidential tickets are identified, as well as those minor party presidential nominees who attained noteworthy support from voters and/or presidential electors. For the sake of completeness, all those who received electoral votes prior to the advent of partisan competition are also noted. Joining their ranks are congressional party leaders, divided into several categories: Speakers of the House of Representatives, presidents pro tempore of the Senate, and floor leaders for both the majority and minority parties in each chamber. Complementing these elected officials are the chairs of the national party committees of the Democratic and Republican Parties. Brief biographical entries sketch the public lives of these subjects.

Party leaders represent two of the three distinct structural components of a modern political party: party-in-office and party organization. In addition to identifying party leaders, this volume includes entries for the institutional offices they occupy and represent in the party-in-office and the party organization.

The third membership component of party, unrepresented in these entries on individuals and offices, is the party-in-the-electorate. Political parties in the United States can be distinguished from their counterparts in other settings by the extraordinary extent to which they focus on electoral activity. Thus, many of the concepts enumerated here pertain to voting behavior and the electoral process, embracing the campaigns that occur for party nominations and for general elections. This differentiation among party-in-office, party organization, and party-in-the-electorate will recur frequently in the entries.

The political parties themselves constitute yet another set of entries. They are roughly divided into major and minor parties. All of the major parties are included, as well as the more significant minor parties, those that have made relatively impressive, albeit unsuccessful, national electoral showings or have persisted for lengthy periods of time. Key issues that united and divided parties are also identified.

The persisting pattern of two-party competition gives rise to another recurring concept, "party-in-power," which designates the party that controls a specific branch of government or the entire government. That entity is also variously labeled the "in-party," or the "majority party." In turn, the "minority party" is also known as the "out-party" or the "party-out-of-power."

Throughout, there is strong emphasis on the national level in the federal system. In addition, the dictionary includes a list of acronyms; a chronology provides an overarching framework; a bibliography points the reader to the impressive array of scholarship on U.S. political parties; and appendixes provide useful reference data. In the body of the dictionary, boldface type within the entries indicates terms that have their own main entries.

The Dictionary

– A –

ABOLITIONIST MOVEMENT. An effort to eliminate slavery in the decades preceding the **Civil War**. Building on foundations in Great Britain, the Abolitionist Movement in the United States emerged in the colonial era. Under the 1787 **Constitution**, the federal principle limited the capacity of the national government to address the slavery issue. By 1804, the northern states had made slavery illegal, but it remained a vital institution in the South. Abolitionists differed with regard to timing of abolition (immediate versus gradual) and the postemancipation status of the slaves in American society (colonization and emigration versus integration). Abolition emerged as a political controversy in the **Second Party System**. Given the strength and significance of its southern wing, the **Democratic Party** was generally hostile toward the abolitionists, although many Democrats expressed concerns about the institution of slavery. In turn, the **Whig Party** had a significant abolitionist constituency that generated noteworthy intraparty conflict. In the mid-1850s, with the Whig coalition deteriorating over the slavery question, the emerging **Republican Party** took a strong antislavery stance that attracted abolitionist support. The Civil War resulted in the proposal and ratification of the 13th Amendment, abolishing slavery.

ABORTION. A procedure that terminates a pregnancy. Abortion emerged as a politically charged and divisive issue in the wake of the landmark Supreme Court decision, *Roe v. Wade* (1973), which legalized the procedure under certain circumstances. The controversy pits "pro-life" abortion opponents against "pro-choice" defenders of women's right to choose whether to terminate a pregnancy. Initially,

1

both major political parties had significant pro-life and pro-choice elements. Over time, issue realignment has made the **Democratic Party** overwhelmingly pro-choice and the **Republican** Party similarly pro-life.

ABSENTEE VOTING. A procedure allowing a registered voter to participate in an election without being present to cast a **ballot** on Election Day. In the federal system, the individual states determine the appropriate conditions regarding access to, and exercise of, absentee ballots. Contemporary variations on the absentee-voting concept include early voting and voting by mail.

ABSOLUTE MAJORITY. More than 50 percent of the total votes of all voters eligible to participate in an **election**. *See also* MAJORITY; PLURALITY.

ACCIDENTAL PRESIDENT. A **president** who occupies the office without having been elected specifically to that office. To date, the accidental presidents have been the nine vice presidents who have become president when a vacancy occurred in the presidential office. They are **John Tyler**, **Millard Fillmore**, **Andrew Johnson**, **Chester A. Arthur**, **Theodore Roosevelt**, **Calvin Coolidge**, **Harry S. Truman**, **Lyndon B. Johnson**, and **Gerald R. Ford**. All but Ford were elected vice president. Ford assumed the vice presidency in 1973 under the provisions of the 25th Amendment to the **Constitution**: **nomination** by the president and confirmation by **majority** vote in each house of **Congress**. Congress establishes the line of presidential succession after the vice president.

ACTIVIST. A person whose commitment to a cause entails a willingness to work for its realization. Activists make up the **party organization**. They are motivated by **material incentives, solidary incentives**, and/or **purposive incentives**.

ADAMS, JOHN. Vice president, 1789–1797 and Federalist president, 1797–1801. (b. 30 October 1735; d. 4 July 1826). A leading revolutionary voice, John Adams served in the Massachusetts General Court and the First and Second Continental Congresses. He was a member of the committee that drafted the Declaration of Independence. Immediately afterward, he held diplomatic posts for the new national government in France, the Netherlands, and Great Britain. In the first presidential election under the **Constitution** in 1789, he ran a distant second to **George Washington** in the **electoral college** balloting and thus became **vice president**. He held that office for two terms prior to winning the presidential election in 1796. Adams was the leader of a **faction** of the emerging **Federalist Party**, but the party's marching orders came more from **Alexander Hamilton**, who sought to undermine Adams's presidential prospects. Adams's bid for reelection failed, and he entered into a lengthy retirement, during which he published his autobiography and maintained an extensive correspondence, most notably with his old friend and **partisan** rival, **Thomas Jefferson**. The two died within hours of each other on Independence Day in 1826. The previous year, the presidential election of **John Quincy Adams** made the elder Adams the first former president to have a child occupy that office.

ADAMS, JOHN QUINCY. Democratic-Republican president, 1824–1829. (b. 11 July 1767; d. 23 February 1848). The son of President **John Adams**, John Quincy Adams followed his father into public life. He represented Massachusetts in the U.S. Senate (1803–1808). From there, he entered into an extended tour of diplomatic assignments. He served as minister to Russia (1809–1814); minister to Great Britain (1815–1817); and finally, secretary of state (1817–1825). In 1820, with President **James Monroe** unchallenged for reelection, one presidential elector, unwilling to see Monroe match the tribute of unanimous support accorded on two occasions to President **George Washington,** cast his vote for Adams.

Four years later, with the dominant **Democratic-Republican Party** torn by rivalries, Adams emerged as the champion of one **faction.** With most states now choosing electors by popular vote, presidential nominees conducted increasingly public campaigns as sponsors of designated candidates for the office of elector. In the popular vote, with several candidates in the contest, Adams received 30.9 percent, running a distant second to **Andrew Jackson** with 41.3 percent. In the subsequent **electoral college** balloting, Adams again ran second, with 84 votes to Jackson's 99. Because no candidate received a **majority**, the **election** went to the **House of Representatives** for a decision. There, support from Speaker **Henry Clay** threw the election to Adams.

Four years later, in a two-man rematch, Adams lost convincingly to Jackson. The popular vote went against him, 56 percent to 43.6 percent, and in the electoral college, Jackson prevailed 178 to 83. Adams's retirement from public life was short lived. He returned to the capital as a member of the House of Representatives in 1831 and remained in that office for the rest of his life.

ADAMS, JOHN T. Republican National Committee Chair, 1921–1924. (b. 20 December 1862; d. 28 October 1939). Adams was an Iowa manufacturer who identified with the **faction** of the **Republican Party** known as the **old guard**. He was initially elected to the **Republican National Committee (RNC)** in 1912 as a supporter of President **William Howard Taft** when Taft was under assault by the **progressive** wing of the party. In 1917, Adams became vice chair of the RNC, serving under **William R. Willcox**. When Willcox resigned as chair, Adams sought to replace him, but the progressive faction on the **committee** blocked his election. **Will Hays** was the compromise choice as chair, with Adams retaining the office of vice chair. When Hays resigned in 1921, Adams initially became acting chair. Then, after President **Warren G. Harding** indicated his approval, Adams was elected chair. He held the office through the 1924 **Republican National Convention**. Harding had died in office in 1923, and the new president, **Calvin Coolidge**, received the nomination. Coolidge installed his Massachusetts political ally, **William M. Butler**, as chair. Adams became the chair of the **campaign** strategy committee. After his stint in national party politics, Adams returned to Iowa to give full-time attention to his manufacturing concern. In 1928, he was an early supporter of the presidential candidacy of Iowa's **favorite son, Herbert C. Hoover**.

ADAMS, SAMUEL. Electoral vote recipient, 1796 (Federalist). (b. 27 September 1722; d. 2 October 1803). Samuel Adams played a key role in events leading up to the American Revolution. He was a member of the Continental Congress prior to and during the Revolutionary War. A signer of the Declaration of Independence, he later served as governor of Massachusetts (1794–1797). While holding that office, he received 15 of Virginia's **electoral college** votes in 1796.

ADMINISTRATION. *Administration* has at least four related but analytically distinct usages with regard to party politics. (1) It is used to refer to the tenure of a particular **president** (e.g., the Bush administration). (2) That same term also pertains to the collective appointees who serve under that president. (3) It means the execution of policy (e.g., the administration of justice). (4) It describes certain organizational entities in the federal executive branch, either within an executive department or standing apart, such as the Food and Drug Administration or the National Aeronautics and Space Administration.

ADVANCE TEAM. Campaign officials assigned the task of making preliminary arrangements for an appearance by a **candidate**. The advance team appears on the scene several days before the scheduled event to work with local officials to ensure that all necessary preparations have been made.

AGNEW, SPIRO T. Republican vice president, 1969–1973. (b. 9 November 1918; d. 17 September 1996). The son of a Greek immigrant, Agnew grew up in Maryland, where he practiced law and became involved in local **Republican Party** politics. After serving as a county executive, he was elected governor in 1966. Nationally, he was initially identified with the party **faction** known as the **Eastern establishment**, but he soon accommodated himself to the party's more powerful **conservative** faction. After nominating Richard M. Nixon for president at the 1968 Republican National Convention, Agnew emerged as Nixon's **dark horse** choice for the vice presidential **nomination**.

After winning election that fall, Agnew emerged as a prominent **administration** spokesman, a role that belied his relative noninvolvement in decision making. Using strong and strident language, he attacked the administration's critics, whose ranks included both members of the **Democratic Party** and the mass media. In 1972, he was renominated and reelected, and he was considered a likely contender for the presidency in 1976.

However, early in the second term, Agnew came under investigation for alleged payoffs he received from contractors during and following his service in local and state offices. He denied the charges, but he reached a plea bargain agreement with the prosecutors in the Justice Department that required his resignation as **vice president**. Following his departure, President Nixon named **Gerald R. Ford** as his successor, under the provisions of the recently ratified 25th Amendment to the **Constitution**.

ALBERT, CARL. Democratic House majority leader, 1962–1971. Democratic Speaker of the House, 1971–1977. (b. 10 May 1908; d. 4 February 2000). Carl Albert served his native Oklahoma for three decades in the **House of Representatives** (1947–1977). His district bordered that of **Sam Rayburn**, the Democratic **floor leader** in the House when Albert arrived. Under Rayburn's influential sponsorship, Albert became part of the chamber's inner club, serving the **majority** as **whip** under Speaker Rayburn and Majority Leader **John W. McCormack** (1955–1962). On Rayburn's death, McCormack moved up to **Speaker** and Albert became **majority leader**. When McCormack retired in 1971, Albert ascended the leadership ladder to Speaker.

During his tenure, the Democratic House pursued the impeachment of Republican president **Richard M. Nixon**, an inquiry that ended with Nixon's resignation in 1974. On two occasions, immediately following the 1973 resignation of Vice President **Spiro T. Agnew** and then that of President Nixon, Speaker Albert was first in the line of presidential succession, until the nomination and confirmation of a vice president under the provisions of the 25th Amendment to the **Constitution**. Albert did not seek reelection in 1976, instead retiring to Oklahoma, where the University of Oklahoma established the Carl Albert Center for Congressional Studies, housing his papers as well as those of other congressional notables.

ALCORN, H. MEADE, JR. Republican National Committee Chair, 1957–1959. (b. 20 October 1907; d. 13 January 1992). Meade Alcorn was a Connecticut lawyer and party politician. He served three two-year terms in the state general assembly (1936–1942) before being elected state attorney-general (1942–1949). He was also active in state and national party politics, serving on both the state **committee** and the national committee. As a prominent member of the **Eastern establishment**, he supported the 1952 presidential candidacy of **Dwight D. Eisenhower**. When **Leonard W. Hall**, the national party **chair**, resigned in 1957 after guiding Eisenhower's reelection effort, the **president** called on Alcorn to replace him. Alcorn embodied the **modern Republican**ism that Eisenhower promoted. Alcorn was at the helm during the 1958 midterm congressional elections, which proved disastrous for the GOP. He resigned in 1959 and was replaced by **Thruston B. Morton**. Alcorn returned to Connecticut, where he practiced law and maintained a low-level involvement in party affairs.

ALIENATION. A perception and/or condition of exclusion or isolation of an individual or group from the political process.

AMATEUR. A category of political activists. An amateur is usually contrasted with a **professional**, in that the former does not consider politics to be a vocation. In the late 1960s and early 1970s, amateurs seized control of the organization of the **Democratic Party**. *See also* NEW POLITICS.

AMERICA FIRST PARTY. Label used by several unrelated minor parties. In 1944, an America First Party nominated Gerald L. K. Smith for the presidency. Smith was a notorious right-wing extremist who had appeared on the national scene almost a decade earlier as the self-proclaimed political heir of assassinated Louisiana Senator Huey Long. Smith had been a visible supporter of the **Union Party** candidacy of William Lemke in 1936. Mounting his presidential candidacy in the midst of World War II, Smith and his America First Party promoted isolationism and nativism, with negligible success.

In 1960, the Tax Cut Party used the America First label, as well as that of the American Party, in some states in promoting the presidential candidacy of Lar Daly of Illinois.

Another America First Party (Populist) contested the 1992 presidential election. Its nominee, James "Bo" Gritz, was identified with the emerging militia movement on the far right wing of American politics.

Most recently, in 2002 a **faction** of the **Reform Party** constituted itself as the America First Party and proclaimed its support for 2000 presidential nominee Pat Buchanan. This version of the America First Party is socially conservative and identifies with the Christian Right.

AMERICAN INDEPENDENT PARTY. The American Independent Party was established in 1968 as a vehicle for the presidential candidacy of **George C. Wallace.** Wallace's core constituency resided in his native South and shared his opposition to the civil rights movement and its advocacy of racial integration. In addition, he appealed to disgruntled rural and blue-collar voters elsewhere with his populist rhetoric and hawkish stance on the Vietnam War. Wallace mounted a relatively successful **minor party** effort, amassing almost 10 million popular votes and 46 electoral votes. In subsequent elections, without Wallace as a **standard-bearer**, the American Independent Party was unable to retain that level of support. It became **faction** ridden in the 1970s, and one group split away to form the **American Party**. In 1976, the American Independent Party nominated Lester Maddox, former Democratic governor of Georgia, for president. In doing so, the party rejected overtures from prominent right-wing ideologues who sought to use the party to assemble a new **conservative coalition**. Maddox ran poorly, and the party disappeared from the electoral landscape in the 1980s.

AMERICAN PARTY. A label used by several minor parties in contesting presidential elections in the past 150 years. The first to use the label were the Know-Nothings. In the mid-1850s, growing opposition to European immigration manifested itself in the formation of the American Party. Reflecting organizational origins in secret societies opposed to immigration, party supporters refused to identify themselves openly with the party and its programs, claiming ignorance. The popular name, Know-Nothings, reflected this stance. Apart from its nativism, the party also appealed by default to voters increasingly disenchanted with the major parties, the **Democratic Party** and the **Whig Party**, which were splintering over the volatile slavery issue.

The party elected 7 governors, 5 senators, and 43 congressmen in 1854 and 1855, positioning itself as a significant factor in the upcoming 1856 presidential contest. However, the slavery issue divided the Know-Nothings as well. Following their presidential nomination of a prominent Whig, former president **Millard Fillmore**, the antislavery wing of the party bolted in favor of the nominee of the new **Republican Party, John C. Fremont**. Fillmore received over 20 percent of the popular vote, an impressive performance, but carried only one state, Maryland. The northern Know-Nothings soon gravitated into the Republican camp as well. Their border-state adherents provided support for the **Constitutional Union Party** in 1860.

Over a century later, the American Party was one of the labels under which the presidential nominee of the Tax Cut Party, Lar Daly (Illinois), conducted his 1960 presidential **campaign**. Yet another American Party emerged subsequently out of a factional split in the American Independent Party in the 1970s. In 1972, the **American Independent Party** shortened its name to the American Party in several states, running Republican congressman John G. Schmitz (California) as its presidential nominee. After that election, the party split into two irreconcilable factions. One, led by Thomas J. Anderson (Tennessee), the 1972 vice presidential nominee, claimed the American Party label. It has contested presidential elections since 1976, thus outlasting its parent body. However, it has never achieved any noteworthy support from the electorate. It locates itself on the **right wing** of the ideological spectrum.

"AMERICAN SYSTEM." A phrase employed by **Henry Clay** in 1824 and afterward to characterize his agenda for national economic improvements funded by a protective **tariff**.

ANDERSON, JOHN B. Independent presidential candidate, 1980. (b. 15 February 1922). Anderson was elected to the **House of Representatives** from northwest Illinois in 1960, serving 10 terms. Within the **Republican Party**, he initially identified with the **old guard** in factional rivalries. Over the years, he moved to the middle of the ideological spectrum, in part in response to demographic changes in his congressional district. In 1980, he gave up his House seat to seek the presidential **nomination** at the **Republican National Convention**. He fared poorly in the presidential primaries and decided to continue his presidential quest as an **independent**. Establishing a **National**

Unity Campaign that won access to the **ballot** in all 50 states, Anderson positioned himself as a centrist, between his **major party** rivals: **Ronald W. Reagan**, the Republican nominee and a strong **conservative**; and the **incumbent, Jimmy Carter**, renominated by the **Democratic Party**, a moderate whose party **coalition** pulled him in a **liberal** direction. Anderson won over 6 percent of the popular vote, but he carried no states. His respectable showing qualified him to receive federal funding for a presidential race in 1984, and he took some tentative steps to establish a partisan vehicle. In the end, he chose not to run and endorsed the Democratic ticket. Retired from politics, he has maintained a measure of political visibility by chairing the nonpartisan Center for Voting and Democracy (1996–) and serving as president of the World Federalist Association.

ANDERSON, JOSEPH. President pro tempore of the Senate, 1805. (b. 5 November 1757; d. 17 April 1837). Anderson was elected to the **Senate** from Tennessee in 1797. He served in that body until 1815. On three occasions in the second session of the 8th Congress, his colleagues named him **president pro tempore**. Three years after his death, Tennessee sent his son, Alexander, to the Senate for a year.

ANDREW, JOE. Democratic National Committee chair, 1999–2001. (b. 1 March 1960). Andrew is an Indiana attorney and entrepreneur. His participation in **Democratic Party** politics in that state led to his selection as state party chair in 1995. He presided over a remarkable series of electoral successes in a state where the **Republican Party** had traditionally dominated. In 1999 he was the choice of President **Bill Clinton** and his **heir apparent,** Vice President **Al Gore,** to replace the retiring **Steven Grossman** as national party **chair.** Former Colorado governor **Roy Romer** briefly retained his position as general chair before giving way to former Philadelphia mayor **Edward G. Rendell.** Andrew served as national party chair during the controversial 2000 presidential **campaign,** leaving office in January 2001. In 2005, he signed on with Diebold Election Systems, maker of electronic voting machines, in a public relations capacity. In 2007, he endorsed Hillary Clinton for the Democratic presidential **nomination,** but in May 2008 he announced that he would support the candidacy of **Barack H. Obama**. His endorsement indicated that the party elders were lining up behind Obama, in anticipation of his likely victory in the nomination contest.

ANTHONY, HENRY B. Republican president pro tempore of the Senate, 1869–1873. (b. 1 April 1815; d. 2 September 1884). Anthony, a former governor of Rhode Island (1850–1851), represented that state in the Senate from 1859 until his death. He served as **president pro tempore** on 15 occasions during the 41st and 42nd Congresses.

ANTI-FEDERALISTS. A **faction** in the 1780s and 1790s, the Anti-Federalists never constituted themselves as a **political party**. As a **coalition** of interests, they opposed the ratification of the 1787 **Constitution** and went on to oppose the **Federalist Party** in **Congress** in the first decade of the new constitutional regime. The Anti-Federalists represented rural, inland regions, and they feared that the stronger national government created by the Constitution would abridge states' rights and individual liberties. They provided the initial opposition to the economic policies of Treasury Secretary **Alexander Hamilton**. As political parties began to form in the 1790s, the interests and sentiments reflected by the Anti-Federalists were subsumed into the **Democratic-Republican Party**.

ANTI-MASONIC PARTY. Appearing on the political scene in 1831, this influential minor party reflected a growing anti-Mason sentiment in New York and neighboring states. It appealed primarily to common people with its avowedly anti-elitist stance. It conducted the first national party nominating **convention**, putting forth **William Wirt** (Maryland) as its presidential nominee. Wirt won seven electoral votes in the 1832 **election**. The party also captured the statehouse in Vermont and elected several congressmen. After the election, most of its supporters gravitated toward the emerging **Whig Party**.

ANTI-MONOPOLY PARTY. The Anti-Monopoly Party emerged in opposition to heightening concentration of businesses in the era of industrialization. It contested the 1884 presidential **election**. Its presidential nominee, Benjamin Butler (Massachusetts), also ran under the banner of the **Greenback Party**.

ARMEY, RICHARD. Republican majority leader of the House of Representatives, 1995–2003. (b. 7 July 1940). An economics professor at North Texas State University, Armey was elected to the **House of Representatives** in 1984. A decade later, when the **Republican Party** won an upset **majority**, his fellow partisans named Armey their **floor leader.** He guided the progress of the **Contract with America** through the House. Subsequently, Armey fell victim to intrigues within the House **Republican Conference** that precluded any prospects of his becoming **Speaker.** He chose not to seek reelection in 2002 and retired to private life. Armey continues to speak out on public issues, especially economic ones.

ARMSTRONG, JAMES. Electoral vote recipient, 1789 (Federalist). (b. 29 August 1748; d. 6 May 1828). Armstrong received one **electoral college** vote from Georgia in the 1789 presidential balloting. He went on to serve a term as a member of the Pennsylvania delegation in the **House of Representatives** (1793–1795).

ARTHUR, CHESTER A. Republican president, 1881–1885. (b. 5 October 1830; d. 18 November 1886). Chester Arthur was a New York lawyer who in 1871 was appointed collector of the Port of New York, one of the most prestigious **patronage** positions then available, by President **Ulysses S. Grant.** President **Rutherford B. Hayes** removed him from that position in 1878, and Arthur returned to his legal practice. At the 1880 **Republican National Convention,** he was a prominent supporter of the presidential candidacy of former president Grant, who was the early leader in **convention** balloting. After the convention finally selected a **dark horse, James A. Garfield,** as its compromise nominee, it quickly turned to Arthur, identified with the **stalwart** faction, for **vice president** to balance the **ticket** and promote **party unity.** The ticket won a close election that fall.

After six months as vice president, Arthur became president following Garfield's assassination by a disappointed office seeker. During his presidency, the Pendleton Act established the Civil Service Commission, promoting reform of the **spoils system** in favor of the alternative **merit system.** Arthur competed unsuccessfully for a presidential nomination in his own right in 1884, but the convention picked party rival **James G. Blaine**. In retirement, Arthur resumed his legal practice.

ATCHISON, DAVID R. Whig president pro tempore of the Senate, 1846–1854. (b. 11 August 1807; d. 26 January 1886). Atchison represented Missouri in the **Senate** (1843–1855). Highly respected by his colleagues, he was elected **president pro tempore** during five separate Congresses between 1846 and 1854: the 29th (three times), 30th (six times), 31st (twice), 32nd (once), and 33rd (once).

On three occasions, his service was performed amid extraordinary circumstances. He was occupying that office on Sunday, 4 March 1849, when **James K. Polk** ended his presidential term. The **vice president, George M. Dallas**, had resigned on 3 March. Because the inauguration of President-elect **Zachary Taylor** was not scheduled to take place until 5 March, the claim has been advanced that Atchison, next in the line of presidential succession, was legally **president** for one day.

On 9 July 1850, President Taylor died, elevating Vice President **Millard Fillmore** to the presidency. Thus, when Atchison was named president pro tempore on 20 December 1852, there was no vice president in office. This situation subsequently recurred. Atchison was chosen president pro tempore on 4 March 1853, in the absence of the ailing vice president, **William R. King**, whose illness precluded his official inauguration. King died less than six weeks later, once again leaving Atchison the constitutionally established presiding officer of the Senate.

AT-LARGE ELECTION. An **election** that chooses representatives based on the entire unit of an electing body rather than its subdivisions. Thus, the body typically represents larger and broader interests than those of specific subdivisions. Within each state, elections to the U.S. Senate are at-large.

ATWATER, LEE. Republican National Committee chair, 1989–1991. (b. 27 February 1951; d. 29 March 1991). Atwater came of political age in his native South Carolina when the fortunes of the **Republican Party** were on the rise. He became a professional campaign consultant, and he moved quickly to the national arena, where he played key organizational roles in the successful presidential campaigns of **Ronald W. Reagan** and **George H. W. Bush** in the 1980s. Atwater proved to be a superb strategist and tactician, one who joyously embraced the **new politics** approach to **election** campaigns. Bush rewarded Atwater for his service by making him the national party **chair** in 1989.

Atwater advocated a **big tent** approach to party development, seeking to accommodate diverse issue and ideological perspectives under the party banner. His short tenure was marked by controversies that related to abiding concerns about the efficacy of his negative **campaign** style, which featured personal attacks on opponents. In the spring of 1990, Atwater was diagnosed with a brain tumor that incapacitated him. He held on to his national party post until his two-year term ended in 1991. At that point, he surrendered it and accepted the titular position of general chair. He died shortly afterward. Atwater's influence loomed large among the next generation of Republican strategists.

AUSTRALIAN BALLOT. A balloting arrangement featuring the **ballot** printed at public expense, distributed at public polling locations, and marked in private. This arrangement was developed in Australia in the mid-19th century. In the context of **Progressive Era** reform, states in the United States began to employ it in the 1880s. It quickly supplanted the existing practice whereby political parties produced, distributed, and collected ballots, giving rise to widespread allegations of corruption and fraud.

AVAILABILITY. Criteria associated with potential candidates for public office. Such background criteria might include previous offices held, issue and ideological positions taken, region, and name recognition. *See also* BALANCED TICKET.

– B –

BACKBENCHERS. Junior members of Congress, those with little seniority. The term originated in Great Britain, where the legislative chamber has the two major parties facing each other. The party leaders sit on the front benches, while the junior members occupy the back ones. In the United States, a similar pattern developed, although the fan-shaped seating arrangements in both houses have the two parties sitting side by side.

BACON, AUGUSTUS O. Democratic president pro tempore of the Senate, 1912, 1913. (b. 20 October 1839; d. 14 February 1914). A Georgia Democrat, Bacon was chosen for a Senate seat in 1895. He held it until his death. During the second and third sessions of the 62nd Congress, the Senate on 10 occasions named Bacon to be **president pro tempore**, in the absence of the ailing **vice president, James S. Sherman.** After Sherman's death on 30 October 1912, Bacon's presiding responsibilities took on increased constitutional significance.

BAILEY, JOHN M. Democratic National Committee chair, 1961–1968. (b. 23 November 1904; d. 10 April 1975). Bailey chaired the state **committee** of the **Democratic Party** in his native Connecticut for almost three decades (1946–1975). In that position, he played the role of **kingmaker** on both the state and national scenes. He was an early and influential supporter of the presidential aspirations of **John F. Kennedy.** Following Kennedy's **election** in 1960, Bailey became chair of the **Democratic National Committee**, while retaining his state party leadership post.

After Kennedy's assassination, President **Lyndon B. Johnson** kept Bailey on at the national party headquarters as a symbol of continuity. However, Johnson did not include Bailey in his inner circle of advisers and confidants. Bailey chaired the national party during the Johnson landslide of 1964, and he stayed on as Johnson's fortunes, and those of the Democratic Party, receded from that pinnacle of success.

Bailey stepped down as party chair in August 1968, after a lengthy tenure. His departure followed the **Democratic National Convention** held in Chicago, which was marred by demonstrations by student activists protesting the Vietnam War and a violent response by the Chicago police. The new presidential nominee, **Hubert H. Humphrey,** named his campaign manager, **Lawrence F. O'Brien,** as Bailey's replacement. Bailey returned to Connecticut, where he continued to serve as state party chair until his death.

BAKER, HOWARD W. Republican Senate minority leader, 1977–1981; Republican Senate majority leader, 1981–1985. (b. 15 November 1925). Both of Howard Baker's parents served in the **House of Representatives**, as did his father-in-law, **Everett M. Dirksen**, who also represented Illinois in the **Senate**. Baker entered the Senate from Tennessee in 1967. A decade later, he became **minority leader**. In 1980, he unsuccessfully sought the Republican presidential **nomination**, which went to **Ronald W. Reagan**. When the Republicans captured the Senate that year, he assumed the position of majority leader. He did not seek reelection in 1984, in anticipation of a second presidential bid in 1988, which never materialized. Instead, he took on the assignment of White House chief of staff at a critical point during President Ronald W. Reagan's second term, when allegations regarding the Iran–Contra scandal threatened that presidency. Baker worked effectively to limit the damage. After leaving the White House, Baker never returned to the electoral arena. Rather, he developed a lucrative clientele as a lawyer-lobbyist. In 2001, President **George W. Bush** named Baker ambassador to Japan. He served until 2005.

BALANCED TICKET. The practice of political parties seeking a diverse **slate** of nominees reflecting a variety of constituency bases, including regional, religious, ethnic, and ideological. Doing so enables a party to appeal to a broad base of potential voters. Examples of geographical balancing at the presidential level include the **Franklin D. Roosevelt** (New York)–**John Nance Garner** (Texas) tickets for the Democratic Party in 1932 and 1936, and the 1960 Democratic **ticket** of **John F. Kennedy** (Massachusetts) and **Lyndon B. Johnson** (Texas). In a variation on this theme, appointments to the position of national party **chair** have been used to achieve broader geographical coverage. A balanced local-level slate of party nominees in a major urban center like Chicago or New York might include representatives of the significant ethnic constituencies of the population.

BALDWIN, ABRAHAM. Federalist president pro tempore of the Senate, 1801–1802. (b. 2 November 1754; d. 4 March 1807). Baldwin represented Georgia in the Continental Congress in 1785 and again in 1788–1789. He was elected to the **House of Representatives** for the first **Congress** and reelected four more times. After a decade in the House, he moved over to the **Senate** in 1799, where he remained until his death in 1807. On two occasions during the 7th Congress (1801–1803), he served as **president pro tempore**.

BALLOT. An instrument through which a vote is cast, as well as the exercise of conducting an **election**. *See also* AUSTRALIAN BALLOT.

BALLOT-BOX STUFFING. A term for voter fraud. Originally, it entailed the physical insertion of illegal paper ballots into a ballot box. The advent of voting machines called forth alternative illegal endeavors, but the term persists.

BANDWAGON EFFECT. The tendency of voters to support a **candidate** with apparent momentum, basing that support on the expectation that such a candidate is likely to win. This phenomenon was traditionally visible in multiballot nominating **convention** decision making. Today it more often applies to sequential **presidential primary** victories.

BANKHEAD, WILLIAM B. Democratic majority leader of the House of Representatives, 1935–1936; Democratic Speaker of the House of Representatives, 1936–1940. (b. 12 April 1874; d. 15 September 1940). Bankhead belonged to a prominent political family in Alabama that also sent his father, brother, and nephew to **Congress**. He won his first election to Congress in 1916. Almost two decades later, he had recently been elected **majority leader** when Speaker **Joseph W. Byrns** died in 1936. Bankhead succeeded Byrns, and he remained in that office until his own death four years later.

BANKS, NATHANIEL P. American Speaker of the House, 1856–1857. (January 1816; d. 1 September 1894). During a congressional career that began in 1853 and spanned almost four decades, Banks represented Massachusetts under the banner of various parties: **Democratic Party** (1853–1855), **American Party** (1855–1857), **Republican Party** (1857, 1867–1873, 1889–1891), **Union Party** (1865–1867), and **Liberal Republican Party** (1875–1879). During his short-lived affiliation with the American Party, Banks was elected **Speaker** on the 133rd ballot by a chamber in partisan disarray over the slavery controversy. To date, he is the only member of a minor party ever to be chosen House Speaker. He left the speakership to become governor of Massachusetts (1858–1861), returning to the House as a Republican in 1865.

In 1872, Banks received one electoral vote for **vice president**. That year, the Democratic Party and the Liberal Republican Party had run a fusion presidential campaign, jointly nominating **Horace Greeley** for **president** and **Benjamin G. Brown** for **vice president**. After the election, in which the ticket lost decisively to the Republican opponents, Greeley died before the **electoral college** met. Several of his pledged electors cast their presidential ballots for Brown, leaving them at liberty to vote as they pleased for vice president. One Georgia elector designated Banks as his choice.

BARBOUR, HALEY. Republican National Committee chair, 1993–1997. (b. 22 October 1947). Haley Barbour rode the rising tide of Southern Republicanism to national prominence. Fresh out of law school, he became executive director of the Mississippi Republican Party (1973–1976). He simultaneously directed the activities of the Southern Association of State Republican Chairmen. After a brief period as a lawyer-lobbyist, he won the party **nomination** for U.S. Senate in 1982, but he lost convincingly to **John C. Stennis**, the entrenched **incumbent**. In 1984, Barbour won a seat on the **Republican National Committee**, and the next year he went to work for President **Ronald W. Reagan** at the White House. In 1987, he returned to private life, but his activities as a lawyer-lobbyist kept him attentive to party politics.

In 1993, Barbour successfully sought election as national party **chair**. He undertook a vigorous campaign to elect a Republican **Congress** in 1994, closely coordinating with the congressional party leadership in the development and promotion of the **Contract with America**. The failure of the Republicans to build on their success in 1994, losing the presidential election in 1996, proved discouraging, and Barbour did not seek reelection as national party chair. He shifted back to his profession as a lawyer-lobbyist. In 2003, he successfully entered the electoral arena in Mississippi, winning election as governor. He won reelection to a second term in 2007, and he remains a significant force in Republican circles.

BARBOUR, JAMES. Democratic-Republican president pro tempore of the Senate, 1819–1820. (b. 10 June 1775; d. 7 June 1842). Barbour came from a prominent Virginia political family. His brother, **Philip P. Barbour,** had a distinguished career in national politics. James Barbour served as governor of Virginia (1812–1814). A year later, he went to the **Senate** and remained there for a decade. In 1819, he was chosen president pro tempore during the 15th **Congress,** and he continued to hold that position for several weeks during the 16th Congress. In 1825, he left the Senate to join the **cabinet** of President **John Quincy Adams** as secretary of war, holding the latter office for three years.

BARBOUR, PHILIP P. Democratic-Republican Speaker of the House, 1821–1823. (b. 25 May 1783; d. 25 February 1841). Philip Barbour belonged to a prominent family of Virginia politicians. His brother, **James Barbour,** was governor, senator, and secretary of war. Philip Barbour entered the **House of Representatives** in 1814 and remained there until 1825, when he temporarily left office. He returned in 1827, serving until 1830. In 1821, he was a compromise choice of the House as **Speaker,** winning election on the 12th **ballot.** Several years after leaving the House the second time, he was named by President **Andrew Jackson** to a seat on the Supreme Court, serving from 1836 until his death in 1841.

BARKLEY, ALBEN W. Democratic Senate majority leader, 1937–1947; Democratic Senate minority leader, 1947–1949; Democratic vice president, 1949–1953. (b. 24 November 1877; d. 30 April 1956). Alben Barkley won **election** to the **House of Representatives** from his Kentucky district in 1912. He served seven terms before moving on to the **Senate** in 1927. After a decade in the Senate, he became **majority leader** for the **Democratic Party.** Holding that position for the next decade, he struggled to maintain unified party support for the **New Deal** promoted by President **Franklin D. Roosevelt,** as the **conservative coalition** arose in opposition and attracted many of Barkley's fellow Southern Democrats to its banner. When the Democrats lost both chambers of **Congress** in 1946, Barkley continued his party leadership for the **minority**.

In 1948, President **Harry S. Truman** selected Barkley as his vice presidential **running mate**. After the **ticket** prevailed in November, Barkley resigned from the Senate on the eve of his inauguration in January 1949. For the next four years, he presided over the Senate and became known affectionately as the **veep**. He briefly retired from public life when his term ended in 1953 but was sent back to the Senate by his Kentucky constituency in 1955. He died in office the next year.

BARNBURNERS. A dissident **faction** of the New York **Democratic Party** during the late 1840s. Their major factional rivals were known as the **Hunkers**. They were attacked as party-wreckers; hence their name. They supported the policies and ambitions of former president **Martin Van Buren**. Their major policy concern was slavery; and they were adamant in their opposition to slavery and its spread. They abandoned the Democrats in 1848, supporting Van Buren's candidacy under the **Free Soil Party** banner. Later on, many Barnburners joined forces with the emerging **Republican Party**.

BARNUM, WILLIAM H. Democratic National Committee chair, 1877–1889. (b. 17 September 1818; d. 30 April 1889). Barnum was elected to the **House of Representatives** from Connecticut in 1866. He served there until 1876, when he was chosen to finish an unexpired Senate term. The next year, the **Democratic National Committee** named him **chair**, to replace **Abram S. Hewitt**. Barnum held the post until his death 12 years later, tying Republican **Edwin D. Morgan** (1856–1864, 1872–1876) and fellow Democrat **August Belmont** (1860–1872) for longevity as national party chair. During his lengthy tenure, the Democrats recaptured the White House in 1884, with nominee **Grover Cleveland**, for the first time in a generation.

BAYARD, THOMAS F. Democratic President pro tempore of the Senate, 1881. (b. 29 October 1828; d. 28 September 1898). Thomas Bayard belonged to a distinguished family of Delaware politicians. He followed his grandfather and his father to the **Senate**, and his son followed him. Thomas Bayard came to the Senate in 1869 and held that office until 1885. In both 1880 and 1884, he sought the presidential **nomination** of the **Democratic Party**, but he fell short in the convention balloting to **Winfield S. Hancock** and **Grover Cleveland**, respectively.

When the Senate reconvened in October 1881, after the death of President **James A. Garfield**, Bayard served briefly as president pro tempore, an assignment that took on unusual significance because there was no **vice president**. Bayard resigned his Senate seat in 1885 to join the incoming Cleveland **administration** as secretary of state. He retired from public life after Cleveland's reelection defeat in 1888.

BELL, JOHN. Whig Speaker of the House of Representatives, 1834–1835; Constitutional Union presidential nominee, 1860. (b. 15 February 1797; d. 10 September 1869). John Bell was a seven-term congressman from Tennessee. Initially elected in 1826 as the nominee of the **Democratic-Republican Party**, he transferred his allegiance to the emerging Whig Party for his first reelection effort. In 1834, a divided House took 10 ballots to decide on Bell as **Speaker**. When the next **Congress** convened, the majority **Democratic Party** replaced him with fellow Tennessean **James K. Polk**. Bell left the **House of Representatives** in 1841 to serve a brief stint as secretary of war under President **William Henry Harrison**. He departed later that year, following the accession of President **John Tyler**. In 1847, Tennessee sent him to the **Senate** for two terms. In 1860, the newly formed **Constitutional Union Party**, committed to maintaining the Union amid growing sectional strife, nominated him for **president**. His campaign won three states with 39 electoral votes: Tennessee, Kentucky, and Virginia.

BELLWETHER. Characterization of an electoral district or precinct that typically reflects the voting behavior of a much larger constituency. Pollsters and political analysts rely on surveys and vote totals in bellwether districts reporting early to make their projections of final electoral outcomes. The old saying, "As Maine goes, so goes the nation," suggests a bellwether status for Maine. The term bellwether can also be used in reference to a trendsetter.

BELMONT, AUGUST. Democratic National Committee chair, 1860–1872. (b. 2 December 1816; d. 24 November 1890). Belmont immigrated to the United States in 1837 from Europe to continue his service on behalf of the financial interests of the powerful Rothschild family. Settling in New York City, he became a naturalized citizen in 1844. He soon emerged as a major financial contributor to the **Democratic Party**. President **Franklin Pierce** rewarded him with a ministerial position at The Hague in 1853. In 1860, he backed **Stephen A. Douglas** for the Democratic presidential **nomination**. When Douglas prevailed, Belmont became **chair** of the **Democratic National Committee**. He held that leadership position for 12 years, a tenure record for national party chairs that he shares with fellow Democrat **William H. Barnum** (1877–1889) and Republican **Edwin D. Morgan** (1856–1864, 1872–1876).

As party chair, Belmont attended to the customary assignments of fund-raising, publicity, and **campaign** management during the disastrous 1860 campaign. Douglas's death the next year, combined with the departure of the Democrats' congressional delegations from the Southern states, left a leadership void in the party that Belmont endeavored to fill. He strongly supported the Union cause in the Civil War, exercising his financial influence in Europe on its behalf. Belmont encouraged General **George B. McClellan** in his successful candidacy for the Democratic presidential nomination in 1864, and he managed the unsuccessful general election campaign. After the war, he became increasingly at odds with the party's presidential nominees, **Horatio Seymour** (1868) and **Horace Greeley** (1872). Indeed, he resigned his national party post rather than campaign for Greeley. In ostensible retirement, Belmont continued to dabble in party politics, vainly promoting the presidential prospects of Senator **Thomas F. Bayard** (Delaware) in 1880 and 1884.

BENTSEN, LLOYD M. Democratic vice presidential nominee, 1984. (b. 11 February 1921; d. 23 May 2006). A member of a prominent south Texas family, Bentsen won a special **election** to the **House of Representatives** in 1948, and he served three full terms before retiring in 1955 to pursue private business interests. In 1970, he reentered the political arena, winning the senatorial **nomination** of the

Democratic Party in a heated **primary** contest with the **incumbent,** Ralph Yarborough. Bentsen then bested Republican Party nominee **George H. W. Bush** in the general election. In 1988, Bentsen had risen to the position of **chair** of the powerful finance committee. He was the choice of the party's presidential nominee, Michael Dukakis, for the vice presidential nomination. Bentsen distinguished himself in the subsequent campaign, but the ticket went down to defeat at the hands of the Republican team headed by old rival George H. W. Bush. Bentsen retained his committee chair and remained a major force in the Senate. In 1993, he joined the incoming **administration** of President **Bill Clinton** as secretary of the treasury, serving almost two years before retiring from public life.

BIDEN, JOSEPH R., JR. Democratic vice president, 2009– . (b. 20 November 1942). Joe Biden was elected to the U.S. **Senate** from Delaware at age 29, attaining the constitutionally prescribed age of 30 before he assumed office. He won reelection on six occasions, the last time in conjunction with his vice presidential election. During his long senatorial tenure, he chaired two influential committees, Judiciary and Foreign Affairs. He unsuccessfully sought the Democratic presidential **nomination** in 1988, which eventually went to Michael Dukakis. Two decades later, he resumed his presidential quest, but his campaign similarly fell short. However, the presidential nominee, **Barack H. Obama**, selected Biden as his **running mate**, in recognition of his foreign policy experience and expertise, as well as his potential electoral appeal to working-class Roman Catholics, with whom he closely identified. After the **ticket** prevailed that fall, Biden became the first Roman Catholic elected **vice president**.

BIG TENT. A phrase used by **Lee Atwater**, among others, to characterize a **political party**, reflecting the belief that a political party's base should be broad enough to encompass identifiers who may differ significantly among themselves on issue positions. The big-tent perspective emphasizes winning elections over ideological cohesion. As such, it can conflict with the tenets of **party responsibility**, which demand a high degree of the latter. *See also* CATCH-ALL PARTY; COALITION.

BINGHAM, WILLIAM. Federalist president pro tempore of the Senate, 1797. (b. 8 March 1752; d. 7 February 1804). William Bingham represented Pennsylvania in the latter days of the Continental Congress (1787–1788). In 1795, he went to the **Senate** for a single term. In February 1797, as the 4th Congress neared adjournment, he became **president pro tempore**.

BIPARTISAN. A term describing cooperation and compromise between political parties in the pursuit of an agreed-upon common interest. A setting of **divided party government** and/or poorly disciplined parties requires high levels of bipartisanship for public policymaking. *See also* NONPARTISAN; PARTISAN.

BIPARTISAN CAMPAIGN REFORM ACT (BCRA). A major piece of **campaign finance** reform legislation enacted in 2002. BCRA outlawed **soft money** contributions to national party organizations and placed $10,000 separate annual limitations on donors contributing to state, district, and local party committees. BCRA also doubled the prevailing individual contribution limit to candidate organizations from $1,000 to $2,000. It also prohibited soft-money funded issue advocacy advertisements within 60 days of a general election and 30 days of a **primary** election. However, in June 2007, the Supreme Court ruled these particular limitations to be unconstitutional constraints on political expression.

BLACK REPUBLICAN. A term applied before the Civil War to the new **Republican Party** by opponents who objected to its avowed antislavery position. After the war, it took on an additional meaning when it characterized the freed slaves who flocked to the party banner.

BLAINE, JAMES G. Republican Speaker of the House of Representatives, 1869–1875; Republican presidential nominee, 1884. (b. 31 January 1830; d. 27 January 1893). Blaine was a prominent figure in post–Civil War national politics. A native of Maine, he arrived on the national scene in 1863, following his **election** to the **House of Representatives**. Reelected six times, he became **Speaker** in 1869, serving until 1875. He became known as the **Plumed Knight**, a

description bestowed on him in a presidential nominating speech. In 1876, he moved from the House to the **Senate**, where he held office until 1881. His next move was to the executive branch, as secretary of state for President **James A. Garfield**.

Garfield's assassination later that year left the issue of party leadership in question. Having strongly contended for the presidential **nomination** in both 1876 and 1880, in 1884 Blaine finally secured the nomination on the fourth **ballot**, prevailing over the **accidental president, Chester A. Arthur**. However, he lost the **general election** and the **electoral college** balloting to Democrat **Grover Cleveland**.

Blaine resumed his public service in 1889, returning as secretary of state during the term of President **Benjamin Harrison**. In 1889, he also served as president of the first Pan-American Congress. Shortly after resigning his office in 1892, he died.

BLAIR, FRANCIS P. Democratic vice presidential nominee, 1868. (b. 19 February 1821; d. 8 July 1875). The son and namesake of a key confidant of President **Andrew Jackson**, Blair settled in Missouri and participated at the national level in the politics of three different political parties. He served several interrupted stints in the **House of Representatives** (1857–1859, 1860, 1861–1862, 1863–1864). Initially elected as a nominee of the **Free Soil Party**, he shifted to the **Republican Party** camp in 1863. His support for the Reconstruction policies put forward by President Abraham Lincoln brought him into conflict with the Radical Republicans in Congress. In 1868, he accepted the vice-presidential nomination of the **Democratic National Convention**, running alongside **Horatio Seymour** in a futile campaign against the Republican ticket headed by **Ulysses S. Grant**. Elected to the **Senate** as a Democrat in 1870, he served only two years, during which he contributed to the successful effort by Horace Greeley to secure the party's presidential **nomination.**

BLANKET PRIMARY. Also known as a "wide-open" **primary**, it allowed primary voters a consolidated **ballot** containing the candidates of all the parties for all of the offices. A voter, without otherwise indicating a party affiliation, could participate in nominating decisions of more than one party. However, such a voter could select only

one **candidate** per office. The candidates receiving the most votes in each party primary went on to contest each other in the **general election**. Washington, Alaska, and California enacted laws providing for blanket primaries. In 2000, the U.S. Supreme Court struck down the California law as a violation of the state parties' freedoms of association guaranteed by the 1st Amendment. Alaska and Washington subsequently abandoned their blanket primaries as well. Louisiana has a unique variation of the blanket primary, a **nonpartisan** primary, in which a candidate who receives a **majority** of the votes cast wins the office without a general election contest. If no candidate achieves a majority, the **runoff primary** pits the top two vote-getters, regardless of party affiliation. See a*lso* CLOSED PRIMARY; OPEN PRIMARY.

BLISS, RAY C. Republican National Committee chair, 1965–1969. (b. 16 December 1907; d. 6 August 1981). Bliss came up through the ranks of the local and state **party organization** in Ohio, serving as county **chair** (1942–1964) and state chair (1949–1965). He devoted himself full time to his party organization responsibilities, for which he received a salary. He promoted this pattern as a model for other state parties and the national party as well.

In 1965, with the **Republican Party** in disarray following the disastrous showing of **Barry M. Goldwater** in the 1964 presidential **election**, the **Republican National Committee** selected Bliss as its chair. He was a pioneer in developing the concept of the **service party**, whereby the national party organization concentrated on providing its state and local counterparts with assistance in the performance of party chores. His leadership efforts contributed to the revitalization of the party organization and the party's successful showings in the 1966 congressional elections and the 1968 presidential election.

In the wake of the election of **Richard M. Nixon** as president, Bliss resigned his party post in 1969, enabling Nixon to place a nominee of his choice, **Rogers C. B. Morton**, in the national party chair. In retirement, he remained a revered figure in the party organization. His understanding of the appropriate role to be played by the national party headquarters has generally been accepted by both major parties.

BLUE DOG DEMOCRATS. A turn-of-the-21st-century term that describes loyal partisans in Congress who are more moderate and centrist than the mainstream Democrats, who lean toward the **left wing** of the ideological spectrum. The blue dogs are amenable to **bipartisan** cooperation with moderate Republicans. In addition to being less committed to partisanship, blue dogs can also be distinguished from another counterpart, the **yellow dog Democrats**, who clearly had Southern roots, in that their geographical base is somewhat broader.

BOEHNER, JOHN. Republican House majority leader, 2006–2007; Republican House minority leader, 2007– . (b. 17 November 1949). John Boehner served in the Ohio House of Representatives (1985–1990). In 1990, he was elected to the **House of Representatives**. He was instrumental in developing the **Contract with America** that advanced the successful Republican campaign to gain **majority** status in the House in the 1994 elections. In 1995, Boehner became chair of the **Republican Conference**, holding that position until 1999. When Majority Leader **Tom DeLay**, embroiled in legal controversy, decided to step down and resign his House seat, Boehner announced his candidacy for the leadership post. He defeated House Majority Whip Roy Blunt in a second ballot, runoff contest. When the Republicans lost their House majority in the 2006 **midterm elections**, Speaker **Dennis Hastert** declined to seek the **floor leader** position; and the **Republican Conference** designated Boehner as **minority leader**. Despite further losses in 2008, Boehner was retained in office by the party conference for the 111th Congress.

BOGGS, THOMAS HALE. Democratic majority leader of the House of Representatives, 1971–1973. (b. 13 March 1916; d. 16 October 1972). Hale Boggs was first elected to the **House of Representatives** from Louisiana in 1940. He served a single term and went on to reclaim his seat in 1946, holding it for the rest of his life. In 1962, he became part of the **Democratic Party** leadership, when he assumed the position of **whip**. Nine years later, he moved up the ladder to **majority leader**. In 1972, while on a **campaign** assignment in Alaska, his plane disappeared. Boggs's body was never found. His seat was declared vacant the following January, and his widow won a special election to succeed him.

BOLL WEEVILS. An informal group of **conservative** Southern Democrats in the **House of Representatives** during the early years of the **Ronald W. Reagan** presidency. They often allied with the Republicans to provide **majority** support for Reagan policy initiatives.

BOLT. To abandon one's **political party**, renouncing an identity with it. Bolting may be done either individually or collectively.

BOND, RICHARD. Republican National Committee chair, 1992–1993. (b. 30 May 1950). Rich Bond got his start in **Republican Party** politics in New York. In 1979, he signed on with **George H. W. Bush** in a **campaign** for the presidential **nomination**. Bond directed the field operations in Iowa that resulted in an impressive victory for Bush. The Bush campaign later faltered, and Bush settled for second place on the presidential **ticket** with **Ronald W. Reagan.** Bond played a key organizational role in the fall campaign that resulted in electoral victory. Bond accompanied Bush to the White House, serving the vice president as his deputy chief of staff (1981–1982). In 1982, he moved over to the **Republican National Committee** as deputy **chair,** with the understanding that he would look out for Bush's interests there. He left the national committee in 1983 to open a political consulting firm. When Bush began assembling a campaign organization for his 1988 run for the presidency, Bond signed on as deputy campaign manager. After the election, he returned to political consulting.

In February 1992, seeking to boost a faltering reelection campaign, President Bush installed Bond as head of the RNC, moving the previous **incumbent, Clayton Yeutter,** over to the White House. As chair, Bond provided quiet support for Bush's successful quest for renomination against challenger Patrick J. Buchanan. However, Bush's failure to win reelection in November meant that Bond had little standing for his continuation as party chair. Bond did not pursue reelection the following January, resuming his career as a political consultant.

BOOM. An energetic attempt to promote popular support for a **candidate** or cause, as well as the product of such an effort. A low-level boom is known as a boomlet.

BOSS. A pejorative term for a powerful **party leader**. It became widely used by **progressive** reformers in the Gilded Age to characterize **party organization** leaders whom the reformers considered corrupt and undemocratic.

BOYD, LINN. Democratic Speaker of the House of Representatives, 1851–1855. (b. 22 November 1800; d. 17 December 1859). Linn Boyd represented Kentucky in the **House of Representatives** for almost two decades. First elected in 1835, he served a single term. He was elected again in 1839, and he remained in office until 1855. He played a key role in the development of the Compromise of 1850, an effort to ease rising tensions associated with the slavery issue that threatened the survival of the Union. His last two terms in the House were as **Speaker**.

BOYLE, WILLIAM M., JR. Democratic National Committee chair, 1949–1951. (b. 3 February 1902; d. 30 August 30 1961). Boyle was a longtime friend and political ally of **Harry S. Truman**'s. He followed Truman to Washington in the early 1940s to work on Truman's Senate staff in an investigation of the national defense program. He also worked closely with fellow Missourian **Robert E. Hannegan**, the national party chair, on the 1944 presidential campaign. Both energetically promoted Truman's candidacy as the vice presidential **running mate** of **Franklin D. Roosevelt**. After Truman became **president**, Boyle informally represented presidential interests at the **Democratic National Committee**, then headed by Senator **J. Howard McGrath**, during Truman's bid for **nomination** and **election** in his own right. When McGrath resigned his party post after the 1948 election to become attorney general, Truman named Boyle to succeed him at party headquarters. Boyle came under suspicion in the influence-peddling scandals that emerged in the latter years of the Truman presidency. Although proclaiming his innocence, he resigned under mounting pressure in 1951, with **Frank E. McKinney** succeeding him. Out of public life, he practiced law in Washington, D.C.

BRADFORD, WILLIAM. President pro tempore of the Senate, 1797. (b. 1 November 1729; d. 6 July 1808). Bradford represented Rhode Island in the **Senate** 1793–1797). During the first session of the 5th

Congress, at the end of his service, he became **president pro tempore**.

BRADLEY, STEPHEN R. Democratic-Republican president pro tempore of the Senate, 1802–1803, 1808. (b. 20 February 1754; d. 9 December 1830). Bradley went to the **Senate** to represent Vermont from 1791 to 1795, and again from 1801 to 1813. He identified himself with the emerging **Democratic-Republican Party**. In 1802–1803, on three occasions during the second session of the 7th Congress, and once again in 1808, during the second session of the 10th Congress, he held the position of **president pro tempore**.

BRANDEGEE, FRANK B. Republican president pro tempore of the Senate, 1912. (b. 8 July 1864; d. 14 October 1924). The son of a Republican congressman from Connecticut, Brandegee followed his father into the **House of Representatives** in 1902. Less than three years later, his state sent him over to the **Senate**, where he remained for the rest of his life. In 1912, during the second session of the 62nd Congress, he was one of several senators who served briefly as **president pro tempore**.

BRECKINRIDGE, JOHN C. Democratic vice president, 1857–1861; Southern Democratic presidential nominee, 1860. (b. 21 January 1821; d. 17 May 1875). Breckinridge came from a prominent Kentucky family. He established a law practice in his home state and became active in the **Democratic Party**, serving first in the state legislature (1849–1851) and then in the U.S. **House of Representatives** (1851–1855). He then resumed his law practice, rejecting a presidential appointment as ambassador to Spain. In 1856, the **Democratic National Convention** designated him for **vice president** on the second **ballot**, pairing him with **James Buchanan** on the presidential **ticket**. Elected that fall, Breckinridge barely met the constitutional requirement that he be 35 years old. While vice president, he was the choice of the Kentucky legislature for a seat in the **Senate**, to be filled on his leaving the former office.

When Southern Democrats could not accept the presidential nominee of the 1860 Democratic National Convention, **Stephen A. Douglas**, they convened in Baltimore and put forward Breckinridge

as their presidential **nominee**, along with Joseph Lane, an Oregon senator, for vice president. Breckinridge swept the 11 Southern states, receiving 72 votes in the **electoral college** to come in second, behind **Abraham Lincoln**, the nominee of the **Republican Party**.

After the election, Breckinridge sought in vain to avert the impending **Civil War**. Returning to Kentucky, he favored secession but concurred with the state's decision to remain neutral. He assumed his Senate seat when **Congress** convened. When Kentucky became a battleground, Breckinridge cast his lot with the Confederate forces. Indicted for treason by the federal government, he served as a general in the field and later became secretary of war. When the war ended, he fled the country to avoid prosecution. Following the 1868 amnesty declaration by President **Andrew Johnson**, Breckinridge returned to Kentucky to public acclaim and resumed his law practice.

BRICE, CALVIN S. Democratic National Committee chair, 1889–1892. (b. 17 September 1845; d. 15 December 1898). Brice was a prominent Ohio lawyer. In 1884, while serving his state **party** on the **Democratic National Committee**, Brice managed the victorious presidential **campaign** of party nominee **Grover Cleveland**. Five years later, following the death of **William H. Barnum**, longtime national party **chair**, Brice became his successor. In 1890, the Ohio legislature sent him to the **Senate** for a single term. Brice resigned his national party post after the 1892 **Democratic National Convention** renominated former president Cleveland for president, a decision that Brice had opposed. Following Cleveland's recommendation, the national committee chose **William F. Harrity** as his replacement.

BRICKER, JOHN W. Republican vice presidential nominee, 1944. (b. 6 September 1893; d. 22 March 1986). Bricker won two terms as attorney general of Ohio (1933–1937), followed by three terms as governor (1939–1945). In 1944, he mounted a **favorite son** candidacy for the presidential **nomination** of the **Republican National Convention**. That assembly instead nominated **Thomas E. Dewey**, but it turned to Bricker as its vice presidential choice to put forward a **balanced ticket** that reconciled competing party factions. Bricker represented the **old guard**, Midwestern, isolationist sentiments within the party coalition. The **ticket** fell that fall as President

Franklin D. Roosevelt, the nominee of the **Democratic Party**, won an unprecedented fourth term.

In 1946, Bricker won election to the U.S. **Senate**, where he served two terms as a faithful member of the old guard. The primary cause he espoused pertained to foreign policy. On several occasions in the early 1950s, he introduced the Bricker Amendment, a proposed constitutional amendment that would have prohibited any treaty provisions that conflicted with the **Constitution** and would have authorized Congress to oversee executive agreements. His proposal met opposition from President **Dwight D. Eisenhower**, a fellow Republican, and it never received the required two-thirds **majority** from his Senate colleagues.

BRIDGES, H. STYLES. Republican Senate minority leader, 1952–1953; Republican president pro tempore of the Senate, 1953–1954. (b. 9 September 1898; d. 26 November 1961). Bridges won the governorship of New Hampshire in 1834. Two years later, he ran successfully for the **Senate**. Following the death of Minority Leader **Kenneth S. Wherry** in 1951, Bridges was chosen by his fellow Republican senators as their floor leader. He filled the office for the remainder of the 82nd Congress. When the Republicans captured control of the Senate in 1952, the new Republican **majority** passed over Bridges in favor of **Robert A. Taft** as their leader. As a consolation prize of sorts, Bridges became **president pro tempore** for the 83rd Congress, strengthening the recent precedent of naming the senior member of the majority party (*see* PARTY-IN-POWER) to that position. When the Democrats retook the Senate in 1954, they replaced Bridges with **Walter George**. Bridges continued to serve in the Senate until his death in 1961.

BRIGHT, JESSE D. (1812–1875). Democratic president pro tempore of the Senate, 1854, 1856, 1860. Jesse Bright went to the **Senate** from Indiana in 1845 and remained there until 1862. A Democrat, he was chosen **president pro tempore** on three occasions: 1854, 1856, and 1860. During the first two periods of service, the office of **vice president** was vacant, owing to the death of **William R. King**.

BROCK, WILLIAM. Republican National Committee chair, 1977–1981. (b. 23 November 1930). Brock's family was prominent in

Tennessee political and economic circles. His grandfather had a short tenure in the **Senate**. Brock was elected to the **House of Representatives** in 1962 and served four terms. In 1970, he moved over to the **Senate** for a single term. Losing his bid for reelection, he became **chair** of the **Republican National Committee** in 1977, replacing **Mary Louise Smith**. Occupying that office for the next four years, he was instrumental in modernizing the headquarters operation of the national **committee**. Brock followed the lead of a former chair, **Ray C. Bliss**, in his **service party** emphasis. His successful tenure came to an end after the 1980 presidential **election**, when president-elect **Ronald W. Reagan** brought Brock into his **administration** as special trade representative. He subsequently became secretary of labor. He left office and entered the private sector in 1987. In 1997, he was unsuccessful in a **general election** bid to return to the Senate, this time from Maryland.

BROKER. Someone who arranges a deal. In party politics, the term was often used to describe national **convention** decision making, whereby state party leaders would come together at the convention and decide whom to nominate. That decision would then be ratified by the compliant delegations. An increasing reliance on presidential primaries in party nominations has greatly diminished the likelihood of a brokered convention. Indeed, the last convention to take more than a single ballot to designate its presidential nominee met in 1952. The term is also widely used in the legislative arena.

BROWN, BENJAMIN GRATZ. Democratic vice presidential nominee, 1872. (b. 28 May 1826; d. 13 December 1885). Gratz Brown was the grandson of **John Brown**, who served in Congress from Virginia and Kentucky. Gratz Brown grew up in Missouri, where he was active in the **Democratic Party** and was elected to the **Senate** in 1863 to finish an unexpired term that ended in 1867. In 1870, he was elected governor for a two-year term, aligning himself with the **coalition** of reform Republicans and fellow Democrats that portended the formation of the **Liberal Republican Party**.

In 1872, a national **convention** of Liberal Republicans met to nominate a presidential **ticket**. Horace Greeley received the presidential **nomination**, and Brown was named for **vice president**. When

the accommodating Democrats met several weeks later, they named the same ticket. This **fusion** effort failed at the polls in November, carrying only eight states. Greeley died shortly afterward, before the **electoral college** met. Eighteen electors who had been pledged to Greeley decided to cast their presidential ballots for Brown, who also received 47 vice presidential votes.

BROWN, JOHN. President pro tempore of the Senate, 1803–1804. (b. 12 September 1757; d. 29 August 1837). John Brown was a member of the Continental Congress, representing the Kentucky region of Virginia, in 1786–1788. When the new government under the **Constitution** got under way, Brown's constituents sent him to the **House of Representatives** (1789–1792). When Kentucky was granted statehood, Brown became one of its first two senators (1792–1805). Once in 1803 and once again in 1804, he was named **president pro tempore**. He left the **Senate** a year later.

BROWN, RONALD H. Democratic National Committee chair, 1989–1993. (b. 1 August 1941; d. 3 April 1996). Upon graduating from law school, Ron Brown continued his previous service on behalf of the National Urban League, working in the Washington office of the **civil rights** organization (1973–1979). Then he joined the presidential **campaign** organization of Senator Edward M. Kennedy (Massachusetts) in an ill-fated effort to wrest the presidential **nomination** of the 1980 **Democratic National Convention** from **incumbent** president **Jimmy Carter**. Brown continued to work for Kennedy on his **Senate** staff. In 1982, he became deputy **chair** of the **Democratic National Committee**, representing the Kennedy constituency in the party.

Brown left the party post in 1985 to become a highly successful lawyer-lobbyist, but he continued his interest and involvement in party politics. In 1988, Jesse Jackson enlisted Brown as a campaign strategist in his quest for the presidential nomination. Brown acquitted himself well in a losing effort, and he went on to work on behalf of the party nominee, Michael Dukakis.

At the January 1989 meeting of the **Democratic National Committee** that followed Dukakis's defeat, Brown was elected chair, the first African American to hold the post. Brown received credit in

party circles for his effective leadership of the party organization, and he impressed the eventual 1992 presidential **nominee, Bill Clinton**, with his ability. Brown was a visible presence in the Clinton **general election** campaign. After his victory, Clinton invited Brown to join his **administration** as secretary of commerce. Brown accepted and did not seek reelection to the national party post.

As secretary of commerce, Brown vigorously promoted the interests of American corporations in international business. He was killed when his airplane crashed on a trade mission to Bosnia in 1996.

BROWNELL, HERBERT, JR. Republican National Committee chair, 1944–1946. (b. 20 February 1904; d. 1 May 1996). A Nebraska native, Brownell graduated from Yale Law School and began to practice law in New York City. As a **precinct** worker for the local **Republican Party**, he made the acquaintance of another young **partisan, Thomas E. Dewey.** Brownell served five one-year terms in the state assembly (1932–1936), but increasingly focused his energies on promoting Dewey's candidacies for higher elective offices. He managed Governor Dewey's successful **campaign** for the 1944 presidential nomination and became national party chair, acquitting himself well in a losing effort and earning plaudits for keeping the national **party** headquarters up and going in the months that followed.

Brownell resigned in 1946 to resume his law practice, but he continued his service on Dewey's behalf, managing the 1948 presidential **nomination** and general election campaigns as well. In 1952, along with Dewey, he shifted his support to the presidential candidacy of **Dwight D. Eisenhower**, securing Eisenhower's willingness to enter the nomination contest, managing his preconvention campaign, and serving as a key campaign strategist. After the November victory, Brownell accepted Eisenhower's invitation to join his **cabinet** as attorney general. He held that post for five years, returning to his lucrative law practice in 1958. He remained a leading representative of the party's **Eastern establishment** as its power waned.

BRYAN, CHARLES W. Democratic vice presidential nominee, 1924. (b. 10 February 1867; d. 4 March 1945). Younger brother of **William Jennings Bryan**, thrice the presidential **nominee** of the **Democratic Party**, Charles W. Bryan was his brother's devoted disciple. In his own right, he served three terms as governor of Nebraska (1923–1925 and 1931–1935). In 1924, the **Democratic National Convention** that took 103 ballots to nominate **John W. Davis** for **president** needed only one to designate Bryan as its vice presidential choice. After the Democratic **ticket** lost in the fall **general election**, Bryan returned to Nebraska, where he pursued business interests and made two unsuccessful runs for governor in 1926 and 1928, before winning again in 1930. After leaving the statehouse in 1935, he was elected mayor of Lincoln (1935–1937). He made a final, unsuccessful bid as an **independent** candidate for governor in 1938.

BRYAN, WILLIAM JENNINGS. Democratic presidential nominee, 1896, 1900, 1908. (b. 19 March 1860; d. 26 July 1925). Bryan led the presidential **ticket** of the **Democratic Party** on three occasions. As a junior member of the **House of Representatives** (1891–1895), he emerged as a strong advocate of a **soft money** policy featuring free coinage of silver. At the 1896 **Democratic National Convention**, he electrified the delegates with a stirring speech on the issue. He emerged as the **dark horse** nominee on the fifth **ballot**. The **People's Party** also nominated Bryan that year, but his presidential **campaign** met defeat at the hands of **hard money** Republican **William McKinley**. The two had a rematch in 1900, with the same outcome. After a 1904 hiatus, in which the Democrats embraced a hard money **candidate**, Alton B. Parker, the party again turned to Bryan in 1908. The Republicans prevailed once more, this time led by **William H. Taft**.

Bryan remained a prominent voice in party politics. When the Democrats regained the White House in 1912 under **Woodrow Wilson**, Bryan became secretary of state. He resigned in 1915, his pacifistic orientation challenged as war raged in Europe.

Out of public life, Bryan continued to attract public attention with his legal practice and his advocacy of fundamentalist religion. He acted as prosecutor in the controversial Scopes trial, promoting Tennessee's anti-evolution law. He died shortly after the historic trial's conclusion.

BUCHANAN, JAMES. Democratic president, 1857–1861. (b. 23 April 1791; d. 1 June 1868). Buchanan capped his distinguished career in public service with a term as **president** (1857–1861). He served five terms in the **House of Representatives** (1821–1831). President **Andrew Jackson** sent him to Russia as minister (1832–1834). Pennsylvania's legislature elected him to the U.S. **Senate** in 1834, and he occupied that seat until 1845, when President **James K. Polk** named him secretary of state for a full term. Buchanan unsuccessfully sought the Democratic presidential **nomination** in 1852. His victorious rival, President **Franklin Pierce**, made him minister to Great Britain (1853–1856). Buchanan's residence abroad served his political interests, enabling him to avoid becoming embroiled in the heightening slavery controversy. He challenged Pierce for the 1856 Democratic nomination, finally besting him on the 17th **ballot**.

Buchanan won the **general election** contest comfortably over **John C. Fremont,** the nominee of the new **Republican Party**, and **American Party** nominee **Millard Fillmore**. His presidential term failed to halt the rising regional tensions generated by the slavery controversy. Frustrated, he did not seek reelection in 1860.

BULL MOOSE. Symbol of the **Progressive Party** in the presidential **election** of 1912. It was put forward by the party nominee, **Theodore Roosevelt**, a former **president** reentering the political arena, who proclaimed himself to be fit as a bull moose.

BULL MOOSE PARTY. *See* PROGRESSIVE PARTY.

BURCH, DEAN. Republican National Committee chair, 1964–1965. (b. 20 December 1927; d. 1 August 1991). An Arizona attorney, Burch was a key supporter of the presidential candidacy of Barry M. Goldwater in 1964. After winning the **Republican Party** presidential **nomination**, Goldwater named Burch the national party **chair.** In seeking to integrate the insurgent Goldwater **campaign** organization into the existing national **party** apparatus, Burch displaced and alienated many of the party faithful. Thus, in the wake of the debacle in November, Burch was positioned to serve as the party scapegoat. He was forced out as party chair in January, replaced by **Ray C. Bliss.**

Burch continued to serve Goldwater's political interests, managing his successful 1968 campaign to return to the Senate. After the Republicans captured the White House that year with **Richard M.**

Nixon, Burch received a presidential appointment to the Federal Communications Commission. In 1974, he joined the White House staff to coordinate President Nixon's defense against charges emerging from the mounting Watergate scandals. He continued to serve as an adviser to President **Gerald R. Ford.** Retiring from an active role in party politics in 1977, he practiced law in Washington, D.C., for another decade.

BURR, AARON. Electoral vote recipient, 1792, 1796, 1800 (Democratic-Republican); Democratic-Republican vice president, 1801–1805. (b. 6 February 1756; d. 14 September 1836). Burr was a rising star in New York state politics when the Constitution authorized the new national government. He served as state attorney general (1789–1790). Elected to the U.S. **Senate** in 1791, he served a six-year term. There, he collaborated with **Thomas Jefferson** and **James Madison** in organizing a **partisan** response to the policy initiatives of **Alexander Hamilton** that birthed the **Democratic-Republican Party**. In his initial presidential contest in 1792, Burr received one electoral vote from South Carolina. Four years later, six states provided him with a total of 30 electoral votes.

In 1800, owing to the balloting arrangement in the **electoral college**, Democratic-Republican electors seeking the election of Jefferson as **president** and Burr as **vice president** produced a tie, with each receiving 73 votes. The **House of Representatives** ultimately chose Jefferson as president, making Burr the vice president; but Burr's willingness to be considered at this stage for the higher office produced ill-will between the two. Out of favor with party leaders, Burr was not renominated in 1804. He then failed in his bid for governor of New York and killed **Federalist Party** leader Alexander Hamilton in a duel. Burr participated in a shadowy scheme for western expansion that allegedly involved forming a new country. Subsequently, he was indicted, tried, and acquitted on charges of treason. He spent most of the rest of his life in Europe but returned home to die in New York.

BUSH, GEORGE H. W. Republican National Committee chair, 1973–1974; Republican vice president, 1981–1989; Republican president, 1989–1993. (b. 12 June 1924). Born into a prominent New

England family, George Bush moved to Texas after serving in World War II and graduating from Yale University. He entered the oil business and prospered. Becoming active in **Republican Party** politics, he was a county **chair** and then sought a seat in the U.S. **Senate** in 1964, but lost in the general election. Two years later, he succeeded in gaining a seat in the **House of Representatives**. After winning reelection, he set his sights once again on a Senate seat. His losing effort in 1970 led to a series of high-level political appointments: United Nations ambassador (1971–1973), chair of the **Republican National Committee** (1973–1974), head of the U.S. Liaison Office in Beijing (1974–1975), and director of the Central Intelligence Agency (1976–1977).

Bush's tenure as party chair coincided with the intensification of the **Watergate** scandals, which culminated in the resignation of President **Richard M. Nixon**. Bush had to walk a fine line between loyalty to his **president** and patron and to the **party organization** whose interests were threatened by the presidential scandals. He received high marks from his party constituency for his performance during this awkward time, and incoming president **Gerald R. Ford** rewarded Bush for his service with additional appointments.

In 1980, Bush sought the Republican presidential **nomination**, settling for the vice presidential nomination offered by **Ronald W. Reagan**. He served two terms as Reagan's **vice president** (1981–1989). In 1988, he received the Republican presidential nomination and went on to win the fall elections, the only **incumbent** vice president to do so since **Martin Van Buren** in 1836.

In foreign policy, Bush achieved noteworthy success. He oversaw the collapse of communism in the Soviet Union and the end of the Cold War. He won great acclaim at home and abroad for his conduct as chief diplomat and commander in chief in the months leading up to and during the First Gulf War (1990–1991). However, his handling of domestic politics was less successful, dealing with **Democratic Party** majorities in both houses of **Congress**, facing mounting budget deficits, and confronting a brief downturn in the economy, which had been booming for several years.

Seeking reelection in 1992, Bush prevailed in a noteworthy challenge to his nomination by Patrick J. Buchanan. However, he was defeated by Democrat **Bill Clinton** in a three-way race that also included **independent** Ross Perot. On leaving office, he retired to his adopted home in Texas. His public visibility heightened when his oldest son, **George W. Bush**, was elected president in 2000. The elder Bush thus joined **John Adams** in the ranks of presidential fathers of presidents.

BUSH, GEORGE W. Republican president, 2001–2009. (b. 6 July 1946). Born in Connecticut, Bush grew up in Texas. His parents relocated to Texas from New England, where both their families had achieved considerable prominence. He returned to the Northeast to attend Yale, and he subsequently earned an MBA from Harvard University. Bush followed his father, **George H. W. Bush**, into the oil business, without achieving comparable success. Like his father, he also sought political office under the rising **Republican Party** banner. He won the Republican **nomination** for seat in the **House of Representatives** from west Texas in 1978, but he lost in the general election. Bush's oil industry involvement ended in the mid-1980s, when he shifted his attention to his father's impending 1988 presidential candidacy and **campaign**. He represented his father's interests in the campaign organization. After that successful endeavor, Bush returned to the private sector, joining a group of investors who purchased the Texas Rangers baseball club and serving quite visibly as the managing partner.

In 1994, Bush reentered the political arena, successfully running for governor of Texas. Reelected in 1998, he emerged as the frontrunner for the 2000 Republican presidential nomination, buttressed by a hefty campaign **war chest**. After an early stumble in New Hampshire, Bush easily won the nomination and engaged in a tight **general election** battle with **Democratic Party** nominee **Al Gore**, the incumbent **vice president**.

The **election** outcome was controversial. Gore won a clear plurality of the national popular vote, but the **electoral college** decision turned on the vote for Florida's 25 presidential electors. On the morning after election day, Bush clung to a narrow popular vote lead in Florida. Over the next five weeks, recounts occurred amid legal challenges from both campaigns in the state and federal courts. Along the way, state officials certified Bush's victory. Ultimately, the Supreme Court ordered a halt to the ongoing recounts, leaving Bush electors authorized to cast Florida's electoral votes, which resulted in Bush's election. The 2000 elections restored **unified party government**, because the Republicans retained control of both congressional chambers.

The Bush presidency began in the wake of unprecedented electoral and legal turmoil. Over the next several months, he achieved surprising successes on the legislative front for his agenda of tax and education reform, but a defection in the evenly divided **Senate** left the Democrats in control of that chamber. The terrorist attacks on 11 September 2001 (9/11) enormously strengthened Bush's political standing. Buoyed by a rally effect that elevated his public opinion support to record highs, Bush undertook aggressive action against Afghanistan, whose government had harbored terrorists, and he shepherded through **Congress** the Patriot Act, empowering the executive branch to deal with domestic threats to national security. In the 2002 midterm elections, Bush campaigned vigorously for Republican candidates, and his action bore fruit. The GOP took back the Senate and increased its majority in the House.

In 2003, the Bush administration undertook an invasion of Iraq, to depose its dictator, Saddam Hussein, fearing that his alleged weapons of mass destruction might be placed at the disposal of America's terrorist adversaries. The invasion was successful, but the aftermath proved less so, as the United States struggled with a persistent insurgency. Bush's popularity, which had remained relatively high in the aftermath of 9/11, began a precipitous slide, imperiling his reelection bid in 2004 against Democratic nominee **John F. Kerry**. Bush narrowly prevailed, and the Republicans continued to control both congressional chambers.

The second term saw continued deterioration of Bush's popular support, rising opposition to the ongoing Iraq War, and an inability to advance an ambitious legislative agenda, the hallmark of which was Social Security reform. Nevertheless, Bush was successful in securing the senatorial confirmation of two Supreme Court nominees in 2006. The **midterm elections** that year transferred party control of both houses of Congress to the Democrats. Bush's **lame duck** status also weakened his political position. In his remaining time in the White House, he never regained momentum. Indeed, a deteriorating economy exacerbated his unpopularity. During the 2008 election campaign, he was the target of **bipartisan** criticisms of his record. As his presidency ended, he looked to history to affirm his decisions and actions that had fallen into disfavor from the public and political elites alike.

BUTLER, NICHOLAS M. Republican vice presidential nominee, 1912. (b .2 April 1862; d. 7 December 1947). Butler was the longtime president of Columbia University (1901–1945) who dabbled in **Republican Party** politics. Clearly identified with the party's **Eastern establishment**, he nevertheless backed President **William H. Taft** in 1912 against the challenge presented by former president **Theodore Roosevelt**—first to Taft's **nomination** and then to Taft's **election**—when Roosevelt bolted from the party and ran as the presidential nominee of the **Progressive Party**. On the eve of the **general election**, the renominated vice president, **James S. Sherman**, died. His name remained on the ballot, and the Taft-Sherman ticket carried only two states. After the election, the **Republican National Committee** convened and designated Butler to be the recipient of the eight **electoral college** votes pledged to the Republican **ticket**. Butler pondered subsequent contests for the Republican presidential nomination, but they never materialized. He continued his distinguished career as an educator and became president of the Carnegie Endowment for International Peace (1925–1945).

BUTLER, PAUL M. Democratic National Committee chair, 1955–1960. (b. 15 June 1905; d. 30 December 1961). Butler was an Indiana lawyer active in state **Democratic Party** politics. In 1952, he was elected to a seat on the **Democratic National Committee**. There, he became a key ally of the new **chair, Stephen A. Mitchell**. Mitchell resigned after the 1954 congressional elections, and he endorsed Butler as his successor. The national **committee** concurred. As national party chair, Butler promoted **party unity**. He bemoaned the growing inclination of Southern Democrats to claim the party label while rejecting the party platform. He sought to heighten interaction and coordination between the national **party organization** and the congressional **party-in-office** by establishing the **Democratic Advisory Council** (DAC). However, the congressional party leaders, Majority Leader Lyndon B. Johnson and Speaker Sam Rayburn, were less than

enthusiastic. The DAC thus emerged as the voice of the liberal **wing** of the party in the late 1950s. In 1960, following the presidential **nomination** of **John F. Kennedy**, Butler was replaced as national party chair by Senator **Henry M. Jackson**.

BUTLER, WILLIAM M. Republican National Committee chair, 1924–1928. (b. 29 January 1861; d. 29 March 1937). In 1924, Massachusetts party leader Butler was designated by President **Calvin Coolidge** to head the **Republican National Committee**, reflecting a rather common pattern whereby the president names a home-state political ally to the national party post. Butler presided over the 1924 Coolidge presidential **campaign.** Immediately after the election, he was named to the **Senate** to finish two years of an unexpired term. He resigned from his national party assignment in 1928, clearing the way for nominee **Herbert C. Hoover** to install **Hubert Work** in that office.

BUTLER, WILLIAM O. Democratic vice presidential nominee, 1848. (b. 19 April 1791; d. 6 August 1880). Butler was elected to the **House of Representatives** from Kentucky in 1838, serving two terms. He served with distinction during the Mexican War as a major general. He won a second-ballot victory in the vice presidential balloting at the **Democratic National Convention**, joining **Lewis Cass** on the presidential ticket. They lost in the fall elections to the **Whig Party** team of **Zachary Taylor** and **Millard Fillmore**. Subsequently, Butler declined the offer of President **Franklin Pierce** to appoint him governor of the Nebraska Territory in 1855.

BYRD, HARRY F. Independent Democratic and States' Rights Democratic presidential candidate, 1960. (b. 10 June 1887; d. 20 October 1966). Byrd was the dominant political figure in Virginia for four decades. He served four years as governor (1926–1930), before moving to the **Senate** in 1933, where he remained until 1965. In the Senate, he was a prominent member of the **conservative coalition.**

In 1960, many conservative Democrats in the South were disenchanted with the party's national **ticket** of John F. Kennedy and Lyndon B. Johnson. A few state parties put forward slates of unpledged electors. In Mississippi, all 8 unpledged electors were chosen; in

Alabama, 6 of the 11 were unpledged. All 14 of them then cast their presidential ballots for Byrd in the electoral college. Byrd also received **electoral college** endorsement from one **faithless elector** in Oklahoma, for a total of 15 presidential votes.

BYRD, ROBERT C. Democratic Senate majority Leader, 1977–1981, 1987–1989; Democratic Senate minority leader, 1981–1987; Democratic president pro tempore of the Senate, 1989–1995, 2001–2003; 2007– . (b. 20 November 1917). Robert Byrd was active in state politics in West Virginia before winning a seat in the **House of Representatives** in 1952. He served three terms there and in 1958 succeeded in winning election to the **Senate**, where he continues to serve. He is now the longest serving U.S. senator in history, having surpassed **J. Strom Thurmond** in June 2006.

Byrd moved into a position in the party leadership in 1971, when he became whip for the majority. Six years later, when Michael Mansfield retired, Byrd was the unanimous choice of his party colleagues to be **majority leader.** He held that position for four years, until the Republican victories in the 1980 elections relegated him to **minority leader** for six years. When the Democrats recaptured control of the Senate in 1986, Byrd returned as majority leader. He stepped aside after the 1988 elections, and his party colleagues named him **president pro tempore**, in recognition of his status as the member of the majority party with the most **seniority.** When the Democrats again lost the Senate in 1994, Byrd surrendered his title. He resumed it briefly in January 2001, in the interim between the convening of **Congress** and the presidential inauguration, after the 2000 elections left the Senate evenly divided between Democrats and Republicans. Thus, outgoing Vice President **Al Gore** initially cast the deciding vote in the Democrats' favor, but incoming Vice President **Richard B. Cheney** shifted the partisan balance in favor of the Republicans. In June 2001, a party switch restored the Democratic majority, and Byrd again served as president pro tempore, until the 2002 elections reinstated the Republican **majority** for the 108th Congress. At that point, the **Democratic Caucus** conferred on him the title president pro tempore emeritus, which had been given to Thurmond in 2001. In 2006, Byrd won reelection to a ninth term, while the Democrats

won control of the chamber, placing Byrd back in the position of president pro tempore.

BYRNS, JOSEPH W. Democratic House majority eader, 1933–1935; Democratic Speaker of the House of Representatives, 1935–1936. (b. 20 July 1869; d. 4 June 1936). Byrns won **election** to the **House of Representatives** from Tennessee in 1908. He became **majority leader** in 1933 and was elevated to the Speaker's **chair** in 1935. He died the next year .

– C –

CABINET. An informal presidential institution traditionally composed of the heads of the executive branch departments. The term itself comes from Great Britain, where the parliamentary form of government specifically provides for collective ministerial action. In the American separation of powers setting, the cabinet has no constitutional standing. Rather, it is an instrument of presidential discretion, to be convened and utilized as the president chooses. Few presidents have relied on the cabinet as an instrument for collective decision making.

The cabinet developed early on in the presidency of **George Washington**, who called together his principal advisers, Secretary of State **Thomas Jefferson**, Secretary of the Treasury **Alexander Hamilton**, Secretary of War Henry Knox, and Attorney General Edmund Randolph. Subsequently, when new executive departments were established by Congress, their heads, presidential nominees, joined the cabinet. In turn, other executive departments have disappeared through reorganization. There are currently 15 executive departments.

The cabinet office traditionally most identified with **party** politics was that of **postmaster general**, the head of the Post Office. That individual customarily linked the **party-in-office** with the **party organization,** on the one hand claiming federal **patronage** on behalf of loyal partisans and on the other dispensing it to them. The rise of the **merit system** gradually undermined this role. During the presidency

of **Richard M. Nixon,** the Post Office was removed from the cabinet and reconstituted as the U.S. Postal Service.

CADRE PARTY. A concept developed by French political scientist Maurice Duverger, who contrasted it with the **mass party** and the **devotee party.** Focusing on **party structure,** Duverger characterized a cadre party as one that concentrates narrowly on winning elections. A few full-time leaders and activists dominate the party's organizational structure, and the party does not pursue formal enrollment of members from the general public. Rather, those who identify with the **party** demonstrate their support primarily through voting for its nominees. **Party organization** leaders control nominations of candidates to represent the party in general elections but have relatively little control over nominees once elected. Traditionally, American parties were appropriately characterized as cadre parties. In recent decades, this has been less the case, as the analytical distinctions between cadre and mass parties have become increasingly blurred.

CALHOUN, JOHN C. Democratic-Republican vice president, 1825–1832. (b. 18 March 1782; d. 31 March 1850). Calhoun belonged to a prosperous South Carolina family. After practicing law and serving in the state legislature, he began his long tenure on the national stage in 1811, when he entered the **House of Representatives,** where he served almost three terms. In December 1817, President **James Monroe** named him secretary of war. Calhoun remained in that office for the rest of the Monroe **administration.**

In 1824, Calhoun sought the presidential **nomination** of the dominant **Democratic-Republican Party,** but his candidacy did not generate much support in the party **caucus.** He indicated his willingness to become **vice president,** and the supporters of presidential candidates **John Quincy Adams** and **Andrew Jackson** endorsed him for the second spot. Calhoun won a comfortable **majority** in the vice presidential balloting in the **electoral college,** but a majority was lacking in the presidential balloting. The House then chose Adams to be **president.**

As vice president, Calhoun proved antagonistic to the policies of President Adams. In 1828, Calhoun supported Jackson's presidential candidacy, and Jackson reciprocated by asking Calhoun to run on his

ticket for reelection. Comfortably elected, the Jackson-Calhoun team proved incompatible. Their differences were both personal and political. Calhoun's growing affection for states' rights placed him at odds with Jackson's nationalism. In 1832, Calhoun stood with his state in the nullification crisis that occurred when South Carolina proclaimed that federal tariffs did not apply within the state. Jackson's threat to send federal troops to enforce federal law led the state to retreat, but Calhoun resigned as vice president and took a seat in the **Senate**, where he continued to champion the states' rights cause.

Calhoun held his Senate seat until 1844, when he served briefly as secretary of state for President **John Tyler**. The next year, he returned to the Senate for the remainder of his life. His distinguished tenure was marked by his strident defense of sectionalism.

CAMERON, J. DONALD. Republican National Committee chair, 1879–1880. (b. 14 May 1833; d. 30 August 1918). J. Donald Cameron was the son of Simon Cameron, a prominent Pennsylvania politician who abandoned the **Democratic Party** that had once named him to the U.S. **Senate** to embrace the newly formed **Republican Party** in the mid-1850s. The elder Cameron went on to serve as secretary of war for President **Abraham Lincoln** and later returned to the Senate. His son followed in his footsteps in **Republican Party** politics at the national level, serving in the **administration** of **Ulysses S. Grant** as secretary of war (1876–1877) and then replacing the elder Cameron in the Senate (1877–1897). Shortly after moving to the Senate, J. Donald Cameron became **chair** of the **Republican National Committee** (1879–1880) during the presidency of **Rutherford B. Hayes**. When **James A. Garfield** won the Republican presidential **nomination** in 1880, **Marshall Jewell** replaced Cameron as national party chair.

CAMPAIGN. An operation undertaken to achieve a goal. The term originated in a military setting. It has been adapted to the political arena, where it most often refers to a quest for elective office. It is also employed with regard to issues and policies. Throughout the 19th and well into the 20th centuries, the **party organization** assumed primary responsibility for a campaign. After World War II, **candidate**-centered campaigns became increasingly prevalent. Party organizations have responded to this situation by developing service capacities that candidates can utilize, such as fund-raising and campaign consulting. In appealing to voters, a campaign can emphasize reinforcement of existing supporters, activation of latent supporters, or conversion of those indisposed to provide support. The last of these is by far the most difficult to achieve.

CAMPAIGN FINANCE. The raising and spending of money in pursuit of public office. **Candidates** and parties raise money from individuals, some wealthy, others less so, and **interest groups** working through their **political action committees**. In the special case of presidential campaigns, public funding is available. However, early 21st-century developments make clear that it is in the interest of candidates who can raise large amounts of money to forgo public funding and the expenditure limits associated with it. Some of this money has always been spent for organizational purposes and for advertising. Increasingly, the latter purpose has come to dominate **campaign** spending.

In 2004, campaign spending reached the $5 billion level for all candidates in all races in the United States, and the 2008 election cycle surpassed this milestone. At this point, early in the 21st century, a local campaign for public office may well cost more than $100,000. A contemporary congressional campaign will likely require over $1,000,000. Statewide campaigns for governor or **senator** in a large state can run over $10,000,000, while presidential campaigns need hundreds of millions of dollars to succeed.

Throughout the 19th century, campaign finance was unregulated, and allegations of corruption were widespread. In the 20th century, successive waves of campaign finance reform have resulted in regulatory legislation and institutions. The first wave followed the Teapot Dome scandal that tainted the presidency of **Warren G. Harding**. In its wake, Congress enacted the Federal Corrupt Practices Act of 1925. This legislation required public disclosure of receipts and expenditures for congressional contests. It also established spending ceilings for these races. However, these restrictions lacked effective enforcement mechanisms and were generally ignored.

Some 15 years later, Congress twice passed the **Hatch Act** (1939, 1940). This legislation established a limit on any contributions to a particular candidate, but it contained a significant loophole that allowed contributors to donate a maximum contribution to several different but loosely related campaign committees, undermining its ostensible purpose.

In the 1970s, in the **Federal Election Campaign Act** (FECA, 1971) and a series of subsequent amendments, Congress refocused on four areas of campaign finance regulation: public disclosure of contributions and expenditures, contribution restrictions, expenditure limitations, and public financing provisions. The developing **Watergate** scandals provided impetus for these reform efforts. These legislative initiatives established a bipartisan **Federal Election Commission** (FEC) to enforce the legislation.

By the 1990s, campaign finance had reemerged as a major public issue, fueled by rising campaign costs and perceived abuses of the rules by campaigns and parties, particularly regarding **soft money**. In response, in 2002 Congress passed the **Bipartisan Campaign Reform Act** (BCRA). Another loophole in campaign finance regulation pertains to issue advocacy undertaken by a **527 group**.

CAMPAIGN MANAGER. An individual responsible for directing a **campaign** for public office. Campaign managers have been present from the outset of contests for public office, but their role has heightened in significance and become increasingly professionalized in recent decades, as campaigns have become more expensive and prolonged. Campaign managers oversee an extensive array of campaign staff, including pollsters, fund-raisers, **advance teams**, media consultants, **speechwriters**, and volunteer overseers. Lines of authority in campaign organizations are often vague, and campaign managers may well compete with other campaign officials, as well as with party organization leaders, for power.

CANDIDATE. An office seeker. A candidate seeks to become a party nominee, with that **nomination** authorizing the candidacy.

CANNON, JOSEPH G. Republican Speaker of the House of Representatives, 1903–1911. (b. 7 May 1836; d. 12 November 1926). Joseph Cannon entered the **House of Representatives** in 1873, and with two brief absences (1891–1893 and 1913–1915), represented

Illinois there for 50 years, retiring in 1923. He was elected **Speaker** in 1903 and enthusiastically and autocratically exercised his authority under existing rules and precedents of the body, becoming known as the "czar" of the House. Cannon's leadership came under attack from a **coalition** of **progressive** Republicans and Democrats, who forced procedural reforms curtailing the power of the Speaker in 1910. Following his fall, Cannon served five more terms, temporarily interrupted by the loss of his seat in 1914.

CARLISLE, JOHN G. Democratic Speaker of the House of Representatives, 1883–1889. (b. 5 September 5 1835; d. 31 July 1910). Carlisle won his first **election** to the **House of Representatives** from Kentucky in 1876, and he was reelected seven times. In 1882, when he won his fourth term, the **Democratic Party** took control of the House and elected him **Speaker**. He held the office during the remainder of the presidency of **Chester A. Arthur**, a brief period of divided party government that made him especially visible as a party leader and enabled him to be extraordinarily assertive in his exercise of the powers and duties of the Speaker's office. He continued as Speaker when unified party government was restored with the presidential election of **Grover Cleveland** in 1884, eventually losing the speakership when the **Republican Party** recaptured the House while winning the presidency in 1888. Carlisle moved to the **Senate** in 1890. When Cleveland finally won a second term in 1892, Carlisle became secretary of the treasury. He retired from politics at the conclusion of the term.

CARPENTER, MATTHEW. Republican president pro tempore of the Senate, 1873–1875. (b. 22 December 1824; d. 24 February 1881). Wisconsin sent Carpenter to the **Senate** in 1869. Early on in the 43rd Congress in 1873, he was named **president pro tempore**, and he was subsequently chosen on three additional occasions. He left the Senate in 1875, but he returned in 1879 for the two remaining years of his life.

CARPETBAGGER. A pejorative term for an outsider who comes into a political setting and seeks to win and exercise political power. The term became popular after the Civil War, when Northerners headed

South to assume political control over that war-ravaged region, carrying their worldly possessions in carpetbags. Increased mobility in modern America has undermined the negative potency of the label, but it endures as a vehicle for attacking the character and motives of newcomers. *See also* SCALAWAG.

CARTER, JAMES E. "JIMMY." Democratic President, 1977–1981. (b. 1 October, 1924). Jimmy Carter mastered state politics in Georgia before making his mark on the national scene. He served in the Georgia legislature (1963–1967). Four years later, he was elected governor (1971–1975).

Leaving office, he embarked on a successful quest to secure the 1976 Democratic presidential **nomination.** His outsider candidacy benefited from reforms in presidential nominating politics and from the **Watergate** scandals. He won the fall elections in a close contest with President **Gerald R. Ford.** His presidency coincided with rising inflation in the economy. The takeover of the U.S. embassy in Iran by Islamic fundamentalists backed by the Iranian government precipitated a lingering foreign policy crisis.

Seeking reelection in 1980, Carter survived a nomination challenge by Senator Edward Kennedy of Massachusetts but lost in the **general election** to Republican **Ronald W. Reagan.** In retirement, he established the Carter Center in connection with his presidential library and devoted himself to humanitarian concerns on both the domestic and international scenes. Acting both on his own initiative and as a diplomatic agent of the U.S. government, he has interceded in tense international situations all over the world. In 2002, Carter became the third American president, following **Theodore Roosevelt** and **Woodrow Wilson,** to receive the Nobel Peace Prize, though Carter's was awarded primarily for his postpresidential initiatives.

CARTER, THOMAS H. Republican National Committee chair, 1892–1896. (b. 30 October 1854; d. 17 September 1911). Carter emerged on the national political scene in 1889, when Montana sent him to **Congress** as its territorial delegate. When Montana achieved statehood later that year, Carter remained in the House of **Representatives,** now as a congressman, for a single term. Shortly afterward, in 1892, he became **chair** of the **Republican National Committee,**

charged with managing the reelection **campaign** of President **Benjamin Harrison**, an endeavor that proved unsuccessful. He continued to occupy the office until the 1896 **Republican National Convention**, when **Mark Hanna** assumed leadership of the national **party organization**. Entering the **Senate** in 1895, Carter served one term, left office for four years, and returned in 1905 for another term.

CASS, LEWIS. Democratic presidential nominee, 1848; Democratic president pro tempore of the Senate, 1855. (b. 9 October 1782; d. 17 June 1866). Lewis Cass was a longtime governor of the Michigan Territory (1813–1831). He served as secretary of war under President **Andrew Jackson** (1831–1836). Jackson sent him to France as minister in 1836, where he remained for six years at the behest of Presidents **Martin Van Buren**, **William Henry Harrison**, and **John Tyler**. Returning to the United States in 1842, Cass served Michigan in the **Senate** (1845–1848). In 1848, he captured the presidential **nomination** of the **Democratic Party** but lost the fall elections to his **Whig Party** rival, **Zachary Taylor**. Michigan sent him back to the Senate (1849–1857). His service as **president pro tempore** occurred when there was a vacancy in the office of vice president, created by the death of the **incumbent**, **William R. King**, on 18 April 1853. President **James Buchanan** named Cass secretary of state in 1857. He retired from public life in 1860.

CATCH-ALL PARTY. A concept developed by political scientist Otto Kirkheimer to characterize a political party that subordinates ideological rigor and purity to embrace a diverse array of individuals and groups in hopes of winning elections. This concept applies well to the major parties in the United States. *See also* BIG TENT.

CAUCUS. A meeting of party leaders to designate leaders and nominees or to determine policy directions and courses of action. When national political parties emerged in the 1790s, partisans in the national legislature met (caucused) to nominate their presidential tickets. Congressional caucuses no longer perform this presidential **nomination** function, but they do designate congressional party leaders and provide forums for discussing and determining party strategy and tactics. In a few states, delegates to national party conventions are named by party activists in caucuses. The Iowa caucuses have assumed great significance in presidential nominating politics because of their location early in the nominating calendar. More broadly, private meetings of political elites can be referred to as caucuses. *See also* KING CAUCUS.

CHAIR. A position of party leadership present at every level of **party organization**. At the national level, the party chair is elected by the national **committee** for a fixed term. Traditionally, that term began immediately after the quadrennial national party **convention**, and the presidential nominee had considerable influence in the selection of the national party chair. In recent years, the beginning of the term has been advanced to January following the presidential election, a development that reduces the role of the nominee. However, for the party winning the presidential election, the **president** typically continues to have a major voice in the selection and tenure of the national party chair.

The office of chair also refers to leaders of legislative committees. In Congress, the chair is usually the senior member of the majority party in the chamber. Finally, to chair is to hold a leadership position.

CHANDLER, ZACHARIAH. Republican National Committee chair, 1876–1879. (b. 10 December 1813; d. 1 November 1879). One of the founders of the **Republican Party**, Chandler went to the Senate from Michigan in 1857 and served three terms. There, he was a prominent spokesman for the Radical Republicans in the Reconstruction era. In 1875, he joined the **administration** of President **Ulysses S. Grant** as secretary of the interior. While holding that office, Chandler took on the assignment of national party **chair** in 1876, overseeing the controversial and ultimately victorious presidential **campaign** of **Rutherford B. Hayes**. In 1879, he resigned his party post to return to the **Senate** for a brief period that ended with his death a few months later.

CHENEY, RICHARD B. Republican vice president, 2001–2009. (b. 30 January 1941). Cheney served briefly as a congressional aide in the late 1960s and then joined the **administration** of President **Richard M.**

Nixon in the Office of Economic Opportunity. When **Gerald R. Ford** became president in 1974, he placed Cheney on his White House staff, and Cheney became chief of staff in 1975. After the Ford presidency, Cheney entered the electoral arena, winning the congressional seat in his home state of Wyoming. He was reelected five times, and he rose in the ranks of the House Republican leadership to the position of **chair** of the **Republican Policy Committee**. He was the choice of President **George H. W. Bush** to become secretary of defense in 1989, serving in that office during the invasion of Panama and the Gulf War. After Bush's defeat in 1992, Cheney entered the private sector, becoming chief executive of Halliburton, a major oil services and contracting firm based in Texas.

In 2000, Cheney undertook an assignment on behalf of the presidential campaign of **George W. Bush** to evaluate vice presidential nominee prospects. Instead, he emerged as Bush's choice. First, he had to reestablish his residence in Wyoming, to meet the constitutional expectation that presidential electors from Texas could cast their ballots for only one candidate from that state. Cheney proved to be an effective campaigner for the presidential **ticket** that eventually prevailed.

As **vice president**, Cheney presided over a closely divided **Senate**. He regularly met with the **Republican party conference** in both chambers, thus establishing a new foundation for vice presidential performance in the role of deputy party leader. More significantly, Cheney emerged as a key presidential adviser on both politics and policy. In this latter role, he engendered considerable controversy related to his advocacy executive prerogatives and the Iraq War. Renominated and reelected in 2004, he became a lightning rod for critics of the Bush presidency. By the end of his second term, his reputation and his influence had declined markedly. Unlike most modern vice presidents, he demonstrated no interest in a presidential bid for himself. Leaving office, ostensibibly retired from public life, he became a leading critic of the national security policies of the **Obama** administration.

CHEVES, LANDON. Democratic-Republican Speaker of the House of Representatives, 1814–1815. (b. 17 September 1776; d. 26 June 1857). Cheves represented South Carolina in the **House of Rep-**

resentatives (1810–1815). In January 1814, Speaker **Henry Clay** resigned his House seat. Cheves was elected as his replacement, serving for the remainder of the 13th Congress.

CITIZENS PARTY. A **minor party** appearing on the national scene in 1979, appealing to **liberal** and **populist** voters. It decried the concentration of economic and political power. Its platform (*see* PARTY PLATFORM) advocated public control of energy industries and multinational corporations, opposition to nuclear power, reduced defense spending, and limited price controls. The party nominated Barry Commoner, a prominent environmentalist, for president in 1980 and put forward more than 20 candidates for lesser offices. Commoner received 0.3 percent of the popular vote. Four years later, the party nominated an avowed feminist from Virginia, Sonia Johnson. Her vote total was 0.1 percent. The party's weak national performance masked rather more impressive showings in selected local contests in environmentalist strongholds such as Burlington, Vermont, where several of its nominees were in fact elected. *See also* GREEN PARTY.

CIVIL RIGHTS. Broadly, the protections afforded citizens under the Constitution and the laws against abusive governmental power. More narrowly, *civil rights* is used in connection with the ongoing efforts of black Americans to overcome the racial discrimination that was a legacy of slavery, notwithstanding the post–**Civil War** constitutional amendments designed to achieve that goal. Early on, the **Republican Party** enthusiastically championed the cause of black civil rights, whereas the **Democratic Party** divided along sectional lines, with the Southern Democrats resistant. In the 20th century, issue **realignment** gradually moved the Democrats toward advocacy, while tempering the Republican commitment.

CIVIL WAR. The 1861–1865 conflict precipitated by the attempt by 11 Southern states to secede from the Union. The slavery controversy loomed large in generating the conflict, as did socioeconomic tensions between the urbanizing, industrializing North and the rural, agricultural South, as well as differing understandings of the federal character of the political order: nationalism versus states' rights. The

Union (Northern) victory in the Civil War left the **Democratic Party** divided and weakened, and it was the catalyst for the rise of the **Republican Party** to power in the **Third Party System** and the ensuing **Fourth Party System**. In turn, the triumph of the Republicans reinforced Democratic loyalties in the defeated South, where they remained solid for over a century following the war.

CLAFLIN, WILLIAM. Republican National Committee chair, 1868–1872. (b. 6 March 1818; d. 5 January 1905). A Massachusetts party leader, Claflin was chosen **chair** of the **Republican National Committee** in 1868, in preparation for the presidential **campaign** of **Ulysses S. Grant**. The next year, he began a two-year term as governor of his state. Departing his national party post in 1872, he was elected to the **House of Representatives** in 1876, where he served two terms.

CLARK, DANIEL. Republican president pro tempore of the Senate, 1864, 1865. (b. 24 October 1809; d. 2 January 1891). Clark represented New Hampshire in the **Senate** (1857–1866). On two occasions in the last year of the 38th Congress, he was elected **president pro tempore**, following several years in which the Senate had routinely named **Solomon Foot** of Vermont to that post whenever necessary.

CLARK, JAMES B. "CHAMP." Democratic minority leader of the House of Representatives, 1908–1911, 1919–1921; Democratic Speaker of the House of Representatives, 1911–1919. (b. 7 March 1850; d. 2 March 1921). "Champ" Clark represented Missouri in the **House of Representatives** for over a quarter of a century. He entered **Congress** in 1893. Losing his first bid for reelection, he persisted and returned to office in 1897, retaining his seat for virtually the remainder of his life. In 1908, Clark replaced **John Sharp Williams** as the **floor leader** for the **minority** Democrats. In 1911, when the Democrats won a **majority** of seats for the first time in over a decade, as their leader, Clark was their choice as **Speaker**. He assumed an office shorn of much of its power under his predecessors **Thomas B. Reed** and **Joseph G. Cannon**. In 1912, he was a strong contender for his party's presidential **nomination**, assembling a clear majority of delegates at the **Democratic National Convention** but falling short of the **two-thirds rule** requirement and eventually losing out to **Woodrow Wilson**. He lost the speakership following the 1918 **midterm elections** won by the Republicans. Continuing to serve as floor leader for the minority in the 66th Congress, he lost his bid for reelection in the Republican **landslide** of 1920; he died shortly afterward.

CLARKE, JAMES P. Democratic president pro tempore of the Senate, 1913, 1915–1916. (b. 18 August 1854; d. 1 October 1916). Clarke served a single term as governor of Arkansas (1895–1897). In 1903, the state legislature selected him for a seat in the U.S. **Senate**. In 1913, early in the 63rd Congress, the Senate named him its **president pro tempore**. Kept on at the beginning of the 64th Congress, he continued to occupy that office until his death in 1916.

CLARKSON, JAMES S. Republican National Committee chair, 1891–1892. (b. 17 May 1842; d. 31 May 1918). Born in Indiana, as a young man Clarkson worked in the underground railroad, transporting slaves fleeing the South to freedom in Canada. He later worked in the railroad industry and became active in the **Republican Party**. Having moved to Iowa, he became **chair** of the state **committee** in 1869. Two years later, he received a **patronage** appointment from President **Ulysses S. Grant** as postmaster of Des Moines, a position he held for six years.

In 1880, his state **party** chose him as its representative on the **Republican National Committee**. There, he became increasingly influential in national party politics. Clarkson was a key player in the 1884 presidential **nomination** and **campaign** of **James G. Blaine**. Four years later, at the **Republican National Convention**, he delivered his state delegation's support to **Benjamin Harrison** at a critical point in the balloting, resulting in Harrison's nomination. At that point, Harrison offered to make Clarkson national party chair, but Clarkson supported the candidacy of **Matthew S. Quay**, in the interests of advancing party unity.

Clarkson was also considered for **postmaster general**, but he settled for the number two spot in that department, where he distributed patronage largesse and decried the progress of **civil service** reform. When Quay resigned as national party chair in 1891, Clarkson succeeded him. However, after the 1892 convention, President Harrison placed Thomas A. Carter in that office. Clarkson remained a member of the national committee until 1896, but he lowered his profile in national party politics and tended to his interests in the railroad industry.

CLAY, HENRY. Democratic-Republican Speaker of the House of Representatives, 1811–1814, 1815–1820, 1823–1825; Democratic-Republican presidential candidate, 1824; National Republican presidential nominee, 1832; Whig presidential nominee, 1844. (b. 12 April 1777; d. 29 June 1852). Henry Clay was a major force in national politics for almost half a century. He went to Washington in 1806 as a senator. After two short stints in the **Senate**, he moved over to the **House of Representatives** in 1811. As a freshman, he was elected **Speaker** of the House, and he spent much of the next 14 years in that body as its leader. In the process, he energized both the Speaker's office and **Congress** in the constitutional system.

In 1824, he contended for the presidency as a factional leader of the dominant **Democratic-Republican Party**. He fared poorly, running last in the field of four candidates. Because no candidate received a **majority** in the **electoral college**, the **election** went to the House, where Clay dominated. He threw his support to **John Quincy Adams**. Once elected, Adams named Clay secretary of state. Controversy surrounding this **nomination**, labeled a "corrupt bargain" by **Andrew Jackson** and his supporters, served as the catalyst for Jackson's successful 1828 presidential **campaign**.

In 1831, Clay returned to the Senate after a two-decade absence. He again proved himself to be a major legislative force. He was the **standard-bearer** for the **National Republicans**, who opposed Jackson in 1832, and a founder of the **Whig Party**.

After leaving the Senate in 1842, Clay headed up the Whig presidential **ticket** in 1844 but lost in the fall elections to Democrat **James K. Polk**. He made a final return to the Senate (1849–1852), during which he sealed his sterling legislative reputation as "the Great Compromiser" in a heroic effort to withstand the sectional conflict that was dividing the nation.

CLEAN SWEEP. An across-the-board party victory, whereby the party **ticket** wins the entire **slate** of public offices being contested in an **election**.

CLEVELAND, GROVER. Democratic president, 1885–1889, 1893–1897; Democratic presidential nominee, 1888. (b. 18 March 1837; d. 24 June 1908). Cleveland burst on the New York state political scene in 1882, when he was elected mayor of Buffalo. The next year, he captured the gubernatorial **nomination** of the **Democratic Party**. Victorious at the polls, he went on to serve a single term. His meteoric rise continued in 1884 when, despite the opposition of New York City's **Tammany Hall** machine, the **Democratic National Convention** nominated him for **president**. In the ensuing fall elections, he defeated Republican **James G. Blaine.**

President Cleveland successfully sought renomination in 1888, but he lost in the **electoral college** to Republican **Benjamin Harrison**, despite having a slight plurality in the popular vote. Four years later, he won an unprecedented third straight Democratic presidential nomination and returned to the White House for a second term. To date, he remains the only president to return to the office after vacating it. His second term featured an economic depression and labor unrest that diminished his political capital. Cleveland was an unabashed Gold Democrat, who embraced a **hard money** position in the currency debate that was then raging. In nominating **William Jennings Bryan** for president in 1996, the Democratic National Convention repudiated the **lame duck** president. In turn, Cleveland declined to support Bryan's candidacy, bolting to the **National Democratic Party**. On leaving office, he retired to Princeton, New Jersey.

CLINTON, DE WITT. Federalist presidential nominee, 1812. (b. 2 March 1769; d. 11 February 1828). Clinton was a major force in New York state politics in the first quarter of the 19th century. He served in the U.S. **Senate** (1802–1803) and then as mayor of New York City. While holding that office, he became the champion of dissidents in the **Democratic-Republican Party** from New York, who abandoned President **James Madison** in 1812 and supported Clinton as their **favorite son**. The opposition **Federalist Party**, seeking to halt its precipitous decline, also embraced Clinton's candidacy. However, in the **electoral college**, Madison easily prevailed. Clinton returned to New York, where he resumed his occupancy of the mayoral office in 1813 and 1814. He went on to serve as governor on two occasions (1817–1823 and 1825–1828). He died in office.

CLINTON, GEORGE. Electoral vote recipient, 1789, 1792, 1796 (Democratic-Republican); Democratic-Republican vice president, 1805–1812. (b. 26 July 1739; d. 20 April 1812). Clinton represented New York in the Continental Congress (1775–1776). From there, he was elected governor (1777–1795 and 1801–1804). He consistently received **electoral college** support in the pre-1800 balloting. In 1789, he won the votes of three Virginians; in 1792, he finished in third place with 50 votes from five states. In 1796, he fell to seventh place, with seven votes from two states.

In 1804, with President **Thomas Jefferson** seeking reelection and Vice President **Aaron Burr** being abandoned, Clinton was the choice of the legislative **caucus** of the **Democratic-Republican Party** as Jefferson's running mate, in recognition of his manifest popularity in the pivotal state of New York. Although he opposed Jefferson's policies, his political standing in New York led party leaders to nominate him for another term as vice president, under **James Madison**. He became even more vocal in his opposition to presidential leadership prior to his death in the last year of that term.

CLINTON, WILLIAM J. "BILL." Democratic president, 1993–2001. (b. 19 August 1946). Bill Clinton was a young law professor at the University of Arkansas when he challenged a firmly entrenched **incumbent** for the third district congressional seat in 1974. Although he lost, the race indicated his political appeal. In 1976, he won a statewide campaign for attorney general and followed up with a successful race for governor in 1978, making him the nation's youngest state chief executive. Defeated for reelection in 1980, he rebounded with a convincing victory in 1982; he held the office throughout the following decade.

As governor, Clinton was active in the National Governors Association, providing him with national visibility. He also was a founding member of the **Democratic Leadership Council**, a group of moderates seeking to pull the Democratic Party back to the center of the ideological spectrum, after moves to the left had proved electorally disastrous.

Clinton sought the 1992 Democratic presidential **nomination**, which few potential competitors desired, given the high public approval ratings that incumbent President **George H. W. Bush** had been enjoying. However, an economic recession sent Bush's popularity plummeting, and Clinton won the presidency in a three-person contest that included a strong **independent** candidacy by businessman Ross Perot.

Clinton experienced a rocky first term that included the loss of both houses of **Congress** by the Democrats for the first time in four decades. Nevertheless, he was unchallenged for the 1996 Democratic presidential nomination. He successfully positioned himself between the **majority** Republicans and minority Democrats in Congress in a strategy of "triangulation" that resulted in his comfortable reelection in 1996 in another three-person race, this time against Republican **Robert J. Dole** and Perot, who ran under the banner of the newly established Reform Party.

Clinton's second term featured continued economic prosperity, sustained charges of improprieties in his private life, and consistently high public job approval ratings. Allegations arising from his actions in the context of a civil suit for sexual harassment while he was governor resulted in impeachment by the **House of Representatives** in 1998 and trial in the **Senate** in 1999 on charges of perjury and obstruction of justice. He was acquitted, but controversy regarding his behavior persisted. He was subsequently cited for civil contempt of court by the federal district judge who received his deposition in the civil suit.

On the foreign policy front, Clinton heightened U.S. involvement in the Balkan conflict, under the auspices of the North Atlantic Treaty Organization. In 1995, he deployed U.S. troops as peacekeepers in support of a treaty the United States had brokered. Subsequently, in 1999, he sent U.S. war planes on bombing missions against the former Yugoslavia, eventually forcing that government to abandon policies and practices of ethnic cleansing. In the Middle East, Clinton eagerly sought a resolution to the Israeli–Palestinian conflict. He achieved limited early success, but this ambitious goal ultimately eluded him.

In 2000, term-limited by the 22nd Amendment, Clinton passed the mantle of presidential party leadership to his **vice president, Al Gore.** The Gore campaign vacillated between its desire, on the one hand, to take advantage of Clinton's record of economic prosperity and his vaunted campaign skills, and on the other hand, to avoid being tarred and feathered by "Clinton fatigue" attributable to the president's scandalous personal behavior. Gore ultimately leaned in the latter direction, leading to rising tensions between the two.

Following Gore's controversial defeat, Clinton ostensibly retired to private life. He has remained a public figure, owing to his celebrity at home and abroad. He oversees humanitarian efforts through the Clinton Foundation. His wife, Hillary, was elected senator from New York in 2000, and her unsuccessful quest for the Democratic presidential nomination in 2008 reengaged Clinton in presidential nominating politics in controversial fashion. He eventually embraced the nominee, **Barack H. Obama**, campaigning on his behalf in the **general election**. In 2009, the United Nations designated him as its special envoy to Haiti.

CLOAKROOM. A partisan meeting place adjacent to a legislative chamber. The name derives from the original use of such a room as a place for legislators to store their coats and hats. Cloakrooms became places where legislators could plot strategy and negotiate compromises.

CLOSED PRIMARY. A **primary** that requires potential voters to declare their party affiliation to become eligible to participate in a primary **election**. Party organizations contend that closed primaries promote **party unity** and responsibility, while preventing the party's choice of nominees from being determined by voters who are not supportive of the party. *See also* BLANKET PRIMARY; OPEN PRIMARY.

COALITION. An array of factions or interests allied to pursue common objectives. In the United States, political parties are broad coalitions of diverse and even competing interests. For example, the **New Deal** coalition assembled by President **Franklin D. Roosevelt** brought together under the **Democratic Party** umbrella the white South, racial and ethnic minorities, organized labor, farmers, and ideological liberals. A **bipartisan** coalition unites factions of more than one party. *See also* CONSERVATIVE COALITION; FACTION.

COATTAIL EFFECT. A situation in which electoral support for the nominee at the top of a party **slate** generates **straight ticket** voting that benefits lower-level **party** nominees. Coattail effects are more likely in states with a **party-column balloti**ng arrangement than those with the office-bloc ballot alternative. Unpopular candidates at the top of the party ticket may encourage negative coattail effects.

COBB, HOWELL. Democratic Speaker of the House of Representatives, 1849–1851. (b. 7 September 1815; d. 9 October 1868). Named for his congressman uncle, Cobb was initially elected to the **House of Representatives** from Georgia in 1842. Six years later, as he undertook his fourth term, the **Democratic Party** had a narrow majority of seats and put him forward as their leader. However, a **bipartisan** array of nominal Democrats and Whigs committed to the free-soil principle deadlocked the proceedings by withholding their crucial support from both Cobb and the designated **Whig Party** leader, Robert Winthrop, the **Speaker** in the previous Congress, in protest over the willingness of congressional party leaders to accommodate slavery. Eventually, the House members agreed to allow the Speaker to be elected by a **plurality** vote, and Cobb prevailed on the 63rd ballot. After his term as Speaker, he returned home to Georgia as governor (1851–1853). He came back to the House for a single term in 1855, and he was the nominee of President **James Buchanan** for secretary of the treasury (1857–1860).

COLFAX, SCHUYLER. Republican Speaker of the House of Representatives, 1863–1869; Republican vice president, 1869–1873. (b. 23 March 1823; d. 13 January 1885). Schuyler Colfax represented Indiana in the **House of Representatives** for seven terms (1855–1869). He was a pioneer in the emergence of the **Republican Party** in the 1850s. Elected **Speaker** during the **Civil War**, he proved to be an energetic **partisan**, setting a new standard of expectation for the office. He was the choice of the 1868 **Republican National Convention** to join its presidential ticket, headed by **Ulysses S. Grant**. Colfax served a single term as vice president. He desired renomination but was dropped from the ticket in 1872 amid allegations of involvement in the Credit Mobilier scandal that were never substantiated.

COMMITTEE. A party organization unit present at national, state, and local levels. It assembles party organization activists nominally chosen by the parallel party **convention**. It exercises the authority of the party organization between meetings of the convention. It typically designates a **chair**, who has considerable day-to-day responsibility.

Committees are also legislative entities. Legislatures typically organize and divide their workload among committees. A legislative party **caucus** assigns its members to committees. In Congress, committee seats are divided between the parties in a manner that roughly approximates the overall party division in the chamber. Usually, the senior member of the majority party (*see* PARTY-IN-POWER) chairs the committee. *See also* DEMOCRATIC NATIONAL COMMITTEE; REPUBLICAN NATIONAL COMMITTEE; SENIORITY SYSTEM.

COMMITTEE TO REELECT THE PRESIDENT (CREEP). The presidential campaign organization promoting the successful 1972 reelection effort of **Richard M. Nixon**. CREEP achieved notoriety for undertaking several illegal and unethical campaign activities that were an integral part of the larger **Watergate** scandals that led to Nixon's 1974 resignation. Operating apart from the **Republican National Committee**, CREEP epitomized the growing separation in presidential politics between the national party committees and the personal campaign organizations of presidential nominees.

COMMUNIST PARTY. Long-standing **minor party** in the 20th century. The leaders of the successful 1917 Bolshevik Revolution in Russia encouraged American leftists to form a communist party. After several years of in-fighting and dissension, in 1921 the Workers' Party of America appeared on the scene with Moscow's endorsement. The party embraced the goal of revolution to overthrow capitalism and create a workers' state. It first contested presidential elections in 1924 and 1928 under the label of the Workers' Party. It did not formally title itself the Communist Party until 1929. Under this label, it continued to nominate presidential candidates through 1940, and again from 1968 through 1984. Its organizational and electoral support peaked in the 1930s. In 1932, perennial nominee William Z. Foster received over 100,000 votes (0.3 percent).

During World War II, with the United States allied with the Soviet Union, party leader Earl Browder proclaimed the dissolution of the party, and the Communists supported the bid of **Democratic Party** nominee **Franklin D. Roosevelt** for a third term, though Roosevelt renounced them. After the war, the party reorganized, supporting **Progressive Party** nominee **Henry A. Wallace** in his 1948 presidential bid, but the onset of the Cold War doomed its efforts to build popular support.

Indeed, during the height of the Cold War, the Communist Party labored under backbreaking legal and normative restrictions that made contesting elections virtually impossible. The easing of Cold War tensions in the late 1960s encouraged the Communist Party to again openly seek electoral support, but these efforts proved futile. With the abandonment of communism in the Soviet Union, the Communist Party, U.S.A., drifted into history.

CONGRESS. The legislative branch of the federal government. The Congress is a bicameral institution, consisting of the **House of Representatives** and the **Senate**. However, some commentators use the term more narrowly, to refer specifically to the House. The first Congress convened in 1789. Consecutively numbered, a new Congress meets every two years, in the wake of the biennial congressional elections. *See also* MEMBER OF CONGRESS; REPRESENTATIVE; SENATOR.

CONSERVATIVE. An ideological label, "conservative" clearly connotes a commitment to tradition and an ensuing resistance to change. In contemporary American politics, it broadly characterizes those who favor limited government, ostensibly opposing government intervention in the daily lives of the citizenry. This principle does not always extend to all dimensions of life, thus differentiating economic from social conservatives, with the latter **faction** favoring government involvement to promote and protect traditional values. Both major political parties have long had conservative wings, but today's **Republican Party** is clearly the more conservative. *See also* LIBERAL.

CONSERVATIVE COALITION. A long-standing **bipartisan** alliance. During the **New Deal** era, a conservative coalition emerged in Congress, joining Southern Democrats with Republicans to oppose the **liberal** initiatives of President Franklin D. Roosevelt. This conservative coalition proved to be a major force in congressional politics for several decades. Party **realignment** in the South, beginning in the 1960s, brought about its gradual demise by the mid-1990s. *See also* COALITION.

CONSERVATIVE OPPORTUNITY SOCIETY (COS). A **caucus** founded by junior members of the **Republican Party** in the **House of Representatives** in the 98th Congress (1983–1985). The group sought out opportunities to challenge in confrontational fashion the procedures and policies put forward by the congressional leadership of the **Democratic Party**, which had long constituted the majority in the chamber. **Newt Gingrich**, a representative from Georgia, quickly emerged as the leader of this ideologically based **faction**. This organizational effort bore fruit a decade later, when the COS policy agenda took the form of the **Contract with America** and the Republicans gained control of the House for the first time in four decades.

CONSTITUTION. The 1787 document that establishes the framework for government in the United States, based on principles of representation, separation of powers, checks and balances, federalism, and judicial review. The Constitution predates the emergence of political parties, and thus it makes no mention of them. However, through informal mechanisms, it quickly accommodated their presence on the political scene. For example, parties quickly asserted themselves in such arenas as presidential selection and congressional organization. In at least one instance, the presence of parties required formal amendment of the Constitution, when the 12th Amendment revised the balloting arrangements in the **electoral college**. *See also* CONSTITUTIONAL AMENDMENTS.

CONSTITUTIONAL AMENDMENTS. The 1787 Constitution provided for a process of amendment with two distinct stages. Amendments may be proposed by either two-thirds majorities of both houses of **Congress** or a convention called for that purpose by at least two-thirds of the states. They may be ratified by either three-fourths of the state legislatures or specially called ratifying conventions in three-fourths of the states. To date, 27 amendments have been ratified and added to the Constitution.

One of these amendments, the 12th, clearly accommodates the emergence of political parties in the United States. It alters the balloting arrangements in the electoral college, shifting from the original process of a single **ballot** with two names on it to the revised process of two ballots, each with a single name, one for **president** and the other for **vice president**. The change was necessary when parties began nominating presidential tickets and seeking the selection of electors committed to that party **ticket.**

In 1800, the nominees of the **Democratic-Republican Party**, **Thomas Jefferson** and **Aaron Burr**, each received 73 electoral votes from loyal electors, giving them a clear lead over their **Federalist Party** rivals, **John Adams** and **Charles C. Pinckney**. However, their tie vote sent the presidential election to the **House of Representatives**, where Jefferson, clearly perceived to be the presidential nominee, prevailed. The 12th Amendment (1804) was quickly proposed and ratified to address a situation that was very likely to recur.

Several other constitutional amendments less directly but still significantly pertain to the presence of political parties in the constitutional system. Several limit the states in their establishment of suffrage requirements. The 15th Amendment (1870) precludes discrimination with regard to race, color, or previous condition of servitude; the 19th Amendment (1920) similarly proscribes gender discrimination; the 24th Amendment (1964) outlaws a poll tax in federal elections; and the 26th Amendment (1971) establishes 18 as the maximum allowable voting age requirement.

In addition, the 17th Amendment (1913) provides for direct popular election of senators. The 20th Amendment (1933) realigns the schedule of presidential and congressional terms and clarifies some ambiguities in presidential succession. The 22nd Amendment (1951) limits presidential tenure to two elected terms. The 23rd Amendment (1961) provides the District of Columbia with representation in the electoral college. The 25th Amendment (1967) addresses presidential disability and succession and provides for filling a vacancy in the vice presidency.

CONSTITUTIONAL UNION PARTY. Minor party that figured prominently in the presidential election of 1860. The Constitutional Union Party came into existence in 1859, organized by former members of the **Whig Party** and the **American Party** (Know-Nothings), both of which had disintegrated. It steadfastly promoted the cause of national unity, as sectional divisions heightened on the eve of the Civil War. It contested the 1860 presidential **election**, with **John Bell**, a former **Speaker** of the **House of Representatives**, as its **standard-bearer**. Bell carried three states on the border between North and South, winning 39 electoral votes. The **party** did not survive the splintering of the Union.

CONTRACT WITH AMERICA. Republican Party legislative agenda developed in advance of the 1994 midterm congressional elections. The impetus for the Contract with America came from the Conservative Opportunity Society, a **faction** within the **House of Representatives** led by **Newt Gingrich**, the **whip** of the **minority** Republicans. The Contract with America was a 12-point plan that embraced both procedural and substantive reforms that the Republican nominees for the House promised to enact if they gained control of the chamber. The proposed reforms included a balanced-budget amendment and line-item veto, welfare reform, tax reductions, term limits, and downsizing of congressional staff.

Surprisingly, the Republicans did win a majority of House seats and proceeded to pass virtually all of the items in the Contract with America. However, resistance in the Senate and the White House kept significant portions of the contract from becoming law. *See also* PARTY RESPONSIBILITY.

CONVENTION. A meeting of party delegates for the purposes of nominating candidates for public office, proclaiming policies, and promoting **party unity** and identity. Conventions occur at county, state, and national levels, with the lower levels typically involved in the selection of delegates to the upper levels. In the Jacksonian era, the convention replaced the **caucus** as the process by which presidential nominees were identified. It quickly became normative at state and local levels for the remainder of the 19th century, only to be largely supplanted by the **primary** at the turn of the century. The nominating convention endures at the presidential level. At the lower levels, modern conventions center on party platforms and rallies.

Beyond the context of party politics, the term "convention" refers to a formal meeting of any assemblage. A noteworthy example is the convention that assembled in Philadelphia in 1787 to draft a new **constitution** for the United States. *See also* DEMOCRATIC NATIONAL CONVENTION; REPUBLICAN NATIONAL CONVENTION.

CONVERTING ELECTION. A rare category in the taxonomy of presidential elections. A converting election features an anticipated victory by the dominant party in the **party system**, but with significant shifts in electoral behavior by voting blocs comprising a party's **coalition** that portend a future **realignment**. For example, in 1928 **Republican Party** nominee **Herbert C. Hoover** won the presidency, as expected in the Republican-dominated **Fourth Party System**, over his **Democratic Party** opponent, **Al Smith**. Hoover's victory came in part through an unprecedented show of strength in the South, where Smith's Roman Catholicism and **wet** stance on **Prohibition** were unpopular. In turn, the losing candidate achieved noteworthy support from urban ethnic voters, which had been lacking for previous Democratic nominees. Four years later, the South returned to its solidly Democratic roots, joining with the urban ethnic voters and other components to produce a realigned party coalition that proved remarkably durable and powerful. *See also* DEVIATING ELECTION; MAINTAINING ELECTION; REALIGNING ELECTION; REINSTATING ELECTION.

COOLIDGE, CALVIN. Republican vice president, 1921–1923, Republican president, 1923–1929. (b. 4 July 1872; d. 5 January 1933). Massachusetts voters elected Calvin Coolidge governor in 1918. Two years later, he was the choice of kingmakers within the **Republican Party** for the second spot on their presidential **ticket**, led by **Warren G. Harding**. The Republicans won a **landslide** victory in 1920, sending Coolidge to Washington. When Harding died in 1923, Coolidge became **president**. Avoiding the scandals of the Harding **administration** and presiding over a booming economy, he won **nomination** and **election** in his own right in 1924, the second consecutive **accidental**

president to do so. Coolidge chose not to run for a second term in 1928. In retirement, he published his autobiography and wrote a newspaper column.

COPPERHEAD. A **Civil War**–era term for Northerners who sympathized with and even supported the South. The Copperheads were a visible and vocal faction within the **Democratic Party**. Since then, the pejorative label has been more broadly applied to challenge the loyalty of individuals and groups to a cause, as well as to attack those whose support is viewed as insufficient.

CORTELYOU, GEORGE B. Republican National Committee chair, 1904–1907. (b. 26 July 1862; d. 23 October 1940). A New York native, Cortelyou was trained as a stenographer. His skill secured him clerical positions in the offices of a series of public officials, peaking with Presidents **Grover Cleveland**, **William McKinley**, and **Theodore Roosevelt**. Roosevelt was particularly impressed with Cortelyou's talent and potential. In 1903, he named Cortelyou the first secretary of the newly created Department of Commerce and Labor. In that capacity, Cortelyou also managed Roosevelt's preconvention **campaign** for the presidential **nomination**, in which Roosevelt shattered precedent by becoming the first **accidental president** to receive that honor from his party. After the convention, Roosevelt made Cortelyou **chair** of the **Republican National Committee** so he could oversee the **general election** campaign. In 1905, Cortelyou moved from Commerce and Labor over to the Post Office, as **postmaster general**, solidifying the connection between the Post Office and the **party organization**.

In 1907, Cortelyou accepted yet another nomination from Roosevelt, this time to lead the Treasury Department. At that point, he resigned his party position. He aspired to the presidential nomination in 1908 but failed to attract sufficient support in a contest that **William Howard Taft** won handily. After the election, Cortelyou retired from public life and embarked on a lengthy career as a corporate executive in New York City.

COX, JAMES M. Democratic presidential nominee, 1920. (b. 31 March 1870; d. 15 July 1957). A prominent Ohio newspaper publisher, James

Cox served two terms in the **House of Representatives** (1909–1913) before his election as governor in 1912. He lost his bid for reelection in 1914 but returned to win two more terms (1917–1921). As he was concluding his last term, he received the 1920 presidential nomination of the **Democratic Party**. His running mate was a young New Yorker with a magical political name, **Franklin D. Roosevelt**. The Democratic **ticket** lost in a **landslide** to Republicans **Warren G. Harding** and **Calvin Coolidge**. Cox left the political arena after the crushing defeat and tended to his wide-ranging business interests.

CRAWFORD, WILLIAM H. Democratic-Republican president pro tempore of the Senate, 1812; Democratic-Republican presidential candidate, 1824. (b. 24 February 1772; d. 14 September 1834). Crawford came to the U.S. **Senate** in 1807, representing Georgia. He served a single term that featured his designation during his last year as the **president pro tempore**. That tenure coincided with the vacancy in the vice presidency created by the death of incumbent **George Clinton** on April 20, 1812.

President **James Madison** named Crawford secretary of war (1815–1816) and then secretary of the treasury (1816–1817). President **James Monroe** kept him in the latter post throughout his **administration** (1817–1825). As the 1824 presidential **election** approached, Crawford appeared to be well positioned to secure the nomination of the dominant **Democratic-Republican Party**. However, in September 1823, he suffered a debilitating stroke. A poorly attended legislative **caucus** the next spring nevertheless made Crawford its nominee. This action undermined the legitimacy of the caucus and did not deter the presidential campaigns of other contenders under the party's umbrella.

In the subsequent presidential balloting, Crawford ran a poor third in both the popular vote and the **electoral college**, trailing **Andrew Jackson** and **John Quincy Adams**. With no candidate receiving a **majority** of electoral votes, Crawford remained in the field of eligibles to be considered by the **House of Representatives**. That body chose Adams to be president. Crawford spent the final decade of his life in retirement from public life.

CRISP, CHARLES F. Democratic Speaker of the House of Representatives, 1891–1895. (b. 29 January 1845; d. 23 October 1896).

Crisp won seven terms to the **House of Representatives** from his Georgia constituents. In 1891, following the Democratic Party successes in the **midterm elections** that gave it a **majority** of seats, he was elected **Speaker**. He followed in the footsteps of his immediate predecessors, **John G. Carlisle** and **Thomas B. Reed**, in providing strong and centralized party-based leadership. When the **Republican Party** returned to power in 1895, Crisp lost the speakership to Reed. He died in office in 1896.

CRITICAL ELECTION. Concept introduced by V. O. Key, who noted that a handful of elections have been associated with fundamental, enduring shifts in **partisan** loyalties by large segments of the electorate. Such an **election** that transforms the landscape of party competition may be called a **realigning election**. Party scholars typically identify the presidential elections of **Thomas Jefferson** in 1800, **Abraham Lincoln** in 1860, **William McKinley** in 1896, and **Franklin D. Roosevelt** in 1932 as critical elections.

CROSSOVER VOTING. Participation by supporters of one **party** in another party's **primary**. The motivations for crossover voting vary. They include genuine support for a particular **candidate** as well as a desire on the part of crossover voters to increase their own party's prospects in the **general election** by supporting an unattractive opposition candidate. The latter act is known as raiding. Both the **open primary** and the **blanket primary** facilitate crossover voting, whereas the **closed primary** seeks to preclude it.

CULLUM, SHELBY M. Republican Senate majority leader, 1911–1913. (b. 22 November 1829; d. 28 January 1914). Collum belonged to a prominent political family. Before the Civil War, two of his uncles served Tennessee and the **Whig Party** in the **House of Representatives**. He was elected to that body as a **Republican Party** nominee from Illinois in 1864. Having served three terms, he returned home. In 1876, he was elected governor, holding that office until 1883, when he was elected to the Senate. In 1911, at the outset of the 62nd **Congress**, his last in office, Collum was the first officially designated Senate **majority leader**.

CUMMINGS, HOMER S. Democratic National Committee chair, 1919–1920. (b. 30 April 1870; d. 10 September 1956). A Yale graduate, Cummings practiced law in Stamford, Connecticut, where he became involved in local **party** politics. In 1900, he was elected mayor and to a seat on the **Democratic National Committee** (DNC). He held the latter for a quarter-century. In 1913, he became vice chair of the DNC. In 1919, when **Vance C. McCormick** resigned as **chair**, the national **committee** elevated Cummings. He served until after the 1920 **Democratic National Convention**, when presidential nominee **James M. Cox** designated fellow Ohioan **George H. White** for the position.

Throughout the decade of the 1920s, Cummings took time off from his law practice to remain active in party politics, increasingly in the service of **Franklin D. Roosevelt**. At the 1932 national convention, he was a **floor leader** for Roosevelt, who named him attorney general after the fall **election**. Cummings served over six years in that capacity, resigning in 1939. He resumed his law practice and pursued literary interests that resulted in several books on legal matters.

CUMMINS, ALBERT B. Republican president pro tempore of the Senate, 1919–1925. (b. 15 February 1850; d. 30 July 1926). Cummins was elected governor of Iowa in 1901. He served six years before moving to the **Senate** in 1908. He remained there until his death in 1926. Elected **president pro tempore** in 1919 for the 66th **Congress**, he retained that post throughout the 67th and 68th Congresses. During the 68th Congress, following the death of President **Warren G. Harding** and the presidential accession of Vice President **Calvin Coolidge**, there was no vice president, so Cummins was the constitutionally prescribed presiding officer. When the 69th Congress assembled in 1925, he was replaced by fellow Republican **George H. Moses** of New Hampshire.

CURTIS, CHARLES. Republican president pro tempore of the Senate, 1911; Republican Senate majority leader, 1923–1929; Republican vice president, 1929–1933. (b. 25 January 1860; d. 8 February 1936). Trained in the law, Curtis represented Kansas in the **House of Representatives** (1893–1907). Elected to the **Senate** in 1907 to finish an unexpired term, shortly afterward he won a full term for himself. In 1911, he was one of several senators who were named **president pro tempore** for brief tenures during the second session of the 62nd **Congress**. Defeated in his reelection bid in the state legislature, in 1914 he successfully sought a vacant Senate seat in a popular **election** under the newly ratified 17th Amendment. He remained there until 1929.

On resuming his Senate seat, Curtis became party **whip**, first in the **minority**, but after 1918 for the **majority**. In 1923, he succeeded the late **Henry Cabot Lodge** as **majority leader**, holding that position for the remainder of his time in the Senate. In 1928, he sought the Republican presidential **nomination** but lost out to **Herbert C. Hoover**. The **Republican National Convention** then nominated him for **vice president**, creating a **balanced ticket**. The Republicans won a **landslide** victory in November. Renominated in 1932, Hoover and Curtis fell victims to the **Great Depression**, which had begun on their watch. Once out of public office, Curtis practiced law in Washington, D.C., until his death.

CURTIS, KENNETH. Democratic National Committee hair, 1977– 1978. (b. 8 February 1931). Curtis is a Maine lawyer who began his pursuit of elective office in 1964, when he lost a congressional bid. Two years later, while serving as secretary of state, he won a race for governor, and he was reelected in 1970. Prohibited by state law from serving another consecutive term, he left office in 1974 and soon became involved in the 1976 presidential **campaign** of **Jimmy Carter**, with whom he had become acquainted as a fellow governor. Curtis's endorsement was one of the more noteworthy early gestures of support received by the relatively obscure candidate. After Carter's **election**, he asked Curtis to become **chair** of the **Democratic National Committee**. Curtis's brief tenure there was marked by tension with the Carter White House, as perceived conflicts developed between the president's political interests and those of the national **party**. Curtis resigned after less than a year in office and accepted a presidential nomination to become ambassador to Canada. He served in that capacity until 1981, when he returned to Maine and his legal practice.

– D –

DALLAS, GEORGE M. Democratic vice president, 1845–1849. (b. 10 July 1792; d. 31 December 1864). Dallas belonged to a prominent Philadelphia family. His father was secretary of the treasury under President **James Madison**. After college, George Dallas joined his father's law practice and served in minor public roles that stemmed from his father's political connections. Dallas gravitated to the **partisan** camp of **Andrew Jackson** in the transition between the **Era of Good Feelings** and the outset of the **Second Party System**. He was elected mayor of Philadelphia in 1828. The next year, he received a presidential appointment as a U.S. district attorney. In 1831, he went to the **Senate** to finish an unexpired term of two years. Back in Philadelphia, he became state attorney general (1833–1835). He accepted the **nomination** of President **Martin Van Buren** as minister to Russia (1837–1839). Dallas then went back to Philadelphia and resumed his law practice.

In 1844, after nominating **James K. Polk** for president, the delegates to the **Democratic National Convention** picked Silas Wright of New York for **vice president**. However, Wright declined the nomination, protesting the refusal of the convention to nominate former president Van Buren. The remaining delegates then turned to Dallas on the third **ballot**. The **ticket** went on to victory that fall.

As vice president, Dallas steadfastly supported the policies of President Polk, even when he found them objectionable. Dallas hoped to build support for a presidential bid in 1848, but he failed to do so. He resumed his private life until 1856, when President **Franklin Pierce** named him minister to Great Britain, a position he retained under President **James Buchanan**.

DARK HORSE. A lightly regarded **candidate** for **election** or party **nomination**. The term is taken from horse-racing slang. It was initially applied to **James K. Polk**, who emerged from the background as the presidential nominee of the Democratic Party in 1844. Much more recently, at the outset of his successful presidential candidacy in 1992, **Bill Clinton** merited this label. *See also* FRONT-RUNNER.

DASCHLE, THOMAS. Democratic Senate majority leader, 2001, 2001–2003; minority leader, 1995–2001, 2003–2005. (b. 9 December 1947). Elected to the House of Representatives by his South Dakota district in 1978, Daschle served three terms before successfully seeking a **Senate** seat in 1986. Reelected in 1992, he won a close contest to replace the departing **George J. Mitchell** as the **floor leader** for the **Democratic Party** in 1995. This shift coincided with the Democrats' loss of **majority** status in the 1994 **midterm elections**. His rival for Senate party leadership, **Christopher Dodd**, was then named general **chair** of the **Democratic National Committee**. As leader of the **minority** Senate Democrats during the last six years of **Bill Clinton**'s presidency, Daschle proved effective at organizing and articulating party interests in opposition to the majority Republicans. His achievement of party unity enabled Clinton to prevail at his impeachment trial in 1999.

The 2000 elections left the Senate evenly divided between Democrats and Republicans. Daschle briefly served as **majority leader** in the interim between the convening of the 107th Congress and the presidential inauguration, because **incumbent** Vice President **Al Gore** cast the deciding vote on organizing the chamber. Daschle resumed his role as **minority leader** when Republican **Richard B. Cheney** succeeded Gore. However, in June 2001, a party defection by Republican Senator James Jeffords restored Daschle as majority leader. After the terrorist attacks on September 11, 2001, Daschle joined President **George W. Bush** and the House Republican leadership in expressions and demonstrations of bipartisanship and national unity. However, this "era of good feelings" was short lived, and Daschle became increasingly critical of the president and the Republicans in **Congress**. In turn, he was successfully targeted by GOP strategists in his 2004 reelection bid.

Since leaving office, he has remained politically visible, serving as a lobbyist and an educator. He emerged as a key **campaign** supporter of and adviser to **Barack H. Obama**, who prevailed in the 2008 Democratic presidential **nomination** campaign and the ensuing **general election**. Obama nominated Daschle for a **cabinet** position as Secretary of Health and Human Services, with the expectation that Daschle would take the lead in advancing health care reform. However, Daschle withdrew his nomination prior to Senate confirmation when problems emerged with regard to his failure to pay taxes on income received from his lobbying activities.

DAVIS, DAVID. Republican president pro tempore of the Senate, 1881–1883. (b. 9 March 1815; d. 26 June 1886). An Illinois lawyer and self-styled independent, Davis was a political ally of **Abraham Lincoln**, who nominated him to the Supreme Court in 1862. When the 1876 presidential **election** featured disputed electoral votes, Congress named Davis to an ad hoc electoral commission, otherwise evenly divided between Democrats and Republicans, to resolve the dispute. However, before the commission decided, Davis was elected to the U.S. **Senate** by his state legislature and resigned his seats on both the Court and the commission. His place on the commission went to fellow justice Joseph Bradley, an avowed Republican, who tipped the **partisan** balance, leading to a decision favoring the Republican cause that resulted in the election of **Rutherford B. Hayes** as president.

In the Senate, where he served a single term, Davis quickly embraced the label of the **Grand Old Party** (GOP). In 1881, during the first session of the 47th Congress, he was elected **president pro tempore**. He held that office until the day of his retirement in 1883, when the **Congress** adjourned. There was no **vice president** throughout Davis's service as the Senate's presiding officer, because **Chester A. Arthur** had become president after the death of **James A. Garfield**.

DAVIS, HENRY G. Democratic vice presidential nominee, 1904. (b. 16 November 1823; d. 11 March 1916). A prosperous industrialist with extensive railroad and lumber interests, Davis served two terms in the **Senate** from West Virginia (1871–1883). He later chaired the Pan American Railway Committee (1901–1916). In 1904, the **Democratic National Convention** tapped him to run for **vice president** alongside presidential nominee Alton B. Parker. At the time, Davis was 80 years old, making him the oldest individual nominated on a national **ticket** by a **major party.** His chief attraction was his enormous personal wealth, which the **party** leaders hoped would be available for the upcoming campaign. The ticket lost in the fall elections, and Davis resumed his oversight of his vast holdings.

DAVIS, JOHN W. Democratic Speaker of the House of Representatives, 1845–1847. (b. 16 April 1799; d. 22 August 1859). Indiana voters first elected Davis to a seat in the **House of Representatives** in 1834, again in 1838, and twice more in 1842 and 1844. During his final term, he served as **Speaker** in the 29th **Congress**. Leaving office in 1847, he returned to public life in 1853 when President **Franklin Pierce** named him governor of the Oregon Territory. He served one year.

DAVIS, JOHN W. Democratic presidential nominee, 1924. (b. 13 April 1873; d. 24 March 1955). Davis represented his native West Virginia for a single term in the **House of Representatives** (1911–1913). President **Woodrow Wilson** named him solicitor general (1913–1918) and ambassador to Great Britain (1918–1921). After the Democrats lost the presidency in 1920, Davis began practicing law on Wall Street. In 1924, he was a **dark horse** prospect for the presidential **nomination** of the **Democratic Party**. The divided convention met for 17 days and took an unprecedented 103 ballots before agreeing on Davis as its compromise choice. After losing in the fall elections to Republican **Calvin Coolidge**, Davis returned to his Wall Street law firm and a lengthy and prosperous legal career. Although he avoided **partisan** politics, he remained in the public eye through arguing a number of important cases before the Supreme Court.

DAWES, CHARLES G. Republican vice president, 1925–1929. (b. 27 August 1865; d. 23 April 1951). Dawes became active in **Republican Party** politics while practicing law in Lincoln, Nebraska. He later moved to Chicago to pursue business interests. There he played a key role in the 1896 presidential **campaign** of **William McKinley**, who named Dawes comptroller of the currency (1897–1902). Failing in a senatorial bid, Dawes returned to private life and became a successful banker. During World War I, Dawes received a commission and eventually became the American Expeditionary Force's chief purchasing agent. After the war, President **Warren G. Harding** named Dawes as the first director of the newly established Bureau of the Budget in 1921. In 1923, he became chair of the Allied Reparations Commission. The Dawes Plan, which he developed, won him the Nobel Peace Prize in 1925.

In 1924, the **Republican National Convention** nominated President Calvin Coolidge for a term in his own right. It then named Frank Lowden, the governor of Illinois, for vice president, despite Lowden's proclaimed unwillingness to accept. When Lowden declined as promised, the convention turned to Dawes on the third **ballot**. The **ticket** won a convincing victory in the fall, and Dawes proceeded to use his status in the **Senate** as presiding officer to play an active role in the politics of the chamber.

Dawes followed Coolidge's lead in not seeking renomination in 1928. Incoming President **Herbert C. Hoover** named him ambassador to Great Britain in 1929 and brought him home in 1932 as head of the Reconstruction Finance Corporation, an institution created to counter the effect of the **Great Depression**. Dawes served briefly in this latter capacity and then resigned to tend to his banking interests.

DAYTON, JONATHAN. Federalist Speaker of the House of Representatives, 1795–1799. (b. 16 October 1760; d. 9 October 1824). Dayton represented New Jersey in the last years of the Continental Congress (1787–1789). Two years later, he was elected to the **House of Representatives**, where he remained for four terms, the last two as **Speaker.** He presided at a time when **party** identities and loyalties were becoming clear. In 1799, Dayton moved to the **Senate** for a single term.

DAYTON, WILLIAM L. Republican vice presidential nominee, 1856. (b. 17 February 1807; d. 1 December 1864). Dayton served in the **Senate** from New Jersey (1842–1851), representing the **Whig Party**. One of the founders of the new **Republican Party**, he was the vice presidential nominee of the inaugural **Republican National Convention** in 1856. The **ticket**, headed by **John C. Fremont,** lost in the fall elections. Subsequently, President **Abraham Lincoln** named Dayton minister to France (1861–1864).

DEALIGNMENT. The tendency of voters to either abandon their previous attachment to a political party or decline to make such an attachment. Historically, a dealignment has preceded a **realignment**. In the contemporary era, some scholars perceive dealignment as an enduring and autonomous phenomenon.

DEAN, HOWARD. Democratic National Committee chair, 2005–2009. (b. 7 November 1948). A Vermont physician, Dean won **election** to the state legislature in 1982 and the lieutenant governorship in 1986. In 1991, the death of the **incumbent** governor elevated Dean to that office. Elected to five two-year terms, he did not seek reelection in 2002. Rather, he embarked on a **dark horse** antiwar **campaign** for the 2004 Democratic presidential **nomination** that catapulted him to **front-runner** status by the beginning of the **presidential primary** season in 2004. However, he stumbled badly in the early caucuses and primaries, and the party nomination went instead to **John F. Kerry.** After Kerry's defeat, Dean successfully sought election to the position of **chair** of the **Democratic National Committee** in February 2005. As party chair, he was a colorful, highly visible, and controversial figure. His vigorous **partisan** attacks outraged Republicans. Meanwhile, he competed with Democratic congressional party leaders for preeminence as a party spokesperson, and they questioned the wisdom of his commitment to an expansive 50-state strategy to broaden the party's base of electoral support, as opposed to a more targeted effort. During his tenure, the Democrats reclaimed their status as the **majority party**, capturing control of both chambers of **Congress** in 2006 and the White House in 2008.

DEBS, EUGENE V. Social-Democratic presidential nominee, 1900; Socialist presidential nominee, 1904, 1908, 1912, 1920. (b. 5 November 1855; d. 20 October 1925). An Indiana native, Debs rose to leadership in the American Railway Union and the larger trade union movement in the United States. In the process, his ideological views became increasingly **radical**. On five occasions, he pursued the presidency as a **minor party** nominee. Initially, he campaigned as a Social Democrat in 1900. In four of the five following elections, he did so as the **standard-bearer** of the **Socialist Party**. His most impressive showing was in 1912, when he garnered 6 percent of the popular vote. Eight years later, unable to campaign because he was incarcerated following his conviction for sedition, Debs actually won more total votes, though his percentage declined. Released from prison in 1921 by President **Warren G. Harding**, Debs remained a leading radical voice until his death.

DELAY, THOMAS D. Republican majority leader of the House of Representatives, 2003–2006. (b. 8 April 1947). DeLay moved from the Texas House of Representatives to the national body in 1985. He identified himself with the ascendant conservatives in the **Republican Conference**, affiliating with the **Republican Study Committee**. In 1995, following the historic elections that propelled the Republicans to a House **majority** for the first time in four decades, DeLay won a conference vote for majority **whip**, defeating a candidate favored by incoming Speaker **Newt Gingrinch**. Nicknamed the "Hammer," DeLay proved extraordinarily effective at mobilizing the GOP **rank and file** on behalf of the legislative initiatives of the **party** leadership. When majority leader **Dick Armey** retired in 2002, DeLay was his obvious successor. DeLay continued to demonstrate his legislative prowess as **floor leader**. His aggressive strategies and tactics to advance the **Republican Party** and **conservative** policies made him increasingly controversial. In 2006, he stepped down as **majority leader** following his indictment in his native Texas for alleged violations of **campaign finance** laws in connection with an effort to redraw that state's congressional districts to give and advantage to the Republicans. That same year, he resigned his congressional seat.

DEMOCRATIC ADVISORY COUNCIL (DAC). A national party policymaking body proposed and established by the **chair** of the **Democratic National Committee, Paul M. Butler**, after the 1956 elections. With the reelection of Republican **Dwight D. Eisenhower** as president maintaining the condition of **divided party government**, Butler sought to coordinate the message of the **Democratic Party**, as developed and delivered through the national **party organization** and the congressional **party-in-office**. However, the leaders of the congressional party, Majority Leader **Lyndon B. Johnson** and Speaker **Sam Rayburn**, were less than responsive to Butler's overtures.

The DAC thus emerged as the voice of a party **faction**, the party's **liberal** wing based outside the South. Throughout the late 1950s, it assembled party leaders to develop positions on issues. The party platform adopted by the 1960 **Democratic National Convention** embodied many of the perspectives embraced by the DAC, as did the subsequent **New Frontier** and Great Society legislative agendas put forward by Democratic presidents **John F. Kennedy** and Lyndon B. Johnson. After Kennedy's election, with a Democrat in the White House, the DAC ceased to function. It provided the model for the subsequent establishment of the **Republican Coordinating Committee.**

DEMOCRATIC CAUCUS. The assembly of Democrats in the **House of Representatives.** The **caucus** convenes in anticipation of an upcoming congressional session and elects its leaders, most notably its nominee for **Speaker.** The caucus also designates **committee** chairs. For decades, this latter responsibility was exercised in nominal fashion, applying the principle of seniority. Beginning in the mid-1970s, the caucus has been more active in this aspect of leadership selection. It has also met with greater frequency during congressional sessions to consider party positions on policy questions. *See also* DEMOCRATIC CONFERENCE.

DEMOCRATIC CONFERENCE. The current name of the **Senate** Democratic **caucus,** the assembly of all Democratic senators. Until relatively recently, the conference met in the wake of senatorial elections to organize the party for the upcoming **Congress,** choosing the leadership and approving recommendations for **committee** assignments. Otherwise, its status was nominal. Since the mid-1980s, it has continued to meet on a weekly or biweekly basis throughout the session to consider party policy and strategy. *See also* DEMOCRATIC CAUCUS.

DEMOCRATIC CONGRESSIONAL CAMPAIGN COMMITTEE (DCCC). A legislative **party organization** whose purpose is to promote the **election** and reelection of party nominees to congressional seats. Established in the wake of the **Civil War,** it provides campaign assistance in a variety of forms, primarily through financial support. The Democratic caucus chooses the chair of the DCCC, who presides over a small staff located at the headquarters of the **Democratic National Committee,** within walking distance of the congressional office buildings on Capitol Hill.

DEMOCRATIC LEADERSHIP COUNCIL (DLC). A centrist **party** body that emerged in the mid-1980s seeking to bring the Democratic Party back to the mainstream of American electoral politics after decisive presidential **election** defeats in 1980 and 1984. Its ranks included noteworthy representatives from **Congress** and the statehouses. In the years that followed, prominent DLC figures such as Bill Clinton and **Richard A. Gephardt** became national party leaders, testimony to the DLC's success in reorienting the party. In turn, during and after Clinton's presidency, **liberal** party activists advocated a more principled, **progressive** identity for the Democrats.

DEMOCRATIC NATIONAL COMMITTEE (DNC). The entity that exercises the authority of the national **party organization** between the quadrennial nominating conventions. It was established in 1848. Its membership consists of representatives designated by the state parties; ex officio members, including each state party **chair** and vice chair; and chairs of various affiliate organizations and additional at-large members. It chooses its chair for a four-year term. When a Democrat occupies the White House, the position of chair effectively becomes a presidential appointment. The DNC typically meets two or three times a year. One of its primary responsibilities is to prepare for the next national **convention**.

In the 19th century, the headquarters of the DNC shifted between New York and Washington, usually for the convenience of the chair. The DNC would expand its staff and operations in anticipation of an upcoming presidential **campaign** and then virtually disband in its wake. Since the 1930s, the DNC offices have remained in Washington, D.C. In the 1980s, the party purchased its own facilities just south of Capitol Hill. There, it maintains a substantial permanent operation.

DEMOCRATIC NATIONAL CONVENTION. A quadrennial assembly of representatives of state parties coming together primarily to nominate a presidential **ticket** but also to put forward a **party platform**. The inaugural Democratic National Convention met in 1832, to nominate President **Andrew Jackson** for reelection, along with vice presidential nominee **Martin Van Buren**. That **convention** established a rule requiring a two-thirds **majority** for nominations, in hopes of building consensus within the party for its nominees. This **two-thirds rule** frequently necessitated numerous ballots and generated considerable controversy, and it was finally overturned in 1936, in favor of a simple majority rule.

Initially, representation of state parties at the national convention followed the model of the **electoral college**. In 1944, partially to compensate the Southern state parties for abandoning the two-thirds rule, the Democrats began to weight representation to reward states that reliably elected party nominees.

In the 19th century, and well into the 20th century, convention decisions were usually tightly controlled by state and local party bosses, who handpicked delegates and gave them marching orders. With the advent of presidential primaries, gradual erosion of this practice began. After 1968, reforms in delegate selection procedures promulgated by the **McGovern–Fraser Commission** effectively ended this practice and opened up the delegate selection process to widespread popular participation. Control over the presidential **nomination** shifted from the assembled delegates to the voters in the previous round of presidential primaries, with the convention ratifying and legitimating those decisions.

DEMOCRATIC PARTY. The oldest **political party** continuously in existence. The Democratic Party traces its origins to **Thomas Jefferson** and **Andrew Jackson**. Its roots clearly rest in Jefferson's **Democratic-Republican Party**. In the 1820s, as the Democratic-Republican Party acquired an unchallenged position on the political landscape, a distinct intraparty faction led by Jackson developed. Beyond its commitment to Jackson's presidential candidacy, it emphasized the party's traditional appeal to the common people. It also reflected the party's bases of support in the new states in the South and West. This **faction** quickly evolved into the Democratic Party. From the time of its founding until the **Civil War**, the Democratic Party generally prevailed in interparty competition with the **Whig Party.**

By the 1850s, the divisive slavery issue was undermining the Democrats' hegemony. The party temporarily split into regionally based factions and lost control of the government to the upstart **Republican Party**. The Civil War further discredited the Democrats, while elevating the Republicans as the party of the victorious Union.

After the war, and until the **Great Depression**, the reunited Democrats generally found themselves at a competitive disadvantage with the Republicans nationally, though they soon reasserted their traditional dominance in the South. Their national coalition uneasily embraced both rural, agrarian sentiments in the South and West and urban, industrial ones in the Northeast. Throughout this era of Republican hegemony, the Democrats remained the major competitive alternative. They occasionally succeeded in winning majorities in **Congress**, but their presidential successes were limited to those of **Grover Cleveland** (1884, 1892) and **Woodrow Wilson** (1912, 1916).

The onset of the Great Depression in 1929 inaugurated a new era of Democratic domination. The Democrats captured both chambers of Congress in 1930. They held the **House of Representatives**, with only two two-year exceptions, for the next 64 years. In the Senate, Democratic control was only slightly less extensive: the Republicans won majorities in only 5 of 32 elections.

At the presidential level, **Franklin D. Roosevelt** won an unprecedented four consecutive terms. His successor, **Harry S. Truman**, won yet another. Roosevelt reconstituted the Democratic **coalition** based on region, socioeconomic class, and ideology. He brought together the white South with ethnic minorities, organized labor, farmers, and liberals. This **New Deal** coalition reinvigorated the Democrats, making them the **majority** party in American politics.

At the presidential level, this Roosevelt coalition began showing strains as early as 1952, when the Republicans captured the White House for two terms, with popular World War II general **Dwight D. Eisenhower** successfully appealing to traditional Democratic voters. The Democrats returned to the White House for two terms in 1960, led first by **John F. Kennedy** and then by **Lyndon B. Johnson**. Johnson's landslide victory in 1964 suggested not only that the New Deal coalition remained largely intact, but also that the Democrats had made major inroads into the traditional Republican base in the business community.

However, severe strains in the Democratic coalition became apparent in the late 1960s. With the national party firmly embracing civil rights for minorities, the white South increasingly abandoned its ancestral home. Strident opposition to the Vietnam War within the party more broadly challenged the internationalist commitments the party had assumed under Wilson and Roosevelt. Rising concerns about "permissiveness" and "law and order" worked to the detriment of the Democrats, who became associated with the **radical** excesses of the 1960s, and fueled a general shift of blue-collar voters away from the Democratic camp, at least in presidential elections.

As a result, the Democrats lost five of the next six presidential elections. Only **Jimmy Carter**, a former governor of Georgia running in 1976 in the wake of the **Watergate** scandals that discredited Republicans, was able to reassemble enough of the traditional Democratic bases of support to win the presidency.

In 1980, Carter failed in his bid for reelection against **Ronald W. Reagan**, and the Democrats lost the Senate for the first time since 1952, although they continued to control the House. They recaptured the Senate in 1986, a victory that was sandwiched between two more presidential defeats at the hands of Reagan and his political heir, **George H. W. Bush**.

Voter rejection of Bush's reelection bid in 1992 returned the Democrats to the White House. The nomination and election of Arkansas governor **Bill Clinton** signaled the triumph of the **Democratic Leadership Council** faction within the party, which sought to move the party right, toward the center of the ideological spectrum. Clinton's success briefly reestablished **unified party government** in Washington for the first time since the Carter presidency. However, two years later the Democrats lost both houses of Congress to Republican majorities. In 1996, Clinton won reelection, the first Democrat to do so since Franklin D. Roosevelt, but the Republicans continued their newfound control of Congress that year and in 1998 as well.

In 2000, Democratic party fortunes took another step backward. **Incumbent** Vice President **Al Gore** met defeat in the **electoral college** in his bid to build on Clinton's foundation, even though he outpolled **George W. Bush** in the popular vote. Despite gaining seats in both the House and Senate, the Democrats failed to win a majority in either chamber. Midway through 2001, they reclaimed control of the evenly divided Senate when a Republican abandoned his party, but they lost their majority in 2002. Their 2004 efforts fell short at both ends of Pennsylvania Avenue, leaving them demoralized and frustrated. However, they rebounded with an impressive showing in the 2006 **midterm elections,** fueled by voter dissatisfaction with the Iraq War and several congressional scandals. Their return to majority status in both congressional chambers presaged a convincing presidential victory in 2008 by their **standard-bearer, Barack H. Obama,** that left Democrats optimistic about their future prospects.

DEMOCRATIC POLICY COMMITTEE. One of three senatorial party organizations, the others being the **Democratic Steering and Outreach Committee** and the **Democratic Senatorial Campaign Committee.** Traditionally chaired by the floor leader, more recently a relatively senior senator has assumed this assignment. This committee, established in 1947, serves as the policy and research arm of the senatorial party. Its House counterpart is the **Democratic Steering and Policy Committee.**

DEMOCRATIC-REPUBLICAN PARTY. One of the first political parties appearing on the national scene. The Democratic-Republican Party constituted the organized opposition to policy initiatives of Treasury Secretary **Alexander Hamilton** during the early stages of the presidency of **George Washington.** Its leaders were Secretary of State **Thomas Jefferson** and Representative **James Madison.** The party originally used the "Republican" label to characterize itself, and its adherents were also known as "Jeffersonian Republicans."

As the loyal opposition, the Democratic-Republicans not only opposed Hamiltonian policies but also represented contending interests in society and reflected an alternative constitutional understanding of the role of the national government. Their supporters were typically more rural and agrarian than Hamilton's more urban, industrial **Federalist Party.** As such, their regional strength rested more in the South and Middle Atlantic states than in the Northeast. They favored a strictly limited role for the central government, leading them to oppose such measures as a protective tariff and a central bank.

In the elections of 1800, the Democratic-Republicans seized control of the national government, electing Jefferson president and gaining majorities in both houses of **Congress.** They firmly held onto power for a quarter-century, with Madison and **James Monroe** succeeding Jefferson in the White House. Indeed, during Monroe's presidency, the domination of the Democratic-Republicans was complete. The Federalists no longer provided even nominal party opposition.

This brief period of one-party rule became known as the **Era of Good Feelings**. It ended when factional division arose among the Democratic-Republicans in anticipation of Monroe's retirement. An intraparty split featured factional competition between the Democrats and the National Republicans. Eventually, the **Whig Party** emerged as the major party challenger to the **Democratic Party** in the **Second Party System**.

DEMOCRATIC SENATORIAL CAMPAIGN COMMITTEE (DSCC). A legislative **party organization** whose purpose is to promote the **election** and reelection of party nominees to seats in the **Senate**. Established in 1913, when the Constitution was amended to provide for direct popular election of senators, it provides **campaign** assistance in a variety of forms, primarily financial support. The legislative party **caucus**, the **Democratic Conference**, chooses the **chair** of the DSCC, who presides over a small staff located at the headquarters of the **Democratic National Committee**, within walking distance of the congressional office buildings.

DEMOCRATIC STEERING AND OUTREACH COMMITTEE. An agency of party leadership in the **Senate**. Formerly known as the Democratic Steering Committee and then the Democratic Steering and Coordination Committee, it continues to serve as the committee on committees, recommending committee assignments to the Democratic Conference. In recent years, in keeping with its new name, it has sought to coordinate and build support for Democratic policy positions.

DEMOCRATIC STEERING AND POLICY COMMITTEE. An agency of party leadership in the House of Representatives. Chaired by the party leader, it serves as the **committee** on committees, having supplanted the Ways and Means Committee in performing that nominating role in the congressional reforms of the mid-1970s. At times, the steering and policy functions have been divided into separate committees, but they are presently combined.

DEMOCRATIC STUDY GROUP (DSG). A long-standing legislative service organization in the **House of Representatives**. Organized in the wake of the party's successful showing in the 1958 **midterm elections**, the DSG advocated congressional reforms that would reduce the power of the **conservative coalition** to block **liberal** legislative initiatives. The DSG policy agenda found expression in the **New Frontier** of President **John F. Kennedy** and the **Great Society** of President **Lyndon B. Johnson**. In the 1970s, the DSG again took the lead in promoting reforms. It succeeded in undermining the **seniority system** as the automatic basis for designating chairs of House committees.

DEVIATING ELECTION. A category in a taxonomy of presidential elections. A deviating **election** occurs when the **candidate** of the **minority party** wins because of short-term candidate and/or issue factors, but the **majority party** retains its dominant position in the **party system**. The 1912 election of Democrat **Woodrow Wilson** and his 1916 reelection qualify as deviating elections in the Republican-dominated **Fourth Party System**. In 1920, voters responded positively to the campaign call of Republican **Warren G. Harding** for a "return to normalcy" and reinstated the Republicans in the White House. *See also* CONVERTING ELECTION; MAINTAINING ELECTION; REALIGNING ELECTION; REINSTATING ELECTION.

DEVOTEE PARTY. A category in Maurice Duverger's taxonomy of **party structure**. A devotee party occupies an intermediate position between the poles of the **mass party** and the **cadre party**. Membership in devotee parties is more open than in cadre parties but less open than in mass parties. In recent years, American parties have moved somewhat into this category by taking limited measures to enlist party supporters as members, primarily in the form of fundraising initiatives.

DEWEY, THOMAS E. Republican presidential nominee, 1944, 1948. (b. 24 March 1902; d. 16 March 1971). Dewey came to public prominence with his attack on organized crime as district attorney of New

York County (1937–1941). He narrowly lost a gubernatorial bid in 1938. In 1942, he was elected governor of New York, an office he held until his retirement from public life in 1955. He received the **Republican Party** presidential nominations in both 1944 and 1948. In 1944, he was virtually unchallenged for the **nomination** and ran a respectable race, losing to **Franklin D. Roosevelt**, who was seeking his fourth term as World War II raged. Four years later, with Republican presidential prospects much more favorable, Dewey won a third-ballot victory at the **Republican National Convention**. In the ensuing **election**, President **Harry S. Truman** won a historic upset victory at Dewey's expense. Still governor of New York, Dewey remained a leader of the Republicans' **Eastern establishment**. He was an enthusiastic and effective supporter of the successful candidacy of **Dwight D. Eisenhower** for the Republican presidential nomination in 1952. Retiring from public office in 1955, he practiced law on Wall Street and continued to be influential in party circles.

DIRECT PRIMARY. *See* PRIMARY.

DIRKSEN, EVERETT M. Republican Senate minority leader, 1959–1969. (b. 4 January 1896; d. 7 September 1969). Dirksen was an eight-term member of the **House of Representatives** from Illinois (1933–1949). In 1950, he successfully sought a **Senate** seat, which he held for the rest of his life. At the outset of his Senate career, Dirksen was identified with the **old guard** within the party. Over the years, he modified his conservative ideology in favor of centrist positions. In 1959, he became **floor leader** for the **minority** Republicans, replacing the more conservative **William F. Knowland**, who had left the Senate. As **minority leader**, he practiced **bipartisan** accommodation with the **majority** Democrats in the Congress, as well as with Democratic presidents **John F. Kennedy** and **Lyndon B. Johnson**. He remained minority leader until his death in 1969.

DIVIDED PARTY GOVERNMENT. Also known as split-party government. It is the condition wherein one party controls the executive and another the legislature, in whole or in part. Divided party government is made possible by the separation of powers. Traditionally relatively rare in the United States, it became increasingly commonplace at the national level after World War II, owing in large measure to an increasing propensity of voters toward ticket-splitting. At the outset of the 21st century, heightened party polarization was reducing the incidence of ticket-splitting, and thus the likelihood of divided party government. *See also* UNIFIED PARTY GOVERNMENT.

DIXIECRATS. Post–World War II Southern Democrats, who broke ranks with the national Democratic Party over the interrelated issues of states' rights and civil rights. They constituted themselves as the **States' Rights Democratic Party** for the presidential election in 1948, nominating **J. Strom Thurmond** as their **standard-bearer**. Returning to the Democratic fold after the election, they continued to be known as Dixiecrats in the ensuing decades, as they became increasingly out of step with the national party.

DODD, CHRISTOPHER. Democratic National Committee general chair, 1995–1997. (b. 27 May 1944). The son of a senator from Connecticut, Thomas J. Dodd, Christopher Dodd was elected to the **House of Representatives** in 1975 and served three terms. In 1980, he won **election** to the **Senate**, and he has won four additional terms. In 1995, he sought the position as **floor leader**, but he lost out to rival **Thomas Daschle**. President **Bill Clinton** then picked Dodd to serve as general **chair** of the **Democratic National Committee**, perceiving him as an attractive party spokesman. Dodd filled this role ably during the 1996 presidential **campaign**. He resigned from his **party organization** position shortly after the election but remains in the Senate. He unsuccessfully sought the Democratic presidential nomination in 2008.

DOLE, ROBERT J. Republican National Committee chair, 1971–1973; Senate majority leader, 1985–1987, 1995–1996; Senate minority leader, 1987–1995; Republican presidential nominee, 1996. (b. 22 July 1923). Severely wounded as a young man in World War II, Dole was elected to the **House of Representatives** in 1960. He served four terms there before successfully seeking a **Senate** seat in 1968. He held that seat until 1996. In 1971, he was the choice of President **Richard M. Nixon** to head the **Republican National Committee** for two years. In 1976, President **Gerald R. Ford**

picked him to be the vice presidential nominee in what proved to be a losing effort.

In 1984, Senate Republicans named him **majority leader** to replace **Howard W. Baker**. When the party lost control of the Senate two years later, he continued as **minority leader**. He made an unsuccessful bid for the party's presidential **nomination** in 1988. The Republican victory in the 1994 **midterm elections** propelled Dole back to the post of majority leader.

Dole's 1996 campaign for the Republican presidential nomination succeeded, and he resigned from the Senate to give the presidential effort his full attention. However, he lost in the fall elections to the Democratic **incumbent, Bill Clinton**. In retirement, Dole has become an **elder statesman** whose continued visibility in Republican and national politics is partly attributable to having had a spouse in the Senate, Elizabeth Dole (R-NC, 2002–2008).

DONKEY. A symbol for the **Democratic Party** since the origins of the party under the leadership of Andrew Jackson, who was characterized by his opponents as a jackass. Gilded Age cartoonist Thomas Nast popularized the symbol in a series of compelling political cartoons in *Harper's Weekly* that portrayed the Democrats as rowdy, outrageous, and unpredictable.

DOUGLAS, STEPHEN. Democratic presidential nominee, 1860. (b. 23 April 1813; d. 3 June 1861). Known as the "Little Giant," Douglas was elected from Illinois to the **House of Representatives** in 1842. He served two terms before going to the **Senate**, where he remained until his death in 1861. He sought valiantly but futilely to keep the **Democratic Party** united as the divisive slavery issue intensified. Douglas was the choice of the Northern **faction** of the party for **president** in 1860, winning the **nomination** of the **Democratic National Convention**, but the Southern partisans did not rally behind him. His fall campaign against old home-state rival **Abraham Lincoln** failed to generate much popular enthusiasm, and the Democrats lost the presidency to the upstart **Republican Party**. Douglas died the next year, as the **Civil War** he had sought to forestall was getting under way.

DRAFT. A call for a noncandidate to become available for and/or accept a party **nomination**. In 1940, supporters of **Wendell L. Willkie** successfully promoted his candidacy for the presidential nomination of the **Republican Party**, in the absence of much iactive campaigning on the part of Willkie. Somewhat similarly, in 1952, **Adlai E. Stevenson II** was the beneficiary of a draft movement to bring him the Democratic presidential nomination. A draft movement was often the product of a divided nomination contest and a brokered **convention**. The advent of presidential primaries has greatly diminished the likelihood and prospective success of a presidential draft effort.

DRY. A supporter of **Prohibition**, the **campaign** to prohibit manufacture, sale, or transportation of intoxicating liquors. Within the **Democratic Party**, the drys were a noteworthy **faction**, based primarily in the rural South and West. They supported the 18th Amendment (1919) establishing Prohibition, and they opposed the 21st Amendment (1933) repealing the 18th. With repeal, the drys declined in significance. *See also* WET.

DUNCAN, ROBERT M. Republican National Committee Chair, 2007–2009. (b. 14 April 1951). An attorney and a banker, Mike Duncan worked his way up the **party organization** ladder, beginning as a precinct captain in Kentucky. He was a county **chair** and state chair prior to his election to the **Republican National Committee**, where he became treasurer (2001) and general counsel (2002). He played prominent roles in **campaign** organizations at local, state, and national levels as well. In anticipation of **Ken Mehlman**'s 2007 departure as national party chair, and in accordance with the wishes of President **George W. Bush**, Senator **Mel Martinez** (Florida) became general chair, and Duncan took on the day-to-day oversight of party headquarters operations. On his watch, which extended beyond Martinez's tenure, the **Republican Party** suffered decisive defeats in the 2008 elections, losing seats in both congressional chambers and, more important, the White House. Duncan nevertheless stood for reelection in 2009, but he was unable to garner the support of a **majority** of the members of the national committee, who elected

Michael S. Steele as his successor. Later that year, he was named chairman of the Tennessee Valley Authority.

DUVERGER'S LAW. Developed by French party scholar Maurice Duverger, it addresses the relationship between electoral arrangements and the number of political parties in a system. Duverger argued that a **single-member district** electoral system promotes a **two-party system**, discouraging **minor party** competition with its **winner-take-all** feature. Conversely, **proportional representation** in a **multimember district** setting encourages a **multiparty system** by allowing minor parties to win some measure of representation.

– E –

EAGLETON, THOMAS F. Democratic vice presidential nominee, 1972. (b. 4 September 1929; d. 4 March 2007). Eagleton rose quickly in **Democratic Party** politics in his native Missouri, serving as circuit attorney (1956–1960), state attorney general (1961–1965), and lieutenant governor (1965–1968). In 1968, he won **election** to a seat in the U.S. **Senate.** Four years later, he was the choice of Democratic presidential nominee **George S. McGovern** to receive the vice presidential **nomination** of the **Democratic National Convention.** Shortly afterward, news reports revealed that Eagleton had suffered from bouts of depression, for which he had been hospitalized and received electroshock treatments. In the aftermath of this revelation, and in response to speculation that the issue would further endanger the Democrats' precarious electoral prospects, Eagleton resigned from the **ticket.** The **Democratic National Committee** replaced him with **R. Sargent Shriver.** Eagleton remained in the Senate, winning reelection in 1974 and 1980. He retired at the end of his third term. Back in Missouri, he practiced law and taught at Washington University.

EASTERN ESTABLISHMENT. An enduring **faction** within the **Republican Party,** identifiable not only by its regional base and the high socioeconomic standing of its adherents, but also by its relatively **liberal** ideology. From the time of **Theodore Roosevelt**

until the mid-1960s, the Eastern establishment competed with the **old guard**, a more **conservative** faction based in the Midwest, for control of the party. Among its champions were such presidential nominees as **Wendell Willkie, Thomas E. Dewey**, and **Dwight D. Eisenhower**. The 1964 presidential **nomination** of **Barry M. Goldwater** signaled the decline of the Eastern establishment in party circles and a power shift ideologically to the **right wing** and geographically to the Sunbelt.

EASTLAND, JAMES O. Democratic president pro tempore of the Senate, 1972–1978. (b. 28 November 1904; d. 19 February 1986). Eastland received a brief interim appointment to the **Senate** from Mississippi in 1941. While out of office the next year, he successfully sought an elected Senate term. He held his seat for six terms, rising to chair the powerful Judiciary Committee, beginning in 1955, whence he sought to impede proposed **civil rights** legislation. In 1972, his status as senior Democrat made him the Senate's choice as its **president pro tempore**. His tenure in this office coincided with two brief vacancies in the office of vice president, following the resignation of **Spiro T. Agnew** and the elevation to the presidency of **Gerald R. Ford**. Eastland did not seek reelection in 1978, and he resigned his seat shortly after the general election to give his successor a seniority advantage.

EDMUNDS, GEORGE. Republican president pro tempore of the Senate, 1883–1885. (b. 1 February 1828; d. 27 February 1891). Edmunds represented Vermont in the **Senate** for four terms (1866–1891). On the last day of the 47th Congress, he was elected **president pro tempore**, and he was reelected at the outset of the 48th **Congress** (1883–1885). Throughout his tenure as the Senate's presiding officer, the vice presidency was vacant, following the death of President **James A. Garfield** and the accession of Vice President **Chester A. Arthur**.

EDWARDS, JOHN. Democratic vice presidential nominee, 2004. (b. 10 June 1953). A prominent North Carolina trial lawyer, Edwards won election to the U.S. **Senate** in 1998. Rather than seek reelection in 2004, he chose to contend for the Democratic presidential

nomination. His **primary** campaign faltered, but he was presidential nominee **John F. Kerry**'s choice for the vice presidential nomination, conferred on him by the **Democratic National Convention**. This **ticket** went down to defeat in November, and Edwards left public office. Soon afterward, he initiated a **campaign** for the 2008 presidential nomination, which failed to garner sustained support beyond the early caucus and primary contests. He abandoned his campaign at the end of January and subsequently threw his support behind the eventual nominee, **Barack H. Obama**.

EISENHOWER, DWIGHT D. Republican president, 1953–1961. (b. 14 October 1890; d. 28 March 1969). A career army officer, Dwight Eisenhower rose from obscurity to international acclaim during World War II. He led the Allied forces in the European Theater. After the war, he became chief of staff of the army (1945–1948). He retired from active duty to become president of Columbia University (1948–1951), but he returned to command the multinational military force of the North Atlantic Treaty Organization (1951–1952). Although he had never been involved in **partisan** politics, both major parties cultivated him as a presidential nominee.

He resigned his command to seek the 1952 presidential **nomination** of the **Republican National Convention**. His campaign succeeded, and he went on to win the fall **election** against **Democratic Party** nominee **Adlai E. Stevenson II**. Surviving a major heart attack in his first term, he accepted his party's nomination for another term and again bested Stevenson in the fall. He presided during a period of economic expansion and Cold War tension. The ratification of the 22nd Amendment to the **Constitution** mandated Eisenhower's retirement after two terms. In retirement, he served reluctantly as a party **elder statesman** and received the continuing **nonpartisan** plaudits of his fellow Americans for his distinguished career in public service.

ELDER STATESMAN. A senior member of a party, who even if not retired is no longer seeking higher office, who serves as a respected **titular leader**, **kingmaker**, and/or conciliator within the party. Such an individual is also known as a party elder. Former presidents, congressional party leaders, and national party chairs are potential prospects to take on this label. The status and authority of an elder statesman are functions of seniority, goodwill, and perceived absence of personal ambition.

ELECTION. A means by which a vote determines the outcome of a contest for office. Popular elections are vehicles for the citizenry to select political leaders. A U.S. **political party** typically designates its nominees through a **primary election**. These nominees then compete for public support in a **general election**. *See also* CONVERTING ELECTION; CRITICAL ELECTION, DEVIATING ELECTION; MAINTAINING ELECTION; MIDTERM ELECTION; REALIGNING ELECTION; REINSTATING ELECTION.

ELECTORAL COLLEGE. The constitutionally prescribed institution that elects the **president** and **vice president**. According to the constitutional design, the electoral college represents states in the federal system. Each state has a number of electors equal to the size of its entire congressional delegation (**House of Representatives** plus **Senate**). Each state chooses how to select its electors. Since the Jacksonian era, popular **election** of electors has been the norm.

Actually, then, the quadrennial November presidential election pertains narrowly to electors committed to supporting presidential candidates. Typically, state political parties nominate trustworthy electors, who are elected by the voters. Again, since the Jacksonian era, a **winner-take-all** arrangement has been used in most states. As such, voters technically vote neither for presidential nominees nor for individual electors. Most contemporary **ballot** forms obscure this reality. Rather, voters cast their presidential ballots for slates of electors. The **slate** receiving the most popular votes in a state gets to cast that state's ballots in the electoral college.

The designated electors convene in their respective state capitals about five weeks after their November election. Originally, the **Constitution** specified that each would cast a single ballot, on which would be written the names of two candidates, only one of whom could be from the elector's home state. The ballots would be sent to the capital of the federal government, where they would be counted before a joint session of **Congress**. The person receiving the most votes, provided that number was a **majority**, would be elected president. The nominee receiving the next most votes would be elected vice president. If no candidate received a majority, or if a tie resulted, the president would be elected by the House of Representatives, where each state delegation would have a single vote.

The procedure was changed by the 12th Amendment to the Constitution. Henceforth, electors would cast two ballots, clearly differentiating their presidential vote from their vice presidential vote. This change came about in the wake of the presidential election of 1800, in which the emergence of political parties seeking selection of presidential tickets made necessary a modification of the framers' design.

That year, the **Democratic-Republican Party** secured the selection of a majority of electors committed to the party's **ticket** of **Thomas Jefferson** and **Aaron Burr**. However, because all these electors cast their ballots in that fashion and no other elector voted for either Jefferson or Burr, the electoral college balloting produced a tie, which had to be resolved by the House of Representatives. To ensure against such an outcome in the future, Congress proposed, and the states quickly ratified, the amendment.

Since then, only once, in 1824, has the electoral college failed to produce a majority choice. That year, **Andrew Jackson** led both the popular and the electoral college balloting, but fell short of a majority. The House subsequently chose **John Quincy Adams**.

In 1876, disputes in several states regarding the selection of electors had to be resolved by a commission established by Congress. That resolution produced a narrow electoral college majority vote for **Rutherford B. Hayes** over **Samuel Tilden**.

In 2000, the electoral college decision turned on the disputed popular vote outcome in Florida. Less than a week before the scheduled date for the electors to cast their presidential ballots, the Supreme Court ruled against continuing recounts, leaving **George W. Bush** with a narrow popular vote victory in Florida, whose 25 electors then provided him with his bare majority in the electoral college.

These three elections, along with the 1888 election, resulted in electoral college victories of nominees whose pledged electors had received fewer popular votes than their **major party** opponents. This is a mathematical possibility, because of the winner-take-all practice adhered to by most states.

On rare occasions, a **faithless elector** has declined to cast the presidential ballots as "instructed" by the voters who chose him or her. The two most recent presidential elections, 2000 and 2004, both featured one faithless electoral vote. As yet, such actions have not affected outcomes. A more common and less arbitrary variation of this practice has occurred on the few occasions when pledged electors were unable to vote for a victorious candidate who had died in the interim.

Reform of the electoral college is a perennial concern. Some proposed reforms would require a **constitutional amendment**. Others would rely on actions in the several states. A rather modest reform proposal would retain the concept of the electoral vote while abolishing the office of elector. The presidential candidate who won the most popular votes in a state would automatically receive all of that state's electoral votes. This would address the problem of the faithless elector. More substantial proposed reforms would allocate a state's electoral votes proportionally or on a congressional district basis, with each state selecting two electors at large. The latter form is already in effect in Maine and Nebraska. In 2008, one Nebraska congressional district chose an elector pledged to Democrat **Barack H. Obama**, while the rest of the state went with electors pledged to Republican **John S. McCain III**. Both these proposals would alter the winner-take-all convention. A more recent reform movement currently under way seeks state legislative commitment to an interstate compact wherein each state would instruct its electors to vote for the winner of the national popular vote, that state's vote notwithstanding. Such a compact would go into effect once states comprising an electoral college majority, 270 votes, agreed to this arrangement. The most drastic reform proposal would simply abolish the electoral college in favor of direct popular election of the president.

ELEPHANT. The long-standing symbol of the **Republican Party**. **Gilded Age** cartoonist Thomas Nast initially portrayed the Republican Party as an elephant to lampoon the alleged foolishness of its voters. Over time, he and others came to see the elephant as an appropriate symbol of the party's size and strength, as well as its ponderousness and unwieldiness. *See also* DONKEY.

11TH COMMANDMENT. A norm for intraparty relations, prescribed for the **Republican Party**. The 11th Commandment, "Thou shalt not speak ill of fellow Republicans," was promulgated in the mid-1960s by California state party **chair**, Gaylord E. Parkinson, in hopes of restoring peace and goodwill to the faction-ridden Republicans of his state. **Ronald W. Reagan**, a candidate for governor of California in 1966, enthusiastically endorsed the commandment and popularized it nationally.

ELLENDER, ALLEN J. Democratic president pro tempore of the Senate, 1971–1972. (b. 24 September 1890; d. 27 July 1972). A member of the powerful Long organization in Louisiana, Ellender was elected to the **Senate** in 1936, and he remained there for the rest of his life. With the death of Senator **Richard B. Russell** in 1971, Ellender became the senior Democrat in the Senate. As such, he was chosen **president pro tempore**. He died 18 months later.

ELLSWORTH, OLIVER. Electoral vote recipient, 1796 (Federalist). (b. 29 April 1745; d. 26 November 1807). Ellsworth represented Connecticut in the Continental Congress (1777–1784). He went home to serve as chief justice of that state's high court. A member of the Connecticut delegation to the Constitutional Convention, he played a key role in the crucial compromise over legislative apportionment. Ellsworth was elected to the newly created U.S. **Senate** (1789–1796). During his Senate years, he distinguished himself by authoring the Judiciary Act of 1789. In March 1796, outgoing President **George Washington** named him chief justice of the Supreme Court. Later that year, he received 11 electoral votes, finishing sixth in the presidential balloting. He remained on the Supreme Court for most of the presidency of **John Adams**. Simultaneously, in 1799, Ellsworth accepted Adams's appointment to the position of minister to France. He retired from political life in 1800.

ENDORSEMENT. A gesture of support by an individual or a group for a **candidate**, a nominee, or a policy. In recent years, celebrities have become increasingly visible in this arena. A noteworthy example is the influential endorsement provided to **Barack H. Obama** by television personality Oprah Winfrey.

ENGLISH, WILLIAM H. Democratic vice presidential nominee, 1880. (b. 22 August 1822; d. 7 February 1896). An Indiana lawyer, English advanced from the state legislature to serve four terms in the **House of Representatives** prior to the **Civil War** (1853–1861). He then pursued banking interests in Indianapolis. In 1880, the **Democratic National Convention** called him back to public service as its vice presidential nominee, designating him by acclamation to run with presidential nominee **Winfield S. Hancock** in what proved to be a losing effort that fall.

EQUAL TIME. A doctrine espoused by the Federal Communications Commission requiring broadcast media to exercise fairness in allocating airtime to public office-seekers. If a broadcast medium makes airtime available to one candidate or political party, it must also make it available to the opposition. The equal time doctrine has proven to be a stumbling bloc in organizing **presidential debates**, in that **minor party** nominees claim the right to participate. A related **fairness doctrine** prescribing even-handed treatment of political and policy issues over the airways was abandoned by the FCC in 1987.

ERA OF GOOD FEELINGS. A brief period (1817–1825), unique for its absence of interparty competition, that provided the transition between the **First Party System** and the **Second Party System**. The Era of Good Feelings coincided with the presidency of **James Monroe**. After the **Federalist Party**'s weak showing in the 1816 elections, it disintegrated, and the Democratic-Republican Party reigned without organized opposition. Growing divisions within the dominant party led to a formal split and the emergence of a new era of party competition. The application of the term to this unique situation evokes an antipathy toward parties and party competition that is an enduring feature of American political culture.

– F –

FACTION. A group that constitutes a part of a larger whole. Legislative factions preceded the emergence of political parties in the United States. In undertaking to nominate candidates for public office, these factions constituted themselves as political parties. In turn, each **major party** contains factions that represent distinct constituencies based on such foundations as region, ideology, issue, and personality. For example, the South constituted a noteworthy **Democratic Party** faction that persisted from the party's founding until the latter decades of the 20th century. Similarly, the Democratic Party was divided in the early decades of the 20th century between **wet** and **dry** factions on the issue of **Prohibition**. In turn, the contemporary **Republican Party** encompasses economic **conservative**, social conservative, and national security conservative factions. A **minor party** likely has factions as well. *See also* POLITICAL PARTY.

FAHRENKOPF, FRANK. Republican National Committee chair, 1983–1989. (b. 28 August 1939). Born in Brooklyn, New York, Fahrenkopf migrated to Nevada, where he practiced law and became active in the state's Young Republican organization. Graduating to the broader arena of state and national party politics, he chaired the state party (1975–1983) and the Association of Republican State Chairs (1981–1983).

In 1983, President **Ronald W. Reagan** wanted to name Senator **Paul Laxalt** as the national party **chair**. However, party rules mandated that the position be full-time and salaried, and Laxalt was unwilling to forfeit his **Senate** seat. The **Republican National Committee (RNC)** then cooperated with the Reagan White House in creating a new position, that of general chair of the **Republican Party**, to be filled by Laxalt and to coordinate the activities of the **party-in-office** and the **party organization**. On the recommendation of Laxalt, the national **committee** next named Fahrenkopf, his longtime state party ally, to the apparently subordinate role of national chair. However, Laxalt was rather lackadaisical in exercising the newly established authority of the general chair, and the position proved to be largely titular.

Fahrenkopf was not constrained in his performance of the traditional responsibilities of his office. He continued stressing the **service party** approach developed by **Ray C. Bliss** and **William Brock**. Under Fahrenkopf, the RNC headquarters played major roles in **campaign** fund-raising and opposition research for Reagan's 1984 reelection effort and the subsequent victory of Reagan's heir, **George**

H. W. Bush, in 1988. Following Bush's election, Fahrenkopf vacated the position of chair, creating a place for Lee Atwater. Fahrenkopf now practices law in Washington, D.C.

FAIRBANKS, CHARLES W. Republican vice president, 1905–1909; Republican vice presidential nominee, 1916. (b. 11 May 1852; d. 4 June 1918). Born in Ohio, Fairbanks moved to Indiana to practice law. Long active in state Republican Party politics, he delivered the **keynote** address at the 1896 **Republican National Convention**. The next year, he was elected to the **Senate** to finish an unexpired term. Harboring presidential ambitions, he resisted overtures to seek the party's vice presidential **nomination** in 1900 as the **running mate** of President **William McKinley**, when a vacancy existed because of the 1899 death of the **incumbent, Garret A. Hobart**. That nomination went to **Theodore Roosevelt**, who became **president** following McKinley's assassination in 1901. Three years later, Roosevelt became the first **accidental president** to win his party's presidential nomination. Fairbanks emerged as the **candidate** of the party's **old guard** faction to join President Roosevelt on the national **ticket**. He campaigned energetically in a winning effort. As **vice president**, Fairbanks's presidential ambitions persisted, but President Roosevelt thwarted them by designating **William H. Taft** as his heir apparent.

After the 1908 **election**, Fairbanks returned to Indiana. While out of office, he continued to play a prominent role in state and national party politics. He mounted a **favorite son** candidacy for the presidential nomination at the 1916 Republican National Convention. It failed, but the assembly again nominated him for vice president, to run alongside **Charles Evans Hughes**. The pair lost narrowly in the successful reelection bid of President **Woodrow Wilson**. Fairbanks then abandoned his political ambitions.

FAIRNESS DOCTRINE. A long-standing policy of the Federal Communications Commission (FCC) requiring broadcasters to address policy and political issues and controversies in a balanced fashion. In 1987, the FCC repealed this policy, contending that, in practice, it discouraged, rather than encouraged, coverage of controversial questions, and that an abundance of broadcasting entities guaranteed the expression of a diversity of perspectives. *See also* EQUAL TIME.

FAITHLESS ELECTOR. An elector who does not follow "instructions" in casting a **ballot** in the **electoral college**. Beginning in the 1790s, with the emergence of political parties, the major parties have sought to secure the selection of presidential electors who will vote for the party nominees. Since the 1830s, the norm has been for states to select their presidential electors by popular vote, with a **slate** of electors standing for election as surrogates of the presidential **ticket** of a **political party**. The slate receiving the most votes is elected, and its members then cast the state's presidential ballots. The great majority of departures from voters' instructions have been necessitated by the death of a victorious candidate before the electoral vote. On a handful of occasions since 1796, electors have departed from the instructions of their sponsors in more arbitrary fashion, most recently in 2000 and 2004. To date, a faithless elector has yet to alter an anticipated election outcome.

FARLEY, JAMES A. Democratic National Committee chair, 1933–1940. (b. 30 May 1888; d. 9 June 1976). Jim Farley's emergence as a major force in New York state party politics paralleled the ascendancy of **Franklin D. Roosevelt** over **Al Smith** in the state party. In 1928, Farley, already secretary of the state party **committee,** managed Roosevelt's successful gubernatorial **campaign.** After Roosevelt won reelection in 1930, Farley, now state party **chair,** embarked on an extensive preconvention campaign that resulted in Roosevelt's presidential **nomination** in 1932. After the **convention,** campaign manager Farley became chair of the **Democratic National Committee.** After the **election,** he was also designated **postmaster general.**

Patronage chief of the Roosevelt administration, Farley also advised the president on congressional and **grassroots** reaction to the **New Deal** programs, for which he lobbied extensively. Farley moved beyond Roosevelt's shadow to become a well-known public figure and a respected political presence in his own right. After managing Roosevelt's landslide reelection campaign in 1936, he dared to dream, not entirely unrealistically, of obtaining a spot on the Democratic presidential **ticket** in 1940. When Roosevelt orchestrated a **draft** for a third term, Farley persisted in a futile opposition candidacy. After the convention, he resigned both his party and his administration posts. In retirement from public service, he became chairman of the board of the Coca Cola Export Corporation, where he was employed for the rest of his life, the last three years in an honorary capacity.

FARMER–LABOR PARTY. A Minnesota-based **minor party** that played an enduring and significant role in Minnesota politics in the first half of the 20th century. Possessing **progressive** ideals, it eventually merged after World War II with the **Democratic Party** to form the Democratic-Farmer-Labor Party in that state.

FAVORITE SON. A presidential **candidate** put forward for consideration at a national **convention** by the home-state delegation. Traditionally, favorite-son candidacies were more honorary than serious. They were a means whereby a state delegation could both pay tribute to a state leader and defer its decision regarding other competing candidacies until a subsequent convention **ballot**. The practice of designating favorite sons has declined dramatically in the past half-century, reflecting broader changes in presidential nominating politics and processes. At the subnational levels, the term "favorite son" is sometimes applied to a candidate whose base of support is clearly regional or local.

FEDERAL ELECTION CAMPAIGN ACT (FECA). Legislation enacted in 1971 and amended in 1974, 1976, and 1979, regulating **campaign finance**. The law initially provided for significantly strengthened disclosure and reporting requirements for candidates for federal office. It also placed limits on campaign spending, independent expenditures, and contributions from candidates and their immediate families.

Amendments in 1974 extended these limitations, provided for public funding of presidential elections, and established a **Federal Election Commission** (FEC) to monitor and enforce the law. These amendments greatly facilitated the organization and operation of political action committees (PACs).

In 1976, the Supreme Court decided in *Buckley v. Valeo* that several provisions of the FECA, as amended, were unconstitutional. These included the limitations on campaign spending and independent expenditures, personal and family campaign contributions, and the staffing procedure for the FEC.

Congress immediately reconstituted the FEC and revised the surviving contribution limits. Subsequent amending legislation in 1979 eased reporting and disclosure requirements and established a significant loophole for **soft money** contributions. Subsequently, the 2002 **Bipartisan Campaign Reform Act** (BCRA) sought to close this loophole.

FEDERAL ELECTION COMMISSION (FEC). Independent regulatory commission established by **Congress** in 1974 to monitor and enforce the **Federal Election Campaign Act** (FECA). A six-member body, it was originally made up of nominees from the **president**, the **House of Representatives**, and the **Senate**. This procedure failed to survive Supreme Court scrutiny in *Buckley v. Valeo* (1976). Congress then provided that the FEC members be nominated by the president and confirmed by the Senate, in keeping with the procedure for other regulatory commissions.

FEDERALISM. A constitutional principle dividing governmental power between the central (national) government and its constituent units (states). The major parties have typically differed with regard to the appropriate distribution of governmental power in a federal system. For example, in the **First Party System**, the **Federalist Party** supported a strong central government, whereas the **Democratic-Republican Party** embraced **states' rights**. Since the **New Deal**, the **Democratic Party** has been more clearly sympathetic toward the claims of the central government in the federal system in the arena of domestic policy, whereas national security concerns have led the **Republican Party** to advocate a strong central government. Intraparty factions have also disagreed on this issue. In confronting the issue of **civil rights** in the mid-20th century, the Democrats were divided into factions disputing th legitimacy of a national response.

FEDERALIST PARTY. One of the first political parties to appear on the American scene, the Federalist Party emerged in the 1790s. It took its name from the supporters of the 1787 **Constitution**. It brought together supporters of Secretary of the Treasury **Alexander Hamilton** and his controversial policy initiatives in the Washington **administration**. The policy initiatives included a national bank, support for manufacturers in the form of a protective tariff, and a proposal that the national government assume the Revolutionary War debts incurred by the states. Undergirding specific policies was the notion that the Constitution authorized a strong, activist central government.

Hamilton's supporters occupied seats in the Congress, the executive branch, the federal courts, and the state governments. Their ranks expanded to include party organizers and **grassroots** voters. The latter generally reflected urban, commercial, and industrial interests in society. In turn, Hamilton's initiatives were generally opposed by Secretary of State **Thomas Jefferson**, whose supporters came to constitute the **Democratic-Republican Party** in the **First Party System**.

A distinctive **faction** of the young Federalist party looked more to Vice President **John Adams** than to Hamilton for leadership. Hamilton left government service at the end of the Washington presidency, while Adams became **president**. Adams's defeat in his reelection bid in 1800 initiated a precipitous decline in the Federalists' electoral fortunes.

Federalist presidential nominees suffered devastating defeats at the hands of Jefferson and his successors, **James Madison** and **James Monroe**. After Monroe's **election** in 1816, the Federalist Party ceased to contest presidential elections and disappeared from the political scene, initiating the **Era of Good Feelings**.

FERRARO, GERALDINE. Democratic vice presidential nominee, 1984. (b. 26 August 1935). Ferraro won election to the **House of Representatives** from Queens, New York, in 1978 and served three terms. In 1984, she was the choice of presidential nominee **Walter F. Mondale** to receive the vice presidential **nomination** of the Democratic National Convention. Her nomination had historic significance, because she was the first woman to be selected on the national **ticket** of a **major party**. After losing in the fall elections, Ferraro returned to New York. She remains in public life, joining the ranks of political pundits, and has twice contended for senatorial nominations.

FERRY, THOMAS W. Republican president pro tempore of the Senate, 1875–1879. (b. 10 June 1827; d. 13 October 1896). Ferry was elected to the **House of Representatives** from Michigan in 1864. He served three terms before moving over to the **Senate** in 1871 for a two-term tenure. During the 44th and 45th Congresses, he was named **president pro tempore** on six occasions, the only senator to be so designated. The 44th Congress convened two weeks after the death of Vice President **Henry Wilson**, so Ferry was constitutionally responsible for presiding over the Senate until the March 1877 inauguration of Vice President **William A. Wheeler**.

FESS, SIMEON D. Republican National Committee chair, 1930–1932. (b. 11 December 1861; d. 23 December 1936). Fess was a college professor who became president of Antioch College in Ohio. He won **election** to the **House of Representatives** in 1912, serving five terms. In 1922, he was elected to the **Senate**, holding this seat for two terms. In 1930, during the presidency of **Herbert C. Hoover**, he became **chair** of the **Republican National Committee**, following the resignation of **Claudius H. Huston**. He was a part-time chair, retaining his senatorial office. After the 1932 **Republican National Convention**, he was succeeded by Everett Sanders. Fess lost his Senate reelection bid in 1934.

FIFTH PARTY SYSTEM. A pattern of party competition that emerged in the 1930s. The Fifth Party System came into being in the midst of the **Great Depression**, beginning in 1929, which undermined the long-standing **Republican Party** domination of national government, initially established in 1860 and substantially consolidated in 1896. In the wake of the Depression, the **Democratic Party**, led by **Franklin D. Roosevelt**, became the new **majority party**, uniting a **coalition** embracing the white South, workers, minorities, farmers, and ideological liberals in support of the **New Deal**. This coalition kept the Democrats in control of the presidency for two decades, and remnants of it produced subsequent presidential victories for the party in 1960, 1964, and 1976. It also gave the Democrats control of **Congress** for most of the next six decades.

For several decades now, some students of party politics have been anticipating a new **critical election** that will inaugurate a **Sixth Party System**. Their critics contend that the **partisan** foundations of electoral behavior have changed, making an enduring period of one-party dominance less likely. Indeed, some argue that the Sixth Party System is already in effect. *See also* PARTY SYSTEM.

FILIBUSTER. An effort by opponents of proposed legislation to prevent a vote being taken by extending debate indefinitely. The rules of the U.S. **Senate** currently make provision for such activity, by requiring the support of an extraordinary 60 percent **majority** to invoke cloture, ending debate. Actual filibusters have become relatively rare. However, the threat to filibuster, particularly when advanced by the leadership of the **minority party**, is often sufficient to achieve the purpose of blocking the progress of proposed legislation. Such threats have increased in recent years, effectively stalling the progress of legislation deemed objectionable by the **minority**. Recent attempts by the majority to eliminate this practice have been labeled the "nuclear option."

FILLMORE, MILLARD. Whig vice president, 1849–1850; Whig president, 1850–1853; American presidential nominee, 1856. (b. 7 January 1850; d. 8 March 1874). Fillmore entered party politics as a New York state legislator identified with the **Anti-Masonic Party**. After three terms, he retired to his native Buffalo and practiced law. Elected to the **House of Representatives** in 1832 for a single term, he soon joined the new **Whig Party** and emerged as one of its more prominent Northern advocates. He returned to the House in 1837 for three more terms. Fillmore ran unsuccessfully for governor of New York in 1844.

In 1848, the Whigs nominated **Zachary Taylor** for **president**. Seeking a **balanced ticket**, the **convention** chose for vice president Fillmore, a party loyalist from the North who opposed slavery. The ticket won that fall, and Fillmore assumed responsibility for presiding over the **Senate** as the slavery controversy intensified. He supported the pending Compromise of 1850, even though President Taylor opposed it and was prepared to veto it following its passage, Then Taylor died unexpectedly.

As the nation's second **accidental president**, Fillmore supported the compromise legislation, and he replaced Taylor's **cabinet** with like-minded enthusiasts. His bid for the Whig presidential **nomination** in 1852 was rebuffed when the national convention chose

General **Winfield Scott.** The Whig Party soon disintegrated, and Fillmore cast his lot with the new **American Party**, better known as the Know-Nothings, whose presidential nomination he received in 1856. He garnered over 800,000 popular votes and carried one state, Maryland, with eight **electoral college** votes. After this rebuff, Fillmore retired from politics. In retrospect, it remains a relatively impressive **minor party** showing.

FIRST PARTY SYSTEM. A reference to an era of party competition that began with the formation of national political parties in the 1790s and lasted through the presidential **election** of 1816. The system pitted the **Federalist Party** against the **Democratic-Republican Party**. Initially, the Federalists controlled the reins of government. However, the **critical election** of 1800 placed the Democratic-Republicans in charge, and the Federalists never recovered electoral momentum. They ceased to contest presidential elections after 1816. Meanwhile, the now-dominant Democratic-Republicans benefited from the brief Era of Good Feelings in the absence of interparty competition. However, they soon began to experience intraparty turmoil, which within a decade produced a split and the onset of the **Second Party System**. *See also* PARTY SYSTEM.

FITZPATRICK, BENJAMIN. Democratic president pro tempore of the Senate, 1857–1861. (b. 30 June 1802; d. 25 November 1869). Fitzpatrick had served as governor in Alabama (1841–1845) before that state's legislature selected him for the **Senate** in 1848 as a Democrat committed to the cause of **states' rights**. He served only a year, but was sent back to the Capitol in 1853. With a brief interruption in 1855, he held office until 1861. Initially designated **president pro tempore** in December 1857, he was reelected on three more occasions during the 35th Congress and four times during the 36th **Congress,** presiding in the absence of the **vice president, John Breckinridge**. In 1860, the Democratic National Convention nominated Fitzpatrick for vice president, but he declined the honor.

527 GROUP. A political organization engaged in issue advocacy and claiming tax-exempt status under section 527 of the Internal Revenue Service Code. Because they do not explicitly support or oppose candidates for federal office, 527 groups are not currently subject to regulation by the **Federal Election Commission (FEC)**.

FLETCHER, HENRY P. Republican National Committee chair, 1934–1936. (b. 10 April 1873; d. 10 July 10 1959). Fletcher was a Pennsylvania lawyer who served under Colonel **Theodore Roosevelt** in the Rough Riders during the Spanish–American War. He returned home and entered the diplomatic service, where he had a distinguished career, holding ambassadorial appointments in Chile, Mexico, Belgium, and Italy, as well as serving briefly as undersecretary of state in the **administration** of President **Warren G. Harding**. After retiring from the Foreign Service, he accepted an appointment from President **Herbert C. Hoover** as chair of the Tariff Commission.

Fletcher proved himself to be an effective party fund-raiser at a time when the party's fortunes were in decline. In 1934, he was a compromise choice to succeed **Everett Sanders** as **chair** of the **Republican National Committee**. During his two-year tenure, he established a research division and sought equal time for the party on the radio airwaves being used so effectively by President **Franklin D. Roosevelt**. After the 1936 Republican National Convention, he resigned as chair, enabling presidential nominee **Alfred M. Landon** to install fellow Kansan **John D. Hamilton**. Fletcher remained on the national **committee** and served as its general counsel until 1944.

FLOOR LEADER. A position in the congressional party leadership, designated by the party **caucus**. In the **Senate**, the floor leaders are the top officials for both the **majority** and **minority** parties. In the House of Representatives, the floor leader for the majority is the chief lieutenant of the Speaker.

The title of floor leader also applies in the setting of a party **convention**. There it refers to a designated representative of a **candidate** for **nomination**, who guides and directs the supportive delegates in their voting behavior.

FLOYD, JOHN. Independent Democratic presidential nominee, 1832. (b. 24 April 1783; d. 17 August 1837). Floyd was elected to the **House of Representatives** from Virginia in 1816, identifying with the dominant **Democratic-Republican Party**. He served six terms and gravitated toward the new **Democratic Party** led by Andrew Jackson. In 1830, Floyd became governor for four years. As governor, he embraced the concept of nullification, whereby a state could assert the nonbinding character of federal law within its boundaries. This position, advocated by Vice President **John C. Calhoun**, brought both men into conflict with President Jackson.

In 1832, after the **general election**, the nullification faction within the Democratic Party met in Charleston, South Carolina, and nominated Floyd for **president**. All 11 South Carolina electors then cast their presidential ballots in the **electoral college** for him. This protest vote did not interfere with President Jackson's reelection.

FLYNN, EDWARD J. Democratic National Committee chair, 1940–1943. (b. 22 September 1891; d. 18 August 1953). A New York City lawyer, Flynn won election to the state assembly in 1917. He soon abandoned his electoral aspirations to concentrate on **party organization** work. Associated with **Tammany Hall**, he became chair of the Bronx County Democratic Committee in 1922, and he remained in that office for the rest of his life, over three decades. In that capacity, he became known nationally as the boss of the Bronx. Flynn became a key supporter of, and adviser to, **Franklin D. Roosevelt**. He became a member of the **Democratic National Committee** in 1930. A decade later, Roosevelt picked Flynn to replace fellow New Yorker **James A. Farley** as national party **chair**. Flynn resigned as chair in 1943 but remained a member of Roosevelt's inner circle of advisers, accompanying the president to the historic Yalta Conference. After Roosevelt's death, Flynn returned to the Bronx and his abiding party leadership responsibilities there.

FOLEY, THOMAS S. Democratic majority leader of the House of Representatives, 1987–1989; Democratic Speaker of the House of Representatives, 1989–1995. (b. 6 March 1929). An attorney active in state and local politics and government and later a committee staff assistant in the U.S. Senate, Foley entered the **House of Representatives** from Washington State in 1965, carried along to victory in 1964 by the **coattail effect** associated with the election of President **Lyndon B. Johnson**. He rose quickly but quietly in the ranks of the congressional leadership of the **Democratic Party**. In 1975, when the **Democratic Caucus** began challenging the **seniority system**, Foley became chair of the powerful Agriculture Committee. In 1977, he was elected chair of the **caucus**. He served as **majority** whip (1981–1987) and **majority leader** under Speaker **James C. Wright** (1987–1989). When Wright resigned under scandal-related pressure, Foley ascended to the speakership. In the 1994 **midterm elections**, Foley lost his bid for reelection to an 11th term, an unprecedented rebuke by his constituents to an incumbent **Speaker**. In 1997, President Bill Clinton named him ambassador to Japan. Replaced by the Bush administration in 2001, Foley later became North American chair of the Trilateral Commission.

FOOT, SOLOMON. Republican president pro tempore of the Senate, 1861–1864. (b. 19 November 1802; d. 28 March 1866). Foot emerged on the national political scene in 1841, following his **election** from Vermont as a Whig Party nominee to the **House of Representatives**. He served two terms. Four years later, the Vermont legislature returned him to the Capitol, this time on the **Senate** side. He held office until his death in 1866. In 1857, following the demise of the Whigs, he shifted his allegiance to the new **Republican Party**. In March 1861, the Republicans, in control of the Senate for the first time, named him **president pro tempore** and renamed him on another five occasions during the 37th Congress, as the Civil War got under way. In the ensuing 38th **Congress**, he was elected president pro tempore on five more occasions. In April 1864, the Senate, again in need of a temporary presiding officer, finally found an alternative, replacing Foot with **Daniel Clark** from New Hampshire.

FORD, GERALD R. House minority leader, 1965–1973; Republican vice president, 1973–1974; Republican president, 1974–1977. (b. 14 July 1913; d. 26 December 2006). Gerald Ford was elected to the **House of Representatives** from Michigan in 1948, and he served in that body until 1973. Most of that time, the **Republican Party** was in the **minority**. In 1965, Ford's party colleagues selected him as the **minority leader**, supplanting **Charles A. Halleck**. He continued to hold this position until 1973, when President **Richard M. Nixon**, acting under the authority of the 25th Amendment to the **Constitution**, nominated him to fill the vacancy in the vice presidency created by the resignation of Spiro T. Agnew. Majorities in both houses of **Congress** confirmed Nixon's nomination, and Ford became the first unelected vice president.

Less than a year later, Nixon's resignation elevated Ford to the presidency. He successfully sought the 1976 Republican **nomination** for a term in his own right, overcoming a spirited challenge by California governor **Ronald W. Reagan**. However, in the **general election**, Ford lost narrowly to **Democratic Party** nominee **Jimmy Carter**.

In retirement, Ford remained active in party politics, even flirting briefly with the idea of becoming Reagan's vice presidential running mate in 1980. He settled comfortably into the role of party **elder statesman**, while the Republican party became notably more conservative in ideology. Dying at age 93, he was the longest-lived former president.

FOSTER, LAFAYETTE S. Republican president pro tempore of the Senate, 1865–1866. (b. 22 November 1806; d. 19 September 1880). Foster represented Connecticut in the **Senate** for two terms (1855–1867). A special session of the newly elected 39th **Congress**, convening in March 1865 as the **Civil War** neared its end, named him **president pro tempore**, to serve in the absence of the **vice president**. The next month, President **Abraham Lincoln** was assassinated, and Vice President **Andrew Johnson** became president. Foster served almost two years in a position that placed him first in the line of presidential succession. As the Congress prepared to adjourn, it replaced him with **Benjamin F. Wade** of Ohio.

FOURTH PARTY SYSTEM. An era of party competition lasting from 1896 to 1932. The **critical election** of 1896 initiated the Fourth Party System. In the preceding **Third Party System** (1860–1896), the **Republican Party** had risen to power nationally, but its hold was precarious. In the election of 1896, the **Grand Old Party** consolidated that power, clearly establishing itself as dominant, especially in the Northeast and Midwest. The Republicans continued their domination until the onset of the **Great Depression**, which led to the emergence of the **Fifth Party System**. *See also* PARTY SYSTEM.

FOWLER, DONALD. Democratic National Committee chair, 1995–1997. (b. 12 September 1935). Fowler received his doctorate in political science and taught at the University of South Carolina. His academic interest in **party organization** gave way to a vocational commitment when he took on the job of executive director of the South Carolina **Democratic Party** (1967–1971). Next he became its **chair** (1971–1980), during which time he also served as chair of the Association of State Democratic Chairs (1975–1977). Joining the **Democratic National Committee**, he played key roles in arranging and conducting the quadrennial national conventions beginning in 1980. Along the way, he also established his own political consulting firm.

In 1995, faced with a vacancy in the position of national party chair, President **Bill Clinton** wanted Connecticut senator **Christopher Dodd** in that position. However, he confronted the same problem that President **Ronald W. Reagan** had experienced over a decade earlier in the **Republican Party**. Party rules required that the chair's position be full time and salaried, and Dodd was unwilling to resign his **Senate** seat. Clinton followed Reagan's lead in seeking the creation of a new position, general chair, for Dodd, in which he could serve in a highly visible role as party spokesman. Clinton then designated Fowler as his choice as party chair, to manage the party headquarters. Fowler presided over a very aggressive fundraising operation during the 1996 presidential campaign, seeking and receiving extraordinary amounts of **soft money**. After the election, amid growing controversy associated with the campaign fund-raising effort, Fowler stepped down as national party chair. He rejoined the political science faculty at the University of South Carolina. Remaining active in party politics, he participated in the Democratic National Conventions in 2000, 2004, and 2008 as a **superdelegate** from South Carolina.

FRANKLIN, JESSE. Democratic-Republican president pro tempore of the Senate, 1804–1805. (b. 24 March 1760; d. 21 August 1823). Franklin represented North Carolina in both congressional chambers, as well as in its statehouse. He served a single term in the **House of Representatives** (1795–1797) at a time when party lines were becoming clearly drawn. His sympathies were with the emergent followers of **Thomas Jefferson**, the **Democratic-Republican Party**. After a two-year hiatus, North Carolina sent him to the **Senate** in 1799. He served two six-year terms, with a two-year interruption. On a single occasion in March 1804, his colleagues in the 8th **Congress** named him **president pro tempore**. Several years after his retirement from the Senate in 1813, he was elected governor. He served a single term (1820–1821).

FREE SOIL PARTY. A noteworthy **minor party** about a decade prior to the **Civil War**, also known as Barnburners-Liberty Party, the Free Soil Party competed in the presidential elections of 1848 and 1852. Its original base came from members of the **Liberty Party**, who were joined by dissident New York Democrats known as the **Barnburners**. The party opposed the extension of slavery into the territories and the admission of new slave states into the union.

Former President **Martin Van Buren** led the Free Soil ticket in 1848. He received almost 300,000 votes but carried no states and thus got no electoral votes. The party elected 13 members to the **House of Representatives** that year, providing it with a crucial voice in the organization of the new **Congress**. In coalition with the Democrats, it elected a **fusion** nominee to the **Senate** in both 1848 and 1851.

In 1852, the Barnburners abandoned the Free Soil Party. This cut voter support for the party's presidential party nominee almost in half, as John Hale received 156,000 votes. By 1856, most of the remaining Free Soilers had embraced the new **Republican Party**.

FRELINGHUYSEN, THEODORE. Whig vice presidential nominee, 1844. (b. 28 March 1787; d. 12 April 1862). Frelinghuysen was state attorney general in New Jersey (1817–1829). He then served a single term in the U.S. **Senate** (1829–1835). Afterward, he became mayor of Newark (1836–1839). He was heavily involved in the activities of several religious organizations. In 1844, the **Whig Party** at a national **convention** unanimously chose **Henry Clay** as its presidential nominee. In the subsequent vice presidential balloting, Frelinghuysen led on the first **ballot,** but he required three ballots to reach the necessary majority. The Clay-Frelinghuysen ticket lost in the fall elections, and Frelinghuysen resumed his religious activities. In 1850, he became president of Rutgers University.

FREMONT, JOHN C. Republican presidential nominee, 1856. (b. 21 January 1813; d. 13 July 1890). Fremont became a national figure through his exploits as an explorer and army officer in the West, for which he became known as "the Pathfinder." The new state of California elected him to the **Senate** in 1850. Serving only a year, he then led two more expeditions that heightened his national prestige.

In 1856, the newly formed **Republican Party** made him their presidential nominee. Enthusiastically embracing the antislavery, free-soil position, he ran a credible race but lost to **Democratic Party** nominee **James Buchanan**. Fremont held noteworthy Union commands during the **Civil War** but did not distinguish himself. After the Civil War, his only public service was a tour of duty as governor of the Arizona Territory (1878–1881).

FRIST, WILLIAM H. Republican Senate majority leader, 2003–2007. (b. 22 February 1952). A highly regarded heart surgeon from a prominent Tennessee family, in 1994 Frist challenged Democratic **incumbent** James Sasser for a seat in the U.S. **Senate** and won a convincing victory. Reelected in 2000, Frist chaired the **Republican Senatorial Campaign Committee** for the 2002 **midterm elections** cycle, which saw the Republicans regain the **majority** they had lost in 2000. Frist became **majority leader** in 2003, following the resignation of Senator **Trent Lott** as **floor leader**, in the wake of Lott's controversial comments on behalf of retiring Senator **J. Strom Thurmond**. Frist's tenure featured efforts to advance judicial nominations to floor votes by challenging the institution of the **filibuster**. He did not seek reelection to the Senate in 2006.

FRONT-PORCH CAMPAIGN. An approach to presidential campaigning that was prevalent around the turn of the 20th century. It called for the presidential nominee to stay at home, delivering occasional public addresses to crowds that would be assembled there. This approach contrasted favorably with a more energetic, peripatetic one, which was considered undignified by the popular culture of that era. Noteworthy practitioners of the front-porch campaign were **Benjamin Harrison, William McKinley**, and **Warren G. Harding**. This approach became less appealing to candidates when advancing transportation technologies enabled presidential nominees to travel throughout the country more easily. *See also* WHISTLESTOP CAMPAIGN.

FRONT-RUNNER. The leading contender for a **nomination** or **election**. The term derives from the analogy between a contest for public office and a race. *See also* DARK HORSE.

FRYE, WILLIAM P. Republican president pro tempore of the Senate, 1896–1911. (b. 2 September 1830; d. 8 August 1911). Frye went to Washington in 1871, following his election to the **House of Representatives** by his Maine constituents the previous year. He won reelection four times. While serving his fifth term, he was chosen by the Maine legislature to occupy a **Senate** seat, which he held for the rest of his life. Initially elected **president pro tempore** by the 54th **Congress** in 1896, he brought an unprecedented stability to that office, serving continuously without being reelected, until his death in 1911. Twice during his tenure, there was a vacancy in the vice presidency. Vice President **Garret A. Hobart** died in 1899, with over a year remaining in his term. Then, in 1901, President **William McKinley** was assassinated, making **Theodore Roosevelt** president and leaving the country without a **vice president** until 1905.

FUSION. A coalition of political parties that agrees before an election to run a single nominee for public office. Fusion has been practiced most notably in large municipalities. At the state level, it finds its most clear contemporary expression in New York, where the Conservative Party and the **Republican Party** often run fusion slates against the Liberal Party and the **Democratic Party** tandem.

– G –

GABRIELSON, GUY GEORGE. Republican National Committee chair, 1949–1952. (b. 22 May 1891; d. 1 May 1976). Gabrielson was an Iowa native who graduated from Harvard Law School. He settled in New Jersey after World War I and practiced law in New York City. For four years (1926–1930) he served in the New Jersey state assembly, rising to the leadership positions of **majority leader**

and **speaker**. Named to the **Republican National Committee** more than a decade later, he was chosen for the executive committee after the 1948 **election**, when the party was trying to reconcile its two increasingly antagonistic factions, the **old guard** and the **Eastern establishment**. Gabrielson identified with the former. Soon afterward, the national party **chair**, Hugh Scott, resigned; and Gabrielson sought the position. He won in a close contest that demonstrated the persistence of the factional rivalries.

While his **Democratic Party** counterpart, **William M. Boyle**, was facing mounting pressures regarding his alleged involvement in influence peddling, Gabrielson found himself enmeshed in similar charges that he sought favors for clients with the Reconstruction Finance Corporation. Unlike Boyle, Gabrielson survived the scandal. Although the national headquarters was expected to be nominally neutral toward competing candidacies for the presidential **nomination**, Gabrielson tilted toward his factional leader, Senator Robert A. Taft. However, the 1952 **Republican National Convention** decided in favor of **Dwight D. Eisenhower**. Gabrielson followed custom and resigned, enabling the nominee to install his choice, **Arthur E. Summerfield**, as national party chair.

GAILLARD, JOHN. Democratic-Republican president pro tempore of the Senate, 1810, 1814–1818, 1820–1825. (b. 5 September 1765; d. 26 February 1826). South Carolina sent Gaillard to the **Senate** in 1804, and he remained there for the rest of his life, faithfully reflecting the values and interests associated with his party leader, **Thomas Jefferson**. On numerous occasions, Gaillard served as **president pro tempore**, including twice during the second session of the 11th **Congress** (1810). During the 13th Congress (1814), he was again chosen twice, the second time following the death of Vice President **Elbridge Gerry**, which left the Senate without its constitutionally prescribed presiding officer. Gaillard held that office throughout the 14th Congress. During the 15th and 16th Congresses, with a new **vice president**, **Daniel D. Tompkins**, on the scene, Gaillard was chosen on a few occasions to be president pro tempore, as was **James Barbour** of Virginia. In 1823, Tompkins abandoned his presiding responsibilities, requesting the Senate to name a standing president pro tempore. Gaillard was the chamber's choice for the remainder of the vice presidential term that included part of the 17th and all of the 18th Congresses. He was chosen president pro tempore for the final time during the early special session of the 19th Congress in 1825.

GALLINGER, JACOB H. Republican president pro tempore of the Senate, 1912, 1913; Republican Senate minority leader, 1913–1918. (b. 28 March 28 1837; d. 17 August 1918). Gallinger was elected to the **House of Representatives** from New Hampshire in 1884, serving two terms. In 1891, he was elected to the **Senate**, where he remained until his death. On two brief occasions during the 62nd **Congress**, he served as **president pro tempore**. On the second occasion, there was no **vice president**, owing to the death of incumbent **James S. Sherman**. Subsequently, at the outset of the 63rd Congress, Gallinger became **floor leader** for the **minority** Republicans. Following his death five years later, the **Republican Party** senators turned to **Henry Cabot Lodge** as their leader and won **majority** control of the chamber in the 1918 **midterm elections**.

GARFIELD, JAMES A. Republican president, 1881. (b. 19 November 1831; d. 19 September 1881). Garfield attained public prominence as a major general in the Union Army during the **Civil War**. His military service propelled him to a seat in the **House of Representatives** in 1863. He held that seat until 1880, when he was the compromise choice of a divided **Republican National Convention** for its presidential **nomination** on the 36th **ballot**.

Garfield easily bested Democratic opponent **Winfield S. Hancock** in a **general election** contest that was also the high tide of the **Greenback Party**, whose **standard-bearer** was **James B. Weaver**. Less than four uneventful months into his presidency, Garfield was shot on July 2, 1881, by Charles Guiteau, a disappointed office seeker. He died some 10 weeks later, and his **vice president, Chester A. Arthur,** assumed the office. Garfield's assassination was the catalyst for the enactment of civil service reform.

GARNER, JOHN NANCE. Democratic minority leader of the House of Representatives, 1929–1931; Democratic Speaker of the House of Representatives, 1931–1933; Democratic vice president, 1933–1941. (b. 22 November 1868; d. 7 November 1967). John Nance Garner spent 30 years representing Texas in the **House of Representatives** (1903–1933), the last two as **Speaker** after the **Democratic Party** won a **majority** of seats in the 1930 **midterm elections**. He sought the Democratic presidential **nomination** in 1932, losing to **Franklin D. Roosevelt** but receiving the vice presidential nomination. After victory in November, he served two terms as **vice president**, grudgingly supporting the **New Deal** reforms of the **administration**. Garner aspired to his party's presidential nomination in 1940 and broke with Roosevelt when the latter shattered the informal two-term limitation on presidential tenure. He retired to his native Texas, where he lived in quiet retirement for more than a quarter-century.

GARRETT, FINIS J. Democratic minority leader of the House of Representatives, 1923–1929. (b. 26 August 1875; d. 25 May 1956). Garrett was elected to the **House of Representatives** from Tennessee in 1904. He served 12 terms. During his last three, he was **the floor leader** of the minority **Democratic Party**.

GENERAL ELECTION. A contest for public office that pits authorized **political party** nominees and occasional independent candidates against one another. *See also* ELECTION; PRIMARY; SPECIAL ELECTION.

GEORGE, WALTER F. Democratic president pro tempore of the Senate, 1955–1957. (b. 29 January 1878; d. 4 August 1957). George went to the **Senate** in 1922 and remained there until his death 35 years later, rising to prominence in the Southern **faction** of the **Democratic Party**, which dominated the institution. As the senior member of the **majority party**, he served as **president pro tempore** during his last two years in office.

GEPHARDT, RICHARD A. Democratic majority leader of the House of Representatives, 1989–1995; Democratic minority leader of the House of Representatives, 1995–2003. (b. 31 January 1941). Gephardt was elected to the **House of Representatives** from St. Louis, Missouri, in 1976. He emerged as a party leader in the mid-1980s, when he was elected chair of the House **Democratic Caucus** and was instrumental in the formation of the **Democratic Leadership Council (DLC)**. In

1988, he contended for the Democratic presidential **nomination**, but he dropped out in time to hold on to his House seat. The next year, he put on hold his preliminary plans for another presidential bid when upheaval in the ranks of the Democratic congressional leadership resulted in an alternative opportunity for advancement. The resignation of Speaker **Jim Wright** elevated **Tom Foley** to that office, leaving a vacancy in the position of **floor leader** for the **majority**. Gephardt was the choice of his **caucus** colleagues. When Foley lost his bid for reelection in 1994 and the Democrats lost their long-standing majority, Gephardt moved into the top leadership post of floor leader for the **minority**. In 2003, preparing for a 2004 presidential nomination bid, Gephardt gave up his position as floor leader, which went to **Nancy Pelosi**. Failing in his presidential bid, he finished out his 14th congressional term and retired in 2005.

GERRY, ELBRIDGE. Democratic-Republican vice president, 1813–1814. (b. 17 July 1744; d. 23 November 23 1814). Gerry represented Massachusetts in the Continental Congress on two occasions (1776–1781 and 1782–1785). During his initial stint, he signed the Declaration of Independence. He attended the 1787 Philadelphia convention that produced the **Constitution**, and he served in the **House of Representatives** it established (1789–1793). In the emerging partisan divisions, Gerry sided with the **Democratic-Republican Party**. Nevertheless, President **John Adams** sent him to France in 1797 as part of what proved to be a controversial diplomatic mission that generated the notorious XYZ Affair, in which the French unsuccessfully demanded a bribe in return for a meeting with the foreign minister, Talleyrand. Gerry came under strong attack from the Federalist Party for his involvement.

Back in the United States, Gerry repeatedly ran unsuccessfully for governor of Massachusetts (1800–1803). Eventually he was elected (in 1810), and he was reelected the next year. As governor, he signed a redistricting bill that redrew boundaries in a manner that aided his party. An oddly shaped district resembled a salamander, giving rise to the term **gerrymander**.

As his governorship drew to a close, Gerry emerged as the choice of the Democratic-Republican **caucus** as the vice presidential **running mate** for President **James Madison**. The previous **incumbent**,

George Clinton, had recently died. The **ticket** prevailed in the fall elections, and Gerry relocated to the capital, where he diligently presided over the **Senate**, despite failing health. He died in office, the second consecutive vice president to do so.

GERRYMANDER. To draw electoral district lines in a manner that benefits the political interests of the **party-in-power**. The term originated in the wake of an 1811 reapportionment bill, passed by the Massachusetts legislature and signed by Governor Elbridge Gerry, that favored the **Democratic-Republican Party** and disadvantaged the rival **Federalist Party**. The boundaries of one particular district were said to resemble a salamander, soon renamed a gerrymander. *See also* SAFE SEAT.

GILDED AGE. The quarter-century after the **Civil War**, when the **Republican Party** was consolidating its position as the dominant political party during the **Third Party System**. The Gilded Age was associated with excesses of capitalism and corruption that brought forth the reform agenda of the **Progressive Era**, beginning in the 1880s.

GILLESPIE, EDWARD W. Republican National Committee chair, 2003–2005. (b. 1 August 1961). Ed Gillespie went to Capitol Hill as a congressional staff assistant in 1983. He spent a decade (1985–1995) in the office of Representative **Richard Armey** (R-TX). There, he developed strategies for bringing about a Republican majority, most notably the **Contract with America**. In 1996, he moved to the **Republican National Committee (RNC)**, where he worked for Chairman **Haley Barbour** as director of communications and congressional affairs. He joined the 2000 presidential campaign of **George W. Bush**, managing the national **convention** program in Philadelphia and serving as a major spokesman for the **campaign** during the Florida recount. After a brief assignment as a public affairs officer in the Commerce Department, Gillespie formed a successful lobbying and consulting firm. In 2003, he became **chair** of the RNC. He presided over a remarkably successful national party campaign in 2004 that featured the reelection of a Republican president and the retention of party majorities in both congressional chambers. He left party headquarters in

2005 to resume his lobbying and consulting roles. In 2006, he guided the successful senatorial confirmation efforts of Bush's two Supreme Court nominees, John Roberts and Samuel Alito. In December 2006, Gillespie was chosen chair of the Virginia Republican Party. In June 2007, he joined the White House staff as a presidential counselor.

GILLETT, FREDERICK H. Republican Speaker of the House of Representatives, 1919–1925. (b. 16 October 1851; d. 31 July 1935). Gillett was a 16-term member of the **House of Representatives** from Massachusetts (1893–1925). In 1919, following the **Republican Party** triumph in the 1918 **midterm elections** that restored Republicans to **majority** status, he was elected **Speaker** of the House. Gillett sought to reestablish the **nonpartisan** leadership initially associated with the speakership, and party leadership devolved on the **majority leader**. In 1923, a party **faction** of progressives threatened his reelection as Speaker, holding him hostage to its demands for more liberal procedural reforms. The Republican leaders met those demands, and Gillett won his final term as Speaker. In 1925, he moved over to the **Senate** for a single term before retiring.

GILMORE, JAMES S., III. Republican National Committee chair, 2001–2002. (b. October 6, 1949). Jim Gilmore was elected Virginia's attorney general in 1993 and its governor in 1997. During his final year as a highly regarded, term-limited governor, he also served as **chair** of the **Republican National Committee**, having been designated for that position by incoming President **George W. Bush**, the former governor of Texas. As party chair, he followed the contemporary practice of subordinating himself to the White House political operation. He left his party post after a year. Once out of office, he maintained both a law practice and his longstanding interest in homeland security, chairing the National Council on Readiness and Preparedness. He briefly and unsuccessfully contended for the 2008 Republican presidential **nomination**. Subsequently, in a **convention** contest, Gilmore won the party nomination for a seat in the U.S. **Senate**. In the 2008 general election, he lost this contest.

GINGRICH, NEWTON L. Republican Speaker of the House, 1995–1999. (b. 17 June 1943). His Georgia constituents elected Newt

Gingrich to the **House of Representatives** in 1978. His energy and aggressive partisanship quickly made him a controversial and formidable figure in the House, where the **Republican Party** had long constituted the **minority**. Gingrich was a founder of the **Conservative Opportunity Society (COS)** during the 98th **Congress** (1983–1985). His heightened visibility led to his election as **whip** in 1989.

When **Robert Michel**, the **minority leader**, announced his intention not to seek reelection to the House in 1994, Gingrich was the obvious choice to succeed him as the leader. Gingrich proceeded to organize and implement an aggressive national **campaign** on behalf of **GOP** congressional candidates in 1994, using the **Contract with America** as the common theme. His efforts met with unexpected success, and the Republicans captured a **majority** of House seats for the first time in four decades. When the 104th Congress convened in January 1995, Gingrich was elected **Speaker**. Under his leadership, the House passed most of the Contract with America, but several items failed to receive the necessary support from the Senate and/ or the president, demonstrating the limitations of responsible party government in the American political system. Gingrich soon found himself under attack from the minority Democrats for alleged ethical improprieties. Subsequently, the **Republican Conference** also began expressing concern, but it was related less to the ethical problems than to Gingrich's ability to continue advancing the Republican agenda.

Nevertheless, Gingrich remained a highly visible presence in the national political arena. He was an enormously successful fundraiser, rallying the party faithful, but he was also a lightning rod for the Democratic opposition in mobilizing its electoral constituencies.

In the two congressional elections that followed the historic 1994 victory, the Republicans remained in the majority, but their margins shrank. After the 1998 elections saw the GOP unexpectedly lose five seats and barely maintain control, Gingrich, facing a formidable challenge to his continuation as Speaker by Robert Livingston, chair of the powerful Appropriations Committee, withdrew as a candidate for reelection to that office and announced his intention to resign his congressional seat. The Republican Conference initially designated Livingston as the heir apparent. Shortly afterward, amid allegations of scandal, Livingston withdrew and similarly announced his intention to resign. The Republican Conference then nominated and elected **Dennis Hastert** as Speaker to replace Gingrich. Although out of office, Gingrich remains a prominent and provocative figure in party politics through frequent publications and public speaking and fund-raising engagements.

GLASS, CARTER. Democratic president pro tempore of the Senate, 1941–1944. (b. 4 January 1858; d. 28 May 1946). Glass entered national public life in 1902, when he was elected to the **House of Representatives**. He served eight terms, resigning in 1918 to become secretary of the treasury for two years under President **Woodrow Wilson**. In 1920, he was appointed to a **Senate** seat that he held until his death. He became **president pro tempore** in 1941, after the death of Senator **Pat Harrison**. He held that position for the rest of the 77th **Congress** and throughout the 78th Congress. He was replaced by Senator Kenneth McKellar of Tennessee at the outset of the 79th Congress, and he died during its second session.

GOLD DEMOCRATS. *See* NATIONAL DEMOCRATIC PARTY.

GOLDWATER, BARRY M. Republican presidential nominee, 1964. (b. 1 January 1909; d. 29 May 1998). Barry Goldwater was elected to the **Senate** from Arizona in 1952. By the time of his reelection in 1958, he had become a noteworthy symbol and spokesman for the **conservative** movement in the **Republican Party** and the nation. His successful candidacy for the Republican presidential **nomination** in 1964 marked the triumph of that party **faction**. Although Goldwater lost overwhelmingly in the fall **election** to **Lyndon B. Johnson**, the conservatives remained dominant within the party apparatus, and they have generally controlled the presidential nomination process in the party ever since.

Goldwater gave up his Senate seat to make his presidential run. Four years later, Arizona voters returned him to the Senate, where he remained a conservative champion until his retirement in 1987. In retirement, he remained an acerbic champion of libertarian conservative values.

GORE, ALBERT A., JR. Democratic vice president, 1993–2001; Democratic presidential nominee, 2000. (b. 31 March 1948). The son and namesake of a prominent Tennessee politician, Albert Gore Jr. followed his father to the **House of Representatives** (1977–1985), and then to the **Senate** (1985–1993). He sought the Democratic presidential **nomination** in 1988 but lost to Michael Dukakis. Four years later, presidential nominee **Bill Clinton** picked Gore as his vice presidential choice, and the **ticket** won **election** that fall. Gore played an active role in the politics and policymaking of the Clinton **administration**. Renominated and reelected in 1996, he became the Democratic presidential nominee in 2000. In the **general election**, Gore outpolled Republican **George W. Bush** by over 500,000 votes, but he failed to achieve the required **majority** in the **electoral college**. Gore unsuccessfully challenged the vote count in Florida, which he lost narrowly, and whose 25 electoral votes would have made him **president**. Once out of office, he became a vocal critic of the policies of the Bush administration, particularly in the realms of foreign affairs, civil liberties, and the environment. In 2007, he was awarded the Nobel Peace Prize for his endeavors on behalf of environmental protection, making him the second vice president (the first was after **Charles G. Dawes**) to be so honored.

GRAFT. A product of political corruption, it is the reward received by those who engage in that corruption. The **Progressive Era** reformers attacked the **political party** organizations of that day for providing and receiving graft.

GRAHAM, WILLIAM A. Whig vice presidential nominee, 1852. (b. 5 September 1804; d. 11 August 1875). Graham served in the **Senate** from North Carolina (1840–1843), representing the Southern **faction** of the **Whig Party**. He returned home and became governor (1845–1849). In 1850, President **Millard Fillmore** named him secretary of the navy. After nominating General **Winfield Scott** for president in 1852, the Whigs in **convention** had problems getting individuals to agree to be considered for **vice president**. Finally, without a roll call, the convention **chair** declared Graham to be the nominee. The ticket lost in the fall to the **Democratic Party** team of **Franklin Pierce** and **William R. King**. Subsequently, Graham followed his state in its secession from the Union, serving in the Confederate senate (1864).

GRAND OLD PARTY (GOP). A nickname the Republican Party embraced in the aftermath of the **Civil War**. First coined in the 1870s, it became widely used in the 1880s. It gave a connotation of legitimacy associated with tradition to what was actually a relatively young **political party**.

GRANGER, FRANCIS. Whig vice presidential nominee, 1836. (b. 1 December 1792; d. 31 August 1868). Granger was a prominent figure in the new **Whig Party** in New York. He served three divided terms in the House of Representatives (1835–1837, 1839–1841, and 1841–1843). As the end of his first term neared, he was chosen by party leaders for the second spot on one of a series of regional tickets the Whigs put forward in the 1836 presidential **election**, in hopes of preventing the dominant **Democratic Party** from receiving a **majority** in the **electoral college**. Whig strategists believed that if the presidential election went to the **House of Representatives** for determination, the Whigs could unite behind the leading nominee and prevail. Granger ran on a New England–based **ticket** headed by **Daniel Webster**. The strategy failed at the presidential level, as the Democrats elected **Martin Van Buren**. However, their vice presidential nominee, **Richard M. Johnson,** fell short of the required electoral college majority. In a singular action provided by 12th Amendment to the **Constitution**, the **Senate** had to elect the **vice president**. Johnson defeated Granger in the balloting.

Granger returned to the House in 1839, and in 1841 he joined the **cabinet** of President **William Henry Harrison** as **postmaster general**. Soon after Harrison's death, Granger clashed with the new **president, John Tyler,** whose party credentials were suspect. Granger resigned and won a special election to a vacant House seat. As factionalism within the Whig Party intensified later in the 1840s, Granger emerged as a leader of the **conservative** wing. His white hair gave rise to the popular name of the **faction**, the **Silver Grays**.

GRANT, ULYSSES S. Republican president, 1869–1877. (b. 27 April 1822; d. 23 July 1885). A West Point graduate, Ulysses S. Grant resumed his military career when the **Civil War** began. After successful campaigns in Mississippi and Tennessee attracted the appreciative notice of President **Abraham Lincoln**, Grant became commander in chief of the Union Army. He defeated the Army of Northern Virginia and brought the war to a victorious close. After the war, President **Andrew Johnson** named Grant to his cabinet as secretary of war.

The Republican Party nominated Grant for president in 1868, and he went on to win two terms in the White House, besting **Democratic Party** adversaries **Horatio Seymour** and **Horace Greeley**. Scandals associated with his **administration** dimmed his presidential luster, but his Civil War service had sealed his meritorious reputation with the American people. After four years of retirement, he made an unsuccessful bid at the 1880 **Republican National Convention** for the presidential nomination. Otherwise, his retirement featured widespread travel and the publication of his memoirs.

GRASS ROOTS. Rank-and-file members of a political party or the larger electorate. The term differentiates the masses from the elite. *See also* NETROOTS.

GREAT COMMONER. A nickname initially given to William Pitt the Elder, an 18th-century British politician who came to dominate the political scene from his position of leadership in the House of Commons. In the United States, despite the relative lack of class consciousness, two noteworthy party politicians became so known: **Henry Clay** and **William Jennings Bryan**. In each case, the leader pursued the interests of the masses against ruling elites.

GREAT DEPRESSION. A severe economic downturn that began in 1929 and persisted until the U.S. entry into World War II in 1941. The Great Depression began during the **Fourth Party System**, with the **Republican Party** in control of the national government and **Herbert C. Hoover** in the White House. Voter dissatisfaction with the apparent inability of the governing party to reverse the decline led to a **party realignment** that placed the **Democratic Party**, led by **Franklin D. Roosevelt**, in a position of dominance in the **Fifth Party System** that persisted for several decades. The Great Depression called for a far more activist national government response to economic and social problems than had been the case previously. Prior to the Great Depression, both major parties had vital progressive factions. Going forward, the Democratic Party clearly took the lead in embracing the modern **liberal** notion of active, positive government.

GREAT SOCIETY. A label applied to the social policies advocated and implemented by President **Lyndon B. Johnson**. The Great Society programs addressed civil rights, medical care, and poverty. Johnson perceived his agenda as complementary to the New Deal of **Franklin D. Roosevelt**.

GREELEY, HORACE. Democratic presidential nominee, 1872. (b. 3 February 1811; d. 29 November 1872). Greeley was a prominent journalist who founded and edited the *New York Tribune*. Initially identifying with the **Whig Party**, he served a partial term in the House of Representatives (1848–1849). Shortly afterward, he was instrumental in the birth of the **Republican Party**. In 1872, the liberal **faction** of that party, disenchanted with the scandal-plagued presidency of **Ulysses S. Grant**, bolted from the party and nominated Greeley for **president**. The **Democratic Party**, despairing of the presidential prospects for a party loyalist, followed suit and endorsed Greeley as their standard-bearer. Grant coasted to an easy reelection victory, and the despondent Greeley died shortly afterward, before the presidential electors were scheduled to meet. His pledged electors divided their votes among several individuals. *See also* LIBERAL REPUBLICAN PARTY.

GREEN PARTY. A **minor party** established in the mid-1990s, committed to environmental protection, **grassroots** democracy, and social justice, and linked with like-minded parties in Europe. The **Citizens Party** in the 1980s paved the way for the emergence of the Green Party. In 1996 and 2000, renowned consumer advocate Ralph Nader served as the party's presidential **standard-bearer** and elevated its national profile. In 1996, the Green Party appeared on presidential ballots in some 20 states and won almost 700,000 votes (0.7 percent). Four years later, competing in 47 states, Nader compiled almost 3 million votes (2.7 percent). More important, he got almost 100,000 votes in Florida, likely tipping the presidential **election** in favor of **George W. Bush**. In 2004, Nader sought the support but not the nomination of the Green Party for his independent presidential candidacy. The Greens nominated their own presidential **ticket**; their popular support dropped precipitously, and their electoral effect was negligible.

GREENBACK LABOR PARTY. A minor party in the **Gilded Age**. The Greenback Labor Party was an attempt by the **Greenback Party** to broaden its base for the 1880 presidential **election**. Led by nominee **James B. Weaver** (Iowa), the Greenback Labor Party moved beyond a **soft money** policy to embrace such progressive ideals as an income tax, an eight-hour day, and women's suffrage.

GREENBACK PARTY. A prominent **minor party** in the **Gilded Age**. The Greenback Party contested presidential elections in 1876, 1880, and 1884. Originating in 1874 as the Independent National Party, it took its popular name from its advocacy of greenbacks, paper notes issued by the government during and after the **Civil War**. It argued that the adoption of these notes would promote prosperity, supporting debtors at the expense of creditors. This **soft money** position was most popular in the West and South. In 1876, the party's first presidential nominee, Peter Cooper, received negligible support. Two years later, the party elected 14 members to the House of Representatives. In 1880, led by **James B. Weaver,** the Greenbacks expanded their platform to embrace a broader array of progressive measures, labeling themselves the Greenback Labor Party. Again, they failed to draw large numbers of voters to their banner, losing seats in Congress. Four years later, the Greenback Party and the **Anti-Monopoly Party** campaigned in **fusion**, led by Benjamin F. Butler (Massachusetts), but electoral response was poor, and the party withered away.

GREGG, ANDREW. President pro tempore of the Senate, 1809. (b. 10 June 1755; d. 20 May 1835). Gregg served eight terms in the **House**, beginning in 1791. In 1807, he was elected to a single term in the **Senate**. During the brief first session of the 11th **Congress**, he was once selected **president pro tempore**.

GROSSMAN, STEVEN. Democratic National Committee chair, 1997–1999. (b. 17 February 1946). A Massachusetts businessman and lifelong Democrat, Grossman became a member of the **Democratic**

National Committee in 1989. He held the position until 1992, and in 1991–1992, he was also **chair** of the state party. Under his leadership, Democrats came to hold every seat in the state's congressional delegation and gave 1992 presidential nominee **Bill Clinton** one of his largest margins of victory. Grossman also gained national attention as president of the American Israel Public Affairs Committee, lobbying for Israeli interests.

After the 1996 elections, a leadership void developed at the Democratic National Committee following the departures of the general chair, Senator **Christopher Dodd**, and the chair, **Donald Fowler**. President Clinton opted to retain the dual structure and designated Colorado Governor **Roy Romer** as the general chair to play the public role of party spokesman. He also asked Grossman to serve as national chair and oversee the party headquarters operation.

Grossman received acclaim for his fund-raising prowess and his administrative ability. Following the 1998 **midterm elections**, in which the Democrats made a surprisingly strong showing in the congressional contests, Grossman resigned. In 2002, he made an unsuccessful bid for Massachusetts' governorship. Remaining active in party politics, he briefly chaired the 2004 presidential nomination **campaign** of **Howard Dean**.

GROUNDSWELL. A demonstration of **grassroots** support for an individual, a group, or a policy.

GROW, GALUSHA. Republican Speaker of the House of Representatives, 1861–1863. (b. 31 August 1823; d. 31 March 1907). Grow was initially elected to the **House of Representatives** from Pennsylvania in 1850 as the nominee of the **Democratic Party**. He clearly identified with the antislavery wing of the national party, styling himself a **Free Soil** Democrat. He switched over to the newly formed **Republican Party** in 1856, holding on to his House seat. In 1861, when Congress convened following the outbreak of the **Civil War**, he was elected **Speaker** for a single term. He left the House in 1863, returning more than three decades later (1894–1903).

GYPSY MOTHS. A small, informal **faction** of the **Republican Party** in the **House of Representatives** in the early 1980s. Based in the

Northeast, these Republicans from urban, industrial districts were ideologically more moderate than the mainstream of the congressional party. They opposed the economic policies put forward by Republican President **Ronald W. Reagan**, viewing them as detrimental to their region.

– H –

HACK. A pejorative term for a second-level, and second-rate, party politician.

"HAD ENOUGH?" A slogan adopted by the **Republican Party** in its successful campaign in the 1946 **midterm elections**. The slogan persuasively suggested that the extended period of **Democratic Party** dominance that began with the **Great Depression** had run its course and that it was time for a change in party power. The Republicans won majorities in both houses of **Congress** for the first time since 1928, but they lost control two years later. Since then, the slogan has occasionally been revived by the **party-out-of-power**, most recently by the Democrats in 2006.

HALF-BREEDS. A faction of the **Republican Party** during the **Gilded Age**. The Half-Breeds were so labeled by party regulars, the **Stalwarts**, for their advocacy of political reform and willingness to abandon the anti-Southern rhetoric of the party. Their champions included **Rutherford B. Hayes** and **James G. Blaine**.

HALL, LEONARD W. Republican National Committee chair, 1953–1957. (b. 2 October 1900; d. 2 June 1979). Hall's father worked for **Theodore Roosevelt** at his Oyster Bay estate on New York's Long Island. Trained in the law, Hall turned to **Republican Party** politics. He won a seat in the **House of Representatives** in 1938, and he held it through 1952, when he chose not to seek reelection. Late in his House career, he chaired the Republican Congressional Campaign Committee.

In the 1952 presidential **campaign**, Hall was a key supporter of the candidacy of General **Dwight D. Eisenhower**, and he traveled on the campaign train. Early in the Eisenhower presidency, when **C. Wesley Roberts, chair** of the **Republican National Committee**, resigned amid allegations of financial impropriety, the **president** tapped Hall to be party chair. He handled that assignment with distinction, orchestrating Eisenhower's reelection in 1956. The next year, he resigned to pursue his own ambition to be governor of New York, but he lost the nomination contest to **Nelson A. Rockefeller**. Hall remained active in national party politics, supporting the presidential candidacy of **Richard M. Nixon** in 1960 by chairing his **campaign organization** and subsequently serving as a prominent **elder statesman**.

HALLECK, CHARLES A. Republican majority leader of the House of Representatives, 1947–1949, 1953–1955; Republican minority leader of the House of Representatives, 1959–1965. (b. 22 August 1922; d. 3 March 1986). Halleck was an Indiana lawyer who had been serving as a prosecuting attorney when he was sent to the **House of Representative** in 1935. He remained there for 17 terms. His initial assignment as a party leader was to head the **Republican Congressional Campaign Committee** in 1943. When the Republican Party captured the House in 1946, Halleck became the **floor leader** under Speaker **Joseph W. Martin Jr.** for a single term. He resumed the position of **majority leader**, again for one term, in 1953. In 1959, Halleck replaced Martin as the **minority leader**. He held that position for three terms, until he was ousted by **Gerald R. Ford** in 1965. He served two more terms in the House, retiring in 1969.

HALLETT, BENJAMIN F. Democratic National Committee chair, 1848–1852. (b. 2 December 1797; d. 30 September 1862). Hallett gained recognition in his native Massachusetts as a radical journalist. He supported the **Anti-Masonic Party** in its 1832 insurgency and then drifted toward the **faction** of the **Democratic-Republican Party** identified with **Andrew Jackson**, which in turn evolved into the **Democratic Party**. In state party politics, he was a conciliator between factions, reflecting the growing sectional divisions.

At the 1848 **Democratic National Convention**, Hallett emerged as a leader of not only the Massachusetts delegation but also those from the neighboring New England states. At a critical point in the presidential balloting, Hallett was able to shift the votes of the regional favorite son, Levi Woodbury, to **Lewis Cass**, securing Cass's **nomination**. That **convention** created the **Democratic National Committee** to direct the national **campaign**, and Hallett became the first national party **chair**.

After the campaign ended in defeat, Hallet continued to serve until the next convention, four years later. He persisted in his attempts to reconcile the regionally based factions that were developing as the slavery controversy intensified. Subsequently, Hallett received a **patronage** appointment as a U.S. attorney from President **Franklin Pierce**. At the 1860 Democratic National Convention, Hallett promoted the presidential candidacy of **John Breckinridge**, then serving as **vice president**. However, the Southern delegates who were expected to provide Breckinridge with his regional base of support withdrew from the proceedings, and the nomination went to **Stephen A. Douglas**.

HAMILTON, ALEXANDER. Federalist Party founder. (b. 11 January 1757; d. 12 July 1804). Hamilton was born in the West Indies, and he came to the United States in 1772 to pursue higher education, first in New Jersey and then in New York. He soon became involved in the revolutionary movement, enlisting in the patriot cause as an effective propagandist. He served with distinction during the Revolutionary War as an aide-de-camp and personal secretary to General **George Washington**. When the pace of war slowed, Hamilton moved to Albany, New York, where he studied law.

Hamilton served in the Continental Congress (1781–1783) and emerged as a leading critic of the form of government provided by the Articles of Confederation. Promoting reform, he was a delegate to the Annapolis **convention** in 1786 and the Philadelphia convention in 1787. He supported the proposed **Constitution** put forward by the latter body, pseudonymously coauthoring the *Federalist Papers*, a series of essays that appeared in the New York press as that state was considering ratification.

Following ratification of the Constitution, Hamilton joined the new **cabinet** being assembled by President George Washington, as secretary of the treasury. In that position, he effectively advocated policies to strengthen the power of the central government in the federal system, to place that government on a solid financial footing, and to promote commercial and manufacturing interests in society. These positions frequently brought him into conflict within the **administration** with the secretary of state, **Thomas Jefferson**. Their policy differences, along with their personal rivalries, resulted in the formation of rival political parties: Hamilton's **Federalist Party** and Jefferson's **Democratic-Republican Party**. President Washington bemoaned the emergence of this **First Party System** while generally embracing Hamilton's policy initiatives.

In 1795, Hamilton left the cabinet but remained an influential voice in both party politics and public policy. Within the Federalist Party, he resisted the rise to leadership of Vice President **John Adams**, seeking to undercut Adams in his successful presidential bid in 1796 and his reelection defeat in 1800. When the latter presidential **election** went to the House of Representatives to resolve the tie between Democratic-Republicans Thomas Jefferson and **Aaron Burr**, Hamilton threw his considerable support behind Jefferson. Almost four years later, he again opposed Burr's ambitions, this time to be elected governor of New York. The two fought a duel that resulted in Hamilton's death.

HAMILTON, JOHN D. M. Republican National Committee chair, 1936–1940. (b. 2 March 1892; d. 24 September 1973). Hamilton was elected to the state legislature in his native Kansas in 1925. He quickly rose to the position of Speaker (1927–1928). He unsuccessfully sought the Republican gubernatorial **nomination** in 1928. The state party placed Hamilton on the **Republican National Committee (RNC)** in 1932. In 1934, he became general counsel for the RNC, but he resigned that position in 1936 to manage the preconvention nomination **campaign** of fellow Kansan **Alfred M. Landon**. Landon's victory at the **convention** resulted in Hamilton's designation as national party **chair**. Hamilton followed the precedent of his predecessor, **Henry P. Fletcher**, in accepting a salary for his full-time party work. As chair, he was an institution builder, remembered with appreciation for his efforts to place the national party headquarters on sounder organizational and financial footings. He left office in 1940, replaced by **Joseph W. Martin**, and joined a Philadelphia law firm. He maintained his interest and involvement in party politics, albeit on a much lower level.

HAMLIN, HANNIBAL. Republican vice president, 1861–1865. (b. 27 August 1809; d. 4 July 1891). Hamlin was a Maine lawyer who initially affiliated with the **Democratic Party**. He was elected to the state legislature in 1836, where he served for five years, including three as speaker. In 1843, he went to the **House of Representatives** for two terms. From there, he moved to the **Senate** (1847–1861). His strong antislavery sentiments led him to bolt from his party in 1856 to join the new **Republican Party**. The next year, he interrupted his Senate tenure when he was elected governor, but he quickly resigned and returned to the Senate.

In 1860, Hamlin was the choice of the **Republican National Convention** for the vice presidential **nomination**. Party leaders seeking a **balanced ticket** perceived his Northeastern base as complementary to the Midwestern strength of presidential nominee **Abraham Lincoln**. Facing a divided **Democratic Party**, the Republican **ticket** won a **plurality** popular vote victory and a **majority** in the **electoral college**.

Hamlin found the vice presidency unsatisfying. He was less than attentive to his constitutional assignment to preside over the Senate. Hamlin advocated a stronger antislavery position than did President Lincoln, but he lacked the influence within the **administration** to push Lincoln further. Rather, Hamlin's stridency led Lincoln to drop him from the reelection ticket in favor of **Andrew Johnson**, a pro-Union Democrat from Tennessee, in a **bipartisan** endeavor labeled the **Union Party**.

Out of elective office, Hamlin secured a **patronage** appointment as collector of the Port of Boston and served as president of a railroad. In 1868, Maine sent him back to the Senate, where he embraced the faction that opposed President Andrew Johnson's Reconstruction policies and sought Johnson's impeachment and removal. Hamlin served two terms and then retired, accepting another patronage appointment, this time as minister to Spain (1881–1882). He then returned to Maine.

HANCOCK, JOHN. Electoral vote recipient, 1789 (Federalist). (b. 12 January 1737; d. 8 October 1793). Hancock was a highly visible revolutionary leader. He served two stints in the Continental Congress (1775–1780 and 1785–1786). Between those terms, he was governor of Massachusetts. From 1775 to 1777, he was the president of the Congress, placing him in a key role in the move toward independence. He was the first signer of the Declaration of Independence. His national reputation made him the recipient of four electoral votes from three states in the first presidential **election** in 1789.

HANCOCK, WINFIELD S. Democratic presidential nominee, 1880. (b. 14 February 1824; d. 9 February 1886). A career Army officer, Hancock served with distinction during the **Civil War**. Remaining on active duty, he figured prominently in postwar **Democratic Party** presidential politics. He contended strongly for the 1868 Democratic presidential **nomination**, which eventually went to **Horatio Seymour**. In 1876, he again contested for the nomination but fared much worse. On his third try, in 1880, he finally succeeded, positioning himself as a candidate acceptable to diverse, antagonistic party factions. The fall elections were closely contested, with Republican Party nominee **James A. Garfield** winning a narrow victory. Hancock returned to active military service.

HANDPICKED. A somewhat pejorative phrase suggesting that a **candidate** or party nominee for public office has been chosen and imposed by a powerful individual or group. *See also* KINGMAKER.

HANNA, MARCUS A. Republican National Committee chair, 1896–1904. (b. 24 September 1837; d. 15 February 1904). Hanna was a prominent Ohio industrialist in the **Gilded Age** who became a major force in state and national Republican Party politics. He successfully managed the preconvention presidential candidacy of **William McKinley** in 1896, and his reward was the position of national party **chair**. There, he orchestrated the **front-porch campaign** that swept McKinley to victory in the **critical election** of 1896, which solidified **Republican Party** dominance of the political landscape, ushering in the **Fourth Party System**. A few months later, Hanna followed McKinley to Washington, and was chosen for a **Senate** seat, making him a significant figure in the **party-in-office** as well as the **party organization**. He was instrumental in maneuvering the vice presidential **nomination** of **Theodore Roosevelt** as McKinley's running mate in 1900, at the behest of the party leadership in New York State, who were discomforted by Roosevelt's **progressive** leanings. After McKinley's assassination elevated Roosevelt to the White House, Hanna continued in his role as national party **boss** until his death in 1904.

HANNEGAN, ROBERT E. Democratic National Committee chair, 1944–1947. (b. 30 June 1903; d. 6 October 1949). Hannegan began his career in party politics in the local **Democratic Party** organization of his native St. Louis, Missouri. In the 1930s, he associated himself with Senator **Harry S. Truman,** based across the state in Kansas City, in a political alliance that proved enduring and mutually beneficial. Hannegan provided vital support for Truman's difficult reelection **campaign** in 1940. In turn, Truman secured a **patronage** appointment for Hannegan as a revenue collector and then successfully lobbied President **Franklin D. Roosevelt** for Hannegan's election as national party **chair** in 1944. Hannegan immediately reciprocated by promoting Truman's vice presidential **nomination.** Following Roosevelt's death, Truman's first presidential appointment was Hannegan, whom he named as **postmaster general.** Health problems forced Hannegan's resignation from both the party and the government post in 1947.

HAPPY WARRIOR. A label that **Franklin D. Roosevelt** bestowed on **Al Smith** in nominating him for president in 1924, calling attention to the obvious pleasure that Smith derived from his vocation. Over 40 years later, supporters of **Hubert H. Humphrey** used the same phrase to describe their candidate, who characterized his 1968 presidential campaign as the "politics of joy."

HARD MONEY. In its original usage, early in the 19th century, "hard money" referred to an economic policy stance that preferred a currency backed by precious metals (gold and/or silver) over a paper-based one. By 1896, the issue had become whether the currency should be backed solely by gold or by a combination of gold and silver. The former position was the hard money one; the latter became known as the easy money, or **soft money,** position.

In contemporary parlance, the term refers to **campaign** funds contributed directly to candidates within the restrictions of **campaign**

finance legislation. Funds contributed to political parties outside these restrictions, or soft money, were a primary regulatory target of the **Bipartisan Campaign Reform Act (BCRA)**.

HARDING, WARREN G. Republican president, 1921–1923. (b. 2 November 1865; d. 2 August 1923). Owner of a small-town Ohio newspaper, Harding became involved in state politics on behalf of the **Republican Party**. He served in the state legislature and as lieutenant governor. After failing twice in bids for the governorship, he succeeded in winning a seat in the U.S. **Senate** in 1914. Six years later, a divided **Republican National Convention** turned to Harding, a **dark horse**, as an acceptable compromise choice. Campaigning for a "return to normalcy" after the disruptions of World War I and the contentious battle over the League of Nations, Harding won a **landslide** victory over Democratic nominee **James M. Cox,** a fellow Ohioan. His presidency became mired in scandal, and Harding died unexpectedly in 1923. Vice President **Calvin Coolidge** became **president**, finishing the remainder of Harding's term and going on to win on his own in 1924.

HARRIS, FRED R. Democratic National Committee chair, 1969–1970. (b. 13 November 1930). Oklahoman Fred Harris won a special election to finish an unexpired **Senate** term in 1964, and he received a full term from the voters in 1966. Two years later, presidential nominee **Hubert H. Humphrey** seriously considered naming Harris as his vice presidential **running mate** but chose Senator **Edmund S. Muskie**. Harris expressed interest in the position of party **chair**, but Humphrey chose **Lawrence F. O'Brien**. Shortly after the election, O'Brien resigned, and this time Harris was the choice of **titular leader** Humphrey. Harris also had broad support within the **liberal** wing of the party. During his brief tenure as party chair, he advanced the cause of party reform through his encouragement of the **McGovern–Fraser Commission**. He resigned as party chair in 1970, and he did not seek reelection to the Senate in 1972, opting instead for what proved to be an unsuccessful quest for the Democratic presidential **nomination**. A subsequent 1976 presidential bid also failed. Out of public life, he moved into academia, teaching and writing about American politics.

HARRIS, ISHAM. Democratic president pro tempore of the Senate, 1893–1895. (b. 20 February 1818; d. 8 July 1897). Harris won a seat in the **House of Representatives** from Tennessee in 1848 and served two terms. Next, he had a five-year stint as governor (1857–1862). Chosen for the **Senate** in 1877, he remained there for the rest of his life. Late in his Senate career, he served as **president pro tempore** for much of the 53rd **Congress**, shortly after the reform that provided that once elected, the president pro tempore would continue to serve at the pleasure of the Senate.

HARRISON, BENJAMIN. Republican president, 1889–1893. (b. 20 August 1833; d. 13 March 1901). Grandson of military hero and president **William Henry Harrison**, Benjamin Harrison served with distinction as a Union officer during the Civil War. In 1881, Ohio sent him to the U.S. **Senate** for one term. In 1888, the **Republican National Convention**, meeting for the first time in a generation without control of the White House, picked him on the eighth **ballot** as its **dark-horse** nominee. Despite trailing in the popular vote to President **Grover Cleveland**, Harrison carried more states and won a narrow **majority** in the **electoral college**. Four years later, Harrison won renomination on the first ballot, but he went down to defeat in a rematch with Cleveland. In retirement, he practiced law.

HARRISON, BYRON PATTON "PAT." Democratic president pro tempore of the Senate, 1941. (b. 29 August 1881; d. 22 June 1941). Harrison served three terms in the **House of Representatives** from Mississippi (1911–1919). Elected to the **Senate** in 1918, he held his seat for the rest of his life. In 1937, he sought the position of **floor leader** but lost to **Alben W. Barkley**, the choice of President **Franklin D. Roosevelt**. In January 1941, at the beginning of the 77th **Congress**, he became **president pro tempore**. He died soon afterward.

HARRISON, ROBERT. Electoral vote recipient, 1789. (b. 1745; d. 1790). Named chief justice of the General Court of Maryland in 1781, he was the favorite son nominee of his state's six electors, who also cast their presidential ballots in the **electoral college** for **George Washington** in the inaugural presidential election.

HARRISON, WILLIAM HENRY. Whig president, 1841. (b. 9 February 1773; d. 4 April 1841). The son of a signer of the Declaration of Independence, Harrison pursued a military career characterized by conflict with Native Americans on the western frontier. He was chosen as a delegate to **Congress** for the Northwest Territory in 1799. In 1801, he became territorial governor of Indiana, a post he held until 1813. It was during this period that he became a national hero, for his successful military leadership in the 1811 Battle of Tippecanoe, providing a significant victory in the Indian Wars. He returned to the **House of Representatives**, this time as a member from Ohio, in 1816, serving until 1819. He went to the **Senate** in 1825 for a three-year stint. In 1836, the newly formed **Whig Party** made him one of its regionally based presidential nominees in an effort to divide the **electoral college** vote and send the presidential election to the House of Representatives. The strategy failed, as **Democratic Party** nominee **Martin Van Buren** prevailed.

In 1840, the Whigs approached the presidential **nomination** in a more normal fashion, meeting as a **convention** and choosing Harrison over party rivals **Henry Clay** and **Winfield Scott**. Pairing Harrison with a dissident Democrat, John Tyler, the Whigs won the presidency, carried along by a historic **campaign** slogan, "Tippecanoe and Tyler Too." Harrison became ill after delivering his inaugural address, and he died a month later, creating the first vacancy in the presidential office.

HARRITY, WILLIAM F. Democratic National Committee chair, 1892–1896. (b. 19 October 1850; d. 17 April 1912). Harrity was a Philadelphia lawyer and banker. He began his career in **Democratic Party** politics at the local level, chairing the municipal **party organization**. This office provided his entree to a position on the executive **committee** of the state party committee. After winning the presidency in 1884, **Grover Cleveland** appointed Harrity postmaster of Philadelphia.

Harrity joined the **Democratic National Committee** in 1891. The next year, following Cleveland's renomination for **president**, Harrity succeeded **Calvin S. Brice** as national party **chair** for what proved to be a victorious presidential **campaign**. Four years later, presidential nominee **William Jennings Bryan**, representing a rival party faction, engineered Harrity's departure in favor of **James K. Jones**. Harrity bolted from the party with other **hard money** advocates to constitute the **National Democratic Party**.

HASTERT, DENNIS. Republican Speaker of the House, 1999–2007. (b. 2 January 1942). Hastert was a high school teacher and coach prior to his **election** to the state legislature in 1980. Six years later, he was the party organization's nominee to replace the Republican **incumbent** in Illinois's 14th District, west of Chicago, who had died following his primary **nomination**. Hastert prevailed in November in what has been a **safe seat** for the **Republican Party**. He toiled in relative obscurity in the **House of Representatives**, becoming a deputy **whip** in 1994.

Extraordinary events following the 1998 **midterm elections** elevated Hastert to the office of Speaker. Following a poor showing by the GOP, in which it lost seats and barely maintained its **majority**, Speaker **Newt Gingrich** came under fire within the **Republican Conference** and announced his intention to resign from both the speakership and his congressional seat. The conference quickly settled on Robert Livingston, **chair** of the powerful Appropriations Committee, as his successor. However, before the inauguration of the 106th Congress, and amid the impeachment proceedings against President **Bill Clinton**, Livingston became embroiled in scandalous allegations, and he followed Gingrich's lead in announcing that he would not be a candidate for Speaker and would resign his congressional seat. At that dramatic moment, Hastert emerged as the consensus choice of the conference. He was elected Speaker two weeks later when **Congress** convened.

In June 2006, Hastert supplanted **Joseph G. Cannon** as the longest serving Republican Speaker. His tenure was marked by his controversial practice of restricting the legislative floor agenda to bills that had the support of a majority of the **Republican Conference**. Republicans losses in the 2006 midterm elections left them in the **minority**, and Hastert declined to seek the office of **minority leader** for the 110th Congress. In 2007, he announced that he would not seek another term in 2009; he resigned his seat that fall.

HATCH ACT. The Political Activities Act of 1939, more popularly known as the Hatch Act after its primary sponsor, **Senator** Carl Hatch, a New Mexico Democrat, prohibited executive branch employees of the federal government from engaging in political activity. The restriction embraced campaigning, political management, and using federal office to interfere with or influence any **partisan** election. A second Hatch Act in 1940 extended these prohibitions to state and local government employees whose salaries come from federal funds. Several states have adopted "little Hatch Acts," imposing similar restrictions on political activity by state employees. The second Hatch Act underwent substantial revision in 1974, reducing the restrictions on political activity for federally funded state and local government employees.

The Hatch Act ostensibly promoted the values of the **merit system** and political neutrality in the federal civil service, while undermining those associated with **patronage** and the **spoils system**. It was enacted at a time of growing congressional concern that the New Deal's dramatic expansion of the scope of the federal government might produce a political machine of federal employees whose loyalty to the **president** could undermine accountability to **Congress**.

HAYDEN, CARL. Democratic president pro tempore of the Senate, 1957–1969. (b. 2 October 1877; d. 25 January 1972). Hayden entered the **House of Representatives** as the first member from the new state of Arizona in 1912. He was subsequently elected to seven full terms. In 1926, he won **election** to the **Senate**, and remained there until 1969. For the last 12 years of his tenure, the 85th through the 90th Congresses, as senior member of the **Democratic Party majority**, he was **president pro tempore**. Following the assassination of President **John F. Kennedy** in 1963, Hayden assumed the constitutional responsibility for presiding over the Senate and moved up to second in the line of presidential succession. Concerns about the advanced age of Hayden and House Speaker **John W. McCormack** fueled the movement for the ratification of the 25th **Amendment** to the Constitution, providing a procedure for filling a vacancy in the vice presidency.

HAYES, RUTHERFORD B. Republican president, 1877–1881. (b. 4 October 1822; d. 17 January 1893). Hayes rose to the rank of major general in the Union Army during the **Civil War**. After the war, he served his Ohio constituents for one term in the **House of Representatives** (1865–1867). He returned home, filling the governorship in 1868–1872 and again in 1876–1877. In 1876, he captured the presidential nomination of the **Republican Party**, when opponents of Senator **James G. Blaine** (Maine) rallied to his candidacy. In the general election, Hayes narrowly lost the popular vote to **Democratic Party** nominee **Samuel Tilden**. Initially, the **electoral college** vote was inconclusive, owing to contending slates of electors casting ballots in three Southern states and an ineligible elector from Oregon. An electoral commission established by **Congress** decided the issue in favor of the Republicans, resulting in a narrow electoral college victory for Hayes. He served a single, uneventful term and retired from politics, turning to philanthropy.

HAYS, WILL. Republican National Committee chair, 1918–1921. (b. 5 November 1879; d. 7 March 1954). Hays was an Indiana lawyer with a corporate clientele who participated in state party politics at a time of rising tension between the old guard and **progressive** factions. Becoming state **chair** in 1914, he successfully reconciled the factional rivals, unifying the state **party organization** in a manner that was the envy of his counterparts across the country. In 1918, Hays replaced **William R. Willcox** as national party chair and led the party to an impressive showing in midterm elections that restored the **Republican Party** to **majority** status in both chambers of **Congress**. His reputation was such that presidential nominee **Warren G. Harding** retained him as chair in 1920. After the victorious **election**, Harding named Hays **postmaster general**. Hays held both positions simultaneously for only a few months, resigning his party post in June 1921. In 1922, he left government service to accept an offer from the motion picture industry to head the Motion Picture Producers and Distributors of America. Known as the Hays Office, it set standards of decency in the industry for over two decades.

HEIR APPARENT. A successor so designated by a political leader. The term has been used most notably in recent years to refer to a **vice president** seeking the presidency under the sponsorship of the sitting **president**. Examples include **Richard M. Nixon (Dwight**

D. Eisenhower), **Hubert H. Humphrey** (**Lyndon B. Johnson**), **George H. W. Bush** (**Ronald W. Reagan**), and **Al Gore** (**Bill Clinton**).

HENDERSON, DAVID B. Republican Speaker of the House of Representatives, 1899–1903. (b. 14 March 1840; d. 25 February 1906). Henderson won **election** to the **House of Representatives** from Iowa in 1882. He served 10 terms. During the last two, the 56th and 57th Congresses, he held the office of **Speaker**, in which he was regarded as conscientious but relatively ineffective. His tenure was sandwiched between two very powerful speakers, **Thomas B. Reed** and **Joseph G. Cannon**. He retired unexpectedly in 1903.

HENDRICKS, THOMAS A. Democratic vice presidential nominee, 1876; Democratic vice president, 1885. (b. 7 September 1819; d. 24 November 1885). Born in Ohio, Hendricks grew up in neighboring Indiana, where he became a lawyer active in the **Democratic Party**. Elected to the state legislature in 1848, he moved up to the **House of Representatives** in 1851. Defeated for reelection in 1854, he secured a **patronage** appointment from President **Franklin Pierce** as commissioner of the general land office. Hendricks ran unsuccessfully for governor in 1860, but he was elected to the **Senate** in 1863. There, he criticized the conduct of the **Civil War** by President **Abraham Lincoln** and later defended the Reconstruction policies of President **Andrew Johnson**, which came under attack from the radicals in the **Republican Party**. Again defeated in his quest to become governor in 1868, he retired from the Senate and returned to Indiana. In 1872, Hendricks won a narrow victory in his third attempt for the governorship. In addition, when the electoral college met in December, following the death of defeated Democratic presidential nominee **Horace Greeley**, Hendricks received 42 presidential votes. Four years later, Governor Hendricks contended for the presidential **nomination** that went to **Samuel Tilden**, but he became the vice presidential choice of the **Democratic National Convention**. The Democratic **ticket** lost a disputed **election** that fall, and Hendricks found himself out of public office. In 1884, Hendricks was called back to public service, when the national **convention** designated him as the **running mate** of presidential nominee **Grover Cleveland**. This time the Democrats prevailed, and Hendricks was inaugurated the following March. He presided over the brief special session of the Senate that confirmed presidential **cabinet** appointees. Shortly before the opening of the scheduled first regular session of the 49th **Congress**, he died, having served fewer than nine months.

HENRY, JOHN. Electoral vote recipient, 1796 (Democratic-Republican). (b. November 1750; d. 16 December 1798). Henry served two stints in the Continental Congress (1778–1781 and 1784–1787). He went on to hold a seat in the U.S. **Senate** (1789–1797). It was near the end of that incumbency that he received two **favorite son** votes in the 1796 presidential balloting of the **electoral college**. In 1797, he was elected governor. He died in office the next year.

HEWITT, ABRAM S. Democratic National Committee chair, 1876–1877. (b. 31 July 1822; d. 18 January 1903). Hewitt was elected to the **House of Representatives** from New York in 1874. Two years later, when fellow New Yorker **Samuel Tilden** became the **Democratic Party** presidential nominee, Hewitt was named national party **chair** to manage the presidential **campaign**, while successfully seeking reelection to his House seat. After the disputed election was resolved in favor of the Republicans, Hewitt resigned as national party chair. He was not reelected in 1878, but he reclaimed his seat in 1880, eventually leaving that office in 1886.

HILL, JOHN F. Republican National Committee chair, 1909–1912. (b. 29 October 1855; d. 16 March 1912). Hill was a Maine physician turned publisher. In 1889, he was elected to the lower house of the Maine legislature; in 1892, he moved over to the state senate. He went on to win two terms as governor (1901–1905). He supported the victorious presidential candidacy of **William H. Taft** in 1908. That connection, along with a longtime association with the incoming **chair** of the **Republican National Committee (RNC)**, **Frank H. Hitchcock** of Massachusetts, secured him a spot on the RNC. In 1909, Hitchcock appointed Hill vice chair, a controversial measure because heretofore that position had been filled via **election** by the national **committee**. It also strengthened Taft's influence on the committee. When Hitchcock resigned later that year, Hill became acting chair. The national committee did not confirm that status by election until 1911. In March 1912, Hill fell ill and died. He was succeeded by his choice as vice chair, **Victor Rosewater**, another loyal Taft supporter, as the presidential **nomination** contest loomed.

HILLES, CHARLES D. Republican National Committee chair, 1912–1916. (b. 23 June 1867; d. 27 August 1949). Hilles was an Ohio native who began a career in youth welfare that soon took him to New York. He played a significant role in the 1908 presidential **campaign** of **William H. Taft**, which led to his appointment as assistant secretary of the treasury in 1909. As the 1912 presidential **nomination** campaign loomed, with former president **Theodore Roosevelt** gearing up to challenge Taft, his successor, Taft designated Hilles as his private secretary and placed him in charge of preconvention operations. At the **Republican National Convention**, Taft was victorious, and Roosevelt bolted, splitting the party. The incumbent national party **chair**, **Victor Rosewater**, who had ascended to the office earlier that year following the death of **John F. Hill**, had been discredited in his home state of Nebraska and was not reelected as a member of the **Republican National Committee**. Taft prevailed on Hilles to take on the duties of national party chair. After the election debacle, Hilles promoted reform of the delegate selection process, which resulted in reducing the representation of the Southern state delegations at the **convention**. These state parties, generally loyal to the **old guard** faction in the national party, were unable to contribute to the **general election** effort, owing to **Democratic Party** dominance in the **Solid South**. Replaced as national party chair in 1916 by William R. Willcox, the choice of presidential nominee **Charles Evans Hughes**, Hilles refused to support the Hughes candidacy, contending that Hughes would be inattentive to **patronage** concerns. Taking a position as an insurance executive, Hilles remained on the national committee until 1946, managing the eastern headquarters in the 1924 election.

HILLHOUSE, JAMES. Federalist president pro tempore of the Senate, 1801. (b. 21 October 1754; d. 29 December 1832). Hillhouse represented Connecticut in the **House of Representatives** (1791–1796). In 1796, he moved over to the **Senate**, where he remained until 1810.

During the notorious **lame duck** session of the 6th **Congress**, held after the **critical election** of 1800, which the Federalists lost decisively, Hillhouse and **John E. Howard** of Maryland each served as **president pro tempore** on a single occasion.

HITCHCOCK, FRANK H. Republican National Committee Chair, 1908–1909. (b. 5 October 1869; d. 5 August 5 1935). Hitchcock was an Ohio native who became active in the Young Republican movement while attending Harvard. After graduating, he moved to Washington, D.C., where he worked as a civil servant in the Agriculture Department and studied law. He became acquainted with **George B. Cortelyou**, who became his party patron, installing Hitchcock in the newly established Department of Commerce and Labor, of which Cortelyou was secretary. Shortly afterward, when Cortelyou became national party **chair**, he named Hitchcock to be secretary of the **Republican National Committee**. In 1905, when Cortelyou moved to the Post Office as **postmaster general**, Hitchcock accompanied him as his top assistant. Later, in 1907, when Cortelyou moved yet again, this time to the Treasury Department, Hitchcock took over the **patronage** function at the Post Office, using this power to promote the interests of **William Howard Taft**, who was preparing his candidacy for the 1908 presidential **nomination** of the **Republican Party**. In early 1908, Hitchcock left the Post Office to devote full time to the Taft presidential **campaign**. After the **Republican National Convention** rewarded those efforts by nominating Taft, Hitchcock became national party **chair**. Following the **election** victory in the fall, he became postmaster general, resigning as party chair to do so. After Taft's reelection defeat in 1912, Hitchcock moved to Arizona, where he practiced law and pursued several diverse business interests. In 1916, he reentered the arena of national party politics, managing the preconvention campaign of Republican nominee **Charles Evans Hughes**.

HOBART, GARRET A. Republican vice president, 1897–1899. (b. 3 June 1844; d. 21 November 1899). Hobart was a New Jersey lawyer who served with distinction for a decade in the state legislature (1872–1882). He was also state **chair** of the **Republican Party** (1880–1891). In 1884, he was elected to the **Republican National Committee**. In private life, he maintained a lucrative legal practice and prospered in his banking and public utility concerns. Relatively obscure, Hobart nevertheless was the first-ballot choice of the 1896 **Republican National Convention** for **vice president**, providing the party with a **balanced ticket** geographically and a uniform position on the currency question. Hobart and his presidential **running mate**, Governor William McKinley of Ohio, shared a strong **hard money** position backing the gold standard. As vice president, Hobart figured prominently in the politics and policy of the McKinley **administration**, as well as conscientiously presiding over the **Senate**. His health failed in early 1899, and he died later that year.

HOOVER, HERBERT C. Republican president, 1929–1933. (b. 10 August 1874; d. 20 October 1964). Hoover had a lucrative career as an international mining engineer before entering public service during World War I. He organized and directed the U.S.-sponsored food relief operation in Europe (1917–1919). Returning home, he joined the presidential **cabinet** of **Warren G. Harding** as secretary of commerce, and he continued in that office under Harding's successor, **Calvin Coolidge**. When Coolidge did not seek the 1928 presidential **nomination**, the **Republican Party** immediately turned to Hoover, who easily won the first-ballot **nomination** of the **Republican National Convention**. He went on to best Democrat **Al Smith** in the fall election, maintaining Republican control of the presidency during the 1920s. Seven months after he assumed office, the stock market collapsed, inaugurating the **Great Depression**. Hoover's public support plummeted as economic conditions worsened. Although the Republicans renominated him, he met electoral defeat in the fall against Democrat Franklin D. Roosevelt. In retirement, he bitterly opposed the **New Deal** policies of his successor. After World War II, Presidents **Harry S. Truman** and **Dwight D. Eisenhower** called on Hoover to chair the Commission on the Organization of the Executive Branch of Government, where his experience and expertise proved invaluable, and the position contributed somewhat to the rehabilitation of his political reputation. Until his death in 1964, he was generally regarded as a party **elder statesman**.

HOSPERS, JOHN. Libertarian presidential nominee, 1972. (b. 9 June 1918). Hospers, a member of the philosophy faculty at the

University of Southern California, was the presidential nominee of the **Libertarian Party** in 1972. His candidacy attracted negligible national support, receiving slightly more than 2,500 popular votes. When the **electoral college** met following the general election, one of the electors chosen from Virginia and pledged to the nominee of the **Republican Party**, President Richard Nixon, proved to be a **faithless elector** by casting his presidential **ballot** for Hospers. Although this action did not affect the presidential outcome, it did provide national attention for the Libertarian Party. Two years later, Hospers was the Libertarian nominee for governor of California. Now retired, Hospers is emeritus professor of philosophy at the University of Southern California.

HOUSE OF REPRESENTATIVES. A chamber of **Congress,** often referred to as the "House," the "lower chamber," or the "people's house," to differentiate it from the **Senate.** Members of the House, traditionally known as congressmen, are elected every two years from congressional districts apportioned among the states according to population. The Constitution authorized 65 districts. As the national population expanded, the number of districts steadily rose following the decennial censuses. After 1930, Congress capped the total number of districts at 435. The Constitution established eligibility for election to the House as follows: 25 years of age, 7 years a citizen of the United States, and an inhabitant of the state from which elected. The presiding officer of the body, elected by its members, is designated as **Speaker.** The term "house" can also be used to refer to either chamber of Congress.

HOWARD, JOHN E. Federalist president pro tempore of the Senate, 1800. (b. 4 June 1752; d. 12 October 1827). Howard was a major force in Maryland politics during the founding era. He served in the Continental Congress (1784–1788). He became governor in 1789 for two years. In 1796, he was chosen for the **Senate,** and he held that office until 1803. When the 6th **Congress** came back for its lame duck session after the **critical election** of 1800, in which the **Federalist Party** suffered a resounding defeat, Howard was named **president pro tempore** on one occasion. In 1816, he was one of four Federalists to receive **electoral college** votes for **vice president** in a losing effort.

HOYER, STENY H. Democratic majority leader of the House of Representatives, 2007– . (b. 14 June 1939). Steny Hoyer grew up in Maryland. Following graduation from law school, he entered the political arena in 1966, winning a seat in the state senate. He ran unsuccessfully for the Democratic party **nomination** for lieutenant governor in 1978. That same year, he received an appointment to the state board of higher education. In 1981, he prevailed in a special primary and the ensuing **general election** to fill a seat in the **House of Representatives** vacated by the death of the **incumbent**. He chaired the **Democratic Caucus** (1989–1994) and served as minority **whip** (2003–2007). When the Democrats won control of the House in the 206 **midterm elections**, the **floor leader**, **Nancy Pelosi**, became **Speaker**, and Hoyer moved into the position of **majority leader**.

HUGHES, CHARLES EVANS. Republican presidential nominee, 1916. (b. 11 April 1862; d. 27 August 1948). Hughes served as a reform-minded governor of New York (1907–1910). President **William Howard Taft** named him an associate justice of the Supreme Court in 1910. He left the Court in 1916 to accept the presidential **nomination** of the **Republican Party**. Losing narrowly to President **Woodrow Wilson**, he practiced law until 1921, when President **Warren G. Harding** named him secretary of state. He retired again to private life after a four-year tenure. In 1930, President **Herbert C. Hoover** returned him to the Supreme Court, this time as chief justice. He held that office for over a decade, leaving the bench in 1941.

HULL, CORDELL. Democratic National Committee chair, 1921–1924. (b. 2 October 1871; d. 23 July 1955). Hull won election to the **House of Representatives** from his East Tennessee district in 1906. He held the seat for seven terms, losing a bid for reelection 1920. While out of office, he was elected **chair** of the **Democratic National Committee**. Hull was the first national party chair to serve in a full-time capacity, establishing a party headquarters operation on a year-round basis in Washington, D.C. In 1922, he won back his House seat, and he resigned the **party organization** post in 1924. He moved over to the **Senate** in 1931, serving only two years before accepting the offer from President-elect **Franklin D. Roosevelt** to become secretary of state. He occupied that position for 11 years, a record tenure, retiring in 1944.

HUMPHREY, HUBERT H. Democratic vice president, 1965–1969; Democratic presidential nominee, 1968. (b. 27 May 1911; d. 13 January 1978). Hubert Humphrey was elected mayor of Minneapolis in 1948. His pro–civil rights speech at the 1948 **Democratic National Convention** made him a national figure. That year, Minnesota voters sent him to the U.S. **Senate**, where over the next 16 years he emerged as a strong voice for the liberal **wing** of the **Democratic Party**. In 1960 he made a brief, unsuccessful run for the Democratic presidential **nomination**, which went to **John F. Kennedy**. In 1964, President **Lyndon B. Johnson**, seeking a term in his own right, picked his former Senate colleague Humphrey as the party's vice presidential nominee. A **landslide** victory in November placed Humphrey in the vice presidency.

As the 1968 presidential **campaign** approached, Humphrey appeared poised to remain Johnson's **running mate**. Then, with public support for the Vietnam War falling, and facing nomination challenges from antiwar senators Eugene McCarthy and Robert Kennedy, Johnson decided not to seek the nomination. Humphrey entered the race, drawing support from the **party organization**, which had remained loyal to President Johnson. In a disruptive nomination campaign season, featuring the assassinations of Robert Kennedy and civil rights leader Martin Luther King Jr., Humphrey won the nomination of the Democratic National Convention. It was a pyrrhic victory, however, as the party was bitterly divided. Humphrey's eventual support was tepid at best. Democratic governor **George C. Wallace** of Alabama mounted a **minor party** challenge. Humphrey lost narrowly in the fall to Republican **Richard M. Nixon**.

In 1970, Humphrey successfully campaigned to return to the U.S. Senate. He sought his party's presidential nomination again in 1972 but lost to **George S. McGovern**, and he briefly flirted with the prospect of a 1976 challenge. In 1977, with his health clearly failing, his Senate colleagues honored Humphrey with the newly created position of deputy **president pro tempore**, to be held by any senator who has served as **president** or **vice president**. He died a year later. So far, he alone has held the office.

HUNKERS. A **faction** of the New York State **Democratic Party** in the 1840s. Their main rivals were the **Barnburners**. The Hunkers remained loyal to the national party when the Barnburners defected to the **Free Soil Party** in 1848.

HUNTER, ROBERT M. T. Democratic Speaker of the House of Representatives, 1839–1841. (b. 21 April 1809; d. 18 July 1887). Hunter was first elected to the **House of Representatives** from Virginia in 1836. After his initial reelection in 1838, he emerged as the 11th-ballot compromise choice as **Speaker** of a severely divided House, in which the **Democratic Party** held a one-vote **majority** while five New Jersey seats remained in dispute. The upshot was that neither party could amass a majority vote for its nominee. Hunter abandoned the Democrats and declared himself an **independent** for purposes of **election**. He assembled a winning **coalition** that united members of the opposition **Whig Party** and fellow alienated Democrats. As Speaker for one term, he conscientiously sought to preside in a **nonpartisan** fashion. He continued to serve in the House in the next **Congress**, left for two years, and came back for an additional term (1845–1847). He then moved over to the **Senate**, where he remained until the onset of the **Civil War**. In 1860, he contended for the presidential **nomination** of the **Democratic National Convention**, which went to **Stephen A. Douglas**.

HUNTINGTON, SAMUEL. Electoral vote recipient, 1789. (b. 3 July 1731; d. 5 January 1796). Huntington represented Connecticut in the Continental Congress (1776–1784), holding its presidency twice (1779–1781 and 1783). Elected governor in 1786, he held the office until his death a decade later. In 1789, he won two **favorite son** votes in the **electoral college** balloting for president.

HUSTON, CLAUDIUS H. Republican National Committee chair, 1929–1930. (b. 15 February 1876; d. 14 August 1952). Huston was an Indiana native who moved to Tennessee as a young man. He headed an oil company and maintained numerous civic and business interests. He assumed some fund-raising responsibilities for the state **Republican Party** in 1920, and his successful efforts drew national attention, leading to his election to the **Republican National Com-**

mittee (RNC). He also received a position in the **administration** of President **Warren G. Harding** in the Commerce Department as assistant secretary, where he worked under **Herbert C. Hoover** (1921–1923). Huston returned to Tennessee to tend to his business interests, but he remained devoted to Hoover and supported Hoover's presidential candidacy in 1928, a year in which the **GOP** made noteworthy inroads in the **Solid South**. In 1929, when **Hubert Work** resigned as national party **chair**, Hoover recommended Huston's election. Huston became the first Southerner to chair the RNC, portending a significant **party realignment** later in the century. Soon after assuming the office, Huston faced allegations of improper financial behavior: using funds provided by lobbyists for personal speculation. He denied the charges but resigned in 1930.

– I –

IDEOLOGY. A worldview, or system of ideas, that prescribes a social, economic, and/or political agenda. The ideological spectrum in U.S. politics ranges from **conservatives** on the **right wing** to **liberals** on the **left wing**, with splinter groups, parties, and party factions at either extreme. The major parties have typically converged toward the center of this ideological spectrum.

INCUMBENT. An officeholder. An incumbent facing an upcoming **election** often has distinct advantages over opponents, most notably name recognition, **campaign finance** capabilities, and opportunities for constituency service. However, incumbency advantages can disappear in the face of such potential disadvantages as a poor record of performance, scandal, or an economic downturn.

INDEPENDENT. A voter, and occasionally an officeholder, who declines to identify with a **political party**. Independent voters of necessity cast ballots for party nominees, and they may well routinely do so on behalf of a particular party; but they do not consider themselves partisans. Rather, they make their electoral choice on the basis of **candidate** and issue-related factors. Self-described independent voters have become more numerous in recent years, as the percentage of party identifiers has declined. *See also* SWING VOTER; TICKET-SPLITTER.

INDEPENDENT PARTY. The name assumed by numerous minor parties over the years. Most have been parties in name only, their identities tied to the office seekers who needed a party banner under which to **campaign**. **John Floyd** of Virginia was the first **standard-bearer** of an Independent Party, in 1832. More recently, the campaign vehicles of Lyndon LaRouche in 1984 and **Ross Perot** in 1992 were similarly labeled.

INGALLS, JOHN J. Republican president pro tempore of the Senate, 1887–1891. (b. 29 December 1833; d. 16 August 1900). Ingalls represented Kansas in the **Senate** for three terms (1873–1891). During his last four years in office, he served as president pro tempore. Initially elected in February 1887, near the end of the second session of the 49th **Congress**, he assumed the office in the absence of a **vice president**, **Thomas A. Hendricks** having died in November 1885. He continued to preside over the Senate throughout the 50th Congress. Following the 1888 election of Vice President **Levi P. Morton**, Ingalls remained in office for virtually all of the 51st Congress, giving way to **Charles F. Manderson** (Nebraska) on the day prior to adjournment.

It was during Ingalls's tenure that the Senate instituted the practice of retaining the designated president pro tempore in that position "until otherwise ordered." Previously, that office was filled only in the absence of the vice president, who presided over the Senate from the chamber, and it was vacated upon his return.

INGERSOLL, JARED. Federalist vice presidential nominee, 1812. (b. 24 October 1749; d. 31 October 1822). Ingersoll represented Pennsylvania in the Continental Congress (1780–1781), and subsequently at the 1787 Philadelphia **convention** that drafted the **Constitution**. In 1812, the **caucus** of the Federalist Party met in New York and chose Ingersoll as its vice presidential nominee to accompany **De Witt Clinton** on the presidential **ticket**. In the **election** that fall, President **James Madison,** running with **Elbridge Gerry** on behalf of the **Democratic-Republican Party**, won an easy reelection victory.

INITIATIVE. The procedure by which citizens in about half of the states may propose a new law by petition, to be considered by either the legislature or the electorate. It reflects the norm of direct democracy, as opposed to representative democracy. The initiative process was advanced by reformers during the **Progressive Era** to heighten citizen involvement in the governing process. *See also* REFERENDUM.

INNER CLUB. A term that came into vogue in the mid-20th century to characterize the informal leaders of both chambers of the U.S. **Congress**, but especially the **Senate**. Although membership in the chamber itself qualified one for admission to the "club," those in the inner club tended to be relatively senior members who held noteworthy party or committee leadership positions. In turn, their inner club status derived less from formal authority than from peer recognition of personal qualities, legislative skills, and loyalty to the congressional institution. By virtue of its smaller membership and longer term of office, the Senate was considered to be the more exclusive club. By the late 20th century, shifting patterns in seniority, party leadership, and partisanship diminished congressional "clubbishness," and the term came to be used much less frequently.

IN-PARTY. *see* PARTY-IN-POWER.

INTEREST GROUP. An entity that seeks to transform its special interests into public policy. Interest groups are also known as pressure groups. Most interest groups advocate for particular and private interests. Others, such as Common Cause, depict themselves as organized and operating in the public interest. Interest groups are key actors in the political process. They represent the concept of pluralism, in which public policy results from the competition and collaboration of diverse forces in the political arena.

An interest group differs conceptually from a **political party** in that it does not formally nominate a **candidate** for public office. Compared with a **major party**, an interest group promotes a narrower agenda. As such, a major party can be envisioned as an aggregation of interest groups, some enduring and others ephemeral. This is not always the case with a **minor party**.

Interest groups relate to political parties on several fronts. They cooperate with political parties in pursuit of common goals, or come into conflict when the goals diverge. In a variety of ways, interest groups interact with all three structural elements of a political party: **party-in-the-electorate**, **party organization**, and **party-in-office**.

Interest groups are key players in campaigns and elections, seeking to secure the selection of public officials supportive of their objectives. An interest group will typically establish a **political action committee** for this purpose. Interest groups raise campaign funds and mobilize voters. They also seek to influence the party platform to reflect the group's demands.

In addition to electoral activity, interest groups are involved in public education and efforts to influence public officials. This latter activity is known as lobbying, and it occurs on two distinct levels, elite and mass. At the elite level, a lobbyist deployed by the interest group will communicate the group's concerns and perspectives to public officials. At the mass level, grassroots sympathizers will be mobilized to make their views known.

Interest groups also relate to political parties with regard to reciprocal recruitment. Parties attract supporters, activists, and candidates from the ranks of interest groups. In turn, former public officials often find employment as representatives of interest groups.

IREDELL, JAMES. Electoral vote recipient, 1796 (Federalist). (b. 5 October 1751; d. 20 October 1799). Named by George Washington as an associate justice of the Supreme Court in 1790, Iredell served until his death in 1799. In 1796, he received three **favorite son** votes from North Carolina when the **electoral college** chose **John Adams** to be the **president** and **Thomas Jefferson** the **vice president**.

IRON LAW OF OLIGARCHY. A term coined by **Robert Michel**, who asserted that in any organization, a few will rule. Michel developed this thesis from his turn-of-the-20th-century study of the German Social Democratic Party. He found that despite the norms proclaiming internal party democracy, a narrow elite dominated that **party organization**. He generalized this finding to all organizations.

IZARD, RALPH. President pro tempore of the Senate, 1794–1795. (b. 23 January 1742; d. 30 May 1804). Izard was a prominent South

Carolinian during the founding era. He was a member of the Continental Congress (1782–1783). Chosen for the **Senate** after its establishment, he served a single term (1789–1795). Toward the end of his tenure, during the first session of the 3rd **Congress**, in May 1794, he was named **president pro tempore** in the absence of Vice President **John Adams**.

– J –

JACKSON, ANDREW. Democratic president, 1829–1837. (b. 15 March 1767; d. 8 June 1845). Jackson entered national public life in 1796, when his Tennessee congressional district sent him to the **House of Representatives**. A year later, he moved over to the **Senate** for a brief tenure. He became a national hero in the War of 1812, when he led the American forces to victory at the Battle of New Orleans. Later, he served as territorial governor of Florida (1821). Tennessee sent him back to the Senate in 1823. From that vantage point, he campaigned for the presidency in 1824, despite his failure to receive the **nomination** of the congressional **caucus** of the dominant **Democratic-Republican Party**. Although leading in both the popular vote and the **electoral college** balloting, he fell short of **majority** support in a multicandidate field. The subsequent decision of the House of Representatives favored Jackson's intraparty rival, **John Quincy Adams**.

Embittered, Jackson immediately began planning his **campaign** for the 1828 presidential **election**. In a rematch with Adams, he prevailed, signifying the ascendancy of his **faction** within the dominant party and leading to a party split that resulted in the emergence of the **Second Party System**. Jackson's faction became known as the Democrats. It soon transformed itself into the **Democratic Party**. The factional opposition also took **partisan** shape. Initially called the **National Republican Party**, it soon assumed the **Whig Party** label. Jackson won reelection in 1832, and he passed on the party nomination to his **vice president** and **heir apparent, Martin Van Buren**, who prevailed in the 1836 presidential contest.

As president, Jackson pursued policies that enhanced popular participation in the political process and expanded the scope of executive power. In retirement for almost a decade before his death in 1845, he embraced the role of party **elder statesman**. In a final act of leadership, he orchestrated the presidential nomination of his protégé **James K. Polk** in 1844. *See also* CALHOUN, JOHN C.

JACKSON, HENRY M. Democratic National Committee chair, 1960–1961. (b. 31 May 1912; d. 1 September 1983). Jackson was elected to the **House of Representatives** from Washington in 1940. He served six terms before his **election** to the **Senate** in 1952. He held his Senate seat until his death, winning reelection five times. In 1960, Democratic presidential nominee **John F. Kennedy** seriously considered tapping Jackson as his vice presidential choice. After he decided in favor of **Lyndon B. Johnson**, Kennedy asked the **Democratic National Committee** to name Jackson its **chair** for the duration of the presidential **campaign**. As chair, Jackson actively campaigned for the ticket, but he was not a key decision maker in the campaign organization. After the election, Jackson resigned as chair, allowing him to give full time to his senatorial responsibilities and clearing the way for Kennedy to name Connecticut party leader **John M. Bailey** to the national party post. In the Senate, Jackson was highly regarded by his colleagues for both his collegiality and his expertise in foreign policy and national security issues. In 1972 and again in 1976, he unsuccessfully contended for the Democratic presidential nomination.

JAY, JOHN. Electoral vote recipient, 1789, 1796, 1800 (Federalist). (b. 12 December 1745; d. 17 May 1829). Jay twice represented New York in the Continental Congress (1774–1777 and 1778–1779). He presided over that body on the latter occasion. He entered diplomatic service as minister to Spain in 1779 and later played a key role in the peace talks to end the Revolutionary War. Jay continued to serve the government of the Articles of Confederation as secretary for foreign affairs. In the aftermath of the Constitutional Convention, he demonstrated his support for its work by assisting **Alexander Hamilton** and **James Madison** in writing the *Federalist Papers*. President **George Washington** named him the first chief justice of the Supreme Court in 1789. While presiding over the court, Jay conducted sensitive diplomatic relations with Great Britain, resulting in the controversial Jay

Treaty. Elected governor of New York in 1794, he served six years. In the emerging party alignments, Jay identified with the **Federalist Party**.

On three occasions, Jay received support in the **electoral college** balloting. In 1789, he finished third, with nine votes coming from three states. In 1796, five of Connecticut's electors named him. Four years later, a Rhode Island elector defected from the Federalist **ticket** of **John Adams** and **Charles C. Pinckney**, substituting Jay for the latter. After leaving the office of governor in 1801, Jay spent almost three decades in quiet retirement.

JEFFERSON, THOMAS. Democratic-Republican president, 1801–1809. (b. 13 April 1743; d. 4 July 1826). Jefferson entered public life in 1768 as a member of the Virginia House of Burgesses. In 1775, he became a part of Virginia's delegation to the Second Continental Congress. He quickly rose to prominence as drafter of the Declaration of Independence. He served a term as wartime governor of Virginia (1779–1781) and then rejoined the Continental Congress (1783–1785). While holding the latter office, in 1784 he was sent to France as minister, where he spent the next five years. Jefferson returned home in 1789 to become secretary of state for President **George Washington**, holding that office for five years.

As a member of the president's **cabinet**, Jefferson led emerging opposition to the policy initiatives of Secretary of the Treasury **Alexander Hamilton**. His pioneering efforts resulted in the formation of the **Democratic-Republican Party**. In 1792, he won four votes in the **electoral college** from Kentucky. His party-building initiatives continued during his recess from public office in Washington's second term. In 1796, he mounted a presidential campaign that accumulated 68 electoral college votes, three short of the total amassed by **John Adams**. Jefferson thus became Adams's **vice president**. During the next four years, he continued to build his partisan base, openly attacking the policies of the Adams administration.

Again seeking the presidency in 1800, Jefferson prevailed, but only after the House of Representatives resolved a tie vote in the electoral college between Jefferson and his party **running mate, Aaron Burr**. The tie resulted from the Democratic-Republican electors, a clear **majority**, all casting ballots for both Jefferson and Burr.

President Jefferson used his status as party leader as a vehicle for energetic presidential leadership at odds with the ideological position of his party. The Democratic-Republicans generally distrusted executive authority and saw the legislature as the centerpiece of national power in a federal system that would limit the role of the central government. Their deference to Jefferson thus derived less from his status as chief executive than as party leader. Jefferson was elected overwhelmingly in 1804, and his second term was marked by growing tension with Great Britain. He retired from public life in 1809. During his lengthy retirement, he focused his energies primarily on the development of the University of Virginia. He also maintained a keen interest in public affairs and a voluminous correspondence addressing that interest. He died on the same day as his old friend and rival, John Adams.

JEWELL, MARSHALL. Republican National Committee chair, 1880–1883. (b. 20 October 1825; d. 10 February 1883). Jewell was a Connecticut publisher and manufacturer who won two terms as governor of Connecticut (1869–1872). His enthusiastic support for **Republican Party** presidential nominee **Ulysses S. Grant** contributed to Grant's electoral success there in both 1868 and 1872. Jewell's reward was an appointment as minister to St. Petersburg, Russia, in 1873. The next year, Grant brought him home to become postmaster general. Jewell resigned two years later, following the presidential nomination of **Rutherford B. Hayes**, and returned to his business interests. In 1880, he was called out of retirement by presidential nominee **James A. Garfield**, who asked him to **chair** the **Republican National Committee**. Garfield considered the outgoing chair, J. Donald Cameron, too beholden to the party bosses; yet he did not want to alienate those powerful party chieftains. Jewell was his choice to balance those competing interests. Jewell oversaw the successful fall campaign, and he remained at the helm of the national party following Garfield's assassination in 1881, until his own death in 1883.

JOHNSON, ANDREW. Democratic president, 1865–1869 (National Union Party). (b. 29 December 1808; d. 31 July 1875). Born in North Carolina, Andrew Johnson moved to neighboring Tennessee as a young man. He represented his adopted state as a **Democratic Party** nominee for five terms in the **House of Representatives** (1843–1853). After a decade in **Congress,** he returned home and was elected governor. Reelected two years later, he then went back to the nation's capital as a **senator** in 1857. A staunch supporter of the Union, he campaigned for **John C. Breckinridge,** the nominee of the **Southern Democratic Party,** in the 1860 presidential **election.**

When the **Civil War** broke out, Johnson remained loyal to the Union, despite the secession of his state. In 1862, President **Abraham Lincoln** made him military governor of Tennessee. Two years later, the **Republican Party,** now styling itself the **Union Party,** promoted bipartisanship by nominating Johnson, still a Democrat, for **vice president.** This **ticket** prevailed in November, and Johnson returned to Washington.

Slightly more than a month after his inauguration, Johnson became **president** when Lincoln was assassinated. He quickly crossed swords with the congressional Republicans over Reconstruction policy. Johnson was disposed to be more lenient toward the defeated South than was the **Congress.** Impeached by the House in 1868, Johnson survived when the **Senate** narrowly failed to marshal the required two-thirds **majority** for conviction and removal.

With the 1868 presidential election looming, the Republicans disregarded Johnson, whom they considered an interloper, and nominated Ulysses S. Grant. Johnson aspired to the Democratic **nomination,** but his old party rejected his overtures in favor of **Horatio Seymour,** who lost to Grant. Johnson went home to Tennessee, where he persisted in his electoral ambitions. Finally, in 1875 the state legislature sent him back to the Senate for the few remaining months of his life.

JOHNSON, HERSCHEL V. Democratic vice presidential nominee, 1860. (b. 18 September 1812; d. 16 August 1880). Johnson represented Georgia in the **Senate** (1848–1849). He returned home and was elected governor (1853–1857). In 1860, after nominating **Stephen A. Douglas** (Illinois) for president, the **Democratic National Convention** chose Senator **Benjamin Fitzpatrick** (Alabama) to run for **vice president** on a geographically **balanced ticket.** However, Fitzpatrick declined the **nomination,** and the **Democratic National**

Committee convened in an unprecedented emergency session to fill the vacant spot on the ticket. Johnson was their unanimous choice. The Democratic team ran second in the popular vote but finished a poor fourth in the subsequent **electoral college** balloting. In the wake of the election, Georgia seceded from the Union. Johnson followed his state, serving in the Confederate Senate (1862–1865).

JOHNSON, LYNDON B. Senate minority leader, 1953–1955; Senate majority leader, 1955–1961; Democratic vice president, 1961–1963; Democratic president, 1963–1969. (b. 27 August 1908; d. 22 January 1973). Having prepared for a career as a Texas schoolteacher, Johnson entered national politics as an aide to Congressman Richard Kleberg. He returned home to work for a **New Deal** agency. Shortly afterward, Johnson won a 1937 **special election** to a vacant seat in the **House of Representatives**. In 1940, he served a stint as the **chair** of the **Democratic Congressional Campaign Committee**. He ran for the **Senate** in a 1941 special election, but lost. Retaining his House seat, he served briefly in the Navy during World War II.

In 1948, Johnson again ran for the Senate, and this time he narrowly prevailed. He held that position for the next 12 years, rising to power and national prominence, first as **whip** for the **majority** (1951–1953), next as **minority leader** (1953–1955), and then, when the Democrats recaptured the Senate, as **majority leader** (1955–1961). He proved extraordinarily effective in these congressional party leadership roles, promoting consensus both within the **Democratic Party** and with congressional Republicans and Republican President **Dwight D. Eisenhower**.

Johnson sought the Democratic presidential **nomination** in 1960, but he fell short, and that prize went to **John F. Kennedy**. Kennedy picked Johnson to be his vice presidential **running mate**, and the ticket prevailed in a tight **election**. When Kennedy was assassinated in 1963, Johnson became **president**. He successfully sought his party's 1964 presidential nomination and won a landslide victory over Republican **Barry M. Goldwater**.

Johnson's presidency featured wide-ranging expansion of the social service programs of the federal government under the label **Great Society**, as well as the widening of the Vietnam War. Under attack within his party by antiwar activists, Johnson unexpectedly decided not to seek another term. He abandoned the volatile political arena for the seclusion of his Johnson City, Texas, ranch, where he wrote his memoirs and observed the construction of his presidential library in nearby Austin. The Democratic Party renounced his foreign policy in 1972. He died shortly afterward.

JOHNSON, RICHARD M. Democratic vice president, 1837–1841. (b. 17 October 1780; d. 19 November 1850). After practicing law and serving in the Kentucky legislature, Johnson was elected to the **House of Representatives** in 1806, where he served six terms. In **Congress**, he was one of the War Hawks who promoted the conflict with Great Britain known as the War of 1812. While remaining in office, Johnson commanded Kentucky troops in battle and gained national renown as the slayer of Tecumseh, the Indian chief and nemesis of the American forces. In 1819, Johnson left the House for a decade to serve in the **Senate**. Defeated for reelection in 1829, he returned to the House for four more terms. Initially a champion of **Henry Clay** and his presidential prospects, Johnson shifted his allegiance to **Andrew Jackson** in the aftermath of the controversial 1824 **election**. After Jackson's two terms in the White House (1829–1837), he handpicked the 1836 presidential **ticket** of the **Democratic Party,** naming his **vice president, Martin Van Buren**, as the presidential nominee, and designating Johnson as the **running mate**. The second **Democratic National Convention** ratified this act of party leadership, despite misgivings about Johnson's flamboyant personal life.

In the **general election** that followed, the Democratic ticket won a narrow **majority**, and Van Buren was comfortably elected by the **electoral college**. However, Johnson fell short of the required majority from that body, throwing the election into the Senate, where he was chosen vice president in a singular procedure. Four years later Johnson, who had continued his scandalous pursuits, was not renominated by the Democratic National Convention. Rather, that body authorized the state parties to put forward their own vice presidential nominees to run with Van Buren. Most of the states named Johnson anyway, but the varying Democratic tickets went down to defeat against the nominees of the **Whig Party**, **William Henry Harrison** and **John Tyler.**

Johnson returned to Kentucky and briefly resumed his service in the state legislature. In 1844, he was a **favorite son** candidate for the Democratic presidential nomination, but his support was negligible. In 1850, he was once again elected to the Kentucky legislature, but he died before assuming the office.

JOHNSTON, SAMUEL. Electoral vote recipient, 1796 (Federalist). (b. 15 December 1733; d. 18 August 1816). During the Revolutionary War, Johnston represented North Carolina in the Continental Congress (1780–1782). That state made him one of its first two members of the U.S. **Senate** (1789 to 1793). In 1796, two Massachusetts electors cast ballots bearing his name in the presidential **election**.

JONES, BENJAMIN F. Republican National Committee chair, 1884–1888. (b. 8 August 1824; d. 19 May 1903). Jones was a prominent Pennsylvania industrialist and ardent protectionist. He was a longtime friend of **James G. Blaine**, the 1884 presidential nominee of the **Republican Party**. Blaine tapped Jones to head the **Republican National Committee**, in part because of their enduring friendship, but also because Jones could bankroll the upcoming **campaign**. After leaving office following the 1888 **Republican National Convention**, Jones devoted himself full time to his business concerns. Several years later, in 1899, he made an ill-fated run for a seat in the U.S. **Senate**.

JONES, JAMES K. Democratic National Committee chair, 1896–1904. (b. 29 September 1839; d. 1 June 1908). Jones was elected to the House of Representatives from Arkansas in 1880. Twice reelected, he resigned in 1885 to become a member of the **Senate**, where he finished an unexpired term and served two full ones as well (1885–1903). In 1896, following the presidential **nomination** of **William Jennings Bryan**, Jones was chosen to **chair** the **Democratic National Committee**. His selection, in the wake of the Bryan nomination, emphasized the ascendance of the Southern-Western, rural **faction** within the **Democratic Party**. Jones also shared Bryan's enthusiasm for **soft money**. His enthusiastic advocacy of the free silver cause led observers to label him the **Plumed Knight** of Arkansas, borrowing a label earlier applied to **James G. Blaine**. With

Bryan's renomination in 1900, Jones stayed on at the helm of the national **party organization** until the conclusion of the 1904 national **convention** that nominated Alton B. Parker of New York. Jones's successor was **Thomas Taggart** of Indiana.

JONES, JOHN W. Democratic Speaker of the House of Representatives, 1843–1845. (b. 22 November 1791; d. 29 January 1848). Virginia sent Jones to the **House of Representatives** in 1835, where he served five terms, the last as **Speaker** of the 28th **Congress**. His leadership was controversial, owing to his disputed **election** to his House seat in 1842. Previously, he had been an early **front-runner** in the contest for the speakership of the 26th Congress, before giving way to fellow Virginian **Robert M. T. Hunter.**

JONES, WALTER B. Independent Democratic presidential candidate, 1956. (b. 16 October 1888; d. 1 August 1963). Jones was a local judge in Alabama who received a single **electoral college** vote for **president** in 1956 from a **faithless elector** in Alabama. The protesting elector was pledged to the presidential **ticket** of the **Democratic Party**, headed by **Adlai E. Stevenson II**, accompanied by **Estes Kefaufer.**

– K –

KAINE, TIMOTHY M. Democratic National Committee chair, 2009– . (b. 26 February 1958). Tim Kaine was born in Minnesota and grew up in Missouri, graduating from the University of Missouri. After serving as a Roman Catholic missionary in Honduras, he received his law degree from Harvard. He married the daughter of a former governor of Virginia and practiced law in Richmond, where he was elected to the city council in 1994 and chosen by that body as mayor in 1998. In 2001, he successfully ran for lieutenant governor, and four years later, he won the governorship. Kaine emerged as a noteworthy new and moderate voice for the national **Democratic Party**, and he figured in 2008 presidential and vice presidential speculation. He declined to run for the former office, and he was not chosen for the latter. In January 2009, President-elect **Barack H. Obama** indicated that Kaine was his choice to **chair** the **Democratic National Committee**. Because Kaine had a full year left in his gubernatorial term, he accepted the office on a part-time basis, with the expectation that his role would be that of party spokesman, while a full-time executive director would manage the party headquarters.

KANGAROO TICKET. A description that likens a party's presidential **ticket** to a kangaroo, whose back legs are stronger than its front legs. This metaphor suggests that the vice presidential nominee has greater political strength and electoral appeal than does the presidential nominee. The 1988 **Democratic Party** ticket of Michael Dukakis and Lloyd Bentsen was so characterized.

KEFAUVER, ESTES. Democratic vice presidential nominee, 1956. (b. 26 July 1903; d. 10 August 1963). Kefauver served five terms in the **House of Representatives** from his east Tennessee district (1939–1949). Elected to the **Senate** in 1948, he held his seat for the rest of his life. Kefauver heightened his national presence in 1950 by presiding over televised Senate hearings on organized crime. He then sought the 1952 presidential **nomination** of the Democratic National Convention, competing with considerable success in the handful of presidential primaries then in existence. However, he had no significant support among the party **bosses** who controlled the bulk of delegate selection, and the nomination went to **Adlai E. Stevenson II**.

In 1956, Kefauver again lost out in a presidential bid as Stevenson bested him in the primaries and won renomination for a rematch with President **Dwight D. Eisenhower**. Stevenson declined to exercise his prerogative to recommend a vice presidential choice to the **convention**, and Kefauver emerged as the second-ballot choice in a heated contest with Massachusetts Senator **John F. Kennedy**. The **ticket** lost in the fall **election**, and Kefauver withdrew from the national scene.

KEIFER, J. WARREN. Republican Speaker of the House of Representatives, 1881–1883. (b. 30 January 1836; d. 22 April 1932). On two separate occasions, Keifer served several terms in the **House of Representatives** from Ohio. Initially elected in 1876, he held his seat for four terms. During the 47th **Congress** (1881–1883), he was

Speaker. Allegations of nepotism led the congressional Republicans to decline to reelect him as their leader when the next Congress convened, and he left the House at the end of that term. In 1904, he was elected once again to the House. This time he served three terms.

KEMP, JACK. Republican vice presidential nominee, 1996. (b. 13 July 1935; d. 2 May 2009). Kemp was a star professional football player who played quarterback for the Los Angeles Chargers and the Buffalo Bills. At the end of his athletic career, he won a seat in the **House of Representatives** from his upstate New York district. Kemp held office for nine terms and became a major power in the congressional **Republican Party**, particularly in the economic arena, where he promoted the controversial doctrine of supply-side economics.

He gave up his House seat to contend unsuccessfully for the 1988 presidential nomination, which went to the **vice president, George H. W. Bush**. While out of office, Kemp retained his high public visibility through frequent speaking appearances. In 1996, he was the choice of presidential nominee **Robert J. Dole** for the party's vice presidential nomination. This **ticket** lost in the fall, as President **Bill Clinton** and Vice President **Al Gore** were reelected. Kemp remained visible on the public lecture and media talk show circuits for more than a decade, until health problems forced his withdrawal from the public arena.

KENNEDY, JOHN F. Democratic president, 1961–1963. (b. 29 May 1917; d. 22 November 1963). The son of a wealthy financier, John Kennedy grew up in the public spotlight. After heroic service in the Pacific during World War II, he returned home and won an open congressional seat in 1946. Reelected twice to the **House of Representatives**, Kennedy successfully challenged the Republican **incumbent, Henry Cabot Lodge Jr.**, for his **Senate** seat in 1952. Four years later, he made a strong run for the vice presidential **nomination** of the **Democratic National Convention**, losing to **Estes Kefauver**. After winning reelection to the Senate in 1958, he set his sights on the 1960 presidential nomination. He utilized **presidential primary** contests to demonstrate his national appeal to skeptical **party organization** leaders, and he won a first-ballot victory at the **convention**. Kennedy chose his chief party rival, Senator **Lyndon B. Johnson**

of Texas, to be his vice presidential nominee, and the **ticket** won an exceedingly narrow **general election** victory over Republicans **Richard M. Nixon** and Henry Cabot Lodge Jr., which was magnified in the subsequent electoral college balloting. Kennedy was the first, and thus far the only, Roman Catholic to win the presidency.

Kennedy's presidency featured momentous conflict and controversy both at home and abroad. The **civil rights** struggle intensified, as did the Cold War. In the fall of 1963, Kennedy was making plans for his reelection campaign. On a political visit to Dallas, Texas, he was assassinated.

KERN, JOHN W. Democratic vice presidential nominee, 1908; Democratic majority leader of the Senate, 1913–1917. (b. 20 December 1849; d. 17 August 1917). In his native Indiana, Kern twice sought and received the gubernatorial **nomination** of the **Democratic Party**, but he lost both times. Nevertheless, he was the vice presidential choice of the 1908 **Democratic National Convention**, running alongside **William Jennings Bryan** in the latter's third futile presidential bid. Two years later, Kern won **election** to a single term in the **Senate** (1911–1917). During the 63rd and 64th Congresses, he was the **floor leader** of the **majority** Democrats.

KERR, MICHAEL C. Democratic Speaker of the House of Representatives, 1875–1876. (b. 15 March 1827; d. 19 August 1876). Kerr was elected to the **House of Representatives** as an Indiana Democrat in 1864. He served four terms, leaving office in 1873, then returning in 1875 for another term, which was interrupted by his death. During that latter term, when the **Democratic Party** was restored to **majority** status for the first time in almost a generation, Kerr was its choice as **Speaker**.

KERRY, JOHN F. Democratic presidential nominee, 2004. (b. 11 December 1943). A Yale graduate, Kerry emerged on the political scene in the early 1970s as a decorated Vietnam War veteran who embraced the antiwar cause, most notably in public testimony before the Senate Foreign Relations Committee. In 1972, he won the **Democratic Party nomination** for a congressional seat from Massachusetts; but he lost in the **general election**. After law school, he worked as a prosecutor. In 1982, he was elected Massachusetts's lieutenant governor, and two years later he won an open-seat contest for the U.S. **Senate**. He has been reelected four times. After initially supporting the resolution authorizing President **George W. Bush** to use force to disarm Iraqi dictator Saddam Hussien, Kerry became an early and strident critic of the ensuing Iraq War. He mounted a successful **campaign** for the 2004 Democratic presidential nomination, in which he emphasized his Vietnam service and his national security credentials in an effort to project electability. In November, he was defeated by President Bush. Kerry remains in the Senate, where his seniority affords him considerable influence, heightened by the success of the Democrats in regaining majority status in 2006. Declining to mount another presidential bid in 2008, he threw his pre**convention** support behind the victorious candidacy of **Barack H. Obama**.

KEYNOTE. A speech scheduled in the early deliberations of a national party **convention**. The keynote address supposedly sets the tone for a successful convention. The convention organizers designate a party luminary to be the keynote speaker. This designation is typically highly prized.

KING, RUFUS. Federalist presidential nominee, 1816. (b. 24 March 1755; d. 29 April 1827). Massachusetts native Rufus King served that state in the post–Revolutionary War national Congress (1784–1787) and at the 1787 Constitutional Convention. He later moved to New York, where he continued his illustrious career in public service. During the presidency of **George Washington**, he occupied a seat in the U.S. **Senate**, where he distinguished himself by his oratorical ability. In 1796, Washington named him minister to Great Britain, where he remained until 1803. In 1804 and 1808, he was the **Federalist Party** nominee for **vice president** in unsuccessful campaigns led by **Charles C. Pinckney**. In 1813, New York sent King back to the Senate, where he vigorously opposed the War of 1812. In 1816, he was the last presidential nominee of the dying Federalists. Leaving the Senate in 1825, he went back to Great Britain as minister, a nominee of President **John Quincy Adams**. He stayed there a year, returning home in 1826.

KING, WILLIAM H. Democratic president pro tempore of the Senate, 1940–1941. (b. 3 June 1863; d. 27 November 1949). King was elected to the **House of Representatives** from Utah in 1897. He was not reelected, but he won a special election the following April and finished that second term. In 1916, he was elected to the **Senate**, where he served four full terms. In November 1940, when Senator **Key Pittman**, who had long been **president pro tempore**, died, the Senate named King, who was nearing retirement, to fill that post for the few remaining days of the session.

KING, WILLIAM R. Democratic president pro tempore of the Senate, 1836–1841, 1849–1852; vice president, 4 March–18 April 1853. (b. 7 April 1768; d. 18 April 1853). Initially elected to the **House of Representatives** from North Carolina in 1810, he became one of the War Hawks promoting the War of 1812. He resigned his House seat in 1816 to participate in a diplomatic mission to Italy and Russia. Back in the United States, he moved to Alabama and became politically active. When Alabama joined the Union in 1819, King was chosen as one of its first two members of the Senate. Associating himself with the person and causes of **Andrew Jackson**, King served almost four terms before resigning in 1844 to accept the **nomination** of **President John Tyler** as minister to France. Twice chosen as **president pro tempore** for the 24th Congress (1836–1837), he was reelected to that position four times during the 25th Congress (1837–1839), twice more during the 26th (1840–1841), and once again at the outset of an early special session of the 27th Congress. Thus, over a five-year period, he alone occupied that office.

King unsuccessfully sought reelection to the Senate in 1846, but he secured a gubernatorial appointment to an unexpired term in 1848. After the 31st Congress convened for its first regular session in 1849, King was chosen again to be president pro tempore on two occasions in 1850. The second followed the death of President **Zachary Taylor**, which elevated Vice President Millard Fillmore to the presidency. King took over Fillmore's assignment of presiding over the Senate.

In 1852, the Democrats selected King as their vice presidential nominee, viewing him as an able complement to Franklin Pierce, in light of his close connections with Pierce's chief rival for the nomination, **James Buchanan**. At that point, King's health was already failing, for he had contracted tuberculosis. After the victorious **election**, King traveled to Cuba in hopes of improving his health. While in residence there he took his oath of office as **vice president** almost three weeks after the presidential inauguration. He remains the only constitutional officer to be sworn in outside the United States. Shortly afterward, he returned directly to his home in Alabama, where he died less than a month after assuming the vice presidency, giving him the distinction of serving the briefest tenure in that office.

KING CAUCUS. The presidential nominating procedure that evolved early on in the **First Party System**. The members of the party holding congressional office met to authorize the party's presidential nominee. This procedure, initiated in the 1790s, broke down in the 1820s for several reasons. First, since interparty competition had ended with the demise of the **Federalist Party**, nomination by the **caucus** of the dominant **Democratic-Republican Party** was tantamount to **election**, undermining the character of the constitutional principle of separation of powers by enabling the legislature to select the executive. Further, in an age of broadening participation of the citizenry in the political process, the caucus appeared narrowly elitist. Finally, the Democratic-Republican Party became increasingly torn by factions, which were either unable to come to a consensus decision in the caucus or unwilling to accept an unsatisfactory outcome. After 1824, the caucus ceased to act as a presidential nominating institution. Soon afterward, the national nominating **convention** emerged in its wake.

KINGMAKER. A party leader who exercises significant leadership in the designation of the party's presidential nominee. The term can also be used with reference to those who are influential in the filling of other high offices. *See also* HANDPICKED.

KIRK, PAUL G., JR. Democratic National Committee chair, 1985–1989. (b. 18 January 1938). A Massachusetts native, Kirk practiced law and gravitated into the political organization of Senator Edward M. Kennedy. When Kennedy sought the presidential **nomination** of the **Democratic Party** in 1980, Kirk managed his **campaign** to unseat **incumbent** president **Jimmy Carter**. In 1983, he became treasurer of the **Democratic National Committee (DNC)**, where he was perceived as being in place to look after the political interests of Senator Kennedy. When **Charles A. Manatt** resigned as chair in 1985, in the wake of a **landslide** loss in the 1984 presidential **election**, Kirk was the choice of the national **committee** as his successor. He quickly transcended his identity as a Kennedy loyalist and set out to invigorate a demoralized party. He abandoned some controversial innovations that had taken hold in recent years, such as special-interest caucuses and midterm conventions; and he followed Manatt's lead in emphasizing the **service party** approach in seeking to narrow the gap in institutional effectiveness that had developed between the DNC and its **Republican Party** counterpart. He retired from party politics following the 1988 presidential election. Afterward, he chaired the National Democratic Institute for International Affairs (1992–2001), and he currently serves as chair of the board of the John F. Kennedy Library Foundation.

KITCHEN CABINET. An informal group of advisers surrounding a political leader. The term originated during the presidency of **Andrew Jackson**, who at times tended to rely less on his appointed department heads than on relatively obscure friends and colleagues. *See also* CABINET.

KITCHIN, CLAUDE. Democratic majority leader of the House of Representatives, 1915–1919; Democratic minority leader of the House of Representatives, 1921–1923. (b. 24 March 1869; d. 31 May 1923). Kitchin belonged to a prominent North Carolina political family. His father, brother, and nephew all served in the **House of Representatives**. He was elected to the House in 1900 and held on to his seat for the rest of his life. In 1915, at the outset of the 64th **Congress**, Kitchin became the **floor leader** of the majority Democrats, holding that title during the 65th Congress as well. When the Democrats lost control of the House in 1918, the outgoing **Speaker**, **Champ Clark**, became the minority leader. After Clark's death in 1921, the **minority** Democrats elevated Kitchin to the position of floor leader. He died two years later.

KNOWLAND, WILLIAM F. Republican majority leader of the Senate, 1953–1955; Republican minority leader of the Senate, 1955–1959. (b. 26 June 1908; d. 23 February 1974). Knowland belonged to a prominent California family. His father, a newspaper publisher, had served in the **House of Representatives** for over a decade. Knowland became involved in party politics at the state and national levels as a young man, serving in the state assembly and on the **Republican National Committee**. In 1945, Governor **Earl Warren** named him to fill a Senate vacancy. Knowland won a full term in 1946 and was reelected in 1952. In 1953, he replaced the late Robert Taft as Senate **majority leader**. In 1954, the Republicans lost their Senate majority, but Knowland remained **floor leader**. He came to the Senate with a reputation as a **progressive**, but he quickly drifted into the camp of the **old guard**, the more **conservative** wing of the party. Harboring presidential ambitions for 1960, he did not seek reelection in 1958, instead seeking the governorship of California, which he thought would provide a better springboard for a presidential bid. However, he lost convincingly in the **general election**, and his political career ended. He remained in California, tending to his family newspaper business while remaining involved behind the scenes in state party politics.

KNOX, WILLIAM FRANKLIN. Republican vice presidential nominee, 1936. (b. 1 January 1874; d. 28 April 1944). Frank Knox served under **Theodore Roosevelt** in the Rough Riders during the Spanish–American War. He returned to Illinois and embarked on a successful publishing career there, and later in New Hampshire as well, that included extensive Republican Party involvement. He supported Roosevelt's unsuccessful 1912 reentry into presidential politics, embracing the minor party effort of the **Progressive Party**. Knox served in France during World War I. After the war, he initially aspired to a role as a Republican **kingmaker**, but he came to harbor personal presidential aspirations. He made poor showings in presidential bids in both 1924 and 1936. On the latter occasion, he was the vice presidential choice of the **Republican National Convention**, running alongside **Alfred M. Landon** in a futile campaign against the reelection of the **ticket** of the **Democratic Party, Franklin D. Roosevelt**

and **John Nance Garner**. In 1940, as war raged in Europe and the likelihood of U.S. intervention heightened, Knox responded to President Roosevelt's **bipartisan** call and joined his cabinet as secretary of the navy.

– L –

LA FOLLETTE, ROBERT M. Progressive presidential nominee, 1924. (b. 14 June 1855; d. 18 June 1925). La Follette initially identified with the **progressive** wing of the **Republican Party** both at the state level in Wisconsin and on the broader national scene. He served in the **House of Representatives** for three terms (1885–1891). Returning home, he became governor (1901–1906). In 1906, he went back to Washington as a **senator**, and he held on to the **Senate** seat for the rest of his life. In 1924, with progressivism in decline within Republican ranks, La Follette accepted the presidential **nomination** of the **Progressive Party**. In November, he attracted the support of almost five million voters, comprising more than 16 percent of the total, and he carried his home state, Wisconsin, with 13 electoral college votes. He ran third, behind the winner, incumbent Republican **Calvin Coolidge**, and **Democratic Party** nominee **John W. Davis**.

LAME DUCK. An incumbent about to leave office because of defeat or retirement, voluntary or required. With the exit from office looming, the power of the officeholder is considered to be weakened, and controversial exercises of power may be viewed as lacking legitimacy. The ratification of the 22nd Amendment to the **Constitution** makes a second-term president a lame duck. The advent of term limits in many states for executives and legislators alike similarly makes lame ducks of those elected for the final term of their allowed tenure.

LANDON, ALFRED M. Republican presidential nominee, 1936. (b. 9 September 1887; d. 12 October 1987). Born in Pennsylvania, Landon was raised and educated in Kansas, where he achieved recognition in legal and banking circles, as well as the oil business. He became involved in state **Republican Party** politics as a member of the progressive **faction**, rising to chair the state's central **committee** and then to serve two terms as governor (1933–1937). As his second term was about to end, he won the Republican presidential **nomination** in 1936. Facing **Democratic Party** nominee Franklin D. Roosevelt in his bid for reelection to a second term, Landon lost in a landslide. He never again sought public office, maintaining a low political profile while pursuing his private business interests. His daughter, Nancy Landon Kassebaum, was elected to the **Senate** from Kansas in 1978.

LANDSLIDE. An overwhelming electoral victory. The size of the victory margin is imprecise. Some commentators consider 55 percent of the vote sufficient. Others require 60 percent.

LANGDON, JOHN. President pro tempore of the Senate, 1789, 1792–1794 (Democratic-Republican). (b. 25 June 1741; d. 18 September 1819). Langdon was a major force in state and national politics during the founding era. He served in the Continental Congress from New Hampshire (1775–1776 and 1783). He subsequently represented his state in the 1787 Constitutional Convention and became its governor the next year. Elected to the **Senate** in 1789, he served two terms.

Langdon was the body's first **president pro tempore**, selected at the outset to preside over the counting of the **electoral college** ballots and continuing to preside until Vice President **John Adams** arrived on the scene some two weeks later. Establishing a custom that endured for a century, that office then became vacant until the next time the **vice president** was absent. In the second session of the subsequent Congress, Langdon was named president pro tempore on two occasions. After leaving the Senate in 1801, he resumed his career in state politics, serving twice again as governor (1805–1809 and 1810–1812). In 1808, nine presidential electors pledged to the **Democratic-Republican Party** designated Langdon as their vice presidential choice, but he ran far behind his fellow **partisan**, **George Clinton,** who received a comfortable majority.

LAST HURRAH. A politician's final **campaign**. Novelist Edwin O'Connor used the phrase as the title of a 1956 novel loosely based on the experience of longtime Boston **boss** James Michael Curley.

LAURANCE, JOHN. President pro tempore of the Senate, 1798–1799. (b. 1750; d. 11 November 1810). Laurance represented New York in the Continental Congress (1785–1787). Initially elected to the **House** in 1788, he won a second term two years later. Entering the **Senate** in 1796, he served slightly less than four years. During the third session of the 5th **Congress**, he was once named **president pro tempore**.

LAXALT, PAUL. Republican National Committee general chair, 1983–1986. (b. 2 August 1922). Laxalt was the governor of Nevada (1967–1971). Entering the **Senate** in 1974, he served two terms. Early in his second term, President **Ronald W. Reagan** asked Laxalt to become general **chair** of the Republican Party, a newly created position. Reagan had wanted Laxalt to be the chair of the Republican National Committee, but party rules required that the position of chair be full time and salaried, and Laxalt was unwilling to leave the Senate. At Reagan's request, the national **committee** created the position of general chair for Laxalt, with the expectation that he would coordinate the activities of the various party bodies, organizational and congressional. A long-standing Laxalt political ally, **Frank Fahrenkopf**, was named party chair, presumably to act as Laxalt's deputy. However, Laxalt proved to be relatively passive in his party leadership role, and Fahrenkopf performed the normal assignments of **party organization** leadership without undue deference to Laxalt. When Laxalt chose not to seek reelection to the Senate in 1986, his party leadership position expired as well. Laxalt considered the possibility of a bid for the Republican presidential nomination in 1988, but he decided not to enter the race. Out of office, he practiced law in Washington, D.C.

LEE, RICHARD HENRY. President pro tempore of the Senate, 1791–1792. (b. 20 January 1732; d. 19 June 1794). A prominent Virginian, Lee twice served in the Continental Congress (1774–1780 and 1784–1787). Elected to the first **Senate**, he served until 1792. During the first session of the 2nd **Congress**, he was named **president pro tempore** on a single occasion.

LEFT WING. A term used to describe individuals and groups who are located on the left, or **liberal**, end of the American ideological spectrum or of a particular political party. The term originated on the eve of the French Revolution in 1789, when the delegates to the Estates General who promoted radical change congregated on the left side of the assembly hall. Traditionally, both major parties have featured a left wing, which has also been called a **progressive** wing. *See also* RIGHT WING.

LIBERAL. An ideological label. Its meaning has shifted over the years. Initially, it characterized those who promoted the value of individual liberty against the authority of the state. In the 20th century, the concept has come to embrace an enthusiasm for government activism to address individual needs. Traditionally, each major **political party** has had a liberal **faction**, but in recent decades, the **Democratic Party** has clearly been the more liberal. *See also* CONSERVATIVE.

LIBERAL REPUBLICAN PARTY. A reform-oriented party **faction** that split from the **Republican Party** in 1872 over dissatisfaction with President **Ulysses S. Grant** and the scandals associated with his **administration**. The Liberal Republicans attacked corruption and advocated civil service reform and abandonment of Reconstruction.

Constituting themselves as a party, the **Liberal Republicans** convened in Cincinnati in May 1872 and nominated *New York Tribune* editor **Horace Greeley** for **president** and **Benjamin G. Brown** for **vice president**. Two months later, the **Democratic Party** followed the Liberal Republicans' lead and nominated the identical **ticket**, in hopes of assembling a victorious **bipartisan** alliance behind the **fusion** nominees. However, the voters convincingly rejected Greeley and his **running mate**. Although this ticket won six states, Greeley died before the electors cast their ballots. Essentially, the Liberal Republican Party did likewise.

LIBERTARIAN PARTY. A well-established **minor party** on the contemporary scene. Organized in 1971, its 1972 presidential nominee, **John Hospers** (California), received the electoral vote of a **faithless elector** from Virginia, who declined to cast his **ballot** as "instructed" for President **Richard M. Nixon**, the nominee of the **Republican Party**. That elector, Roger MacBride, went on to become the party's presidential nominee in 1976. The Libertarians have taken advantage of decreasingly restrictive ballot-access requirements in the states to gain a small but durable and enthusiastic national constituency and identity in recent years. Indeed, they have been a standard-setter among minor parties in achieving ballot access. However, their electoral appeal has remained negligible.

Libertarians call for minimizing the role of government in both economy and society. Their policy positions thus have appeal to extremists at both poles of the ideological spectrum, **liberal** and **conservative**. Social liberals appreciate their opposition to laws restricting social behavior, whereas economic conservatives find their antiregulation commitments attractive.

At the ballot box, the Libertarian Party appears to draw more support from disenchanted Republicans than from their **Democratic Party** counterparts. Its 1988 presidential nominee, Ron Paul, had been a Republican **member** of the **House of Representatives** from Texas, and he subsequently resumed that office, whence he contested the 2008 Republican presidential nomination. Its 2008 presidential nominee, Bob Barr from Georgia, was also a former GOP member of **Congress**. Among the more prominent Democrats in the Libertarian camp is former senator Mike Gravel (Arkansas), who ran unsuccessfully for the presidential nominations of both the Democratic and the Libertarian parties in 2008.

LIBERTY PARTY. A noteworthy **minor party** in the 1840s, the Liberty Party embraced an unequivocal antislavery position at a time when both major parties were seeking to accommodate their constituencies who were committed to **slavery**. The Liberty Party represented the segment of the antislavery movement that wanted to seek slavery's **abolition** within the conventional political process. This commitment distinguished party adherents from their unconventional counterparts, led by William Lloyd Garrison.

In 1840, the newly organized Liberty Party nominated James G. Birney (New York) for **president**. He sought without much success to appeal to abolitionist sentiments in both the **Democratic Party** and the **Whig Party**, receiving only 0.3 percent of the popular vote. Four years later, amid heightening tensions over slavery, the Liberty Party, again led by Birney, increased its popular vote total to 2.3 percent but carried no states. In 1848, the Liberty Party, having already nominated John P. Hale (New Hampshire) for president, abandoned the field, integrating into the **Free Soil Party**, led by former president **Martin Van Buren**.

LIEBERMAN, JOSEPH I. Democratic vice presidential nominee, 2000. (b. 24 February 1942). A Yale graduate, Lieberman served 10 years in the Connecticut state senate (1971–1981). He lost a congressional bid in 1980. Two years later, he was elected state attorney general. In 1988, he defeated a Republican **incumbent** for a seat in the U.S. **Senate**. In 2000, Democratic presidential nominee **Al Gore** designated Lieberman as his vice presidential **running mate**, making Lieberman the first Jew to hold a place on a major party's presidential **ticket**. Gore and Lieberman prevailed in the popular vote, but lost in a disputed **electoral college** contest. Nevertheless, Lieberman remained in the Senate, having followed a precedent set by **Lyndon B. Johnson** in 1960 of running for reelection as well as for the vice presidency. He undertook a **campaign** for the 2004 presidential **nomination** that failed to catch fire, owing in large part to his support for the Iraq War, which estranged him from antiwar party activists, who constituted a significant portion of the **presidential primary** electorates. In 2006, he won reelection to a fourth senate term, despite losing the state party's **primary** nomination. Elected as an Independent, he styled himself an independent Democrat, and he continued to **caucus** with the Democrats, enabling them to claim **majority** control and him to **chair** a **committee**. In 2008, he endorsed the presidential candidacy of John McCain, the Republican Party nominee. The Democrats expanded their majority, making his Democratic party connections more problematical. Nevertheless, he continues to claim the party label.

LINCOLN, ABRAHAM. Republican president, 1861–1865 (Union Party presidential nominee, 1864). (b. 12 February 1809; d. 15 April 1865). Born in Kentucky, Lincoln moved to Illinois as a young man and read law. He became a successful attorney and developed political ambitions. He was elected to a single term in the **House of Representatives** (1847–1849), as the nominee of the **Whig Party**. When the Whigs collapsed a few years later, Lincoln quickly shifted his allegiance to the newly formed **Republican Party**. He ran unsuccessfully for the **Senate** in 1858 and then secured the presidential **nomination** of his new party in 1860. With the opposition **Democratic Party** deeply divided along regional lines by the slavery issue, Lincoln won a popular vote **plurality** and a **majority** in the electoral college, although his support came exclusively from the Northern states.

Shortly after his inauguration, 11 Southern states seceded from the Union and the **Civil War** began. Lincoln made the survival of the Union his primary objective. In responding vigorously to the rebellion, he vastly expanded the scope of presidential power. In 1864, he pursued reelection as the war raged, jettisoning his **vice president, Hannibal Hamlin**, in favor of **Andrew Johnson**, a pro-Union Democrat from Tennessee, and campaigning under the improvised **Union Party** label. He won reelection convincingly and brought the war to a successful close. Days afterward, he was assassinated. His crisis presidency brought the Republicans into a position of sustained dominance in American national politics that largely endured until the onset of the **Great Depression**.

LINCOLN, BENJAMIN. Electoral vote recipient, 1789 (Federalist). (b. 24 January 1733; d. 10 May 1810). Lincoln, from Massachusetts, held the office of major general in the Continental Army (1777–1781). From that post, he went on to serve as secretary of war (1781–1783). In the inaugural presidential **election** of 1789, one Georgia elector placed his name on the **ballot**.

LIST SYSTEM. A form of **proportional representation** whereby parties prepare lists of candidates equal to the number of seats available in an electoral district. When the percentages of party electoral support are known, each party receives its equivalent percentage of legislative seats. These seats are filled by the listed candidates, moving from the top of the list down as far as the party's percentage authorizes.

LITERACY TEST. A suffrage requirement formerly imposed by many states. Historically identified with, but not restricted to, the

South, literacy tests were ostensibly designed to ensure that voters could read and thus presumably were capable of making informed voting decisions. In practice, selectively administered literacy tests were an effective means of preventing African Americans from voting in the post-Reconstruction South. The use of literacy tests began to decline in the decade after World War II. By the early 1970s, federal legislation, the Voting Rights Act (1965) and subsequent amendments, and a Supreme Court decision, *Oregon v. Mitchell* (1970), effectively eliminated this long-standing practice.

LIVERMORE, SAMUEL. President pro tempore of the Senate, 1796, 1799–1800. (b. 14 May 1732; d. 18 May 1803). Livermore represented New Hampshire in the Continental Congress on two occasions (1780–1782 and 1785). Elected to the **House of Representatives** in 1788, he won reelection two years later. Chosen for the Senate in 1793, he served eight years, leaving in 1801. On two occasions, initially in the first session of the 4th **Congress** and once again in the first session of the 6th Congress, he was named **president pro tempore**.

LODGE, HENRY CABOT. Republican president pro tempore of the Senate, 1912; Republican minority leader of the Senate, 1918–1919; Republican majority leader of the Senate, 1919–1924. (b. 12 May 1850; d. 9 November 1924). Lodge descended from a prominent New England family. He was elected to the **House of Representatives** in 1886, serving three terms before moving over to the **Senate** in 1893. He held his Senate seat for the rest of his life. In 1912, Lodge briefly served as **president pro tempore**, during the second session of the 62nd **Congress**. In 1918, after the death of **Jacob H. Gallinger**, Lodge became **floor leader** of the **Republican Party**, then in the **minority**. When the GOP captured the Senate later that year, he became **majority leader**, and kept the post until his death. In that capacity, he played the key role in successfully marshaling opposition to the ratification of the Treaty of Versailles, as proposed by President **Woodrow Wilson**. Two of his grandsons succeeded him in the Congress. His namesake, **Henry Cabot Lodge Jr.**, was the unsuccessful vice presidential nominee of the Republican Party in 1960.

LODGE, HENRY CABOT, JR. Republican vice presidential nominee, 1960. (b. 5 July 1902; d. 27 February 1985). Grandson of a prominent senator and **Republican Party** leader, Lodge followed his namesake into the **Senate** from Massachusetts in 1937. He resigned his seat in 1944 to serve in World War II, but he won reelection in 1946. Defeated in 1952 by **John F. Kennedy**, Lodge joined the **administration** of President **Dwight D. Eisenhower** as United Nations ambassador. During this time of Cold War tension, Lodge maintained high public visibility. In 1960, he was the choice of presidential nominee **Richard M. Nixon** for the vice presidential slot on the Republican **ticket**. In the fall, they lost to Lodge's old Massachusetts rival, Kennedy, and his **running mate**, **Lyndon B. Johnson**. Lodge later joined the Kennedy administration as ambassador to the Republic of Vietnam (1963–1964). After Kennedy's assassination, Lodge returned home to seek the 1964 Republican presidential **nomination**, which went to Barry M. Goldwater. In 1965, President Johnson sent Lodge back to Vietnam for a second tour of duty as ambassador. He returned home in 1967 and retired from public life.

LOGAN, JOHN A. Republican vice presidential nominee, 1884. (b. 9 February 1826; d. 26 December 1886). Running under the banner of the **Democratic Party**, Logan won **election** to the **House of Representatives** from his southern Illinois district in 1858. The Civil War interrupted his service in 1862, but after distinguished service in the Union effort, he returned to office in 1867, now as an enthusiast for the **Republican Party**, for two more terms. Rising in prominence at both the state and national levels, Logan went to the **Senate** (1871–1877 and 1879–1886). Devoted to President **Ulysses S. Grant**, he identified with the **Stalwarts** in the factional rivalries within the party. In 1884, he contended for his party's presidential **nomination**, which went to **James G. Blaine**. Afterward, he was the overwhelming choice of the **Republican National Convention** for the second spot on the **ticket**. Defeated in that endeavor, he was reelected to the Senate and served there until his death.

LONG BALLOT. A ballot that features a large number of offices to be filled by competing candidates. It may also include issues to be addressed by the voters. Voters in the United States typically encounter a long ballot. Students of voting behavior associate the long ballot with roll-off, a decline in voter participation in low-level contests toward the bottom of the ballot. *See also* SHORT BALLOT.

LONGWORTH, NICHOLAS. Republican majority leader of the House of Representatives, 1923–1925; Republican Speaker of the House of Representatives, 1925–1931. (b. 5 November 1869; d. 9 April 1931). Elected to the **House of Representatives** from Ohio in 1903, Longworth soon after married the daughter of President **Theodore Roosevelt** in a White House ceremony. He served five terms in the House before losing his bid for reelection in 1912. Reelected two years later, he held his seat for the rest of his life. In 1923, he served as **majority leader** for the **Republican Party** during the 68th **Congress**, under Speaker **Frederick H. Gillett**. When Gillett won election to a **Senate** seat in 1924, Longworth became **Speaker**. Not content merely to preside and moderate, he consciously sought to act as the chamber's political leader. His success restored to the office a considerable measure of the power and prestige that had been sacrificed with the downfall of Speaker **Joseph G. Cannon** in 1910.

LOTT, TRENT. Republican majority leader of the Senate, 1996–2001, 2001; Republican minority leader, 2001–2002. (b. 9 October 1941). Lott went to **Congress** in 1968, to serve on the staff of Mississippi Representative William Colmer, a senior, conservative Democrat. In 1972, when Colmer retired, Lott successfully sought his seat as a **Republican Party** nominee. He held the seat for eight terms, moving to the **Senate** in 1988. Six years later, he won both reelection and the position of **whip** for the newly established Republican **majority**. When Majority Leader **Robert J. Dole** won the presidential **nomination** in 1996, he left the Senate to devote his full attention to his **campaign**, and Lott replaced him as **majority leader**. As **floor leader**, Lott focused more on process than substance.

The 2000 election left the Senate evenly divided between Republicans and Democrats. When the 107th Congress convened on 3 January 2001, outgoing Vice President **Al Gore** cast the deciding vote, giving temporary control of the chamber to the Democrats, relegating Lott to **minority leader** until 20 January, when incoming Vice President **Richard B. Cheney** voted to restore the Republicans and Lott to power in the chamber. Later on that spring, Senator James Jeffords (R-VT) decided to identify himself as an **independent** and **caucus** with the Democrats. Lott thus found himself again leading the **minority**. When the Republicans regained their majority in the 2002 elections, Lott was poised to reclaim the post of majority leader. However, shortly afterward he resigned his leadership position, following reports of controversial remarks he had made in connection with the retirement of Senator **J. Strom Thurmond** that appeared to endorse Thurmond's 1948 **Dixiecrat** presidential campaign. **William H. Frist** replaced him as floor leader. Lott remained in the Senate, and he reestablished his status as a party leader in late 2006, when the **party conference** designated him minority whip. However, in December 2007 he resigned his seat and became a lobbyist.

LOYAL OPPOSITION. A characterization of the **minority** party, or the **party-out-of-power**, in the American **two-party system**. It is most often applied in a legislative context. It suggests that the party's opposition to the agenda of the **majority** party, or **party-in-power**, is legitimate and should not be viewed as unpatriotic or treasonous. The term was originally used in 18th-century Great Britain, and from there it was imported to the new Republic. During the **First Party System**, there was substantial opposition to the idea of party competition. However, the notion became well grounded in the American political culture during the **Second Party System**. **Martin Van Buren** was a key figure in facilitating this shift.

LUCAS, SCOTT. Democratic majority leader of the Senate, 1949–1951. (b. 19 February 1892; d. 22 February 1968). Lucas served two terms in the House of Representatives from Illinois (1935–1939). He won a **Senate** seat in 1938, which he held for two terms. During the 80th Congress (1947–1949), with the **Democratic Party** in the minority, he became **whip**. The Democrats regained control of **Congress** in the 1948 elections, when their **floor leader, Alben W. Barkley**, won the vice presidency. Lucas thus rose to the position of majority leader for the 81st Congress. He was defeated for reelection in 1950 by **Everett M. Dirksen**, who later rose to the position of floor leader for the minority Republicans.

– M –

MACHINE. A derogatory term often applied to a strong **party organization** at the local and state levels. In the late 19th century, such party organizations came under assault from **Progressive Era** reformers, who viewed them as corrupt and undemocratic.

MACK, NORMAN E. Democratic National Committee chair, 1908–1912. (b. 24 July 1858; d. 26 December 1932). Mack was a newspaper publisher from Buffalo, New York, who initially came on the national party scene as a supporter of the 1884 presidential candidacy of his hometown's **favorite son**, Grover Cleveland. In 1896, after the **Democratic National Convention** embraced a **soft money** stance and nominated **William Jennings Bryan** for president, Mack proved himself to be a party regular. He steadfastly supported Bryan even as many Gold Democrats were abandoning the party standard in favor of the **National Democratic Party**. Subsequently, Bryan demonstrated his appreciation for Mack's endorsement, first by using his influence to promote Mack for a seat on the **Democratic National Committee** in 1900, then in 1908, after Bryan had been nominated for the presidency for the third time, by naming Mack national party **chair**. Mack oversaw the conduct of the unsuccessful fall **campaign** and remained as party chair until the next national **convention**, continuing to promote Bryan's interests. After stepping down in 1912, Mack remained involved in presidential nominating politics for another two decades.

MACON, NATHANIEL. Democratic-Republican Speaker of the House of Representatives, 1801–1807; Democratic-Republican president pro tempore of the Senate, 1826–1827. (b. 17 December 1757; d. 20 June 1837). A prominent **Anti-Federalist** opponent of the 1787 **Constitution**, Macon was elected from North Carolina to the House of Representatives for the 2nd **Congress** in 1790 and reelected on 11 subsequent occasions. When the 7th Congress convened in 1801, after the **critical election** of 1800 that transferred national political power to the **Democratic-Republican Party**, Macon was chosen as **Speaker**, at the behest of President **Thomas Jefferson**. During the three terms Macon held the office, he deferred to the **president as party leader**, though he took care to promote and protect the constitutional prerogatives of his position. When the 10th Congress convened in 1807, **Joseph Varnum** of Massachusetts replaced Macon as Speaker. Macon stayed on in the House for another four terms.

In 1815, Macon moved over to the Senate, where he remained for 13 years, leaving office in 1828. In the 1824 **electoral college** balloting, he received the votes of Virginia's 24 electors for vice president. During the 19th Congress, he was named **president pro tempore** on three occasions in 1826 and 1827.

MADISON, JAMES. Democratic-Republican president, 1809–1817. (b. 16 March 1751; d. 28 June 1836). His native Virginia sent Madison to the Continental Congress on two occasions (1780–1783 and 1786–1788). During the latter tenure, he represented his state at the Constitutional Convention, where he played a key role in developing a new charter for national government. Subsequently, he pseudonymously coauthored the *Federalist Papers*, profound and persuasive arguments for ratification of the **Constitution**. Madison won election to a seat in the newly formed **House of Representatives**, where he served three terms and became a chief spokesman for the emerging **Democratic-Republican Party** opposition to the **Federalist Party**, led by **Alexander Hamilton**. Returning home in 1797, he was instrumental in developing the party apparatus and arguing against the policies of President **John Adams**. He anonymously authored the Virginia Resolutions, advocating a states'-rights position against national encroachments.

Madison essentially managed the successful **campaign** of **Thomas Jefferson** for the presidency in 1800, and Jefferson named him secretary of state. He held that position throughout Jefferson's presidency. When Jefferson left office, Madison was his obvious successor. He was elected without difficulty in 1808. Toward the end of his first term, the War of 1812 broke out with Great Britain. He won a second term and brought the war to a successful conclusion. Madison respectfully observed the two-term tradition of **George Washington** and Thomas Jefferson, retiring in 1817. During his lengthy retirement, he served as rector of the University of Virginia and was a delegate to Virginia's constitutional revision convention. He died in 1836, the last surviving signer of the **Constitution**.

MAGNUSON, WARREN G. Democratic president pro tempore of the Senate, 1979–1981. (b. 12 April 1905; d. 20 May 1989). Washington sent Magnuson to the **House of Representatives** in 1937. In 1944, he moved over to the **Senate,** where he served six terms. When Senator **James O. Eastland** of Mississippi did not seek reelection in 1978, Magnuson became the senior member of the **Democratic Party**, which controlled the chamber. As such, he was named **president pro tempore** at the outset of the 96th Congress. He lost his bid for reelection in 1980, contributing to the Democrats' first loss of **majority** status in the Senate since 1954. **J. Strom Thurmond** replaced him as president pro tempore.

MAINTAINING ELECTION. An election in which the **majority party** retains control of a public office or institution. For example, in the **Fifth Party System,** the reelections of President **Franklin D. Roosevelt**, the nominee of the Democratic Party, were maintaining elections. *See also* CONVERTING ELECTION; DEVIATING ELECTION; REALIGNING ELECTION; REINSTATING ELECTION.

MAJOR PARTY. A political party that competes successfully in electoral contests and has reasonable prospects to win control of some, if not all, of the offices of government at some level. In the United States, at any given time only two parties have been considered major parties. In the **First Party System,** they were the **Federalist Party** and the **Democratic-Republican Party**. This pattern of party competition eventually gave way to a **Second Party System**, which featured competition between the **Democratic Party** and the **Whig Party**. Since the end of this era, the two major parties have been the Democratic Party and the **Republican Party**. *See also* MINOR PARTY; TWO-PARTY SYSTEM.

MAJORITY. A number more than half the total number in a given group. This term applies to votes cast, as well as to the division of seats in a legislative body between or among political parties. *See also* ABSOLUTE MAJORITY; MINORITY; PLURALITY.

MAJORITY LEADER. A party leadership position for the party in control of the legislative chamber; the term is used in both the **House**

of **Representatives** and the **Senate**. The individual occupying this position is also known as the **floor leader**. In the House, the majority leader is the deputy party leader, serving under the **Speaker**. In the Senate, the majority leader occupies the top leadership position. In each chamber, the party **caucus** chooses its leader.

MAJORITY-MINORITY DISTRICT. A legislative district within which a racial **minority** of the larger population comprises the numerical **majority**. The creation of majority-minority districts for the **House of Representatives** and state legislatures was systematically pursued in several states following the 1990 census, in keeping with Justice Department interpretations of the Voting Rights Act of 1965, as amended in 1982. At issue was whether district lines encouraged or discouraged the election of minority legislators. Majority-minority districts presumably provide encouragement, and they have indeed heightened the presence of African Americans in state and federal legislatures. Majority-minority districts have arguably contributed to the rise of the **Republican Party** in the South, by concentrating black voters, who are typically very loyal to the **Democratic Party**, in homogenous districts and creating a more favorable political environment for Republicans in the more numerous surrounding districts. Supreme Court rulings have provided qualified endorsement for majority-minority districting, so long as race is not the explicitly controlling factor in drawing district lines.

MAJORITY PARTY. *See* PARTY-IN-POWER.

MAN ON HORSEBACK. A reference to a military leader who enters the political arena to assume command. American political parties have repeatedly looked to men on horseback to advance their fortunes. Noteworthy examples include Presidents **George Washington, Andrew Jackson, William Henry Harrison, Zachary Taylor, Ulysses S. Grant, Theodore Roosevelt**, and **Dwight D. Eisenhower**. Losing presidential races were nominees **Lewis Cass, Winfield Scott, George B. McClellan**, and **Winfield Scott Hancock**. Recent examples of this phenomenon include the cultivation of General Colin Powell by some in the **Republican Party** and General Wesley Clark's 2004 candidacy for the Democratic presidential nomination.

MANATT, CHARLES A. Democratic National Committee chair, 1981–1985. (b. 9 June 1936). Born in Chicago and raised in Iowa, Manatt relocated to California to practice law. There, he became involved in state party politics and demonstrated his abilities as a fund-raiser. In 1981, he energetically sought **election** as **chair** of the **Democratic National Committee**, in the wake of the 1980 elections in which the **Democratic Party** lost both the White House and the **Senate**. As chair, he emphasized the **service party** approach that the **Republican National Committee** had earlier taken under **Ray C. Bliss** and **William Brock**. He also maintained the commitment to centralization and regularization of delegate-selection procedures to the national party convention that had been initiated a decade earlier by the **McGovern–Fraser Commission**.

At the 1984 **Democratic National Convention**, presidential nominee **Walter F. Mondale** considered exercising his time-honored prerogative to install his **candidate** as national party chair. Manatt's supporters on the national **committee** discouraged the move, and Mondale declined to press the issue. This development strengthened the recent precedent of a fixed term for Democratic national party chairs that begins in January following the presidential election. After Mondale's defeat in November, Manatt resigned as party chair and resumed his law practice.

MANDERSON, CHARLES F. Republican president pro tempore of the Senate, 1891–1893. (b. 9 February 1837; d. 28 September 1911). Nebraska sent Manderson to the **Senate** in 1883, where he served two full terms. On the eve of the adjournment of the 51st **Congress**, in March 1891, he was elected **president pro tempore**. He continued to serve throughout the 52nd Congress. He resigned shortly after the 53rd Congress took office. Manderson was the first to be elected president pro tempore in the wake of a new rule that specified that an individual, once elected, would serve until otherwise ordered. Previously, presidents pro tempore had been chosen to preside over the

Senate only in the absence of the **vice president**, generally vacating the office upon the return of that **incumbent**.

MANGUM, WILLIE P. Whig president pro tempore of the Senate, 1842–1845. (b. 10 May 1792; d. 7 September 1861). Mangum was elected to the **House of Representatives** from North Carolina in 1822. He left office in his second term. In 1831, he won **election** to the **Senate** and left office in 1836, before the end of his term. In the **electoral college** balloting that year, Mangum won the 11 presidential ballots of members of the South Carolina delegation, who were proclaiming their dissatisfaction with the nominee of the **Democratic Party**, Vice President **Martin Van Buren**, who won the election, and the regional nominee of the **Whig Party**, Tennessean **Hugh Lawson White**.

Four years later, Mangum returned to the Senate, and retained that office until 1853. During the 27th **Congress**, he was the last of three senators chosen **president pro tempore**. He continued in that capacity during the 28th Congress. His tenure as presiding officer had extraordinary constitutional significance in that there was no **vice president**, **John Tyler** having succeeded to the presidency following the death of **William Henry Harrison**.

MANN, JAMES R. Republican minority leader of the House of Representatives, 1911–1919. (b. 20 October 1856; d. 30 November 1922). Elected to the **House of Representatives** from Illinois in 1896, Mann held his seat for the rest of his life. In 1910, the **Republican Party** lost control of the House, which it had held since 1895. In the **minority**, the party chose Mann as its **floor leader**, replacing **Sereno E. Payne** of New York, the first officially designated **majority leader**. Mann remained floor leader for four terms. In 1918, the Republicans recaptured **majority** status. They passed over Mann in favor of **Frederick H. Gillett** of Massachusetts as their choice for **Speaker** and named **Franklin W. Mondell** of Wyoming as their floor leader. Mann stayed on in the House for almost two more terms, until his death in 1922.

MANSFIELD, MICHAEL J. Democratic majority leader of the Senate, 1961–1977. (b. 16 March 1903; d. 5 October 2001). Mansfield was a professor of Far Eastern history at the University of Montana when he successfully ran for Montana's **House of Representatives** seat in 1942. After five terms in the House, he moved over to the **Senate**, defeating a Republican **incumbent** in 1952. In 1957, he became **whip** for the Democratic **majority**, serving under **Lyndon B. Johnson**. When Johnson became **vice president** in 1961, Mansfield assumed the office of **majority leader**. He held the post for 15 years, a record tenure. His leadership style was more accommodating and low key than his predecessor's. Mansfield did not seek reelection in 1976 but remained a presence in national politics as the choice of President Jimmy Carter as ambassador to Japan. President **Ronald W. Reagan** retained him in that capacity. Mansfield retired from public life in 1988.

MARSHALL, THOMAS R. Democratic vice president, 1913–1921. (b. 14 March 1854; d. 1 June 1925). An Indiana attorney, Marshall entered the arena of **partisan** politics in 1908, when he secured the gubernatorial **nomination** of the **Democratic Party**. He went on to win a narrow **general election** victory in a state with a reputation for being reliably Republican. Ineligible for reelection as governor in 1912, he was successfully promoted as a vice presidential candidate by the former national party **chair, Thomas Taggart**, at the Democratic National Convention. Marshall joined presidential nominee Woodrow Wilson on the ticket, and they went on to win a **plurality** in the popular vote and a comfortable **majority** in the **electoral college** balloting.

During his tenure as vice president, Marshall appealingly displayed his self-deprecating, dry wit to a national audience. Renominated and reelected in 1916, he maintained his low profile even after President Wilson became incapacitated in 1919. Marshall retired from public life at the end of his term in 1921, the first vice president to serve two full terms since **Daniel D. Tompkins** almost a century earlier.

MARTIN, JOSEPH W., JR. Republican minority leader of the House of Representatives, 1939–1947, 1949–1953, 1955–1959; Republican Speaker of the House of Representatives, 1947–1949, 1953–1955; chair, Republican National Committee, 1940–1942. (b. 3 November 1884; d. 6 March 1968). Joseph Martin was a Massachusetts state **representative**, state **senator**, and state **party organization** leader prior to his **election** to the **House of Representatives** in 1924. He remained there for the remainder of his career.

Martin became part of the congressional leadership team of the **Republican Party** in 1933, when he was chosen assistant minority leader. In 1939, he became leader of the House Republicans, a position he held for two decades. In addition, he chaired the **Republican National Committee** for two years, beginning with the 1940 presidential **campaign** of nominee **Wendell L. Willkie**. For most of Martin's tenure as congressional party leader, the Republicans were in the minority, but they constituted a **majority** of the chamber in the 80th and 83rd Congresses, during which he became **Speaker**. In 1959, his party colleagues replaced him with **Charles A. Halleck**. Martin continued as a member of the House for four more terms, leaving office in 1967.

MARTIN, THOMAS S. Democratic minority leader of the Senate, 1911–1913, 1919; Democratic majority leader of the Senate, 1917–1919. (b. 29 July 1847; d. 12 November 1919). Entering the **Senate** from Virginia in 1895, Martin held his seat for the rest of his life. At the outset of the 62nd **Congress** (1911), when the parties in the Senate each began officially designating a **floor leader**, Martin was the choice of the **Democratic Party**, then in the minority. However, when the Democrats took control of both houses of Congress in 1912, they passed over Martin in favor of **John W. Kern** of Indiana. Kern died in 1917, and the party conference again chose Martin as its leader. When the Republicans recaptured the Senate in 1918, Martin resumed his earlier status as **minority leader**. Following his death in 1919, Gilbert Hitchcock of Nebraska served as acting minority leader for several months, with **Oscar W. Underwood** of Alabama officially taking over in 1920.

MARTINEZ, MELQUIADES R. General chair of the Republican National Committee, 2007. (b. 23 October 1946). Born in Cuba, Mel Martinez immigrated to Florida in 1962. After earning his law degree, he became active in state **Republican Party** politics. In 2000, he was a leading fund-raiser for **George W. Bush**, and he co-chaired the presidential **campaign** organization in that critical state. President Bush brought Martinez to Washington as secretary of the department of housing and urban development. In 2003, Martinez resigned to undertake a successful campaign to win an open **Senate** seat from Florida, making him the first Cuban American to serve in that chamber. When national party chair **Ken Mehlman** resigned his post after **GOP** losses in the 2006 **midterm elections**, Martinez became general chair, while retaining his Senate seat. Day-to-day responsibility for managing the national party headquarters, along with the designation as chair, went to **Robert M. Duncan**. Ten months after assuming this office, Martinez resigned, and the position was not filled. At the end of 2008, Martinez announced that he would not seek reelection in 2010.

MASON, JAMES M. Democratic president pro tempore of the Senate, 1856–1857. (b. 3 November 1798; d. 20 April 1871). James Mason served a single term in the **House of Representatives** from Virginia (1837–1839), solidly identifying with the emerging **Democratic Party** led by **Andrew Jackson**. Chosen for the **Senate** in 1847, he held that office until 1861, when the outbreak of the **Civil War** forced his departure. For two days during the 34th **Congress**, once in 1856 and again in 1857, he held the office of **president pro tempore**. On those occasions, he had extraordinary constitutional standing as the presiding officer, because there was no **vice president** following the death in 1853 of **William R. King**.

MASS PARTY. A party that systematically and formally seeks to enroll members from the ranks of the general public. Maurice Duverger (*Political Parties*, 1963) compares and contrasts mass, cadre, and devotee parties. Mass parties are generally guided by an ideological vision. A mass party features strong, bureaucratized **party organization** that exercises considerable control over the **party-in-office**. Historically, European parties better fit this description than do their American counterparts. More recently, mass and cadre parties appear to be converging. *See also* CADRE PARTY; DEVOTEE PARTY.

MATERIAL INCENTIVES. Motivations for **partisan** activity that are economic in character. For example, expectations of **patronage** positions or **preferments** are material incentives for partisan activity.

Peter B. Clark and James Q. Wilson developed a taxonomy of incentives: material, purposive, and solidary. *See also* PURPOSIVE INCENTIVES; SOLIDARY INCENTIVES.

MCAULIFFE, TERRENCE R. Democratic National Committee chair, 2001–2005. (b. 1957). Terry McAuliffe is a lawyer, banker, and real estate developer who entered national politics in 1980 on behalf of the presidential reelection bid of **Jimmy Carter**. He reemerged in the 1990s as a prominent **Democratic Party** fund-raiser, particularly successful at attracting **soft money**. During the presidency of **Bill Clinton**, he served as finance director for both the **Democratic National Committee** and the **Democratic Congressional Campaign Committee**. McAuliffe achieved considerable public notice as a close friend of Clinton's. Coinciding with Clinton's departure from the presidency in 2001, McAuliffe was elected national party **chair**, a development that suggested Clinton might aspire to a postpresidential party leadership role. During his years as chair, McAuliffe was a strong critic of President **George W. Bush** and an energetic party fund-raiser. After serving a four-year term, he stepped down in 2005. McAuliffe demonstrated his abiding loyalty to the Clinton family by chairing the unsuccessful 2008 presidential **nomination** campaign of Hillary Clinton. He subsequently expressed interest in running for governor in Virginia.

MCCAIN, JOHN S., III. Republican presidential nominee, 2008. (b. 29 August 1936). John McCain was born into a family of distinguished naval officers. His father and grandfather, for whom he was named, both attained the rank of admiral. McCain graduated from the U.S. Naval Academy and flew bombing missions over North Vietnam in the Vietnam War. Shot down in 1967, he spent more than five years in captivity as a prisoner of war. Following his release in 1973, he remained on active duty in stateside assignments until his 1981 retirement with the rank of captain.

McCain relocated to Arizona, where he undertook a successful 1982 **campaign** for **election** to the **House of Representatives** under the auspices of the **Republican Party**. Reelected in 1984, he went on in 1986 to win the seat in the U.S. Senate that had been occupied by **Barry M. Goldwater**. His involvement in the Keating

Five influence-peddling scandal contributed to his commitment to **campaign finance** reform, which culminated in the 2002 enactment of the McCain–Finegold bill restricting the use of **soft money** in election campaigns. McCain won reelection in 1992, 1998, and 2004. In 2000, he contended for the Republican presidential nomination, which went to **George W. Bush**.

In 2008, McCain undertook another presidential bid, and this time he succeeded in winning the Republican nomination, despite a lack of enthusiasm from the party **rank and file**, owing to suspicions regarding the depth of his commitment to **conservative** ideology, especially social conservatism. He also suffered from the declining popularity of President Bush, his former rival, whom he had embraced in his efforts to ingratiate himself with the party faithful. In November, McCain and his **running mate**, **Sarah Palin**, were soundly defeated by the Democratic Party **ticket** of **Barack H. Obama** and **Joseph R. Biden Jr**. McCain remained in the Senate in anticipation of a bid for a fifth term in 2010.

MCCLELLAN, GEORGE B. Democratic presidential nominee, 1864. (b. 3 December 1836; d. 29 October 1885). McClellan was a career army officer who rose to command the Army of the Potomac during the Civil War. Differences with President **Abraham Lincoln** over military strategy and tactics led to McClellan's replacement. Northern Democrats nominated him for **president** in 1864, on a platform seeking a negotiated peace. The Democrats hoped that popular disenchantment with the progress of the war would lead voters to reject President Lincoln's reelection bid. However, the fortunes of the Union improved over the course of the **campaign**. With the Southern states not participating in the **election**, the potential Democratic constituency was vastly diminished, and McClellan went down to a convincing defeat. In later years, he served as governor of New Jersey (1878–1881).

MCCOMBS, WILLIAM F. Democratic National Committee chair, 1912–1916. (b. 26 December 1875; d. 22 February 1921). Born in Arkansas, McCombs attended Princeton, where he studied under Professor **Woodrow Wilson**. Years later, as a lawyer in New York City, McCombs played the leading role in the advancement of Wilson's

1912 candidacy for the presidential **nomination** of the **Democratic Party**. He dealt effectively with the state party leaders, who controlled delegate selection and who had reservations about Wilson's reputation as a reformer. However, McCombs's efforts to allay the concerns of the party bosses generated tension in his relationship with Wilson. Nevertheless, after Wilson's nomination, McCombs received Wilson's endorsement for the position of national party **chair**, which he coveted. The personal tensions persisted throughout the **campaign** and afterward, as the two principals clashed over campaign strategy and **patronage** considerations. McCombs declined Wilson's offer to become ambassador to France, preferring to remain party chairman and practice law. Increasingly estranged from the president, McCombs resigned as party chair in 1916.

MCCONNELL, A. MITCHELL, JR. Republican minority leader of the Senate, 2007– . (b. 20 February 1942). Mitch McConnell grew up in Louisville, Kentucky. After service on **Capitol Hill** as an intern and staff assistant to two Republican senators from Kentucky, McConnell joined the **administration** of President **Gerald R. Ford** as deputy assistant attorney general. He then returned home, where he became county judge-executive in Jefferson County in 1978. In 1984, he defeated a Democratic **incumbent** in a close contest for a seat in the U.S. **Senate**. He won reelection in 1990, 1996, 2002, and 2008. In 1998 and 2000, he chaired the **Republican Senatorial Campaign Committee**. In 2003, he became **whip** for the **majority**, serving in that capacity for the 108th and 109th Congresses. With the retirement of majority leader **Bill Frist** in 2006, McConnell became the **floor leader** for the Republicans, now in the **minority**, for the 110th Congress, and the **Republican Conference** retained him in that role for the 111th Congress.

MCCORMACK, JOHN W. Democratic majority leader of the House of Representatives, 1940–1947, 1959–1953, 1955–1962; Democratic Speaker of the House of Representatives, 1962–1971. (b. 21 December 1891; d. 22 November 1980). A Boston native, McCormack practiced law and participated in local party politics. In 1920, he was elected to the Massachusetts state legislature, where he served in both chambers. After a brief retirement from public life occasioned by a primary defeat in 1926, he was elected to the **House of Representatives** in 1928. He remained there until his retirement in 1971. In 1940, McCormack became **floor leader** for the **majority** under Speaker **Sam Rayburn**. He held that position for more than two decades, except for the 80th and 83rd Congresses, when the **Republican Party** constituted the majority and Rayburn served as **minority leader**. When Rayburn's health failed in 1961, McCormack became Speaker pro tempore. Following Rayburn's death that fall, McCormack was elected **Speaker** when **Congress** came back into session in January 1962. He held that office for nine years, until his retirement in 1971. During his tenure, Congress enacted the **Great Society** legislation proposed by President **Lyndon B. Johnson**.

MCCORMICK, VANCE C. Democratic National Committee chair, 1916–1919. (b. 19 June 1872; d. 16 June 1946). McCormick began his career in party politics at the local level, serving on the city council and then as mayor in his native Harrisburg, Pennsylvania. He also maintained publishing and banking interests. He identified with the progressive wing of the **Democratic Party**, where he found himself allied with **Woodrow Wilson**, the reform governor of neighboring New Jersey. McCormick was an early and influential supporter of Wilson's 1912 presidential candidacy. President Wilson appointed him a director of the Federal Reserve Bank in Philadelphia. Backed by **progressive** forces, McCormick ran for governor in 1914 but lost.

In 1916, preparing for a reelection **campaign**, President Wilson named McCormick **chair** of the **Democratic National Committee**. McCormick oversaw the successful reelection bid and emerged as a key figure in the second term. While serving as party chair, he also chaired the War Trade Board and accompanied the **president** to Europe for the postwar peace talks. McCormick resigned as party chair in 1919. In later years, he bolted from the party and supported the presidential candidacies of Republicans **Herbert C. Hoover** and **Wendell L. Willkie**.

MCFARLAND, ERNEST W. Democratic majority leader of the Senate, 1951–1953. (b. 9 October 1894; d. 8 June 1984). McFarland was elected to the **Senate** from Arizona in 1940. He served two terms.

During the 82nd Congress (1951–1953), he held the office of **floor leader** for the Democratic **majority,** replacing **Scott Lucas** of Illinois, who had been defeated for reelection in 1950. In turn, McFarland lost his own bid for reelection to Republican **Barry Goldwater** in 1952, an **election** in which the Democrats lost control of both houses of **Congress.** McFarland returned to Arizona, where he won election as governor in 1954, serving two terms before losing a rematch with Goldwater in 1958. In the mid-1960s, he was appointed to the state supreme court, rising to the position of chief justice in 1967. McFarland retired from politics in 1971.

MCGOVERN, GEORGE S. Democratic presidential nominee, 1972. (b. 19 July 1922). The son of a Methodist minister, McGovern flew bombing missions over Europe in World War II and went on to earn a Ph.D. in history from Northwestern University. He taught college briefly and then entered political life, winning a seat in the **House of Representatives** in 1956. He twice secured reelection, leaving in 1961 to join the **administration** of **John F. Kennedy** as director of the Food for Peace program in the Department of Agriculture. In 1962, McGovern successfully sought a **Senate seat,** which he held through two more electoral cycles. In 1972, he was a **dark horse** contender for the presidential **nomination** of the **Democratic Party,** campaigning on an anti–Vietnam War platform. He took advantage of reforms he had advocated in the delegate-selection process mandating more popular involvement, taking the form of participatory caucuses and presidential primaries, to emerge as the choice of the **Democratic National Convention.** In November, McGovern went down to an overwhelming defeat at the hands of the incumbent, **Richard M. Nixon.** He remained in the Senate until his 1980 defeat for reelection. He has been politically active in retirement, giving speeches and lectures, appearing in national media forums, contemplating additional campaigns, and pursuing diplomatic assignments. *See also* MCGOVERN–FRASER COMMISSION.

MCGOVERN–FRASER COMMISSION. A catalyst for **Democratic Party** reform in the late 1960s and early 1970s. The McGovern–Fraser Commission promoted substantial reform in delegate-selection procedures for the **Democratic National Convention** between 1968 and 1972. Authorized at the tumultuous 1968 Democratic National Convention, the Commission on Party Structure and Delegate Selection took its popular name from its cochairs, South Dakota senator **George S. McGovern** and Minnesota congressman Donald M. Fraser. The commission's recommendations encouraged state parties to expand opportunities for popular participation in national convention delegate selection. The recommendations were embraced by the national party and effectively imposed on the state parties in an unprecedented assertion of national party authority. As a result, participatory caucuses and presidential primaries increased dramatically, and competing in them became essential for aspirants to the party's presidential **nomination**. *See also* PRESIDENTIAL PRIMARY.

MCGRATH, J. HOWARD. Democratic National Committee chair, 1947–1949. (b. 28 November 1903; d. 2 September 1966). Proclaimed the "boy wonder" of Rhode Island politics, McGrath was elected governor in 1940 at the age of 36. He held that office for four years and then won election to the **Senate** in 1946. The next year, President **Harry S. Truman** called on him to head the **Democratic National Committee**. McGrath guided the national **party organization** through the 1948 **campaign** that saw the Democrats hold on to the White House and win back **majority** control of both houses of **Congress**. Several months after the election, Truman brought McGrath into his **cabinet** as attorney general, leading the latter to leave both Capitol Hill and his party leadership position. After his tour of duty with the Truman **administration**, McGrath retired from party politics.

MCKELLAR, KENNETH. Democratic president pro tempore of the Senate, 1945–1947, 1949–1953. (b. 29 January 1869; d. 25 October 25 1957). A product of the Crump **machine** in West Tennessee, McKellar won a **special election** to the **House of Representatives** in 1911, and he was reelected on two successive occasions. In 1916, he won a **Senate** seat, which he held for six full terms. As senior member of the Democratic **majority**, he was named **president pro tempore** for the 79th (1945–1947), 81st (1949–1951), and 82nd (1951–1953) Congresses. For most of his initial tenure in that office, he had extraordinary constitutional standing, in that there was a vacancy in the vice presidency following the death of President **Franklin D. Roosevelt** and the elevation of Vice President **Harry S. Truman**.

MCKINLEY, WILLIAM. Republican president, 1897–1901. (b. 29 January 1843; d. 14 September 1901). McKinley was elected to the **House of Representatives** from Ohio in 1876. He won reelection to three more terms, but his bid for the third was the subject of a successful postelection challenge by his **Democratic Party** opponent. He eventually surrendered his seat in May 1884 but won it back the following November. He served three additional terms before losing in 1890, an election in which the high-tariff policy he advocated proved unpopular. He returned home and successfully ran for governor the next year. His supporters promoted his candidacy for the 1892 presidential **nomination** of the **Republican Party**, but **incumbent** President **Benjamin Harrison** firmly controlled the party machinery. McKinley chaired the **convention**. Four years later, Governor McKinley was an easy first-ballot victor, the beneficiary of an astute preconvention campaign conducted by **Mark Hanna**. Hanna then directed the **front-porch campaign** that produced a comfortable fall victory over **William Jennings Bryan**. That **critical election** inaugurated the **Fourth Party System**, an era of Republican dominance.

During McKinley's first term, the Spanish–American War erupted. Following its successful conclusion, McKinley was joined on the 1900 Republican ticket by war hero **Theodore Roosevelt**. He won an easy reelection victory over his Democratic opponent, Alton B. Parker. Six months into his second term, McKinley was assassinated.

MCKINNEY, FRANK E. Democratic National Committee chair, 1951–1952. (b. 16 June 1904; d. 9 January 1974). McKinney rose through the ranks of state and local party politics in Indiana, where he also pursued banking interests. By the 1940s, he had become visible on the national stage as a successful party fund-raiser. In 1951, McKinney was the choice of President **Harry S. Truman** to become chair of the **Democratic National Committee**, replacing **William M. Boyle**. Sensitive to suggestions of financial impropriety and influence peddling that had bedeviled his predecessor, McKinney divested himself of his corporate connections during his tenure as chair. After Truman chose not to run for renomination in 1952, the **Democratic National Convention** named **Adlai E. Stevenson II**, who replaced McKinney with **Stephen A. Mitchell**. McKinney returned to Indianapolis and resumed his banking career.

MCLANE, ROBERT M. Democratic National Committee chair, 1852–1856. (b. 23 June 1815; d. 16 April 1898). Robert McLane was the son of Louis McLane, a prominent figure in Delaware and national politics, having held seats in the **House of Representatives**, the **Senate**, and the **cabinet** of President **Andrew Jackson**. Robert McLane won **election** to the House from Maryland in 1846 and served two terms. Shortly after leaving the House to practice law, he was named the second chair of the **Democratic National Committee**, replacing **Benjamin F. Hallet**. From his base adjacent to the nation's capital, McLane oversaw the presidential **election** of **Franklin Pierce**, who handed him some diplomatic assignments. After leaving the national party post, he received diplomatic appointments from Presidents **James Buchanan** and **Grover Cleveland**. He also remained active in the electoral arena, returning to the House for two more terms (1879–1883), and serving as governor of Delaware (1884–1885).

MCNARY, CHARLES L. Republican minority leader of the Senate, 1933–1944. (b. 12 June 1874; d. 25 February 1944). McNary held an interim appointment as a **senator** from Oregon (1917–1918). **Progressive** in domestic policy and isolationist in foreign affairs, he won **election** in his own right in 1918 and held his seat until his death. In 1933, with the **Republican Party** in the **minority** in the **Senate**, he was chosen to be **floor leader**. In 1940, the **Republican National Convention** nominated him to be the vice presidential **running mate** of **Wendell L. Willkie**. The **ticket** went down to defeat in November, and McNary continued as the minority leader in the Senate until his death.

ME TOO. A phrase suggesting the willingness of a candidate or party to embrace the agenda of another candidate or party, thus conveying a lack of originality and initiative. More specifically, in the **New Deal** era and for several years following, the **conservative** wing of the **Republican Party** criticized more **liberal** party colleagues for accepting the basic tenets of the New Deal. More recently, when President **Bill Clinton** sought to move the **Democratic Party** toward the center of the ideological spectrum, some disgruntled liberal Democrats characterized him as a "me too" Democrat who embraced the Republican policy agenda.

MEDIA. A term referring to the mass means of communication, embracing traditional print media, consisting of newspapers and magazines; modern electronic media, specifically television and radio; and the very contemporary online Internet media, adapted by the earlier institutions, but also including **web-logs**, or blogs. Like a **political party** or an **interest group**, a medium of communication is an intermediary institution in society, linking the public, or segments thereof, with the government. Media are important components of the environment within which political parties operate.

At the outset of the American party system, political parties established and supported newspapers, which could be expected to promote the **party line** while reliably criticizing opponents. Toward the end of the 19th century, a new journalistic norm of objectivity supplanted **partisanship**, effectively distancing the print media from political parties in the presentation of news, even as editorial stances continued to reflect sympathy or antagonism toward parties and their policy stances. The emergence of electronic media occurred in the wake of this development, and they similarly maintained separation from political parties, a commitment enhanced by the greater measure of governmental regulation they experienced, attributable to the limitations on bandwidths available for broadcasts. In the contemporary Internet age, political parties are reclaiming a place in the mass media, albeit in a much more limited, cluttered, and competitive setting than was the case when parties sponsored newspapers. In addition, parties can use contemporary technologies such as e-mail and text messages to communicate immediately and directly with the public.

Parties, **candidates**, and office-holders rely on the media to present their messages to the public, in both **campaign** and governing settings. There is a basic distinction between free media, which cover developments, and paid media, which receive payments to advertise messages. Paid electronic media are the major cause of the dramatic escalation of campaign expenses in recent decades.

The media play an agenda-setting role in American politics, and they also frame expectations regarding performance. This role is particularly pertinent to presidential selection. Prior to the presidential primaries, the media assess the anticipated strengths and weaknesses of the various aspirants. Throughout the campaign, candidates and their **campaign managers** seek to **spin** the media to embrace their assessments of the state of the contest. Below the presidential level, similar dynamics govern contests for lesser offices.

MEHLMAN, KEN. Republican National Committee chair, 2005–2007. (b. 21 August 1966). Mehlman served as a congressional staff assistant before joining the 2000 presidential **campaign** of **George W. Bush** as field director. After the **election** victory, he became the White House director of political affairs. He managed Bush's 2004 successful reelection campaign, and he became **national party chair** in its wake, succeeding **Ed Gillespie**. Throughout his service on Bush's behalf, he operated in the shadow of preeminent Bush campaign strategist Karl Rove. Mehlman is Jewish, the first of his faith to chair the RNC. Following the **Republican Party** losses in the 2006 midterm elections, Mehlman chose not to seek another term as chair. He was replaced by Senator **Mel Martinez** (FL) as **general chair** and **Robert M. Duncan** as chair.

MEMBER OF CONGRESS. A national legislator serving in either the **House of Representatives** or the **Senate**. The term is usually used to refer more specifically to the House. *See also* REPRESENTATIVE; SENATOR.

MERIT SYSTEM. A method for staffing the bureaucracy whereby positions are assigned on the basis of qualifications and expertise, as demonstrated in open, competitive examinations. In the United States, the merit system arose out of criticism of the traditional staffing method, **patronage**, also known as the **spoils system**. The merit system was instituted by the Pendleton Act of 1883, in response to long-standing concerns about government corruption and the recent assassination of President **James A. Garfield** by a disappointed office seeker. Initially, it covered only a small percentage of federal employees. Gradually it has grown to include well over 90 percent of government workers. The chief benefits derived from the merit system are technical proficiency of workers and equal opportunities of access. The major pathology is the lack of accountability and responsiveness to elected political leaders.

MICHEL, ROBERT. Republican minority leader of the House of Representatives, 1981–1995. (b. 2 March 1923). Michel won **election** to the **House of Representatives** from Illinois in 1956 and held that office for 19 terms. When **John J. Rhodes** of Arizona left office in 1981, creating a vacancy in the office of **floor leader** for the **minority** Republicans, the **Republican Conference** chose Michel as his replacement. Michel filled the position for seven terms. He decided not to seek reelection in 1994, when the **Republican Party** captured control of the House for the first time in four decades.

MIDTERM ELECTIONS. Elections held for seats in **Congress** in the middle of a four-year presidential term. The **Constitution** requires two-year terms for the members of the **House of Representatives**, six-year terms for the **Senate**, and a four-year presidential term. This means that all of the House and one-third of the Senate seats are up for **election** at midterm. From 1938 until 1998, the president's party always lost seats in the House in midterm elections. However, in both 1998 and 2002, the president's party made marginal gains. In 2006, the more customary pattern reasserted itself, with the **Republican Party**, led by President **George W. Bush**, losing its majorities in both congressional chambers.

MILLEDGE, JOHN. President pro tempore of the Senate, 1809. (b. 1757; d. 9 February 1818). Milledge served in the House of Representatives from Georgia on three separate occasions (1792–1793, 1795–1799, and 1801–1802). On leaving the House, he became governor for four years. In 1806, he began a short Senate career that lasted slightly more than three years. At the end of his tenure, during the second session of the 10th Congress, the Senate named him president pro tempore on one occasion.

MILLER, WILLIAM E. Republican National Committee chair, 1961–1964. (b. 22 March 1914; d. 24 June 1983). Miller served seven terms in the **House of Representatives** from his upstate New York district. In 1960, he chaired the **Republican Congressional Campaign Committee** in what proved to be a successful effort, as the **GOP** increased its representation in the chamber. The next year, the **Republican National Committee** chose him to replace Senator **Thruston B. Morton** of Kentucky as its **chair.** Miller proved to be a slashing **partisan** in attacking the candidates and policies of the opposition **Democratic Party.** In 1964, after the **Republican National Convention** nominated **Barry M. Goldwater** for **president,** Goldwater indicated that Miller was his choice for the vice presidential **nomination,** and the delegates gladly embraced the designation of the **party organization** leader. Goldwater said that he wanted Miller on the **ticket** because Miller "drives [**Lyndon**] **Johnson** nuts." Miller was the first Roman Catholic to win a spot on a Republican presidential ticket. The Republicans lost in a **landslide** in November, and Miller retired from party politics to his law practice in upstate New York.

MILTON, JOHN. Electoral vote recipient, 1789. (b. ca. 1740; d. ca. 1804). Milton was a Georgia public servant, holding office as that state's secretary of state at various times between 1778 and 1783. He received two **favorite son** votes from Georgians in the 1789 **electoral college** balloting.

MINOR PARTY. Also known as third party. A minor party is one that does not normally compete successfully in elections. Minor parties typically reflect and promote relatively narrow and specific issue positions and/or the personal ambitions of the party leader. In the United States, minor parties have often emerged to address issues that the major parties have avoided. In turn, any success they achieve in doing so usually encourages the major parties to co-opt their supporters.

In the United States, minor parties face formidable institutional obstacles in their efforts to gain electoral support and shape public policy. The prevailing **single-member district** electoral arrangement, with its **plurality, winner-take-all** features, benefits the two major parties at any given time against third-party challengers. The constitutional separation of powers establishes an indivisible executive office, undermining the credibility of minor-party efforts. **Nomination** by **primary** encourages a party **faction** to compete for electoral support within the party rather than to **bolt** and form another party.

In addition, socioeconomic, geographic, and cultural factors contribute to the persistent problems faced by minor parties in the United States. Many observers point to an abiding dualism in American society that takes alternative forms: rich versus poor, urban versus rural, north versus south, **liberal** versus **conservative**. This dualism manifests itself in two, and only two, major parties. In addition, minor parties are inhibited by a sweeping social consensus on fundamental political issues that is lacking in many, more divided, societies. This general agreement on the "rules of the game" facilitates compromise and accommodation both within and between the major parties, to the detriment of minor parties.

Despite the obstacles, minor parties have persistently emerged, though rarely endured, and played key roles in American politics at all levels, national, state, and local. Eight minor parties have carried at least one state in a presidential **election** and thus won votes in the **electoral college**: the **Anti-Masonic Party** (1832), the **American Party** (**Know-Nothings**) (1856), the **Constitutional Union Party** (1860), the **People's Party** (**Populist**) (1892), the **Progressive Party** (**Bull Moose**) (1912), the **Progressive Party** (1924), the **States' Rights Democratic Party** (**Dixiecrat**) (1948), and the **American Independent Party** (1968). *See also* MAJOR PARTY.

MINORITY. A number less than half of the votes cast or members making up an assembly. *See also* MAJORITY; PLURALITY.

MINORITY LEADER. The top congressional party leadership position in the political party that does not control the legislative chamber; the term is used in both the **House of Representatives** and the Senate. In each chamber, the party **caucus** chooses its leader. This individual is also known as the **floor leader**.

MINORITY PARTY. *See* PARTY-OUT-OF-POWER.

MISSOURI PLAN. A **nonpartisan** method for judicial selection, developed in Missouri and now used in several states. It provides for an initial judicial appointment by the governor from an array of qualified candidates recommended by an impartial nominating commission. After a period of incumbency, a judge must then receive popular consent to continue in office. The Missouri Plan was developed to insulate judges from **partisan** elections.

MITCHELL, GEORGE J. Democratic majority leader of the Senate, 1989–1995. (b. 20 August 1933). A protégé of **Edmund S. Muskie**, longtime **senator** from Maine and a powerful figure both on Capitol Hill and in Maine state politics, Mitchell entered the **Senate** in 1980 by appointment to finish the unexpired term of Muskie, who had resigned to become secretary of state. Mitchell held the seat two years later and won reelection to a second full term in 1988. As head of the **Democratic Senatorial Campaign Committee** in 1986, he was instrumental in the party's electoral successes that enabled it to regain **majority** control of the body after six years of **Republican Party** rule. Mitchell received favorable national coverage for his televised performance on the committee investigating the Iran-Contra controversy. Following the 1988 elections, when **Robert C. Byrd** stepped down as **majority leader**, Mitchell was the surprise choice of the **Democratic Conference** as the replacement. He served effectively in that role for six years, until his retirement from the Senate in 1994. In retirement, he has practiced law and been called on for special diplomatic assignments, most notably involving Northern Ireland.

MITCHELL, STEPHEN A. Democratic National Committee chair, 1952–1954. (b. 3 March 1903; d. 23 April 1974). Born in Iowa, Mitchell practiced law in Chicago, where his civic activity introduced him to **Adlai E. Stevenson II**. He became a key Stevenson supporter in state and national campaigns. In 1952, Mitchell was presidential nominee Stevenson's choice to **chair** the **Democratic National Committee**. Setting up shop at party headquarters in Washington, D.C., he maintained awkward liaisons with Stevenson's personal **campaign** organization in Springfield, Illinois, where Stevenson continued to serve as governor, and the White House, where

Democratic President **Harry S. Truman** remained in residence. After the fall campaign ended in defeat, Mitchell sought to promote Stevenson as the party's **titular leader**, positioning him to speak officially on the party's behalf. This effort met with resistance from the congressional party leadership: **Sam Rayburn** in the **House of Representatives** and **Lyndon B. Johnson** in the **Senate**. Mitchell resigned after the 1954 **midterm elections**, which saw the Democrats win majorities in both houses.

MODERN REPUBLICAN. A designation associated with the presidential party leadership efforts of **Dwight D. Eisenhower** to carve out a centrist identity for the **Republican Party**. Eisenhower sought to characterize his party's governing philosophy as **liberal** in human affairs and **conservative** in fiscal affairs.

MONDALE, WALTER F. Democratic presidential nominee, 1984. (b. 5 January 1928). Fritz Mondale was a Minnesota protégé of **Hubert H. Humphrey**. Highly visible in state politics as attorney general, he replaced Humphrey in the **Senate** in 1964 when Humphrey became **vice president**. In 1976, **Democratic Party** presidential nominee **Jimmy Carter** designated Mondale as his vice presidential choice, and the **ticket** prevailed in the fall **election**.

As vice president, Mondale was unusually visible and helped link Carter, an outsider and a centrist, to the Washington political community and to the party's **liberal** wing. In 1980, the Carter-Mondale ticket lost its reelection bid to Republicans **Ronald W. Reagan** and **George H. W. Bush**.

Once out of office, Mondale nominally practiced law, while laying the groundwork for a successful run for the presidential **nomination** of the 1984 **Democratic National Convention**. His vice presidential choice, **Geraldine Ferraro**, was the first woman to occupy a spot on the presidential **ticket** of a **major party**. Challenging Reagan's reelection bid, Mondale lost in a **landslide** and returned to private life. A party **elder statesman**, he was the choice of President **Bill Clinton** to become ambassador to Japan. He unexpectedly returned to the electoral arena in 2002 as the Minnesota state party nominee for the Senate seat that had been occupied by Paul Wellstone, following Wellstone's death in a plane crash late in the campaign. Mondale lost the election. In retirement in Minnesota, he remained visible in presidential party politics.

MONDELL, FRANKLIN. Republican majority leader of the House of Representatives, 1919–1923. (b. 6 November 1860; d. 6 August 1939). Initially elected to the **House of Representatives** from Wyoming in 1894, Mondell lost his bid for reelection, but he recovered his seat in 1898 and held it for 12 terms. During his last two terms, he was the **floor leader** of the Republican **majority**.

MONROE, JAMES. Democratic-Republican president, 1817–1825. (b. 28 April 1758; d. 4 July 1831). James Monroe was the last representative of the Virginia dynasty that dominated American politics during the early years of the Republic. Shortly after the new government got under way, Monroe went to the **Senate** (1790–1794). President **George Washington** sent him to France as minister (1794–1796). He returned home and won **election** as governor (1799–1802). He reentered diplomatic service under President **Thomas Jefferson** as minister to France (1803) and England (1803–1807). Monroe served another brief period as Virginia's governor (1811) before becoming secretary of state for President **James Madison** (1811–1817). He was the clear choice of the legislative **caucus** of the **Democratic-Republican Party** to succeed Madison. With the opposition **Federalist Party** in disarray, he won easily in 1816 and without opposition in 1824, presiding over the unique **Era of Good Feelings** in national politics, which featured no significant interparty competition. He retired from public life after two presidential terms.

MORGAN, EDWIN D. Republican National Committee chair, 1856–1864, 1872–1876. (b. 8 February 1811; d. 14 February 1883). A New York merchant and founding father of the **Republican Party**, Morgan served as the first **chair** of the **Republican National Committee** (1856–1864). In 1859, he became the governor, and in 1863 he entered the **Senate** for a single term. After leaving the Senate, he once again took on the challenge of chairing the national party (1872–1876). His initial tenure as national party chair established a record for longevity that no Republican has yet broken. Combining his tenures, his 12 years at the helm of the national party tie him for the record with Democrats **August Belmont** and **William H. Barnum**.

MORTON, LEVI P. Republican vice president, 1889–1993. (b. 16 May 1824; d. 16 May 1920). Morton was a successful Wall Street banker who provided generous financial support to the **Republican Party**. In 1878, he won **election** to a seat in the House from his affluent Manhattan district. Two years later, he was offered the vice presidential **nomination** by presidential nominee **James A. Garfield**. Morton declined, out of a sense of obligation to his state party **boss,** Senator Roscoe Conkling, who had opposed Garfield's nomination. Morton won reelection to the **House of Representatives** in 1880 and raised and contributed funds for the presidential **campaign**. His reward for the successful effort was a prestigious appointment as minister to France. He returned to the United States in 1885 in vain hopes of winning a seat in the **Senate**, an ambition that again eluded him in 1887.

In 1888, Morton again received an invitation to accept the vice presidential nomination, this time from presidential nominee **Benjamin Harrison**. Morton accepted, and the **ticket** won in the **electoral college** despite trailing in the popular vote. As **vice president**, Morton presided over the Senate in an impartial fashion. In doing so, he lost the support of influential Republicans, who demanded a more **partisan** leadership style, and he was not renominated in 1892.

Morton reentered the political arena in 1895, when he was elected governor of New York. He mounted a **favorite son** candidacy for the 1896 presidential nomination of the **Republican National Convention**, which went to **William McKinley**. Morton then retired to private life, where he expanded his vast financial holdings.

MORTON, ROGERS C. B. Republican National Committee chair, 1969–1971. (b. 19 September 1914; d. 19 April 1979). Morton belonged to a prominent Kentucky family; his brother, **Thruston B. Morton**, preceded him as national party **chair**. Elected to the **House of Representatives** from Maryland in 1962, he served four full terms and part of another. In 1969, President **Richard M. Nixon** designated him to replace **Ray C. Bliss** as the national party **chair**. He held the post for almost two years, serving primarily as a party spokesman, while the Nixon White House tightly controlled political operations. Shortly after the 1970 **midterm elections**, Nixon asked Morton to join his **cabinet** as secretary of the interior. Morton resigned both his congressional and party offices to do so.

After Nixon's resignation in 1974, Morton remained a member of the **administration** of the new president, **Gerald R. Ford.** In 1975, President Ford moved Morton from the Department of the Interior to the Department of Commerce. At the latter, he played a key role in the **campaign** organization set up on behalf of Ford's successful bid for presidential **nomination** of the **Republican National Convention.** In 1976, he resigned his position in the administration to assume a full-time campaign role. When the Ford campaign went down to defeat in November, Morton, in failing health, left the political arena.

MORTON, THRUSTON B. Republican National Committee chair, 1959–1961. (b. 19 August 1907; d. 14 August 1982). Thruston Morton was the scion of a prominent Kentucky family. Elected to the **House of Representatives** in 1946, he served three terms. He joined the **administration** of President **Dwight D. Eisenhower** in 1953, working on congressional relations in the State Department. In 1956, he successfully sought a **Senate** seat. In 1959, Eisenhower tapped Morton to replace the retiring **H. Meade Alcorn Jr.** as **chair** of the **Republican National Committee.** At the **Republican National Convention** the next year, **Richard M. Nixon,** the presidential nominee, seriously considered designating Senator Morton as his vice presidential choice but opted instead for **Henry Cabot Lodge Jr.** During the **campaign,** Morton was a key figure on the campaign trail, but as party chair he was not a central campaign organization decision maker. He resigned the position of chair in 1961, in anticipation of his reelection bid for the Senate. In 1964, Morton took on the responsibility of chairing the **Republican Senatorial Campaign Committee.** He did not seek reelection in 1968, instead retiring from public life.

MOSES, GEORGE H. Republican president pro tempore of the Senate, 1925–1933. (b. 9 February 1869; d. 20 December 1944). Moses went to the **Senate** from New Hampshire in 1918, finishing an unexpired term. He went on to win two full terms on his own. He had an extended period of service as **president pro tempore** (1925–1933), which ended when he left the Senate in the wake of an **election** in which the **Republican Party** lost its long-standing **majority**.

MOUNTAIN REPUBLICAN. A characterization of minority Republicans in the traditionally Democratic South, because they typically resided in the mountainous regions of such states as Tennessee, North Carolina, Alabama, and Arkansas, where the institution of slavery never took hold. Mountain Republicans occasionally constituted a regional **majority**, enabling them to select members of the **House of Representatives**, but they routinely met with defeat in statewide competition. The regional **realignment** that brought the **Republican Party** to power in the South typically reduced the standing of the mountain Republicans within the party, in favor of residents in the fast-growing suburbs.

MUGWUMPS. A **faction** of the **Republican Party** that supported the presidential candidacy of Democrat **Grover Cleveland** in 1884. Ideologically **progressive**, the Mugwumps bolted from their party rather than endorse presidential nominee **James G. Blaine**, whom they considered corrupt. As a party faction, they were the lineal descendants of the Liberal Republicans who had opposed the presidential renomination and reelection of **Ulysses S. Grant** in 1872. "Mugwump" is an Indian word for "chief." It came to be identified more broadly with both party bolters and political independents.

MUHLENBERG, FREDERICK A. C. Speaker of the House of Representatives, 1789–1791, 1793–1795. (b. 1 January 1750; d. 5 June 1801). Muhlenberg was a leading figure in Pennsylvania and national politics during the founding era. He served briefly in the Continental Congress (1779–1780). When the new government was established, he won election to the **House of Representatives**, and held his seat for four terms. The inaugural House elected him **Speaker**, and he was chosen again for the 3rd Congress. His initial service as Speaker predated the emergence of parties. By his second tour of duty, however, parties were a fact of life in the chamber. Nevertheless, he maintained a **nonpartisan** stance.

MULTIMEMBER DISTRICT. A district that elects several representatives to the legislature on the basis of **proportional representation**, whereby a political party receives representation proportionate to its demonstrated electoral support. Multimember districts are relatively rare in the United States, being restricted to a few states and municipalities. *See also* SINGLE-MEMBER DISTRICT.

MULTIPARTY SYSTEM. A system featuring many parties realistically competing for public offices. A multiparty system limits the prospects for a single party to win a **majority** of legislative seats, necessitating the formation of a **coalition** government. Many observers view such **bipartisan** governments as less stable than those featuring a majority party. In the contemporary world, France, Italy, and Japan are examples of multiparty systems. A country's electoral system can contribute to the nature of the **party system**, and vice versa. *See also* SINGLE-PARTY SYSTEM; TWO-PARTY SYSTEM.

MULTIPLE PARTISANSHIP. A capacity of voters in the American federal system to identify with one party at one level of competition and governance and another at a separate level. Currently, this tendency is most pronounced in the South, where traditional **Democratic Party** loyalties persist at the state and local levels alongside growing **Republican Party** identification at the national level. *See also* TICKET-SPLITTER.

MUSKIE, EDMUND S. Democratic vice presidential nominee, 1968. (b. 28 March 1914; d. 26 March 1996). Muskie was elected governor of Maine in 1954. Four years later, he ran for a seat in the U.S. **Senate**, where he served until 1980. In 1968, Muskie received the vice presidential **nomination** of the **Democratic National Convention** as the **running mate** of Vice President **Hubert H. Humphrey**. Muskie's impressive showing in a losing effort positioned him as the **front-runner** for the 1972 presidential nomination. His **campaign** faltered, and that nomination went to Senator **George S. McGovern**. Muskie remained in the Senate, where his seniority and stature made him a formidable figure. In 1980, President **Jimmy Carter** prevailed on Muskie to join his administration as secretary of state. After Carter lost his reelection bid that fall, Muskie retired from public life.

– N –

NATIONAL DEMOCRATIC PARTY. The National Democrats were a faction of the **Democratic Party** in the late 19th century, **conservative** in their **ideology** and committed to the maintenance of the gold standard. For this reason, these hard money advocates were also known as Gold Democrats. Disenchanted by the party's 1896 decision to nominate **William Jennings Bryan** and embrace a free silver platform, the National Democrats were disinclined to affiliate with the **Republican Party**, similarly committed to the gold standard, because of differences over the **tariff** issue. The Republicans were avowedly protectionist, offending the free-trade National Democrats.

Thus, the National Democrats perceived no alternative but to put forward their own presidential nominee, Senator John M. Palmer (Illinois). Palmer received the support of outgoing Democratic President **Grover Cleveland**, along with many members of his administration. The National Democrats received only 1 percent of the popular vote, because many conservative Democrats obviously chose to support the Republican nominee, **William McKinley**, who won comfortably over Bryan and the Democrats.

The party split proved short lived, and the National Democrats rejoined the Democratic Party. However, the equilibrium between the major parties that had previously characterized the **Third Party System** had now shifted convincingly toward the Republicans with the advent of the Fourth Party System.

NATIONAL REPUBLICAN PARTY. A short-lived party label arising from a **faction** that developed within the **Democratic-Republican Party**. When the Democratic-Republican **coalition** splintered irrevocably in 1824, the National Republicans emerged as a wing of the party supportive of the person and principles of President **John Quincy Adams** and opposed to those of **Andrew Jackson** and the Democrats. As their name suggested, the National Republicans were strong nationalists. They supported the Bank of the United States, a protective **tariff,** and nationally sponsored internal improvements. They unsuccessfully contested the next two presidential elections, as first Adams and then **Henry Clay** lost to Jackson and the Democratic

Party. By 1836, the National Republicans had reconstituted themselves in more enduring fashion as the **Whig Party**.

NATIONAL STATESMAN PARTY. The label adopted by the **Prohibition Party** for the 1980 presidential election. After the election, the party reverted to its traditional label.

NATIONAL UNION PARTY. *See* UNION PARTY.

NATIONAL UNITY CAMPAIGN. The **campaign** vehicle for the **independent** presidential bid in 1980 of Illinois Representative **John B. Anderson.** Earlier that year, Anderson had competed unsuccessfully for the presidential **nomination** of the **Republican Party**. When it became clear that he would not prevail and that the **Republican National Convention** would nominate **Ronald W. Reagan,** considered by Anderson to be a **right-wing** extremist, Anderson decided to mount an independent presidential candidacy. Positioned at the center of the ideological spectrum, he advocated policies that were economically **conservative** and socially **liberal**. He won more than 6 percent of the presidential vote that year, qualifying for federal campaign funding and reserving a position on presidential ballots. Anderson gave up his seat in the House of Representatives to make the presidential bid. Over the next four years, Anderson labored to establish his campaign organization as a partisan institution, the National Unity Party. However, he decided not to contest the 1984 presidential election and endorsed the ticket nominated by the **Democratic Party**. The National Unity Party disappeared from the national scene.

NATURAL LAW PARTY. A noteworthy contemporary **minor party**. The Natural Law Party was founded in 1992. It stood for prevention-oriented government, conflict-free politics, and proven solutions designed to bring national politics into harmony with natural law. In 1996, the party fielded candidates in more than 400 races in 48 states, including the presidential contest, winning over 2.5 million votes. From this peak, it lost support, and it formally disbanded in 2004, with many of its adherents shifting their allegiance to a new entity, the United States Peace Government.

NEOCONSERVATIVE. A contemporary ideological label, sometimes abbreviated to "neocon," that describes a **faction** within the **Republican Party**. This faction emerged in the late 1960s. It was initially relatively centrist and reflected the intellectual perspectives of a group of disenchanted liberals associated with the publication *Public Interest*. This founding generation of neoconservatives was more willing to accept the legitimacy of governmental activism than their more libertarian colleagues within the conservative movement. However, they contended that the liberalism of the **Great Society** advanced the frontiers of government activism too far. By the turn of the 21st century, the term was being more typically applied to those advocates of an aggressive, interventionist foreign policy committed to the establishment of democratic ideals and values internationally. As such, the term has lost much of its original centrist connotations. *See also* CONSERVATIVE; LIBERAL; NEOLIBERAL.

NEOLIBERAL. A contemporary ideological label that describes a **faction** within the **Democratic Party**. This faction, like its original **neoconservative** counterpart, is relatively centrist. Neoliberals are less committed to activism by the national government than are mainstream liberals. They embrace the free market in the economic arena. Neoliberals emerged on the political scene in the last quarter of the 20th century. *See also* CONSERVATIVE; LIBERAL.

NETROOTS. A contemporary term referring to supporters of a candidate, party, or cause who are organized and mobilized for political action through the Internet, netroots are a 21st-century phenomenon. The netroots are a modern, technologically sophisticated expression of **grassroots** support (the neologism joins "Internet" and "grassroots"). One mechanism through which information is passed along is the **web-log**, or blog. To date, they have been more influential in the **Democratic Party** than in the **Republican Party**. In the former, the **liberal** wing of the party is much better represented in the netroots.

NEW, HARRY S. Republican National Committee chair, 1907–1908. (b. 31 December 1858; d. 9 May 1937). Harry New was the publisher of the *Indianapolis Journal* and served on the **Republican National**

Committee from Indiana. In 1907, with Republican **Theodore Roosevelt** occupying the White House, New became **chair** of the national **committee**, serving only one year. In 1916, he was elected to the **Senate** for a single term. On leaving that office in 1923, he became **postmaster general** for President **Warren G. Harding**. Both President **Calvin Coolidge** and President **Herbert C. Hoover** retained him in that role, which was traditionally reserved for a prominent party politician. He retired from public life following Hoover's reelection defeat in 1932.

NEW DEAL. The label used by **Franklin D. Roosevelt** in seeking electoral support for his 1932 presidential **campaign** and the program he put forward following his election. Responding to the crisis of the **Great Depression,** the New Deal constituted unprecedented activism by the national government in addressing the economic and social problems facing the country.

Roosevelt's initial efforts were wide ranging and experimental. In a historic 100 days following his inauguration, he secured congressional support for efforts to foster economic recovery that embraced direct relief assistance, national planning, and heightened federal government regulation. Much of this legislation was struck down by the Supreme Court in the next few years. Beginning in 1935, the New Deal entered a second phase, in which more enduring institutions emerged, with Social Security preeminent among them. As a result, the role of the national government in promoting and providing welfare expanded dramatically.

Politically, the coming of the New Deal coincided with the realigning election of 1932 that elevated the **Democratic Party** to **majority** status in the **Fifth Party System**. Its policies proved enormously attractive to voters, who rewarded its **partisan** sponsors with their electoral support. As a result, the **Republican Party** generally came to accept the New Deal's legitimacy. The New Deal set the stage for a subsequent wave of reforms known as the **Great Society**.

NEW FREEDOM. The slogan employed by **Woodrow Wilson** in his 1912 presidential **campaign** to characterize his agenda of domestic initiatives. The New Freedom reflected **Progressive Era** ideals. Generally, it embraced the cause of government intervention on behalf of imperiled small-business interests at a time of unprecedented concentration of economic power.

NEW FRONTIER. The rhetorical slogan associated with the 1960 presidential **campaign** and subsequent **administration** of **John F. Kennedy**. It aroused expectations of advancement in a climate of uncertainty. It also resonated with the frontier image in American popular culture at the dawn of the age of space exploration.

NEW NATIONALISM. The slogan used by President **Theodore Roosevelt** to describe his **progressive** agenda for the Republican Party. Influenced by journalist Herbert Croly, Roosevelt promoted the values of nationalism over sectionalism and held a stewardship conception of executive power. The slogan is most clearly associated with Roosevelt's 1912 unsuccessful **campaign** to win the Republican presidential **nomination** away from President **William Howard Taft**. After failing to deny Taft the nomination, Roosevelt mounted a **minor party** effort, officially under the label of the **Progressive Party**, but popularly known as the Bull Moose Party.

NEW POLITICS. A phrase that became popular in the late 1960s to characterize a new political style associated with the insurgent presidential campaigns of Eugene McCarthy in 1968 and **George S. McGovern** in 1972. The New Politics style emphasized participatory values and ideological commitment and was therefore associated more with party **amateurs** than **professionals**.

NICHOLSON, JAMES. Republican National Committee chair, 1997–2001. (b. 4 February 1938). Jim Nicholson is an Iowa native who relocated to Colorado after attending West Point and serving in the army. He pursued a career as a home builder and real estate developer while becoming active in state party politics. He was elected to the **Republican National Committee** in 1988, where he took on a variety of responsibilities pertaining to party rules, budgeting, and scheduling **convention** delegate selection contests. In 1997, he sought the position of national party chair, prevailing in a heated contest that took several ballots to resolve. Two years later, he was reelected, despite the party's unexpectedly poor showing in the 1998 **midterm elections**. He oversaw the national party effort in 2000 that resulted in regaining the presidency and maintaining control of the **Congress**. Nicholson joined the **administration** of **George W. Bush** in 2001 as ambassador to the Vatican. In 2005, he entered the **cabinet** as secretary of veterans affairs, where he served until 2007.

NIXON, RICHARD M. Republican vice president, 1953–1961; Republican president, 1969–1974. (b. 9 January 9 1913; d. 22 April 1994). Richard Nixon left his law practice in Southern California during World War II, first to work in Washington for the Office of Price Administration and then for active duty in the navy in the South Pacific. He returned from the war to win a **House of Representatives** seat in 1946. Reelected in 1948, he won a statewide **campaign** for the U.S. **Senate** in 1950. Two years later, General **Dwight D. Eisenhower** chose Nixon to accompany him on the presidential **ticket** of the **Republican Party**. Nixon served two terms as **vice president** and then won his party's 1960 presidential **nomination**. He lost narrowly to **Democratic Party** nominee **John F. Kennedy**.

Returning to California, Nixon ran for governor in 1962 but lost in the **general election**. His political career apparently at an end, he moved to New York to practice law, but he remained politically active, particularly in supporting Republican candidates for **Congress**. In 1968, he again entered the presidential picture, winning the Republican nomination over rivals **Nelson A. Rockefeller** and **Ronald W. Reagan**. In the fall **election**, he faced Democrat **Hubert H. Humphrey** and **American Independent Party** nominee **George C. Wallace**. Nixon prevailed, with a popular vote **plurality** and a **majority** in the **electoral college**.

Foreign policy concerns were paramount for President Nixon. He sought to wind down the Vietnam War, ease Cold War tensions with the Soviet Union, and establish diplomatic relations with the People's Republic of China. On the domestic political front, he pursued a **Southern strategy** to bring Wallace's supporters into the Republican Party, and he governed as a centrist.

In 1972, Nixon won a **landslide** reelection victory over antiwar Democrat **George S. McGovern**. However, the **Watergate** scandals associated with his reelection effort resulted in the collapse of his political support. Facing impeachment and likely conviction and removal from office, he resigned the presidency on August 8, 1974. His successor, **Gerald R. Ford**, soon afterward issued a controversial pardon to Nixon, freeing him from criminal charges.

Throughout his two decades in retirement, Nixon labored with some success to restore his political reputation, focusing on his foreign policy accomplishments and his insights as a political strategist. Since his death in 1994, however, the Watergate scandals have continued to dominate assessments of his presidency.

NOMINATION. The act of putting forward a candidate for appointment or **election** to public office. In the electoral arena, nomination is done explicitly under the banner of a **political party**. The candidate receiving a party nomination becomes its nominee. Nomination is a key **party function**. It most clearly distinguishes parties from other political organizations, notably **interest groups**. Historically, parties have developed a variety of institutions to nominate candidates: **caucus**, **convention**, and **primary**. Each institution empowers a different component of the **party structure: party-in-office**, **party organization**, and **party-in-the-electorate**, respectively.

NOMINEE. *See* NOMINATION.

NONPARTISAN. A stance that disregards considerations of party politics. In the United States, many local offices and some judicial offices are filled in nonpartisan elections. *See also* BIPARTISAN; PARTISAN.

NONPARTISAN PRIMARY. *See* BLANKET PRIMARY.

NOVEMBER REPUBLICANS. A phrase traditionally used to describe voters who participate in the **primary** of the **Democratic Party** despite their intention to vote for **Republican Party** nominees in the **general election**. The phrase originated in Texas, but it quickly came to have broader application throughout the South. Today, the once dominant Democratic Party in the South has lost support in national and even statewide contests, but it remains strong at the local level in numerous locales. Thus, voters who wish to participate in

choosing local nominees remain disposed to vote in the Democratic primary. *See also* MULTIPLE PARTISANSHIP.

– O –

OBAMA, BARACK H. Democratic president, 2009– . (b. 4 August 1961). Barack Obama was born in Honolulu, Hawaii, to biracial parents. His father, for whom he was named, was an international student from Kenya, and his mother was a Kansas native whose family had relocated to the 50th state. After his parents divorced, his mother married an Indonesian national, and Obama spent part of his childhood in Jakarta. He returned to Hawaii at age 10 and lived with his maternal grandparents until he graduated from high school. He initially attended Occidental College in Los Angeles, transferring to Columbia University in New York City, where he received his undergraduate degree. After a brief interlude as a community organizer in Chicago, he went on to Harvard Law School, where he distinguished himself as an editor and then president of the *Law Review*. After graduating, he returned to Chicago, where he joined the law school faculty of the University of Chicago and published an acclaimed memoir. He also practiced law and was engaged in community development.

In 1996, he was elected to the state senate, winning reelection in 1998 and 2002. He ran an unsuccessful **campaign** for a seat in the U.S. **House of Representatives** in 2000. In 2004, he won **election** to the U.S. **Senate**, and his campaign gained national exposure when he delivered the **keynote** address at the **Democratic National Convention**.

As a junior senator, Obama maintained an extraordinarily high profile, attributable to his compelling biography and his outspoken opposition to the Iraq War. He entered the race for the 2008 presidential **nomination** of the **Democratic Party** as a decided underdog, but early on he demonstrated an outstanding capacity to raise funds, and his antiwar stance generated enthusiasm from party activists. His main rival was Senator Hillary Clinton (New York), the spouse of former president **Bill Clinton**, who was the favorite of the party establishment. Obama's decisive victory in the Iowa caucus elevated

him above Clinton as the **front-runner**. The two battled through a lengthy series of primaries and caucuses, with Obama narrowly prevailing in these contests and securing the necessary support of **superdelegates** as well.

In the **general election**, Obama faced **Republican Party** nominee **John S. McCain III**. Obama won a comfortable popular vote victory, garnering 53 percent of the vote, the largest percentage won by a Democratic nominee since the 1964 landslide of **Lyndon B. Johnson**.

O'BRIEN, LAWRENCE F. Democratic National Committee chair, 1968–1969, 1970–1972. (b. 7 July 1917; d. 28 September 1990). O'Brien got his start in Massachusetts party politics in the 1940s. He quickly gravitated into the camp of the rising star of state politics, **John F. Kennedy**, playing key organizational roles in Kennedy's successful **Senate** races in 1952 and 1958. He moved with Kennedy onto the national stage in 1960, serving as a top deputy to **campaign** manager Robert Kennedy in the successful **nomination** and **general election** efforts. After the election, O'Brien joined the Kennedy White House staff, heading up the congressional relations office and addressing **patronage** issues.

After Kennedy's assassination, O'Brien stayed in the White House to work for the new **president, Lyndon B. Johnson**, in a successful effort to get the **Great Society** legislation through **Congress** as a tribute to Kennedy. As compensation for his effective work, Johnson made O'Brien **postmaster general** in 1965, the traditional reward for the party politician in the cabinet.

In 1968, when Robert Kennedy challenged Johnson for the presidential nomination of the **Democratic Party**, O'Brien left the **administration** and went to work for Kennedy, reprising the campaign role he had played for John Kennedy. After Robert Kennedy's assassination, O'Brien ended up supporting the candidacy of **Hubert H. Humphrey**. When Humphrey won the nomination, he named O'Brien to **chair** the Democratic National Committee, replacing John M. Bailey. The disappointing loss in November briefly removed O'Brien from the arena of party politics, as he surrendered the position of chair to Senator **Fred R. Harris**. O'Brien soon returned to the helm of the national party in 1970 for a second tour of duty.

O'Brien backed the reform movement then under way at the behest of the **McGovern–Fraser Commission**, which transformed delegate selection procedures for the national **convention**. In June 1972, his office at party headquarters was the target of a burglary undertaken by agents of **CREEP**, the personal reelection campaign organization of President **Richard M. Nixon**, precipitating the **Watergate** scandals. After the Democratic National Convention nominated **George S. McGovern**, O'Brien turned over the reins of national party leadership to **Jean Westwood**, McGovern's choice to succeed him, and retired from public life.

OFFICE-BLOC BALLOT. A ballot form grouping candidates competing for a specific office in a general election. Although it lists party affiliations, the office-bloc arrangement, unlike its **party-column ballot** counterpart, does not provide the voter with a readily ascertainable list of party nominees for all offices from the top to the bottom of the ballot. As such, it discourages **straight-ticket** voting in favor of the split-**ticket** alternative.

The office-bloc arrangement was developed in Massachusetts when that state introduced the **Australian ballot** in 1888. A slight minority of states currently make use of the office-bloc arrangement.

OLD GUARD. An enduring **faction** in the **Republican Party** that appeared on the scene around the turn of the 20th century. Originally centered in the Midwest, the old guard was steadfastly **conservative** in both **ideology** and adherence to tradition. It resisted the temptation to embrace **liberal** or **progressive** policies and candidates put forward by the rival **Eastern establishment**.

OLD HICKORY. A nickname given to General **Andrew Jackson** by an admiring soldier who served under him and judged him to be "tough as a hickory nut." The nickname carried over to Jackson's political campaigns.

OLD ROUGH-AND-READY. A nickname given to General **Zachary Taylor** during the Mexican War. It was widely used in Taylor's subsequent 1848 presidential **campaign**.

O'NEILL, THOMAS P. "TIP." Democratic majority leader of the House of Representatives, 1973–1977; Democratic Speaker of the House of Representatives, 1977–1987. (b. 9 December 1912; d. 5 January 1994). Tip O'Neill was a Massachusetts state legislator when he ran for the **House of Representatives** seat being vacated by **John F. Kennedy** in 1952, when Kennedy challenged **Henry Cabot Lodge Jr.** for his **Senate** seat. O'Neill won the **safe seat** and held it until his retirement in 1987. His close association with **John P. McCormack** gave him an entree to the party leadership. Early on, he obtained a coveted seat on the powerful Rules Committee; and in 1971, when McCormack retired, O'Neill became **whip** for the **majority** Democrats. Two years later, following the death of **Hale Boggs**, O'Neill moved up the leadership ladder to **majority leader**. In 1977, upon the retirement of **Carl Albert**, he won the speakership. He held it for a decade, attracting considerable national attention as party spokesman during the early 1980s, when the opposition **Republican Party** controlled both the White House and the Senate. He did not seek reelection in 1986, retiring to his native Massachusetts.

ONE-PARTY SYSTEM. *See* SINGLE-PARTY SYSTEM.

OPEN CONVENTION. A convention that assembles with no **candidate** having secured sufficient delegate support for **nomination**. Open conventions were commonplace at the national party level from the inception of the nominating **convention** in the 1830s until midway through the 20th century. State party leaders served as **brokers** in negotiating an agreement on a nominee. More recently, with the expansion of **presidential primaries**, the identity of the presidential nominee has become known well in advance of the convention.

OPEN PRIMARY. A **primary** that does not require voters to be affiliated with a specific party. About a dozen states currently make use of open primaries. Proponents of strong parties contend that open primaries are destructive, because they allow **independent** and crossover voters undue influence in the determination of the party's nominees. *See also* BLANKET PRIMARY; CLOSED PRIMARY.

ORR, JAMES L. Democratic Speaker of the House of Representatives, 1857–1859. (b. 12 May 1822; d. 5 May 1873). Orr was elected to the **House of Representatives** from South Carolina in 1848. He was chosen **Speaker** of the 35th Congress, his last. After the **Civil War**, he became the Republican governor of his state (1865–1868).

OUT-PARTY. *See* PARTY-OUT-OF-POWER.

– P –

PACKING THE GALLERIES. A tactic employed at a party **convention**, whereby a candidate's vocal supporters are seated in the convention hall, and opposition supporters are denied seats, in hopes of influencing the decision of the convention delegates.

PALIN, SARAH. Republican vice presidential nominee, 2008. (b. 11 February 1964). Born in Idaho, Palin's family moved to Alaska in her infancy. She grew up in the small town of Wasilla. She briefly pursued a career in sports reporting before entering politics in 1992 as a successful candidate for the Wasilla city council. She went on to serve as mayor, and ran second in the **Republican Party** primary for lieutenant-governor in 2002. She then received a gubernatorial appointment to the Alaska Oil and Gas Conservation Commission, resigning after a year in office. In 2006, she defeated the **incumbent** governor in the Republican **primary** and went on to defeat a former governor in the **general election**, becoming both the first female and the youngest governor of Alaska.

In 2008, Republican presidential nominee **John S. McCain III** surprisingly chose her to be his **running mate**, a decision enthusiastically endorsed by the **Republican National Convention**. She excited and energized the **rank-and-file** base, who appreciated her strong social conservatism and her combative campaign style, but McCain's expectation that she would appeal to disaffected Democrats, particularly women, did not come to pass. Nevertheless, her performance elevated her stature within the party, and she is now viewed as a likely contender for a future presidential **nomination**.

PARTISAN. A pattern of attitude and behavior characterized by intense **party loyalty** and opposition to those who do not share that loyalty; also one who conforms to this pattern. *See also* BIPARTISAN; NONPARTISAN.

PARTY BASE. *See* RANK AND FILE.

PARTY-COLUMN BALLOT. A **ballot** form that aligns all of the **political party** nominees in a single column on the ballot, with national-level offices at the top and local ones at the bottom. This ballot form originated in Indiana in 1889. As opposed to its **office-bloc ballot** counterpart, a party-column ballot encourages **straight-ticket** voting behavior.

PARTY ELDER. *See* ELDER STATESMAN.

PARTY FAITHFUL. *See* RANK AND FILE.

PARTY FUNCTIONS. Tasks performed by a political party. Gabriel Almond pioneered functional analysis in political science. He identified several functions performed by political systems: political socialization, political recruitment, interest articulation, interest aggregation, political communication, rule making, rule application, and rule adjudication. Political parties can and do perform all of these. This array can be compressed into three clusters of party activity: electing, propagandizing, and governing.

PARTY IDENTIFICATION. The inclination or tendency of voters to develop an enduring attachment to a **political party**. This attachment is primarily psychological. It requires neither legal recognition, evidence of formal membership, nor even a consistent record of party support. This concept was developed by the authors of *The American Voter* (1960) and became the foundation for subsequent scholarship on electoral behavior.

PARTY-IN-GOVERNMENT. *See* PARTY-IN-OFFICE.

PARTY-IN-OFFICE. Also known as party-in-government. This is an analytical element of **party structure**. It embraces the officials who occupy public office under the banner and sponsorship of a **political party**. This category includes not only elected officials but also appointees who are identified with the party. *See also* PARTY-IN-THE-ELECTORATE; PARTY ORGANIZATION.

PARTY-IN-POWER. Also known as the in-party, or the **majority party**. It refers to the **political party** that controls a branch of government or a legislative chamber. In the executive branch, it is the party of the chief executive. In the legislature, it is the party with the **majority** in a given chamber. *See also* PARTY-OUT-OF-POWER.

PARTY-IN-THE-ELECTORATE. An analytical element of **party structure**. It consists of those members of the electorate (voters) who, with varying degrees of commitment and intensity, support the policies and candidates of a **political party**. The vote is the primary demonstration of such support. *See also* PARTY-IN-OFFICE; PARTY ORGANIZATION.

PARTY LINE. The authoritative position taken by the party leadership and/or **party organization** on an issue. A party platform provides a basic statement of issue positions. In a somewhat different sense, the plural, "party lines," refers to the issue and ideological boundaries separating the parties.

PARTY LOYALTY. A commitment to support the candidates and policies of one's **political party**, even when cross-pressures pull in a different direction.

PARTY OF THE PEOPLE. A slogan regularly employed by the **Democratic Party** over the years to characterize itself and to distinguish it from its opposition. It reflects the long-standing perception that the Democrats are the party of the masses, as opposed to elites.

PARTY ORGANIZATION. An analytical element of **party structure**. It refers to the machinery of the party: the formal network of

conventions, committees, and headquarters that are loosely linked at the national, state, and local levels. In the United States, party organization has been relatively weak and decentralized, compared with other Western industrial democracies. In part, this is due to the federal structure of the government. It also reflects the absence of a **mass party** tradition here. Party organization once tended to be strongest in the United States at the local level, in the form of urban political **machines** like **Tammany Hall**. The rise of civil service and the welfare state undermined local party organizations. By the mid-20th century, party organizations at all levels found their traditional control over campaigns being challenged by emerging candidate-centered entities. However, the latter decades of the 20th century saw an enhancement of national party organization power, as both major parties embraced the **service party** model. Party organizations rely heavily on volunteers supervised by relatively small numbers of full-time, paid workers. Typically, the ranks of the party organization swell during campaigns and shrink in their aftermath. *See also* PARTY-IN-OFFICE, PARTY-IN-THE-ELECTORATE.

PARTY-OUT-OF-POWER. Also known as out-party, or **minority party**. In a **two-party system**, it does not control a particular branch of government or legislative chamber. *See also* PARTY-IN-POWER.

PARTY PLATFORM. An official statement of the **party line**, or party position, on public policy issues, domestic and foreign, such as **abortion**, **civil rights**, and trade. Typically, a party platform is put forward by a party **convention**. At the presidential level, modern party platforms typically are in general accord with the perspectives of the party nominee. This was not always the case when **open conventions** took several ballots to determine their nominees. However, contemporary party platforms continue to reflect tensions within the party **coalition**, sometimes resulting in a triumph of one **faction** over another, or perhaps a compromise. **Interest groups** pressure the platform drafters to embrace their policy perspectives. The party platform usually emphasizes fundamental differences with other parties. **Party responsibility** entails a willingness and ability by the **party-in-office** in the **majority party** to use its governmental power

to translate the party platform into public policy, but structural and cultural obstacles to party responsibility limit the likelihood that the party platform will constitute a governing agenda.

PARTY RESPONSIBILITY. Also known as responsible party government, it is a norm prescribed by many political scientists pertaining to the role political parties should play in the conduct of government. Responsible parties manifest the following interrelated features. First, they develop coherent and cohesive platforms, statements of party positions on issues reflecting underlying ideological principles. Second, they nominate candidates committed to the realization of these policy positions. In a **general election**, voters confront competing party visions for public policy and authorize one by majority vote. That **party-in-office** exercises discipline within its ranks and enacts and implements the **party platform** as public policy.

Adherents of party responsibility contend that it maximizes citizen control over public policymaking by holding officeholders accountable for their promises. It expects officeholders to perceive the relationship between themselves and their constituents primarily in **partisan** terms. That is, representatives should subordinate personal perceptions of conscience and constituent interest to the expectations and demands of party leaders, on the grounds that the **majority** of voters expressed their commitment to that party in the previous elections. This model received its most significant expression in a 1950 report of the Committee on Political Parties of the American Political Science Association. Detractors assert that by promoting polarization, it would intensify conflict within the political order. Further, it would make that the system more vulnerable to majority tyranny.

The American political system presents several noteworthy obstacles to the realization of the party responsibility model. One is constitutional. The principles of separation of powers and federalism both establish impediments. Separation of powers makes possible **divided party government**, which renders responsible party government impossible. Federalism decentralizes party nominations, undermining the prospects for shared values among party nominees. Staggered elections mean that not all elected officeholders face the electorate at the same time. The American political culture also promotes values that impede party responsibility. First, it embraces an

antiparty ethos. Second, it promotes an individualism that is at odds with the expectations of party responsibility. Nevertheless, enhanced ideological cohesion within the major parties, along with increasing polarization between them, has heightened party responsibility in the United States in recent years.

PARTY STRUCTURE. The configuration of elements constituting a **political party** or, more broadly, a **party system**. Analytically, the elements of a political party include **party-in-office, party organization**, and **party-in-the-electorate**. Party systems are typically categorized with reference to the number of parties competing in the electoral arena. This approach differentiates a one-party system, a **two-party system**, and a **multiparty system**.

PARTY SYMBOL. *See* BULL MOOSE; DONKEY; ELEPHANT.

PARTY SYSTEM. An enduring pattern of competitive interaction with regard to the political parties in a political order. Party systems are typically differentiated with respect to the number of parties competing in that setting. This approach gives rise to a threefold categorization: one-party system, **two-party system**, and **multiparty system**.

Fundamental changes in the pattern of interaction and/or the setting produce a new party system. In American politics, a two-party system has consistently prevailed. There have been at least five distinctive historical eras of party competition. The **First Party System**, originating in the 1790s, pitted the **Democratic-Republican Party**, led by **Thomas Jefferson**, against **Alexander Hamilton** and his **Federalist Party**. After the **critical election** of 1800, the Democratic-Republicans came to dominate this system. The Federalists ceased competing nationally after 1816.

About a decade later, a **Second Party System** emerged, growing out of profound factional divisions within the dominant Democratic-Republican Party. It featured the **Democratic Party**, the followers of **Andrew Jackson**, in competition with the **Whig Party**, those opposed to Jackson and his policies that enhanced executive power. The Democratic Party generally prevailed during this period. The grow-

ing slavery controversy produced intraparty divisions in both parties, and the Whigs were unable to survive. They disappeared from the electoral scene in the mid-1850s.

The simultaneous rise of the **Republican Party** signaled the onset of the **Third Party System**, one in which the weakened Democrats now competed with the Republicans. The ensuing party systems reflected not new party participants but rather shifting balances of power between the two major parties. After over three decades of close competition, in which the Republicans tended to prevail, the critical election of 1896 ushered in a new era of national Republican dominance, the **Fourth Party System**. It endured until the onset of the **Great Depression** in 1929 paved the way for the **realigning election** of 1932, which began an extended period of dominance of the national electoral landscape by the Democratic Party, known as the **Fifth Party System**.

More recently, the pattern of party competition has taken on new forms and characteristics, most notably in the regular alternation of party control of the White House; the enhanced prospects for divided party government, wherein one party controls the presidency and the other at least one chamber of Congress; shifting foundations of the major party coalitions; and heightened ideological cohesion between the two major parties and polarization between them. Party identification in the electorate, in apparent decline around 1970, has rebounded. Some observers use the concept of the **Sixth Party System** to describe these contemporary conditions.

PARTY UNITY. The capacity of a **political party**, particularly its **party-in-office**, to hang together, behaving in a coherent, responsible fashion.

PATRONAGE. Governmental appointments made on the basis of political loyalty, so as to enhance political strength. Patronage is a means by which a political party seeks both to reward its followers and to transform its party platform into public policy. In a broader sense, patronage can refer to **preferments**, preferential treatment in awarding government contracts, and favors, similarly rewarding loyalists. *See also* MERIT SYSTEM; SPOILS SYSTEM.

PAYNE, HENRY C. Republican National Committee chair, 1904. (b. 23 November 1843; d. 4 October 1904). Payne was a Wisconsin insurance executive who developed broader business interests in telephone and streetcar companies. His involvement in state **Republican Party** politics led to his appointment as postmaster of Milwaukee (1876–1886). In 1888, he joined the **Republican National Committee (RNC)**. Offered the position of national party **chair** by President **Benjamin Harrison** in 1892, Payne declined, but he subsequently agreed to become vice chair. While serving in that capacity in 1900, he promoted the vice presidential **nomination** of **Theodore Roosevelt**. Shortly after becoming president in 1901, Roosevelt made Payne **postmaster general** in January 1902. He continued to serve as vice chair of the RNC.

In February 1904, the chair, **Mark Hanna**, died. Payne served as acting chair until the **committee** met in June on the eve of the **Republican National Convention**. At that point, he was elected chair, but his tenure proved exceedingly brief. When the committee held its customary postconvention meeting, he was replaced by **George B. Cortelyou**, the choice of the presidential nominee, Theodore Roosevelt, to manage Roosevelt's **campaign** for a presidential term in his own right. Payne remained postmaster general for the few remaining months of his life.

PAYNE, SERENO E. Republican majority leader of the House of Representatives, 1899–1911. (b. 26 June 1843; d. 10 December 1914). Payne was initially elected to the **House of Representatives** from New York in 1882. He served two terms, then lost his seat in 1886. He regained it in 1888 and held it until his death. Beginning with the 56th **Congress** (1899–1901), each party **caucus** in the House began designating a **floor leader**. Payne was the initial choice of the **Republican Party**, then in the **majority**. He retained that position for the five following Congresses. In 1910, the **Democratic Party** captured the House, and Payne lost his leadership position when the minority Republicans named **James R. Mann** of Illinois as their leader for the 62nd Congress.

PEACE AND FREEDOM PARTY. A California-based **minor party**, formed in the 1960s and loosely linked to the **People's Party**, which has continued to field presidential tickets in that state. In 1974, it associated itself with the socialist ideology. Its popular support typically ranges between 10,000 and 30,000 voters.

PELOSI, NANCY. Democratic minority leader of the House of Representatives, 2003–2007; Democratic Speaker of the House of Representatives, 2007– . (b. 26 March 1940). The daughter of a congressman who also served as mayor of Baltimore, Nancy Pelosi won a **special election** to a **House of Representatives** seat from San Francisco in 1987. In 2001, she became minority **whip.** Two years later, she succeeded **Richard A. Gephardt** as **floor leader,** the first woman to hold that position. She emerged as a strong and visible critic of the **administration** of President **George W. Bush.** After the **Democratic Party** won a **majority** of House seats in the 2006 **midterm elections,** Pelosi became the first woman to be elected **Speaker.** The 2008 elections enhanced her party majority and also reinstated **united party government** under Democratic rule, resulting in a shift in her relationship to the executive branch, from a confrontational stance to a more collaborative one.

PENDLETON, GEORGE H. Democratic vice presidential nominee, 1864. (b. 19 July 1825; d. 24 November 1889). Pendleton was elected to the **House of Representatives** from Ohio in 1856 and served four terms. In 1864, the **Democratic National Convention** designated him as its vice presidential nominee, to run alongside presidential nominee **George B. McClellan.** Pendleton was the favorite of the **Copperheads,** a party **faction** committed to ending the **Civil War** immediately by accommodating Southern interests. The ticket lost convincingly in the fall to the **Union Party,** a **bipartisan** team featuring **incumbent** President **Abraham Lincoln,** representing the **Republican Party,** and vice presidential nominee **Andrew Johnson,** a pro-Union Democrat.

Pendleton returned to public life in 1879, following his election to the **Senate.** He sponsored the Pendleton Act, initiating reform of the spoils system by establishing a merit-based civil service. After a term in the Senate, he accepted appointment by President **Grover Cleveland** as minister to Germany.

PENNINGTON, WILLIAM. Whig Speaker of the House of Representatives, 1859–1861. (b. 4 May 1796; d. 16 February 1862). Five times elected governor of New Jersey (1837–1843), Pennington served a single term in the **House of Representatives** as a member of the **Whig Party**. When the 36th **Congress** convened, the emergent **Republican Party** claimed a nominal **majority** amid considerable fluidity in party affiliations. The slavery controversy immediately impinged on the process of **Speaker** selection. The Republicans failed to amass majority support for their preferred antislavery choice, **John Sherman**, in repeated balloting over almost two months. Finally Pennington, an unknown, emerged as a compromise choice who would preside in an impartial fashion. His inexperience marred his service. He stands with **Frederick Muhlenberg**, the first Speaker, and **Henry Clay** as the only Speakers to be chosen in their first term.

PEOPLE'S PARTY. The name assumed by two minor parties over the years. The far more notable of these was better known as the Populist Party. It appeared during the **Progressive Era**, organized in 1891 in the Midwest by farmers frustrated by deteriorating economic conditions. The party quickly found substantial popular support there and in the South, attacking the railroad interests and the **hard money** policies then in vogue. It sought without much success to include industrial workers in its **coalition** of interests.

In 1892, the Populists nominated **James B. Weaver** for president. Weaver had previously mounted a presidential campaign as the nominee of the **Greenback Party** in 1880. In November, Weaver received over 1 million votes and carried five Midwestern and Western states in the **electoral college**. Two years later, the Populists increased their national presence by electing to **Congress** six senators and seven representatives.

In 1896, the Populists decided in **convention** to endorse **Democratic Party** presidential nominee **William Jennings Bryan**, whose **fusion** candidacy lost decisively to **William McKinley**, the nominee of the **Republican Party**. Four years later, the same scenario prevailed. That year, these Populists became known as the Populist Party-Fusionist when a rival party **faction**, Populist Party-Anti-Fusionist, decided to field its own candidate, Wharton Barker (Pennsylvania), who received negligible popular support. Although the Populists continued to run presidential candidates throughout the decade, their standing with the public declined precipitously, and they disappeared from the scene after 1908.

Another People's Party organized in 1971 and went on to contest presidential elections in 1972 and 1976. This party sought to unite anti–Vietnam War activists with poor voters and their advocates. Its 1972 nominee was Dr. Benjamin Spock, a well-known pediatrician. The party garnered only 0.1 percent of the popular vote nationally, with two-thirds of that coming from California. Four years later, the party named an African American civil rights activist, Margaret Wright, as its presidential nominee. The party's policy focus was on empowering ordinary citizens to exercise political responsibility and governmental power. It received fewer than 50,000 votes nationally, 85 percent from California, where the party labeled itself the **Peace and Freedom Party**. After these two unimpressive showings, the party folded.

PERENNIAL CANDIDATE. A negative term for a persistent office seeker who has often failed in that quest. It was applied most notably to Harold Stassen, who unsuccessfully sought the presidential **nomination** of the **Republican Party** on nine occasions from 1948 to 1992.

PERIODIC REGISTRATION. Voter registration procedure requiring aspiring voters to re-register at specified intervals to maintain their eligibility. Most states currently allow the act of voting to qualify as re-registration. *See also* PERMANENT REGISTRATION.

PERMANENT REGISTRATION. Voter registration provision that allows a voter who satisfies registration requirements to remain eligible so long as other requirements remain in effect. *See also* PERIODIC REGISTRATION.

PEROT, H. ROSS. Independent presidential candidate, 1992; Reform Party presidential nominee, 1996. (b. 27 June 1930). Perot is a Texas businessman who first attracted national political attention during the presidency of **Richard M. Nixon**, when he sought to provide assistance and public support for American prisoners of war in the Vietnam War. In 1992, Perot entered the presidential **contest** as an

independent. His erratic campaign was grounded in **populist** principles. It found substantial support in what came to be called the radical center, voters disaffected by the perceived extreme liberalism of the **Democratic Party** and the extreme conservatism of the **Republican Party**. This base secured him access to the presidential **ballot** in all 50 states. Perot received an impressive 19 percent of the popular vote in the November election, but he carried no states and won no votes in the **electoral college**. Four years later, he undertook another presidential campaign, this time under the auspices of the Reform Party, whose creation he had sponsored. His electoral support dropped to 8 percent, signaling the demise of his presidential prospects and his leadership of the Reform Party.

PIERCE, FRANKLIN. Democratic president, 1853–1857. (b. 23 November 1804; d. 8 October 1869). As a young lawyer, Franklin Pierce was named to the New Hampshire legislature, and he became Speaker two years later. In 1832, he won the first of two consecutive terms to the U.S. **House of Representatives**. In 1836, his former colleagues in the state legislature sent him to the U.S. **Senate**. He resigned in 1842 to accompany his ailing wife home to New Hampshire, where he continued to dabble in state politics. During the Mexican War, Pierce received a commission as brigadier general, and he served with General **Winfield Scott** in the march on Mexico City.

In 1852, the relatively obscure Pierce emerged as a **dark horse** presidential candidate at the **Democratic National Convention**. With the **convention** deadlocked among more visible candidates, the delegates finally endorsed Pierce on the 49th **ballot**. He won the fall **election** against his former superior officer, General Scott, the **Whig Party** nominee. Pierce's presidency was marked by growing sectional tension inflamed by the slavery controversy. Pierce sought to accommodate the combatants and hold the Union together. His commitment to the Kansas–Nebraska Act cost him party support in the North, while Southern Democrats considered him unreliable. The 1856 Democratic National Convention declined to nominate him for a second term. To date, he remains the only elected **president** since the advent of the nominating convention to be rejected by the party convention in a bid for renomination to a second term. Out of public office, he embarked on an extended European tour. On his return to the United States, he discouraged supporters who sought to nominate him for another term as president in 1860. He then became a vocal critic of the **Civil War** policies of President **Abraham Lincoln**, destroying what remained of his political credibility in the Union.

PINCKNEY, CHARLES C. Electoral vote recipient, 1796, 1800 (Federalist); Federalist presidential nominee, 1804, 1808. (b. 25 February 1746; d. 16 August 1825). Charles Cotesworth Pinckney was a South Carolina planter. During the Revolutionary War, he held the rank of brigadier general and also presided over the state senate in 1779. He was a member of the Constitutional Convention and traveled to France as minister for President **George Washington** in 1796. That year, one North Carolinian named him in the **electoral college** balloting.

Four years later, the **Federalist Party** named him its vice presidential choice. Sixty-five electors sympathetic to the Federalist cause were chosen. All but one named Pinckney, but the **ticket** lost to the opposition **Democratic-Republican Party** tandem of **Thomas Jefferson** and **Aaron Burr**, though the House of Representatives had to break the electoral college tie. Pinckney moved up to the top spot on the Federalist presidential ticket in 1804 and 1808, losing convincingly on both occasions, first to Jefferson and then to **James Madison**.

PINCKNEY, THOMAS. Electoral vote recipient, 1796 (Federalist). (b. 23 October 1750; d. 2 November 1828). Like his older cousin, **Charles C. Pinckney**, Thomas Pinckney was a South Carolina planter and lawyer. He served a term as his state's governor (1787–1789). During the Washington **administration**, he entered into the diplomatic service as minister to Great Britain (1792–1796). During this stint, he also was minister to Spain (1794–1795).

In 1796, the **Federalist Party** promoted a presidential **ticket** of **John Adams** for **president** and **Thomas Pinckney** for **vice president**. As the vote neared, party leader **Alexander Hamilton** attempted to manipulate the choices of the electors so that Pinckney would narrowly outpoll Adams and become president. However, New England electors loyal to Adams responded by substituting the name of **Thomas Jefferson** for Pinckney's, in addition to the **favorite son**, Adams. The upshot was that Jefferson ran second to Adams and was elected vice president. Pinckney's South Carolina district elected him to the **House of Representatives**, where he served two terms (1797–1801). He then retired to his plantation, where he devoted himself to agricultural pursuits for the remainder of his life.

PITTMAN, KEY. Democratic president pro tempore of the Senate, 1933–1940. (b. 19 September 1872; d. 10 November 1940). Pittman began his extended career in the **Senate** from Nevada in 1913. He served until his death in 1940. At the outset of the 73rd **Congress** in 1933, he initiated his tenure as **president pro tempore**, which continued until his death.

PLATFORM. *See* PARTY PLATFORM.

PLUMED KNIGHT. Nickname of **James G. Blaine**, a **Gilded Age** Republican leader. In nominating Blaine for **president** in 1876, Robert Ingersoll likened him to a plumed knight, and the flamboyant description took hold in popular discourse. Some two decades later, Democrat **James K. Jones** became known as the Plumed Knight of Arkansas.

PLURALITY. A term applying to an **election** outcome when the winning vote total falls short of a **majority**.

POINDEXTER, GEORGE. President pro tempore of the Senate, 1834 (b. 1779; d. 5 September 1855). Poindexter went to the **House of Representatives** in 1807 as a territorial delegate from Mississippi, serving for six years. After Mississippi achieved statehood, he finished a term (1817–1819). The next year, he was elected to a two-year term as governor. In 1830, he went to the **Senate** for a stint of slightly less than five years. During the first session of the 23rd **Congress**, he was named **president pro tempore** in June 1834.

POL. An abbreviation for **politician** that is frequently employed in a disparaging fashion.

POLITICAL ACTION COMMITTEE (PAC). An organization that raises and distributes **campaign** funds to **candidates** and **political**

parties, while maintaining a formal separation from party organizations. Most PACs are associated with **interest groups**, but other sponsoring entities include individuals and corporations. PACs operating without economic-based sponsorship likely pursue single-issue and/or avowedly ideological agendas. PACs became major forces in party and campaign politics in the 1970s, in the wake of **campaign finance** reforms embodied in the **Federal Election Campaign Act** and subsequent amendments.

PACs play a central role in financing congressional elections. Incumbents typically benefit far more from PACs' largesse than do challengers. After the **Republican Party** captured both houses of **Congress** in 1994, a seismic shift in PAC contributions occurred, as PACs hurried to curry favor with the new Republican majorities. In the case of many business-oriented PACs, this was a welcome move toward incumbents more ideologically attuned to business concerns than their predecessors. Nevertheless, when the **Democratic Party** regained control of both congressional chambers in 2006, the PACs rewarded members of the new majority with financial support.

Critics of PACs express concern that PAC donations buy access to public officials and influence over public policy. In turn, such donations may be the product of shakedowns on two levels: pressure on individuals to make "voluntary" contributions to the PAC, and pressure on PACs to contribute to incumbents. Most observers of PACs believe that they operate to the detriment of political parties, reducing the key intermediary role parties have traditionally played by dealing directly with policymakers and giving rise to single-issue politics.

Defenders of PACs view them as providing essential resources for electoral politics, not only financial but also organizational. They are sources of information for the public and policymakers alike, and they encourage popular participation in the political process. *See also* 527 GROUP.

POLITICAL PARTY. A political entity that aggregates individuals and groups with common public concerns for the purpose of nominating and electing candidates for public office who will work to enact and implement those concerns as public policy. *See also* DEMOCRATIC PARTY; MAJOR PARTY; MINOR PARTY; REPUBLICAN PARTY.

POLITICIAN. One who pursues political activity as a vocation. The activity may embrace holding public office or serving a **party organization.** *See also* POL; PROFESSIONAL.

POLK, JAMES K. Democratic Speaker of the House of Representatives, 1835–1839; Democratic president, 1845–1849. (b. 2 November 1795; d. 15 June 1849). A protégé of fellow Tennessean **Andrew Jackson,** Polk served seven terms in the U.S. **House of Representatives** (1825–1839), rising to the office of **Speaker** in 1835. He went home in 1839 to run successfully for a single term as governor (1839–1841), but he was defeated in two subsequent reelection efforts (1840 and 1842). In 1840, when the Democrats declined to nominate a **vice president,** Polk received one vote from Virginia in the **electoral college** balloting.

In 1844, former president **Martin Van Buren** initially had the support of a simple **majority** of the **Democratic National Convention** delegates, but the **two-thirds rule** mandated an extraordinary majority. With the **convention** deadlocked, Polk emerged as the choice of the party's **elder statesman, Andrew Jackson.** Jackson's followers embraced his decision, nominating **dark horse** Polk on the ninth ballot. In November, Polk defeated **Whig Party** mainstay **Henry Clay.**

During his presidency, Polk successfully pursued an expansionist foreign policy, adding Texas and Oregon to the Union. He declined to seek another term, and retired from public life. He died a mere three months after leaving office in 1849.

POLL. A place where people can vote, the act of casting and registering votes, or a survey of public opinion. One common usage of *poll* refers to a specific location, or set of locations, where elections are conducted, along with the actions that take place in that setting, as in "going to the polls."

Poll also refers to a survey that seeks to measure public opinion and its direction, stability, and intensity. In the 19th century, straw polls began to gauge the political winds by questioning a hopefully representative sample of the larger group being considered. Increasingly, pollsters became concerned with the method by which this sample is drawn, recognizing that a key factor in the accuracy of the poll is the extent to which the sample reflects the larger public opinion. In 1936, a national survey conducted by *Literary Digest* incorrectly forecast a **landslide** presidential **election** victory for **Republican Party** nominee **Alfred M. Landon** over **incumbent** President **Franklin D. Roosevelt**, the nominee of the **Democratic Party**, based on respondents identified on lists of automobile owners and in telephone directories. This sampling method vastly underrepresented the large numbers of rural and working-class voters who were central components of Roosevelt's electoral **coalition** and whose overwhelming support led to his landslide reelection.

In the wake of this episode, public opinion polling became far more scientific, particularly in the development of the sample. Pollsters like George Gallup and Louis Harris convincingly demonstrated that a relatively small number of respondents, if chosen at random, could accurately represent the larger universe being considered, because of the statistical laws of probability. In turn, telephone usage became sufficiently widespread to enable pollsters to use this method to identify their sample, facilitating quicker and broader polling. Contemporary polls tend to be far more accurate than their traditional counterparts. In the later decades of the 20th century, methodological concerns about polls tended to focus less on sampling issues than on biases introduced through the wording of the questions, whether or not to structure responses, and whether the questions encourage socially desirable responses. In the early 21st century, sampling concerns have been revived, due to technological innovations like telephone caller identification, which reduces response rates, and the advent of cell phones, whose numbers are not readily available to pollsters.

Polls can provide accurate snapshots of public opinion at any given point in time. The projected victory of **Thomas E. Dewey** in the 1948 presidential contest was based on ostensibly reliable polls taken well in advance of the election. Indeed, Dewey's lead appeared so comfortable that most of the major polling organizations suspended operations. However, a late surge by President **Harry S. Truman** propelled him to an unexpected victory. Today, systematic tracking polls seek to measure the dynamics of shifts in public opinion. As a result of these developments, today's policymakers are far better attuned to public opinion than ever before. However, some critics of the increasing use of, and reliance on, polls contend that polls are undermining the representative character of the American political system.

POLL TAX. A tax levied on registered voters. It became prevalent in the South after Reconstruction as a means of discouraging voting by blacks. After World War II, a series of judicial decisions, congressional legislation, and the 24th Amendment to the Constitution (1964) outlawed the practice.

POMEROY, THEODORE M. Republican Speaker of the House of Representatives, 1869. (b. 31 December 1824; d. 23 March 1905). Pomeroy was elected to the **House of Representatives** from New York in 1860, and he served four terms. On the eve of his departure from office, the House named him **Speaker** for one day, to replace **Schuyler Colfax** of Indiana, who had resigned in anticipation of his inauguration as **vice president**.

POPE, JOHN. Democratic-Republican president pro tempore of the Senate, 1811. (b. 1770; d. 12 July 1845). Pope served a single term in the **Senate** from Kentucky (1807–1813). During the third session of the 11th **Congress**, he was elected **president pro tempore** on one occasion. Subsequently, he served as governor of the Arkansas Territory (1829–1835) and won three terms in the **House of Representatives** (1837–1843).

POPULIST. One who identifies with the needs and interests of the common people and who, in their name, advocates redistribution of wealth and power. Populist themes have appeared repeatedly in the history of party competition in the United States, dating back at least to **Andrew Jackson**. They were perhaps most clearly and distinctively pronounced in the 1890s, when they emerged in the protests of rural, agrarian interests against an increasingly industrialized economy and society. The term remains relevant in the 21st century, finding expression in public criticism of growing economic inequality amid declining economic circumstances. *See also* PEOPLE'S PARTY.

POPULIST PARTY. *See* PEOPLE'S PARTY.

POSTMASTER GENERAL. The head of the Post Office, the executive department that traditionally linked the **party-in-office** with the **party organization** in American national government and politics. The postmaster general performed this linkage role through federal **patronage**, dispensed by the Post Office and claimed by the party organization.

Several postmasters general had formal ties to the national party organizations, either before, during, or after their tenures in the Post Office. In the **Republican Party**, three postmasters general served simultaneously as national party chairs: **Henry C. Payne, George B. Cortelyou,** and **Will Hays**. Two incumbent party chairs resigned their party posts to become postmasters general: **Frank H. Hitchcock** and **Arthur E. Summerfield**. More than a decade after leaving his position of national party leadership, **Harry S. New** became postmaster general. Two former postmasters general subsequently became national party chairs: **Marshall Jewell** and **Hubert Work**.

For the **Democratic Party**, the simultaneous occupants were **James A. Farley, Frank C. Walker,** and **Robert E. Hannegan**. Lawrence F. O'Brien had been postmaster general shortly before his first designation as national party chair.

The rise of the civil service gradually reduced the patronage role of the Post Office, along with the original basis for the connection of its leader with **partisan** concerns. During the administration of President **Richard M. Nixon**, the Post Office was reconstituted as the U.S. Postal Service, a government corporation, and its head was removed from the **cabinet**, severing the long-standing link with party politics.

PRECINCT. A voting district. It is also the foundation of **party organization**.

PREFERMENTS. Political and governmental favors granted, often on the basis of partisanship. Preferments thus constitute **material incentives** for **partisan** activity. *See also* PATRONAGE.

PRESIDENT AS PARTY LEADER. A presidential role, not derived from the **Constitution**, which preceded the formation of national political parties. Rather, it quickly developed in response to the presidential nominee's position at the head of the party **ticket** in an **election**. This new leadership role empowered the office of chief executive, providing the **incumbent** with a link with the public and enabling the president to claim to be leader of the entire government, rather than of a single branch. The president as party leader also asserts preeminence over the **party organization**, primarily through the traditional prerogative of designating the **chair** of the national **committee**.

However, the party leadership role of the president also potentially conflicts with the unifying responsibilities of the office of chief executive. It is particularly problematic in an era of **divided party government**. Several recent presidents have delegated certain party leadership chores to their vice presidents, establishing a new role for the **vice president** as deputy party leader.

PRESIDENT OF THE UNITED STATES. The chief executive in the American constitutional system. The president heads the executive branch in the separation of powers system. The **Constitution** establishes eligibility requirements: a candidate must be a natural-born citizen, at least 35 years of age, and at least 14 years a resident of the United States. The **electoral college** selects the president. The 22nd Amendment limits presidential tenure to two elected terms of four years. *See also* PRESIDENT AS PARTY LEADER.

PRESIDENT PRO TEMPORE OF THE SENATE. A constitutional office of the **Senate** that establishes a presiding officer in the absence of the **vice president**, who is president of the Senate. Until 1890, the Senate designated such an individual only on the specific occasions when the vice president was absent. Since then, the designation has been until otherwise ordered. Since World War II, the custom has been to award the title to the senior member of the **majority party**. On several occasions in the first six decades of the 19th century, the Senate authorized its president pro tempore to name members to standing committees. More recently, the office has been largely honorific, with little power accruing to it alone. But because of the seniority of its occupant, who may well be a major force within the chamber and the entire Congress, the office should be considered a party leadership position.

Presidents pro tempore have occupied high-level positions in the line of presidential succession established by Congress. From 1792 until 1886, that line placed the president pro tempore immediately after the vice president. In 1886, the office was removed from the line of succession in favor of the executive department heads who comprised the **cabinet**, beginning with the secretary of state. In 1947, legislation reestablished the president pro tempore in the order of presidential succession, after the vice president and the **Speaker**. To date, no president pro tempore has had to assume the presidential office, though some observers claim that **David R. Atchison** was eligible to do so in 1849. With the ratification of the 25th Amendment to the Constitution in 1967, which provides a procedure for filling a vacancy in the vice presidency, the prospects of ever resorting to this supplementary line of succession have been reduced substantially.

PRESIDENTIAL DEBATES. Events in the presidential selection process wherein presidential aspirants assemble to confront each other publicly in discussions of issues and other topics. Such gatherings may be divided into two categories: intraparty and interparty. The former pertains to the **nomination** stage of the presidential **campaign**, and the latter to the **general election**. The historic event that triggered subsequent presidential debates was a series of debates between **Abraham Lincoln** and **Stephen Douglas**, who were contending for a U.S. Senate seat from Illinois in 1858.

The interparty presidential debates began in 1960, with a series of four nationally televised confrontations between Vice President **Richard M. Nixon**, the **Republican Party** nominee, and Senator **John F. Kennedy**, the **standard-bearer** of the **Democratic Party**. The format called for a moderator and a panel of journalists who posed questions for the contestants to field. The next three presidential contests featured no interparty debates, in part because presidential incumbents raised questions about whether debates might violate the **equal time** provisions associated with the **Fairness Doctrine**, which had been suspended for the 1960 debates by congressional action. In 1975, the Federal Communications Commission ruled that presidential debates were news events and thus not subject to equal time standards.

In 1976, President **Gerald R. Ford** agreed to debate his Democratic opponent, **Jimmy Carter**, in forums sponsored by the **nonpartisan** League of Women Voters. This organization hosted similarly structured debates in 1980 and 1984, amid growing controversy about whether **third-party** nominees should be invited to participate and campaign organizations' objections to proposed moderators and panelists. In 1988, the two major national **party organizations** established a **bipartisan** Commission on Presidential Debates to gain greater **partisan** control over the process. The League of Women Voters declined to continue its sponsorship, and the Commission on Presidential Debates has emerged as the forum through which the major party nominees come together for joint campaign appearances featuring questions from a moderator. In variations on this theme, vice presidential debates began in 1976 and resumed in 1984. One 1980 debate pitted Republican **Ronald W. Reagan** against Independent **John B. Anderson**. The 1992 presidential debates included third-party challenger **Ross Perot**. Some debates have featured audience involvement in town hall-like settings.

Debates are credited with influencing outcomes of several presidential contests. Kennedy's strong showing and attractive appearance in his first debate with Nixon helped him overcome a concern that he was insufficiently experienced and prepared for the presidency. A gaffe by Ford in his second debate with Carter regarding the Soviet presence in Eastern Europe undermined his own claims to superior preparedness for the job. Reagan's wit and stage presence served him well in his debates with Carter in 1980 and **Walter F. Mondale** in 1984. Generally, it is considered easier to lose a debate, through an unforced error, than to win one through one's debating prowess.

Debates between candidates for the nomination began in 1948 on the Republican side and in 1956 for the Democrats. They increased in frequency and regularity following the expansion of presidential primaries after 1968. Various entities sponsor these state-based events, most often state parties and the news **media**.

PRESIDENTIAL PRIMARY. A **primary** that addresses the process of presidential selection. Presidential primaries emerged as a **Progressive Era** reform of presidential nominations. Their purpose was to allow voters to influence the selection and voting behavior of state **party** delegates to a national party **convention**. For several decades after their inception, presidential primaries played a peripheral role in presidential nominations. In the late 1960s, the actions of the **McGovern–Fraser Commission** led to a dramatic expansion in the employment and significance of presidential primaries in the states. Since then, presidential primaries have constituted the battleground for contesting presidential nominations. In 1968, there were 17 **Democratic Party** presidential primaries and 16 **Republican Party** counterparts. In 2008, the Democrats hosted 35 and the Republicans 36. Over time, the primary calendar has become increasingly front-loaded, as state parties and state legislatures schedule their contests early in the nominating season, in hopes of exercising greater influence over the eventual outcome. In the federal system, there are significant variations among presidential primaries, most notably with regard to whether they are open or closed. The Democrats require **proportional representation** of primary votes in the allocation of convention delegates, whereas the Republicans allow **winner-take-all** contests. Presidential primaries differ from direct primaries in that they play an intermediary role in the process of nominating a candidate. National party conventions continue to assemble to perform the **nomination** function. However, in recent decades this action has become pro forma, ratifying the aggregated results of the presidential primaries. *See also* SUPER TUESDAY.

PRIMARY. A party **election** to determine a nominee to contest the **general election**, also known as the direct primary. A primary empowers the **party-in-the-electorate** at the expense of the **party organization** in identifying contenders to represent the **party-in-office**. The **Progressive Movement** at the turn of the 20th century promoted the primary as the appropriate method of party **nomination**, as opposed to the then prevalent party **convention**. Primaries quickly became the norm for elective offices beneath those of **president** and **vice president**, for which the national convention continues to prevail. Even here, however, primaries have become extremely important in delegate selection to the party conventions.

Primaries have had a significant impact on American politics. They have weakened, but by no means eliminated, the influence of the party organization over nominations. They have empowered voters, but participation in party primaries is typically well below that in general elections. They have dramatically increased the financial costs of running for office, because candidates must now compete in two separate contests. They can prove divisive within the party, undermining its prospects in the general election. They promote decentralization, and arguably impede the prospects for **party responsibility**, by enabling unorthodox candidates to secure party nominations. At the same time, they may well buttress the two-party system, by encouraging disenchanted individuals and groups to work within a **major party** rather than to establish a minor party. Although ubiquitous in the United States, primaries are rarely found elsewhere. *See also* BLANKET PRIMARY; CLOSED PRIMARY; OPEN PRIMARY; PRESIDENTIAL PRIMARY; RUNOFF PRIMARY.

PROFESSIONAL. A term applied to those who pursue party politics as a vocation. Professionals can thus be distinguished in the political arena from **amateurs**. *See also* POLITICIAN.

PROGRESSIVE. A term in use since the **Progressive Era** to characterize factions and individuals in both major parties and several minor parties who generally can be located on the **left wing** of an ideological spectrum. The term suggests a reformist, forward-looking approach to public policy concerns.

PROGRESSIVE ERA. A period in late 19th and early 20th-century American politics when the reform movement that gave the era its name pursued and achieved noteworthy transformations in the character and process of American politics. *See also* PROGRESSIVE MOVEMENT; PROGRESSIVE PARTY.

PROGRESSIVE MOVEMENT. A cause promoting social and economic reform in the United States around the turn of the 20th century. Urban and middle class in its membership, and thus distinguished from the contemporaneous Populists, the Progressive Movement called for an end to the political corruption that had infested American politics in the **Gilded Age**. It targeted **political party** organizations as major culprits, bemoaning their undemocratic character and promoting the institution of the **direct primary** as a remedy. In similar fashion, Progressives also promoted the state-level institutions of the **initiative, referendum,** and **recall**. Like the primary, these practices placed responsibility for decisions directly in the hands of the electorate, rather than its elected representatives, who were presumably subject to corruption. Other voting-related reforms embraced by the progressives were the **Australian ballot** and voter **registration**. The Progressive Movement also called for increased activism by the national government in dealing with crises attributed to industrialism. It had adherents constituting factions within both the **Republican Party** and the **Democratic Party**. It also manifested itself as a **minor party**. Noteworthy party leaders associated with the Progressive Movement were **Theodore Roosevelt, Woodrow Wilson,** and **Robert M. La Follette**.

PROGRESSIVE PARTY. Name taken by several minor political parties over the years. In 1912, former Republican president **Theodore Roosevelt** came out of retirement to challenge his handpicked successor, President **William Howard Taft**, for the Republican presidential **nomination**. When this effort failed and the **Republican National Convention** renominated Taft, Roosevelt bolted from the party and formed the Progressive Party, under whose banner he sought the presidency. Roosevelt adopted the **bull moose** as his party symbol, having referred to himself as feeling as fit as a bull moose. The party thus became known popularly as the Bull Moose Party.

The Progressive Party was more than simply an electoral vehicle for Roosevelt. It reflected the decades-old sentiments of the **Progressive Movement**, which were well represented in both major parties. This movement, appealing to the urban middle and upper classes, advocated a much stronger role for the national government in promoting extensive social and economic reform.

Roosevelt's hopes of **bipartisan** voter support were dashed when the Democrats also nominated a progressive, Governor **Woodrow Wilson** of New Jersey. Although Roosevelt received the highest popular vote total for a **minor party** before or since (27.4 percent) and carried six states, his support clearly came at the expense of the Republicans. Wilson earned an overwhelming **majority** in the **electoral college** with only 43 percent of the popular vote.

In 1916, the Progressives sought to reenlist Roosevelt, but he declined their nomination and endorsed the Republican nominee, **Charles Evans Hughes**, also identified with progressivism. Although the Bull Moose Party died as a result, another manifestation of a Progressive Party reflecting the ideals of the Progressive Movement quickly emerged.

In the mid-1920s, Senator **Robert M. La Follette**, a Wisconsin Republican, led in the establishment of a new Progressive Party and headed its 1924 presidential **ticket**. This version incorporated some policies and constituencies of the earlier Bull Moose incarnation, but it pitched its appeal more toward farmers and laborers. It identified corporate monopolies as its major target.

La Follette won 16.6 percent of the popular vote, a very impressive third-party showing, but he only carried one state, Wisconsin. His support came primarily from rural voters in the Midwest and Western states. His death in 1925 ended the party's national presence.

Yet another Progressive Party incarnation occurred in 1948. It represented an ideological party **faction**, liberal Democrats who opposed the increasingly hard-line position taken by President **Harry S. Truman** against the Soviet Union in the early stages of the Cold War. The leader of this Progressive Party was **Henry A. Wallace**, who had served in the **cabinet** of President **Franklin D. Roosevelt** and as his **vice president**. He departed the Truman **administration** under fire for his public advocacy of peaceful coexistence with the Soviet Union.

The Progressive Party received the controversial endorsement of the **Communist Party**, which proved to be a kiss of death electorally. It also developed noteworthy support among minority groups. On **election** day, the Progressives received only 2.4 percent of the popular vote, almost half of which came from New York, and failed to carry any states. After the election, it moved even further toward the extreme **left wing** of the ideological spectrum, opposing the Korean War in 1950 and alienating its more moderate adherents, including Wallace. It contested the 1952 presidential election, running as its nominee an obscure Californian, William Hallinan, who garnered only 0.2 percent of the popular vote. The party did not survive this electoral debacle.

PROHIBITION. A movement to outlaw the manufacture and sale of intoxicating beverages. It arose in the mid-18th century, and its influence peaked in the second decade of the 20th century, when the 18th Amendment to the **Constitution** (1919) authorized its objective. The cause of prohibition generated factions in both major parties, more notably the Democrats, as well as an enduring **minor party**. The Prohibition Era ended in 1933, when the 21st Amendment repealed the 18th, although the cause continued to attract small numbers of adherents to the **Prohibition Party**. *See also* DRY; WET.

PROHIBITION PARTY. The Prohibition Party has maintained its minor-party identity for well over a century, making it the most durable, though far from the most successful, minor party in American politics. It emerged on the scene in 1869 with a clear and narrow policy focus: the prohibition of the manufacture and sale of intoxicating beverages. Although it espoused the objective of the preexisting temperance movement, that movement continued to operate through interest groups outside the confines of the party, attracting loyal Democrats and Republicans. Compared with such groups as the Women's Christian Temperance Union and the Anti-Saloon League, the Prohibition Party played a relatively minor role in the noteworthy successes of the temperance movement. Over the years, the Prohibition Party has embraced additional reform proposals, such as women's rights and religious liberty.

Since 1872, the Prohibition Party has contested presidential elections. In 1980, it did so under a new name, the **Statesman Party**. Four years later, it resumed its traditional label. The party has never carried a single state and thus has received no electoral votes. Its best percentage showing was in 1892, when its nominee, John Bidwell, captured 2.2 percent of the popular vote. The party almost always achieved over 1 percent for some three decades, between 1884 and 1916. *See also* DRY; PROHIBITION; WET.

PROPORTIONAL REPRESENTATION. A principle governing electoral arrangements whereby seats in a legislature are divided among the competing parties in proportion to their electoral support. In practice, proportional representation takes on several specific forms.

These include the list system, the Hare system, and the D'Hondt system. Proportional representation is relatively rare in U.S. electoral politics. It exists most notably in contemporary national convention delegate selection procedures within the **Democratic Party**.

However, several European political systems utilize proportional representation. There, it tends to encourage a **multiparty system** by enabling several parties to win some representation in the legislature. Proponents of proportional representation applaud its fairness in giving voice to a broad range of views. Detractors view it as potentially unstable, fragmenting the electorate and forcing the creation of coalitions between and among parties to achieve the **majority** of legislative support required to form and maintain a government. *See also* MULTIMEMBER DISTRICT; SINGLE-MEMBER DISTRICT.

PURGE. A response to opposition within a **political party** or other organization that entails the removal of the opponents from the organization.

PURPOSIVE INCENTIVES. Motivations for **political party** activity. Purposive incentives rely on underlying issue and ideological orientations. Those who enter the political arena primarily to advance issues and/or promote ideological objectives can be said to be motivated primarily by purposive incentives. In the new politics of recent decades, empowered **amateurs** have been more likely than their traditional **professional** counterparts to act on the basis of purposive incentives. *See also* AMATEUR; MATERIAL INCENTIVES; SOLIDARY INCENTIVES.

– Q –

QUAY, MATTHEW S. Republican National Committee chair, 1888–1891. (b. 30 September 1833; d. 28 May 1904). Quay was a prominent Pennsylvania **Republican Party** leader who long held a seat on the **Republican National Committee (RNC)**. He went to the **Senate** in 1887 and served two terms. He began a three-year tour of duty as **chair** of the RNC in 1888, following the presidential **nomination** of **Benjamin Harrison**. Quay resigned in 1891, enabling Harrison to name **James S. Clarkson** to that post. After leaving the Senate in 1899 at the end of his second term, he returned in 1901 to hold that office until his death three years later.

QUAYLE, J. DANFORTH. Republican vice president, 1989–1993. (b. 4 February 1947). Dan Quayle grew up in Indiana and Arizona, where his family had profitable publishing interests. In 1976, he was elected to the **House of Representatives** from Indiana. He served two terms and went on to win a **Senate** seat in 1980. Reelected in 1986, he was the surprise choice of presidential nominee **George H. W. Bush** at the 1988 **Republican National Convention** for the vice presidential **nomination**. This decision proved controversial, initially because of Quayle's relative obscurity. Then allegations quickly surfaced that Quayle had relied on family connections to avoid military service in the Vietnam War, joining the National Guard instead. Nevertheless, the Bush-Quayle **ticket** prevailed that fall, and Quayle was inaugurated as **vice president**.

Despite abiding concerns that he was a lightweight, not up to the challenges and responsibilities of high office, Quayle was renominated in 1992. The Republican ticket was soundly defeated that fall, and Quayle temporarily left the electoral arena. He remained visible on the national scene by speaking out on public policy questions. He reemerged as a candidate for his party's 2000 presidential nomination, but his campaign generated little public support, and he withdrew before the first primary contest. Since then, his national profile has been low.

– R –

RACICOT, MARC. Republican National Committee chair, 2002– 2003. (b. 24 July 1948). Racicot was elected attorney general in Montana in 1988. Four years later, he won the governorship, which he held for two terms, leaving office in 2001. Racicot was heavily involved in the post-2000 presidential **election** development in Florida that resulted in a triumph for **George W. Bush**. He figured prominently in speculation regarding an administrative appointment, but none was forthcoming. Then, in 2002, President Bush designated

Racicot as **James S. Gilmore III**'s successor as national party **chair**. Having served for a year, he became the chair of the Bush reelection **campaign**. After the election, he returned to private life.

RADICAL. A label usually employed in a pejorative fashion to describe or locate an individual or a policy at an extreme of an ideological spectrum. In a unimodal, centrist opinion distribution, such an extreme **right-wing** or **left-wing** position has little public support. By the early 1990s, polarizing tendencies in the electorate had produced a more bimodal opinion distribution, increasing the significance of left-wing ideologues in the **Democratic Party** and their right-wing **Republican Party** counterparts. The term "radical center" came into vogue to characterize the electoral independents disenchanted with these **partisan** developments who flocked to the banner of the presidential candidacy of **Ross Perot**.

RADICAL REPUBLICANS. A **Civil War**–era **faction** of the **Republican Party**, based in **Congress**, that initially criticized the conduct of the war by President **Abraham Lincoln**, a fellow Republican. Subsequently, the Radicals opposed the Reconstruction policy that President **Andrew Johnson** inherited from Lincoln. The Radical Republicans promoted harsher retaliatory measures against the defeated South than President Johnson would countenance. This controversy masked the larger question of whether the **president** or **Congress** would dominate the national government after the war. The Radical Republicans in the **House of Representatives** brought charges of impeachment against Johnson, but their **Senate** counterparts failed by one vote to muster the required two-thirds **majority** vote to remove him from office. Nevertheless, the Radical Republicans were a major force in national government and politics throughout the 1860s. Their status diminished as the issues and passions generated by the war receded.

RAINEY, HENRY T. Democratic majority leader of the House of Representatives, 1931–1933; Democratic Speaker of the House of Representatives, 1933–1935. (b. 20 August 1860; d. 19 August 1934). Rainey was elected to the **House of Representatives** from Illinois in 1902. He was reelected nine times before losing his bid in 1920. He won back his seat in 1922 and held it until his death 12 years later. When the Democrats won control of the House in 1930, the party **caucus** named Rainey **floor leader**, to serve under the incoming **Speaker, John Nance Garner**, during the 72nd **Congress**. Two years later, following Garner's **election** as **vice president**, Rainey succeeded him as Speaker. He presided over the House during the introduction and passage of major **New Deal** legislation favored by President **Franklin D. Roosevelt**. Rainey died two months after the historic 73rd Congress adjourned.

RANDALL, SAMUEL J. Democratic Speaker of the House of Representatives, 1876–1881. (b. 10 October 1828; d. 13 April 1890). Initially elected to the **House of Representatives** from Pennsylvania in 1862, Randall retained his seat until his death. After the **Democratic Party** captured control of the House in the 1874 elections, its leader, **Michael C. Kerr** of Indiana, became **Speaker** for the 44th Congress. Kerr died after less than a year in office, whereupon the Democrats named two of their number, Samuel S. Cox of New York and Milton Saylor of Ohio, as Speakers pro tempore for the remainder of the first session. When the second session convened, they named Randall their leader, resulting in his **election** as Speaker. He held the office through the following Congress but relinquished it when the **Republican Party** gained a **majority** of seats in the 1880 elections.

RANK AND FILE. Lower-level members of the **party structure**, sometimes referred to as the party faithful or party base. The term originated in the military, where it refers to enlisted personnel. In the setting of party politics, it may be applied within the **party organization**, the **party-in-office**, and the **party-in-the-electorate**.

RANKING MEMBER. The senior member of the **minority party** on a congressional **committee**.

RANSOM, MATT W. Democratic president pro tempore of the Senate, 1895. (b. 8 October 1826; d. 8 October 1904). North Carolina sent Ransom to the **Senate** in 1872 to finish an unexpired term. He subsequently won three terms in his own right. During the brief third session of the 53rd **Congress** (December 1894–March 1895), Ransom, about to leave office, was named **president pro tempore**. He served for three days.

RASKOB, JOHN J. Democratic National Committee chair, 1928–1932. (b. 9 March 1879; d. 15 October 1950). Raskob rose from modest circumstances in New York to become a top corporate executive for DuPont and General Motors. Operating in an economic and social environment more favorable to the **Republican Party**, his belated introduction to **Democratic Party** politics came through his association with New York Governor **Alfred E. Smith**, who shared his antiprohibition sentiments. When Smith won the presidential **nomination** in 1928, he prevailed on Raskob to **chair** the **Democratic National Committee**, in an effort to reach out to and reassure the corporate community. This unusual move heightened concerns about Smith in the Southern and Western bases of the Democratic **coalition**.

After Smith's defeat, Raskob stayed on as chair, but he delegated much of his authority to the head of the party executive committee, Jouett Shouse, who set up permanent party headquarters in Washington. Raskob supported Smith in the latter's vain quest for renomination in 1932, whereupon the presidential nominee, **Franklin D. Roosevelt**, unceremoniously replaced Raskob with **James A. Farley**, his own **campaign** manager. Two years later, Raskob joined with Smith and other conservative Democrats to form the Liberty League, an organization opposed to Roosevelt and the **New Deal**, thus separating himself from the Democratic Party.

RAYBURN, SAMUEL T. Democratic majority leader of the House of Representatives, 1937–1940; Democratic Speaker of the House of Representatives, 1940–1947, 1949–1953, 1955–1961; Democratic minority leader of the House of Representatives, 1947–1949, 1953–1955. (b. 6 January 1882; d. November 16, 1961). Sam Rayburn served in the Texas legislature, rising to the office of Speaker in only his third term. In 1912, he won **election** to the **House of Representatives**, holding that seat until his death almost half a century later. Rayburn's close friendship with fellow Texan **John Nance Garner** positioned him in the **inner club** of congressional influence and leadership. In 1937, he was named **majority leader**, and he became

Speaker three years later, after the death of **William B. Bankhead**. Rayburn led the congressional party for the rest of his life, surrendering the speakership for two nonconsecutive terms as **minority leader** when the Democrats lost control of the House (1947–1949 and 1953–1955).

During his lengthy tenure as Speaker, Rayburn strongly endorsed the traditional norms of congressional behavior, advising new members, "if you want to get along, go along." His party leadership featured close cooperation with his protégé and fellow Texan, **Lyndon B. Johnson**, Senate **floor leader**, in representing the **Democratic Party** from Capitol Hill during the period of **divided party government** (1955–1961), which prevailed when that party had majorities in both houses of **Congress** while the GOP controlled the White House under President **Dwight D. Eisenhower**. In 1961, Rayburn's health failed. In August, the party **caucus** named **John W. McCormack** Speaker pro tempore to preside in Rayburn's absence. He died later that fall.

RAYMOND, HENRY J. Republican National Committee chair, 1864–1866. (b. 24 January 1820; d. 18 June 1869). A New York newspaper publisher who founded the *New York Times*, Raymond was active in New York politics, serving in the state legislature and as lieutenant governor. He embraced the newly formed **Republican Party** and rose quickly in its ranks. In 1864, he was named head of the **Republican National Committee**, succeeding **Edwin D. Morgan**, the first Republican national party **chair**. That same year, as he oversaw the party's successful effort to reelect President **Abraham Lincoln**, Raymond was also elected to the **House of Representatives**. He served for two years in each post.

As national party chair, Raymond got caught in the middle of the conflict that developed between the new **president, Andrew Johnson**, and the Radical Republicans in **Congress** over Reconstruction policy. The Republicans had campaigned for the presidency in 1864 under the **Union Party** label, reaching out to pro-Union Democrats by nominating Johnson for **vice president**. Lincoln's assassination left Johnson as president not only without a strong party base of support but also with an increasingly virulent Republican **faction** in control of Congress. Raymond tried without success to heal the widening breach. When Johnson sought to revive the Union Party in 1866, in hopes of developing his own political base, Raymond made an appearance at a meeting Johnson had called. This move angered the Republicans, who sought to expel him as chair. Raymond resisted the move, but his effectiveness ended, and he resigned shortly afterward.

READ, JACOB. Federalist president pro tempore of the Senate, 1797–1798. (b. 1751; d. 17 July 1816). Read represented South Carolina in the Continental Congress (1783–1785). A decade later, he served a single term in the **Senate** (1795–1801). During the second session of the 5th **Congress**, he was named **president pro tempore** on 22 November 1797.

READ OUT OF THE PARTY. An act by party leaders to ostracize or shun an individual or **faction** for behavior considered detrimental to the party.

REAGAN, RONALD W. Republican president, 1981–1989. (b. 6 February 1911; d. 5 June 2004). Ronald Reagan was a prominent movie star who abandoned the **Democratic Party** in the early 1960s to embrace the rising tide of Republican conservatism. He quickly emerged as a leading spokesman for the **right wing** of the **Republican Party**. He ran for governor of California in 1966 and served two four-year terms. In 1968, he ran a tentative, unsuccessful **campaign** for the Republican presidential nomination, which went to **Richard M. Nixon**.

After leaving the governor's office, Reagan challenged the **incumbent, Gerald R. Ford**, for the 1976 Republican presidential nomination but fell short. However, he prevailed in 1980 and went on to defeat incumbent **Jimmy Carter** and independent **John B. Anderson** in the fall election. Four years later, he won a **landslide** reelection victory over Democrat **Walter Mondale**.

Reagan vigorously opposed the idea of "big government." He advocated tax cuts and other measures to reduce the role of the federal government in the lives of its citizens. He presided over a period of economic expansion and a resurgence of Cold War tension, just prior to the collapse of the Soviet Union. Reagan came into office in the wake of a series of incomplete or failed presidencies going back to that of John F. Kennedy. By dint of his abiding popularity, his appealing personal style, and his steadfast commitment to conservative principles, Reagan can be credited with restoring much of the legitimacy the presidency had lost in the two decades since **Dwight D. Eisenhower** occupied the office, as well as with spearheading the Republican resurgence toward the **majority** status that it had lost with the coming of the **Great Depression** and the **New Deal**. Precluded from another presidential bid by the 22nd Amendment to the **Constitution**, Reagan retired to private life in California.

REALIGNING ELECTION. In a taxonomy of presidential elections, an **election** that results in a new **party system**, owing to a fundamental reordering of the pattern of party competition demonstrated in the election. A realigning election typically brings forth a new **majority party** through a substantial conversion in voter loyalties and/or the mobilization of new voters. Examples of realigning elections include those of 1800, 1860, 1896, and 1932. *See also* CONVERTING ELECTION; CRITICAL ELECTION; DEVIATING ELECTION; MAINTAINING ELECTION; REALIGNMENT; REINSTATING ELECTION.

REALIGNMENT. A substantial reordering of the pattern of party competition, wherein the group basis of party coalitions changes and a new **majority party** usually emerges. A realignment occurs through conversion of voters from one party to another and/or through the mobilization of new voters. In the history of party competition in the United States, for about 150 years, realignments tended to occur on a generational basis. An initial alignment in 1800 established the **Democratic-Republican Party** as the dominant party in the **First Party System**. About three decades later, a realignment ushered in a period of **Democratic Party** hegemony in the **Second Party System**. In 1860, the new **Republican Party** staked its tentative claim to voter loyalties as the **Third Party System** emerged. The Republicans consolidated that claim in 1896, establishing the **Fourth Party System**. In turn, the Democrats took advantage of the onset of the **Great Depression** in 1929 to become the new majority party of the **Fifth Party System**. Since then, no clear realignment has taken place. However, the South has experienced a substantial regional realignment, with the decline of the once-dominant Democrats and the rise of the Republicans. In considerable measure because of this regional development, the pattern of national party competition has changed as well, leading some observers to perceive the evolution of a **Sixth Party System**. *See also* DEALIGNMENT; PARTY SYSTEM; REALIGNING ELECTION.

RECALL. A procedure by which a public official may be removed from office by a popular vote. The recall was a **Progressive Era** reform embraced by several states, 18 of which currently authorize it. Two state governors have been recalled: Lynn Frazier of North Dakota in 1921 and Gray Davis of California in 2003.

REECE, B. CARROLL. Republican National Committee chair, 1946–1948. (b. 22 December 1889; d. 19 March 1961). Reece was a **mountain Republican** from east Tennessee who was a dominant figure in his state **party organization.** He won 17 divided terms in the **House of Representatives** (1921–1931, 1933–1947, and 1951–1961), with his death interrupting his final term. In 1946, while serving in **Congress,** he replaced **Herbert Brownell Jr.** as **chair** of the **Republican National Committee.** He lost his bid for House reelection that year. Reece occupied his national party post for two years, vacating the office in 1948 when he vainly sought election to the U.S. **Senate.** He subsequently returned to Congress in 1951.

REED, THOMAS B. Republican Speaker of the House of Representatives, 1889–1891, 1895–1899. (b. 18 October 1839; d. 7 December 1902). Reed was elected to the **House of Representatives** from Maine in 1877. He held his seat for over two decades, vacating it in 1899. In 1889, he was elected **Speaker** for the 51st **Congress,** losing the position two years later when the **Democratic Party** won the House. The **Republican Party** returned to power in 1895 and again chose Reed as its leader. He served for an additional two terms, departing the House after the 55th Congress adjourned. "Czar" Reed was a strong leader of both his party and the entire chamber. His controversial parliamentary rulings limited the opportunities of the **minority** Democrats to impede the actions of the **majority** Republicans and also substantially enhanced the standing of the Speaker within the body.

REFERENDUM. The submission of a proposed public measure or an actual statute to a direct popular vote for authorization. The referendum was a **Progressive Era** reform currently embraced by about half of the states. Perhaps most notable among them is California. A referendum differs from an **initiative** in that the former is submitted by the legislature to the voters for resolution, whereas the latter is initiated in the electorate and bypasses the representative nature of the normal legislative process. Less precisely, the term is often used to characterize the meaning of an electoral outcome. For example, **midterm elections** and **special elections** are often depicted as referenda on the presidential **incumbent** and the **majority party**.

REGISTRATION. Requirement employed by every state except North Dakota as a condition that aspiring voters must meet. Registration, which involves certification from **election** officials that other suffrage requirements have been met, limits the possibility of voter fraud. A **Progressive Era** reform, registration requirements resulted in reduced voter turnout.

In initially adopting such requirements, most states established them on a periodic basis, requiring that voters re-register at specified intervals to maintain their eligibility. This system of **periodic registration** kept the voter rolls up to date and inhibited fraud, but it also discouraged electoral participation by placing a substantial hurdle in the way of voting. Thus, several states shifted to a system of **permanent registration**, whereby a voter who satisfies registration requirements remains eligible so long as other requirements continue to be met. In a hybrid development, many states consider the act of voting as satisfying the requirement to re-register.

In recent years, under a national mandate, states have substantially eased the other traditional obstacles associated with registration through such devices as motor-voter registration, whereby a voter can satisfy voter registration requirements in conjunction with obtaining or renewing a driver's license. *See also* RESIDENCE REQUIREMENTS.

REGULAR. A loyal **partisan**. In a **primary**, a **candidate** with the support of the **party organization** is often identified as the regular, whereas an opponent lacking such support is labeled the insurgent. Regular voters can be counted on to vote a **straight ticket**.

REID, HARRY M. Democratic minority leader of the United States Senate, 2005–2007; Democratic majority leader of the United States Senate, 2007– . (b. 2 December 1939). Reid grew up in a small Nevada mining town. While attending law school at George Washington University, he served on the Capitol Hill Police Force. He returned to Nevada to practice law and entered the political arena in 1967, when he was elected to the state legislature. Elected lieutenant governor in 1970, he ran for the U.S. **Senate** in 1974, losing narrowly to **Paul Laxalt**. He served as state gaming commissioner (1977–1981) and won two terms in the U.S. **House of Representatives** (1983–1987). In 1986, he successfully sought the Senate seat vacated by Laxalt. In 1999, he became minority **whip**. In June 2001, he became **majority** whip, when a party switch by Senator James Jeffords (VT) gave the **Democratic Party** control of the narrowly divided chamber. When the Democrats lost control in the 2002 **midterm elections**, Reid resumed the position of **minority** whip. In 2004, the **minority leader**, **Thomas Daschle**, lost his reelection bid, and Reid moved up to **majority leader**, where he became one of the leading public voices in opposition to President **George W. Bush** and the congressional **Republican Party** leadership. Democratic victories in the 2006 midterm elections reestablished the majority status of the party in both houses of **Congress,** and Reid became majority leader at the outset of the 110th Congress. **Divided party government,** as well as supermajority requirements for conducting Senate business, limited Reid's prospects to advance the party agenda. The 2008 election of Democratic presidential nominee **Barack H. Obama** reinstituted united party government under Democratic direction for the first time since 1998, improving but by no means guaranteeing Reid's capacity to do so.

REID, WHITELAW. Republican vice presidential nominee, 1892. (b. 27 October 1837; d. 15 December 1912). Reid was a longtime editor of the *New York Tribune* (1872–1905). Active in **Republican Party**

politics, he served as the minister to France for President **Benjamin Harrison** (1889–1892). At the 1892 **Republican National Convention**, strong support from his home-state delegation led the assembly to nominate Reid for **vice president** by acclamation, passing over the **incumbent, Levi P. Morton**. The party **ticket** went down to defeat in November, and Reid resumed his editorial position.

REINSTATING ELECTION. A category in a popular taxonomy of presidential elections that also includes **maintaining election, deviating election, converting election,** and **realigning election.** A reinstating election follows one or more deviating elections. It restores the traditional dominant party in the **party system** to power. Examples of reinstating elections over the years include 1844, when **James K. Polk** led the **Democratic Party** back to its accustomed occupancy of the White House in the **Second Party System**; 1888, when Republican **Benjamin Harrison** won back the **White House** from Democrat **Grover Cleveland** in the Third Party System; 1920, when **Warren G. Harding** similarly resumed **Republican Party** control in the **Fourth Party System**; and 1960, when **John F. Kennedy** regained the presidency for the Democrats under the **Fifth Party System**.

RENDELL, EDWARD G. General chair of the Democratic National Committee, 1999–2001. (b. 5 January 1944). Following graduation from the University of Pennsylvania (1965) and Villanova Law School (1968), Rendell went to work in the district attorney's office in Philadelphia. In 1978 he was elected district attorney, serving until 1986. In 1991 he was elected mayor of Philadelphia. In his two terms as mayor, he proved himself to be an extraordinarily effective fund-raiser for the **Democratic Party**. As President **Bill Clinton** was winding down his second term, he tapped Rendell to replace the retiring **Roy Romer** as the general **chair** of the **Democratic National Committee (DNC)**. Rendell's selection addressed growing concerns within the **party organization** that the DNC needed to become more aggressive in its fund-raising efforts as the 2000 presidential **campaign** approached. The choice of Rendell also reflected Clinton's enthusiasm for the presidential candidacy of his **vice president, Al Gore**, whom Mayor Rendell had already endorsed for the Democratic presidential **nomination**. In addition, Gore's reported involvement in the decision indicated a willingness on Clinton's part as a **lame duck** to begin transferring portions of his party leadership responsibilities to his **heir apparent**. After the Gore campaign went down to defeat, Rendell did not seek reelection as national party chair. Returning to Pennsylvania, he was elected governor in 2002.

REPRESENTATIVE. A legislator. In the national Congress, this term is usually restricted to a member of the **House of Representatives**, with a member of the **Senate** labeled **senator**. Representatives understand their roles in various fashions. Some view themselves as trustees, employing their allegedly superior wisdom and judgment on behalf of their constituents. Others, known as delegates, or deputies, perceive an obligation to reflect the demonstrated positions of their constituents, even if those positions conflict with the individual legislator's personal views. Finally, others see themselves as partisans, seeking to follow their party leaders in translating the **party platform** into public policy in accordance with the concept of **party responsibility**. Most legislators balance these alternative representative role orientations in varying degrees. *See also* MEMBER OF CONGRESS.

REPUBLICAN COMMITTEE ON COMMITTEES. A legislative **party organization** in the **Senate** that makes recommendations to the **Republican Conference** regarding **committee** assignments.

REPUBLICAN CONFERENCE. A legislative **party organization** in each house of **Congress** that assembles all of the **Republican Party** members in that chamber. The conferences meet prior to the beginning of a new Congress to select their leaders and assign members to congressional committees. In recent years, the conferences have continued to meet on a weekly to biweekly basis throughout the session when Congress is convened to discuss party policy and strategy.

REPUBLICAN CONGRESSIONAL CAMPAIGN COMMITTEE (RCCC). A legislative **party organization**, created shortly after the **Civil War**, that provides **campaign** support for party nominees for congressional seats. This assistance takes various forms but is primarily financial. The House **Republican Conference** designates the **chair,** who presides over a staff headquartered just off Capitol Hill, between the congressional office buildings and the headquarters of the Republican National Committee.

REPUBLICAN COORDINATING COMMITTEE. An entity uniting the Republican **party organization** and the **party-in-office** (1965–1968). Inspired in part by the **Democratic Advisory Council**, the Republican Coordinating Committee emerged in the wake of the devastating electoral defeat suffered by the party in 1964. It integrated the congressional party leadership, the national party organization, and the state parties, including the Republican governors. Financed and staffed by the **Republican National Committee** chaired by **Ray C. Bliss**, the Republican Coordinating Committee divided into task forces to develop and put forward policy statements. After the party recaptured the White House in 1968 under **Richard M. Nixon**, the Republican Coordinating Committee quietly dissolved. It was briefly and ineffectually revived in 1973 as the party's fortunes began to sink under the weight of the **Watergate** scandals.

REPUBLICAN MAIN STREET PARTNERSHIP. A group of moderate Republicans, centered in the **Congress**. They came together after the 1994 elections that brought the **Republican Party** to power in both houses of Congress, in the context of rising conservatism within the party. Their name connotes their contention that Republicans need to appeal to mainstream, centrist voters rather than ideological zealots. Like the **Blue Dog Democrats**, they seek to pull their party toward the center of the ideological spectrum.

REPUBLICAN NATIONAL COMMITTEE (RNC). Entity that exercises the authority of the national party organization between the quadrennial nominating conventions. It was created in 1856. Its membership consists of representatives designated by the state parties and state chairs as ex officio members. It now chooses its **chair** for a two-year term. When a vacancy occurs while a Republican occupies the White House, that position effectively becomes a presidential appointment. The RNC typically meets two or three times a year. For over a century after its establishment, the RNC rented office space in Washington, D.C., expanding staff and operations in anticipation of an upcoming presidential campaign and then virtually disbanding in its wake. In the 1970s, the party purchased its own facilities just south of Capitol Hill. There, it maintains a substantial permanent operation.

REPUBLICAN NATIONAL CONVENTION. Quadrennial assembly of delegations from state parties, beginning in 1856, who come together primarily to nominate a presidential **ticket** but also to put forward a **party platform**. Initially, seats at the **convention** were apportioned among the state parties in accordance with the **electoral college** formula based on the size of a state's congressional delegation, **House of Representatives** and **Senate**. Since 1912, the **GOP** has weighted convention representation to reward state parties that prove successful in electing the party's nominees to public office. Traditionally, state party leaders tightly controlled delegate selection. More recently, this control has diminished as **candidate** organizations of presidential contenders have played an increasingly significant role, via presidential primaries. The expanded role of presidential primaries in presidential selection has also altered the significance of the national convention's nominating function. Contemporary conventions typically ratify and legitimate a **nomination**.

REPUBLICAN PARTY. Party label employed by two major parties, one in the 1790s and the other since the 1850s. In the political struggles of the 1790s, **Thomas Jefferson** and his supporters referred to themselves as Republicans. They did so to demonstrate their commitment to a republican form of government and to suggest that their opponents, the supporters of **Alexander Hamilton** who made up the **Federalist Party**, were closet monarchists. Gradually, this political organization became better known as the **Democratic-Republican Party**.

Over half a century later, in the 1850s, a new party bearing the Republican label appeared on the political scene. It emerged while the two major parties, the **Democratic Party** and the **Whig Party**, struggled without success to reconcile their respective slavery and antislavery factions. Articulating a strong antislavery position, it initially appealed primarily to farmers, workers, and small businessmen in the Midwest. With the Whig **coalition** disintegrating, the new Republicans became the major beneficiaries, embracing the nationalist sentiments of the Northern Whigs and immediately emerging as the major party alternative to the Democrats. Initially contesting the **midterm elections** of 1854, they gained effective control of the **House of Representatives**. Their first presidential nominee, **John C. Fremont**, ran a solid second to Democrat **James Buchanan** in 1856, easily outpacing the **American Party** nominee, former president **Millard Fillmore,** who obtained the support of the **Silver Grays**, a Whig **faction**.

In the 1858 midterm elections, the Republicans again won a **majority** of seats in the House, and they captured both the **Senate** and the presidency two years later. Republican presidential nominee **Abraham Lincoln** faced a Democratic Party that had divided into two factions, each mounting a presidential **campaign**. He secured a popular vote **plurality** and a comfortable majority in the **electoral college**. In 1864, with the **Civil War** raging and the Southern states not participating in the presidential contest, Lincoln won reelection comfortably.

Building on these early successes, and with the Democrats both divided and discredited by the war, the Republicans emerged from the Civil War as the dominant party in American politics. Styling itself the **Grand Old Party (GOP)**, the party successfully expanded its initial electoral coalition to embrace the powerful commercial, industrial, and financial interests that dominated postwar America. It also received the appreciative support of newly enfranchised black voters.

In the 18 presidential elections from 1860 through 1932, the Republican nominee won on 14 occasions. The Republican presence in **Congress** in this era reflected a similar pattern of domination. The party won majorities in the House in 25 out of 32 elections and controlled the Senate 80 percent of the time. Initially, the victories tended to be narrow. Beginning in 1896, they became more convincing, as the Republicans solidified their regional support in the Northeast and Midwest.

This age of Republican ascendance came to an end with the onset of the **Great Depression** in 1929. This economic disaster discredited the Republicans for over a generation, while Democrat **Franklin D.**

Roosevelt won an unprecedented four presidential elections, and his party heir, **Harry S. Truman**, won yet another. Meanwhile, Democratic control of Congress became the norm, beginning in 1930. The bases of the Republican electoral coalition shrank dramatically.

In 1952, Republican presidential prospects revived, when the GOP took a page from the Whig Party campaign strategy textbook and nominated a man on horseback, General **Dwight D. Eisenhower**. Eisenhower's victory inaugurated a new era of party competition at the presidential level in which the Republicans have held a slight advantage in presidential elections, winning six of the next nine. **Ronald W. Reagan** was the most noteworthy Republican presidential party leader during this era (1981–1989). In turn, the most notable addition to the Republican electoral coalition was the white South, with blue-collar workers also increasingly sympathetic. However, the Republicans were much less successful in congressional contests, as Democratic dominance continued. In the 1990s, these trends reversed themselves, as the Republicans lost the presidency in both 1992 and 1996 but gained control of both houses of Congress in 1994.

Republicans sustained their congressional dominance electorally for over a decade, although a post-2000 election defection by a Republican senator placed the Democrats in control of that chamber until 2003. Meanwhile, the **George W. Bush**–led GOP won the presidency in 2000, despite losing the popular vote, and Bush won reelection in 2004, elevating the political fortunes of the Republicans to heights not seen since the decade of the 1920s. However, Bush's declining popularity, public concerns over the Iraq War, and congressional scandals contributed to the loss of party majorities in both chambers in the 2006 midterm elections. The 2008 elections resulted in a further party decline in both congressional chambers. More significantly, the party lost control of the White House, placing it out of power in the nation's capital for the first time since 1994.

REPUBLICAN POLICY COMMITTEE. The legislative **party organization** that discusses and recommends policy proposals for the consideration of the party leadership and the party conference. There is a policy **committee** in both the **House of Representatives** and the **Senate**.

REPUBLICAN SENATORIAL CAMPAIGN COMMITTEE (RSCC). A legislative **party organization,** formed in 1913 with the institution of direct popular election of senators, that provides **campaign** support to party nominees for **Senate** seats. This assistance takes various forms, but it is primarily financial. The **Republican Conference** designates one of its members as **chair,** who presides over a staff headquartered between the House office buildings and the offices of the **Republican National Committee** south of Capitol Hill.

REPUBLICAN STUDY COMMITTEE. A group of congressional Republicans who seek to promote **conservative** ideological conformity on the **Republican Conference.** As such, they roughly parallel the **Democratic Study Group.** The entity was established in the early 1970s. After the Republicans took control of the House in 1994, the incoming **Speaker, Newt Gingrich,** disbanded the group as unnecessary. Nevertheless, the group reformed, briefly styling themselves the Conservative Action Team, before reinstating their traditional title in 2001.

RESIDENCE REQUIREMENTS. Typical provisions of state law for voting eligibility. Initially rather formidable, as late as 50 years ago they averaged about one year. More recently, residence requirements have been reduced substantially, and even eliminated, not only at the initiative of the states themselves but also at the behest of the federal government. *See also* REGISTRATION.

RHODES, JOHN J. Republican minority leader of the House of Representatives, 1973–1981. (b. 18 September; d. 24 August 2003). John Rhodes was a Kansas native who moved to Arizona after serving in the U.S. Army during World War II. He became active in state Republican politics and won **election** to a **House of Representatives** seat in 1952. After two decades of service, his colleagues rewarded him by naming him their **floor leader** in 1973, following the extraordinary elevation of **Gerald R. Ford** to the vice presidency. Rhodes surrendered his position as **minority leader** to **Robert Michel** in 1981 and served one additional term in the House before retiring to Arizona.

RICHARDS, RICHARD. Republican National Committee chair, 1981–1983. (b. 14 May 1932). A Utah lawyer, Richards was heavily involved in **Republican Party** politics in that state, rising to the position of state party **chair**. In 1980, he served as the **campaign** coordinator for the victorious Republican presidential **ticket** of **Ronald W. Reagan** and **George H. W. Bush**. After the election, Reagan chose him to chair the **Republican National Committee**. In that position, he emphasized party fund-raising. He left office after two years and began practicing law in Washington, D.C.

RICHARDSON, JAMES D. Democratic minority leader of the House of Representatives, 1899–1903. (b. 10 March 1843; d. 24 July 1914). Richardson served 10 terms in the **House of Representatives** from Tennessee (1895–1905). In the 56th **Congress** (1899–1901), each party in the House began officially designating its **floor leader**. Richardson was the choice of the **Democratic Party**, a **minority** in the chamber. He stayed on in that position in the next Congress, but in 1905 he was replaced by **John Sharp Williams** of Mississippi.

RIGHT WING. A term designating a **conservative** position on an ideological spectrum. It originated at the beginning of the French Revolution in 1789, when the Estates General was debating the direction to take in dealing with its conflict with the monarchy. Those who pushed for a moderate response, one that essentially maintained the status quo, gathered on the right wing of the assembly hall; those seeking more radical change sat together on the **left wing**. Each **major party** has typically featured a right-wing **faction**, along with a left-wing counterpart. **Minor parties** traditionally flourish on the ideological extremes. *See also* NEOCONSERVATIVE.

ROBERTS, C. WESLEY. Republican National Committee chair, 1953. (b. 14 December 1903; d. 9 April 1975). Roberts was a Kansas newspaper publisher who became active in state **Republican Party** politics, becoming state **chair** (1947–1950). He played a prominent role in the presidential **campaign** organization of fellow Kansan **Dwight D. Eisenhower** in 1952, coordinating the professional operations at the headquarters of the **Republican National Committee** with its **amateur** counterpart, labeled Citizens for Eisenhower-

Nixon. After the **election**, Roberts replaced **Arthur Summerfield** as national party chair. Almost immediately, allegations surfaced that Roberts had violated a Kansas state lobbying law, and he soon resigned, returning to his business interests in Kansas.

ROBINSON, JOSEPH T. Democratic minority leader of the Senate, 1923–1933; Democratic majority leader of the Senate, 1933–1937. (b. 26 August 1872; d. 14 July 1937). Robinson began a decade of service in the **House of Representatives** from Arkansas in 1903. In 1912, he won election as governor, but he only served a few weeks before moving to the **Senate** to finish an unexpired term. He remained in the Senate for the rest of his life. He quickly ascended to a position of party leadership, becoming **floor leader** of the **minority** Democrats in 1923. He held that office for a decade.

In 1928, the **Democratic National Convention** nominated him for **vice president**, presenting a **balanced ticket**, headed by New York Governor **Alfred E. Smith**. Robinson's presence was not sufficient to stem significant erosion of traditional Southern support for the **Democratic Party**, and the **ticket** lost convincingly in November. Robinson remained a force in the Senate.

In 1933, when the Democrats assumed control of the chamber, he became **majority leader**. In that position, he played a key role in the enactment of the **New Deal**. Rumored to be in line for appointment to the Supreme Court, he died in the midst of the controversy over the proposal by President **Franklin D. Roosevelt** to "pack" the Court by adding new justices.

ROCKEFELLER, NELSON A. Republican vice president, 1974–1977. (b. 8 July 1908; d. 26 January 1979). Rockefeller was a grandson of John D. Rockefeller, the immensely wealthy founder of Standard Oil, and Nelson Aldrich, a powerful U.S. senator from Rhode Island. He worked in family enterprises until 1940, when he began a career in public service that absorbed his time and energies for the rest of his life. A lifelong member of the **Republican Party**, he served Presidents **Franklin D. Roosevelt**, **Harry S. Truman**, and **Dwight D. Eisenhower** in a variety of bipartisan diplomatic and administrative assignments. In 1958, he was elected governor of New York, an office he held until 1973.

Rockefeller contended unsuccessfully for the presidential **nomination** of the **Republican National Convention** in 1960, 1964, and 1968. He was identified with the **Eastern establishment** in the party, a once-powerful **faction** whose influence was declining precipitously.

Shortly after his resignation as governor in 1973, a vacancy developed in the office of **vice president**, following the resignation of President **Richard M. Nixon** and the accession of Vice President **Gerald R. Ford**. In accordance with the provisions of the 25th Amendment to the **Constitution**, President Ford nominated Rockefeller to be vice president, an action confirmed by **majority** vote in each chamber of **Congress**.

As vice president, Rockefeller played an active and visible role in the Ford **administration**. However, he continued to generate opposition within the party from his old factional rivals, conservatives who failed to appreciate Rockefeller's increasing accommodation of them. Facing a **conservative** challenge to his presidential nomination by **Ronald W. Reagan**, Ford encouraged Rockefeller to announce that he would not be a candidate for the vice presidential nomination in 1976. After leaving the vice presidency, Rockefeller devoted himself to his family business and philanthropic concerns.

ROMER, ROY. Democratic National Committee general chair, 1997–1999. (b. 31 October 1928). Romer rose to national party prominence from a base in state politics in Colorado. Initially elected to the state legislature in 1958, he was a key member of Governor Richard Lamm's administration, serving as chief of staff and later treasurer. In 1986, he succeeded Lamm as chief executive and was reelected twice. In 1997, President **Bill Clinton**, who had previously worked with Romer as a fellow governor, named him general **chair** of the **Democratic Party**. Initially, Romer served part-time, while continuing to hold gubernatorial office. His primary national party role was that of spokesman. In 1999, he retired as general chair, and **Edward G. Rendell** was named his replacement. In 2001, Romer became superintendent of the Los Angeles public school system.

ROOSEVELT, FRANKLIN D. Democratic president, 1933–1945. (b. 30 January 1882; d. 12 April 1945). Born into a prominent New

York family, Franklin Roosevelt carried the banner of the Hyde Park Roosevelts, differentiated from their Oyster Bay cousins by their loyalty to the **Democratic Party**. Coming of age when his distant cousin, **Theodore Roosevelt**, was a dominant force in state and national politics, Franklin Roosevelt was elected to the state senate in 1910. In 1913, he entered national politics when he joined the incoming **administration** of President **Woodrow Wilson** as assistant secretary of the navy. The next year, he unsuccessfully pursued a seat in the U.S. Senate. Remaining in the Navy Department throughout World War I, he was the vice presidential choice of the 1920 **Democratic National Convention**, in large measure because of the perceived voter appeal of the Roosevelt name. When the Democratic **ticket** lost in November, Roosevelt returned to New York, where he practiced law and pursued business opportunities.

In 1921, he contracted a severe case of polio that left his legs paralyzed for life. He remained visible on the state and national political scenes, nominating New York Governor **Al Smith** for president in both 1924 and 1928. In 1928, he ran successfully for Smith's vacated governorship. He was reelected in 1930 and emerged as the **front-runner** for the 1932 Democratic presidential **nomination**, which he secured on the fourth **ballot**. Elected in November, he took office in March 1933, with the nation mired in the depths of the **Great Depression**. He pursued an expansive and innovative policy agenda, popularly known as the **New Deal**, to enable the national government to respond to the unprecedented economic distress. His actions received public approval in a **landslide** reelection victory in 1936.

Four years later, with war raging in Europe and Asia, Roosevelt broke the two-term tradition established by George Washington when he accepted the Democratic nomination for a third term. The voters endorsed that decision by reelecting him in November. During his third term, the United States entered World War II, which continued throughout the 1944 presidential **campaign**. Roosevelt stood again for nomination and election to a fourth term, and his party and the voters responded affirmatively. In April 1945, five weeks after his inauguration, with victory in sight in Europe and the Pacific, Roosevelt suffered a fatal stroke. His unprecedented presidential tenure coincided with the establishment of the **Fifth Party System** and the restoration of the Democratic Party to the national dominance it had lost when the slavery controversy generated the Civil War.

ROOSEVELT, THEODORE. Republican president, 1901–1909. (b. 27 October 1858; d. 6 January 1919). "Teddy" Roosevelt's political career began in 1881, with his **election** to the New York State Assembly. In 1886, his reform candidacy for mayor of New York was unsuccessful. Three years later, he was introduced to national politics when President **Benjamin Harrison** appointed him to the Civil Service Commission. In 1895, he turned to local politics, accepting an appointment to the New York City board of police commissioners. Two years later, he returned to Washington as assistant secretary of the navy for President **William McKinley**. When the Spanish–American War broke out in 1898, Roosevelt organized the Rough Riders and achieved national acclaim for his military exploits in Cuba.

Returning home later that year a hero, he was elected governor of New York, campaigning as a reformer. Two years later, the Republicans selected him as their vice presidential nominee for McKinley's successful reelection bid, in part to satisfy the party leaders in New York, who were uncomfortable with his performance as governor.

When McKinley was assassinated in 1901, Roosevelt became the nation's youngest **president**. He won **nomination** and election in his own right in 1904, the first accidental president to do so. His presidency emphasized **progressive** themes, most notably "trust busting" by an energized national government, and an unprecedented activism in foreign policy.

In 1908, Roosevelt declined to seek a second full term, passing the torch to his party protégé, **William Howard Taft**. In retirement, he traveled abroad, leading an African safari. Disillusioned by Taft's tilt toward the **old guard** party conservatives, he made a bid for the party's 1912 presidential nomination. Taft's control of the party machinery doomed Roosevelt's comeback effort, and Roosevelt then bolted from the **Republican Party** to mount a **campaign** on behalf of the Progressive Party. This **minor party** effort was symbolized by the **bull moose**, to which Roosevelt likened his fitness. He secured significant popular and electoral vote support, but it came at the expense of President Taft and the Republicans, enabling **Democratic Party** nominee **Woodrow Wilson**, also identified as a progressive, to win a **plurality** of popular votes and a **majority** of electoral votes.

Roosevelt then resumed his foreign travels. With the outbreak of war in Europe, Roosevelt sought to organize an updated version of the Rough Riders, but Wilson withheld permission. Roosevelt died in January 1919, shortly after the end of World War I.

ROSEWATER, VICTOR. Republican National Committee chair, 1912. (b. 13 February 1871; d. 12 July 1940). The son of German immigrants, Victor Rosewater was a journalist, economist, and civic leader in his native Nebraska. His support for the **progressive** policies of President **Theodore Roosevelt** led to his **election** to the **Republican National Committee** in 1908. Rosewater followed Roosevelt's lead in backing the presidential candidacy of Roosevelt's **heir apparent, William Howard Taft.** When Roosevelt came out of retirement and challenged President Taft for the 1912 presidential **nomination**, Rosewater remained loyal to Taft. He had been appointed vice chair of the national committee by the **chair, John F. Hill.** When Hill died that spring, Rosewater took over. At the **Republican National Convention**, his parliamentary rulings aided the Taft cause. However, his disgruntled Nebraska party colleagues declined to reelect him to the national committee, and he was replaced as national party chair by another loyal Taft supporter, **Charles D. Hilles.** Rosewater returned to Nebraska and resumed his publishing career.

ROSS, JAMES. Federalist president pro tempore of the Senate, 1799. (b. 12 July 1762; d. 27 November 1847). Pennsylvania sent Ross to the **Senate** in 1794 to finish an unexpired term, and he went on to serve one additional term, leaving office in 1803. As the third session of the 5th Congress was about to end, Ross was elected **president pro tempore** on one occasion.

RUMP SESSION. A meeting of party dissidents. Within the **party organization**, rump sessions occur when a party **faction**, dissatisfied with **convention** deliberations, departs and convenes its own meeting. Within the party-in-office, rump sessions can take the form of a **caucus** of legislators unsympathetic to the party leadership.

RUNNING MATE. A junior member of a party **slate** of nominees for elective office. It is most often used more specifically to identify the vice presidential nominee. In designating a running mate, the presidential candidate and the party organization often seek a **balanced ticket**.

RUNOFF PRIMARY. A **primary** between the top two contenders in the regular primary. It occurs if state law requires that a primary victor receive a **majority** of votes cast. Runoff primaries have been widely used in the South, where the traditional dominance of the **Democratic Party** made **general election** contests superfluous and a legitimating majority vote at some point in the electoral process desirable.

RUSH, RICHARD. National Republican vice presidential nominee, 1828. (b. 29 August 1780; d. 30 July 1859). Rush was a Philadelphia lawyer who joined the **administration** of President **James Madison** as attorney general (1814–1817). President **James Monroe** retained him in that office briefly but soon sent him to Great Britain as minister (1817–1824). In that key role, Rush was centrally involved in the behind-the-scenes maneuvers that led to the issuance of the Monroe Doctrine. In 1820, one **Democratic-Republican Party** elector named him on the vice presidential **ballot**. President **John Quincy Adams** enlisted Rush as the secretary of the treasury. In 1828, when Adams sought reelection as the nominee of the **National Republican Party**, he designated Rush as his vice presidential **running mate**. They were soundly defeated in the fall **election**, and Rush retired to private life. Much later, President **James K. Polk** named him minister to France (1847–1849).

RUSK, THOMAS J. Democratic president pro tempore of the Senate, 1857. (b. 5 December 1803; d. 20 July 1857). Texas sent Rusk to the **Senate** in 1846. He remained there until his death just over a decade later. When the 35th **Congress** convened in special session in March 1857, prior to its scheduled beginning in December, Rusk was named **president pro tempore** on March 14. He died later that year.

RUSSELL, RICHARD B. Democratic president pro tempore of the Senate, 1969–1971. (b. 2 November 1897; d. 21 January 1971). Russell was elected governor of Georgia in 1931. He served two years before moving to the **Senate** in 1933. He held his Senate seat for the rest of his life, rising to chair of the powerful Armed Services and Appropriations Committees and becoming the leader of the Southern wing of the congressional party. In 1969, the departure of **Carl Hayden** made Russell the senior member of the **Democratic Party** in the chamber long controlled by his party, and he thus became the **president pro tempore.** He occupied that titular position for just over two years.

RUTLEDGE, JOHN. Electoral vote recipient, 1789 (Federalist). (b. September, 1739; d. 23 July 1800). Rutledge served two terms in the Continental Congress (1774–1776 and 1782–1783). Between those terms he was governor of his state (1779–1782). He represented South Carolina at the 1787 Constitutional Convention. He received six **favorite son** votes in the initial **electoral college** balloting. When the new government got under way, he was one of the initial nominees of President **George Washington** to the position of associate justice of the Supreme Court. He occupied his seat from 1789 to 1792.

– S –

SABIN, DWIGHT M. Republican National Committee chair, 1883–1884. (b. 25 April 1843; d. 22 December 1902). A Minnesota lumberman, Sabin served in the state legislature and began a single term in the U.S. **Senate** in 1883. That same year, with an **accidental president, Chester A. Arthur,** in the White House, the **Republican National Committee** named Sabin **chair** when the **incumbent, Marshall Jewell,** died. Sabin held the post for less than two years, resigning after the 1884 **Republican National Convention,** which nominated **James G. Blaine** for **president.** He failed in his bid for reelection to the Senate.

SACHEM. A party leader. The word, meaning chief, is of Indian origin. The **Tammany Hall** organization in New York City adopted Indian terminology for its leaders, members, and activities, popularizing the term's more general political usage.

SAFE SEAT. A legislative district whose electorate routinely chooses the nominee of a particular party to represent it. A safe seat is occasionally the product of a **gerrymander**. In the contemporary **Congress**, safe seats appear to be on the rise, as fewer and fewer districts feature meaningful party competition.

SANDERS, EVERETT. Republican National Committee chair, 1932–1934. (b. 8 March 1882; d. 12 May 1950). Sanders served four terms in the **House of Representatives** from Indiana (1917–1925). After leaving the House, he joined the White House staff of President **Calvin Coolidge**, serving as his secretary and performing certain tasks relating to party liaison. After practicing law briefly, Sanders returned to the political arena in 1932. In the midst of the **Great Depression**, which was devastating the electoral fortunes of the **Republican Party**, President **Herbert C. Hoover** followed Coolidge's recommendation and named Sanders **chair** of the **Republican National Committee**, in anticipation of the upcoming reelection **campaign**. Sanders represented the Midwestern region, which had generally remained loyal to the GOP despite the economic downturn. Although criticized within the party for the disastrous **election** outcome, he held his party post for two years before resigning.

SATRAP. A low-level party official. The word is of Persian origin and is used in the Bible in the book of Daniel. Its association with party politicians developed in the years following the **Civil War**.

SAULSBURY, WILLARD. Democratic president pro tempore of the Senate, 1916–1919. (b. 17 April 1861; d. 20 February 1927). Saulsbury followed his father and uncle to the **Senate** from Delaware. He served a single term (1913–1919). During the 64th **Congress**, the **president pro tempore, James P. Clarke** of Arkansas, died. Saulsbury replaced him and continued in that office throughout the 65th Congress.

SCALAWAG. The term, meaning rascal, was widely used by unreconstructed Southerners after the **Civil War** to refer to those from the South who collaborated with the **Republican Party**. *See also* CARPETBAGGER.

SCHELL, AUGUSTUS. Democratic National Committee chair, 1872–1876. (b. 1 August 1812; d. 27 March 1884). Schell was a New York financier who began his career in party politics in the 1840s as a district leader for **Tammany Hall**, the New York City **Democratic Party** political **machine**. In 1852, Tammany Hall backed him in an unsuccessful bid for governor. The next year, he began a three-year tour of duty as state party **chair**. After the presidential victory of **James Buchanan** in 1856, Schell received the prestigious **patronage** appointment as a customs collector of the Port of New York. He played a leading role in the presidential **campaign** of **Horatio Seymour** in 1868.

By 1872, Schell had risen to the top leadership position in Tammany Hall, grand **sachem**. That same year, the Democrats somewhat begrudgingly rallied to the presidential candidacy of **Liberal Republican Party** nominee **Horace Greeley**, making him their **fusion** choice. Long close to Greeley in New York politics, Schell became chair of the **Democratic National Committee** for the futile bid to block the reelection of **Ulysses S. Grant**, the nominee of the **Republican Party**. Schell was somewhat more successful in bringing the Liberal Republican **faction** into the Democratic **coalition** and in healing long-standing sectional divisions within the party.

SCOTT, HUGH D., JR. Republican National Committee chair, 1948–1949; Republican Senate minority leader, 1969–1977. (b. 11 November 1900; d. 9 July 1994). Scott won a seat in the **House of Representatives** from Pennsylvania in 1940. He served two terms, lost in 1944, but retook the seat in 1946 and held it for a decade. In 1948, he was the choice of **Republican Party** presidential nominee **Thomas E. Dewey** to **chair** the **Republican National Committee**. Like Dewey, Scott represented the **Eastern establishment** within the Republican **coalition**. His national party position provided him with a highly visible **campaign** role that fall. In the wake of Dewey's unexpected **election** defeat, Scott came under attack from the frustrated **old guard** wing of the party and resigned as party chair in 1949.

In 1958, Scott left the House when he succeeded in his bid for a **Senate** seat. He occupied that seat for three terms. In 1969, his **minority party** colleagues named him their **floor leader**, succeeding **Everett M. Dirksen**. Scott held his leadership position until his retirement from the Senate in 1977.

SCOTT, WINFIELD. Whig presidential nominee, 1852. (b. 13 June 1786; d. 29 May 1866). A career military officer, Scott served with distinction in the War of 1812 and the Black Hawk War. For two decades (1841–1861), he was general in chief of the U.S. Army. His tenure embraced the Mexican War and the outbreak of the **Civil War**. In 1852, the **Whig Party**, hoping to emulate its previous successes with military heroes **William Henry Harrison** and **Zachary Taylor**, turned to Scott as its presidential nominee. He lost convincingly to **Democratic Party** nominee **Franklin Pierce** and resumed his position of military leadership for almost another decade. He retired from active duty in 1861.

SECOND PARTY SYSTEM. Era of party competition that prevailed from about 1830 until the mid-1850s. The Second Party System emerged in the wake of the demise of the **Federalist Party** and the heightened intraparty tensions that beset the dominant **Democratic-Republican Party** as the **Era of Good Feelings** came to a close in the mid-1820s. This **party system**, or pattern of party competition, became increasingly clear after the **election** of **Andrew Jackson** to the presidency in 1828. It pitted Jackson's supporters, the **Democratic Party**, against his opponents, who came to call themselves the **Whig Party**. Typically, the Democrats prevailed in national-level competition, but the Whigs elected two presidents in the decade of the 1840s. In addition, they controlled both chambers of the 27th **Congress** (1841–1843) and one house on two other occasions. The intensification of the slavery controversy split both the Democrats and the Whigs along sectional lines. The Whigs could not survive the division and disintegrated in the mid-1850s, bringing to a close the Second Party System on the eve of the **Civil War**.

SEDGWICK, THEODORE. Federalist president pro tempore of the Senate, 1798; Federalist Speaker of the House of Representatives, 1799–1801. (b. 9 May 1746; d. 24 January 1813). Sedgwick served Massachusetts in the Continental Congress (1785–1788). When the first congressional elections under the 1787 Constitution were held, he won a seat in the **House of Representatives**. He held that seat until 1796, when he moved over to the **Senate** following his designation by the Massachusetts legislature to finish an unexpired term. In

1798, he was named **president pro tempore** on one occasion. That same year, with his Senate term about to end, he again sought election to the House. Victorious, he was elected **Speaker** when the 6th **Congress** convened, in a contest that clearly demonstrated the **partisan** divisions. He left the House after the term, in the wake of the **critical election** of 1800, which shifted control to the **Democratic-Republican Party**.

SENATE. A chamber of the U.S. **Congress**, as well as most state legislatures. At both national and state levels, the senate is typically known as the upper house, as opposed to the **House of Representatives**. Nationally, a senator is elected for a six-year term, with roughly one-third elected every two years. The **Constitution** provides that each state will have equal representation in the Senate, two apiece, so there are currently 100 senators. Originally, senators were designated by state legislatures, thereby providing representation for the states in the federal system. In 1913, the 17th Amendment to the Constitution altered this arrangement in favor of direct popular **election**. Eligibility requirements for senators are as follows: at least 30 years of age, 9 years a citizen, and an inhabitant of the state from which elected. The presiding officer, or president, of the Senate is the vice president of the United States. The Constitution also authorizes the Senate to choose a **president pro tempore** to preside in the absence of the **vice president**.

SENATOR. A member of the U.S. **Senate**. Most of the states in the federal system also have legislative chambers known as senates. Occupants of those offices are also known as senators. *See also* MEMBER OF CONGRESS; REPRESENTATIVE.

SENIORITY SYSTEM. An informal but well-established principle in both houses of **Congress** that links power and status to tenure within the congressional institution. In particular, the position of **chair** of a congressional committee has typically gone to the member of the **majority party** with the most years of continuous service on that committee.

The seniority system gradually emerged in Congress in the first half of the 19th century. When the new Republican Party came to power with the **Civil War**, it initially disregarded the seniority system, but it subsequently embraced and institutionalized it as the norm. A century later, in the 1970s, reformers within the **Democratic Party** attacked the automatic designation of committee leadership according to seniority and succeeded in authorizing the House **Democratic Caucus** to elect the committee chairs. However, most of the time, seniority remained in effect. After gaining control of Congress in 1995, the House **Republican Conference,** under the leadership of the new **Speaker, Newt Gingrich,** disregarded the seniority system in several instances in making committee leadership assignments. Further, it committed itself to the principle of term limits with regard to the tenure of committee. Currently, **Senate** Republicans place a higher value on seniority than either Senate Democrats or House Democrats and Republicans.

SERGEANT, JOHN. National Republican vice presidential nominee, 1832. (b. 5 December 1779; d. 23 November 1852). Sergeant represented Pennsylvania in the **House of Representatives** on several occasions (1815–1823, 1827–1829, and 1837–1841). When the dominant **Democratic-Republican Party** began experiencing strains, Sergeant identified with the **faction** opposing **Andrew Jackson.** In 1831, while out of public office, he was designated the vice presidential **running mate** of **Henry Clay** by a **convention** of the emergent **National Republican Party.** The **ticket** lost convincingly to Jackson and **Martin Van Buren** in the 1832 presidential **election**.

SERVICE PARTY. An approach to **party organization** revitalization that involves developing and providing services for party constituencies. These pertain primarily to fund-raising support and campaign assistance. **Ray C. Bliss** developed this approach during his tenure as **chair** of the **Republican National Committee** (1965–1969). **Charles A. Manatt** brought a similar perspective to the **Democratic National Committee** in the early 1980s. In both instances, doing so enhanced the role and status of the national party organizations.

SEVIER, AMBROSE H. Democratic president pro tempore of the Senate, 1845. (b. 10 November 1801; d. 31 December 1848). Sevier served as Arkansas's territorial delegate in the **House of Represen-**

tatives (1828–1836), identifying with the **Whig Party** in that time of turmoil with the emergence of the **Second Party System**. When Arkansas entered the Union, Sevier was elected to the **Senate** under the banner of the **Democratic Party**. He served there until 1848, when he resigned to accept a presidential appointment as minister to Mexico, where he played a major role in the diplomatic negotiations required by the end of the Mexican War. In 1845, Sevier was designated by Vice President **George M. Dallas** to serve as **president pro tempore** in Dallas's absence.

SEWALL, ARTHUR. Democratic vice presidential nominee, 1896. (b. 25 November 1835; d. 5 September 1900). Sewall was a Maine shipbuilder who was chosen for a seat on the **Democratic National Committee** in 1888. Eight years later, when the **Democratic National Convention** nominated **William Jennings Bryan** for **president**, Bryan declined to participate in the deliberations regarding his **running mate**. Several candidates were nominated, and Sewall emerged as the convention's choice on the fifth **ballot**. The **ticket** went down to defeat in November, and Sewall returned to private life.

SEYMOUR, HORATIO. Democratic presidential nominee, 1868. (b. 31 May 1810; d. 12 February 1886). Seymour was elected to two terms as governor of New York, separated by a decade (1853–1855 and 1863–1865). In 1868, in the first presidential election after the **Civil War**, the reunited **Democratic Party** convened in New York to nominate its presidential **ticket**. Seymour was selected permanent chair. After the **convention** became deadlocked, a reluctant Seymour became the compromise nominee on the 22nd **ballot**. He lost overwhelmingly to General **Ulysses S. Grant** in the fall **election**. In a lengthy retirement from politics that spanned almost two decades, Seymour practiced law in his hometown of Utica, New York.

SHADOW CABINET. British term referring to the parliamentary leaders of the **party-out-of-power**, who organize themselves in a formal fashion to oppose the **party-in-power** and in anticipation of gaining control of the government. In the United States, this term is occasionally used more broadly and less formally to refer either to the leadership of the **minority party** or to the advisers surrounding a presidential aspirant.

SHAVER, CLEMENT L. Democratic National Committee chair, 1924–1928. (b. 22 January 1867; d. 1 September 1954). Shaver was a West Virginia lawyer who served in the state legislature, chaired the state party, and managed successful statewide gubernatorial and senatorial campaigns. When fellow West Virginian **John W. Davis** received the 1924 presidential **nomination** of the **Democratic National Convention** after a record 103 ballots, Shaver became the national **chair** of the **faction**-ridden party. During and after the losing presidential **campaign**, he sought to conciliate the rival factions and foster party unity, without notable success.

SHERMAN, JAMES S. Republican vice president, 1909–1912. (b. 24 October 1855; d. 30 October 1912). Sherman got his start in **Republican Party** politics in 1884, when he was elected mayor of Utica, New York. Two years later, he won election to the **House of Representatives**, where he served two terms (1887–1891, 1893–1909). Sherman was closely allied with party leaders **Thomas B. Reed** and **Joseph G. Cannon**, both of whom served as **Speaker**. Cannon successfully promoted Sherman's candidacy for the vice presidential **nomination** at the 1908 **Republican National Convention**, which had previously nominated **William H. Taft** for **president**. During the fall **campaign**, Sherman faced unsubstantiated charges of influence-peddling and bribery, but the **ticket** easily prevailed.

Sherman's relationship with Taft was initially strained by the campaign allegations, but the two gradually became rather friendly. Sherman enjoyed his constitutional responsibility as **vice president** to preside over the **Senate**, but health problems often incapacitated him. Renominated in 1912, he died less than a week before the **election** that would have otherwise signaled the end of his tenure. The eight **electoral college** ballots awarded him were cast for Nicholas M. Butler.

SHERMAN, JOHN. Republican president pro tempore of the Senate, 1885–1886. (b. 10 May 1823; d. 22 October 1900). Sherman was a prominent Ohio **Republican** who served with distinction in the **House of Representatives**, the **Senate**, and in the **cabinet** for two presidents. He entered national political life in 1854, winning a House seat along with enough of his fellow Republicans to give that new party a **majority** in the chamber. He held that seat until 1861, when he moved over to the Senate, where he remained until 1877. Upon taking office, President **Rutherford B. Hayes** named him treasury secretary. When the Hayes **administration** left office, Sherman went back to the Senate for another 16-year stint. During the first session of the 49th Congress (1885–1886), he was elected **president pro tempore**. By the time **Congress** convened, the new **vice president, Thomas A. Hendricks,** had died, so Sherman's responsibility to preside over the Senate took on heightened significance. In 1897, Sherman joined the administration of incoming President **William McKinley** as secretary of state, holding the office for a year.

SHERMAN STATEMENT. A statement that irrevocably declines a party **nomination**. In 1884, General William Tecumseh Sherman, under pressure to seek the presidential nomination of the **Republican Party**, declared, "If nominated, I will not accept; if elected, I will not serve." Henceforth, an indication of the true intentions of an apparently reluctant **candidate** is whether he or she will follow Sherman's emphatic lead.

SHOO-IN. A prohibitive favorite in an **election** contest, one who is assured of victory.

SHORT BALLOT. A ballot in which few offices are subject to popular **election**. In the United States, elections generally feature a **long ballot**, wherein voters vote on a large number of public offices and some issues as well.

SHRIVER, R. SARGENT. Democratic vice presidential nominee, 1972. (b. 9 November 1915). Married to a daughter of financier Joseph Kennedy, Shriver managed the Merchandise Mart in Chicago, a Kennedy holding. When his brother-in-law **John F. Kennedy** became **president**, Shriver joined the **administration** as head of the Peace Corps (1961–1966). Subsequently, President **Lyndon B. Johnson** called on Shriver to lead his War on Poverty as director of the Office of Economic Opportunity (1964–1968). Johnson then named Shriver ambassador to France (1968–1970).

In 1972, Shriver unexpectedly won a place on the presidential **ticket** of the **Democratic Party**, following the withdrawal of vice presidential nominee Thomas Eagleton, the initial choice of presidential nominee **George S. McGovern** accepted by the **Democratic National Convention**. A few weeks later, Eagleton left the ticket under pressure, after reports of bouts with mental illness surfaced. The **Democratic National Committee** convened a special meeting to choose a replacement, and it accepted McGovern's recommendation of Shriver. The ticket lost in a **landslide** in November. Shriver remained active in presidential politics in the following years, but less on his own behalf than that of his brother-in-law, Senator Edward M. Kennedy.

SILENT MAJORITY. That large segment of the public that does not vocalize its opinion on controversial issues but that can potentially be relied on as a bulwark of political support. The term became popular in the late 1960s and early 1970s. President **Richard M. Nixon** used it to mobilize support for his Vietnam policy, in the face of demonstrators who had taken to the streets to oppose it.

SILVER GRAYS. A **faction** of the disintegrating **Whig Party** that convened in 1856 to nominate **Millard Fillmore** for **president**. Former president Fillmore, who had been the Whig nominee for **vice president** in the successful 1848 campaign and then succeeded to the presidency upon the death of **Zachary Taylor** in 1850, had been rejected by the Whigs in his bid for the 1852 nomination. In early 1856, he received the presidential **nomination** of the new **American Party** (the Know-Nothings). The Silver Grays in effect endorsed his candidacy. They received their name because one of their prominent leaders, **Francis Granger**, had a full head of silver-gray hair and because they embodied old-line, traditionalist elements within the Whig **coalition**.

SILVER REPUBLICANS. A small **faction** of the **Republican Party** around the turn of the 20th century. They embraced a **soft money** position on the currency issue. In 1900, they bolted from the party and nominated the previously designated presidential **ticket** of the **Democratic Party** to run under the Silver Republican Party banner in a **fusion** effort. After the resounding loss of nominee **William Jennings Bryan** to **William McKinley**, the Republican nominee that year, the Silver Republicans disintegrated as both party and faction.

SINGLE-MEMBER DISTRICT. A district that selects only one legislative representative. In contrast, a **multimember district** simultaneously selects several representatives. Single-member districts are the norm in the United States. French political scientist Maurice Duverger credits this institutional feature, and its **winner-take-all** character, with promoting a **two-party system**. It does so by discouraging **minor party** competition, because such parties lack sufficient support to finish first in an **election**.

SINGLE-PARTY SYSTEM. Also known as a one-party system, it features political domination by a single party. Single-party systems can be distinguished according to whether the ruling party tolerates competition, as is the case in the United States. During the presidency of **James Monroe**, the **Democratic-Republican Party** totally but briefly dominated the national political landscape, resulting in a single-party system known as the **Era of Good Feelings**. On a subnational level, the Democratic Party was similarly dominant in the post-Reconstruction South for about a century. *See also* MULTIPARTY SYSTEM; TWO-PARTY SYSTEM.

SINGLE TAX PARTY. A short-lived **minor party,** the Single Tax Party made its only appearance on the presidential **election** scene in 1920, nominating Robert C. Macauley of Pennsylvania, who made an insignificant showing. The party was identified with the 19th-century economic theories of Henry George, who claimed that private ownership of land caused the economic and social problems that beset society. His solution was a single tax on rental value.

SIXTH PARTY SYSTEM. A term sometimes used to describe the current era of party competition. The erosion of the foundations of the **Fifth Party System**, initiated in the 1930s with the **New Deal**, led some observers to argue that a Sixth Party System exists, and has done so since about 1968. This new pattern initially featured an unprecedented norm of **Republican Party** control of the White House and **Democratic Party** control of **Congress**. In the 1990s and after 2006, this pattern reversed itself. From 2000 to 2006, unified Republican **party government** generally prevailed, albeit by narrow margins. Regardless, contemporary party competition appears much more fluid and volatile than was usually the case in earlier party systems. Then, the occasional appearance of unusual volatility portended a **realignment**. **Dealignment**, or the weakening of **partisan** attachments in the electorate, has been credited as a major factor in this recent evolution in patterns of party competition. However, partisan attachments currently appear to be on the rise.

SLATE. A list of party nominees on a **ballot** for election. *See also* BALANCED TICKET; TICKET.

SMALLEY, DAVID A. Democratic National Committee Chair, 1856–1860. (b. 6 April 1809; d. 10 March 1877). A Vermont lawyer, Smalley was a lifelong friend and political supporter of **Stephen A. Douglas**. At the state level, he served the **Democratic Party** in the legislature and as party **chair**. After **Franklin Pierce**, from neighboring New Hampshire, won the presidency in 1852, Smalley received a **patronage** appointment as a customs collector, as Pierce reached out to supporters of his party rivals. In 1856, Smalley supported Douglas for **president** and pled for sectional reconciliation, whereas the **Democratic National Convention** nominated **James Buchanan** and the party divisions continued to widen. Smalley was named national party **chair** primarily because of his previous service on the **Democratic National Committee**. After Buchanan's election, Smalley became a federal district judge, a position he held for the rest of his life. When the **Civil War** broke out, he emerged as an ardent War Democrat, enthusiastically promoting the Union cause.

SMITH, ALFRED E. Democratic presidential nominee, 1928. (b. 30 December 1873; d. 4 October 1944). Alfred E. Smith was a veteran New York state legislator who represented **Tammany Hall**, the New York City **Democratic Party** political **machine**. He was elected governor of New York in 1918. Defeated in his bid for reelection in 1920, he persevered and won again in 1922, 1924, and 1926. In 1924, he mounted a strong challenge for the Democratic presidential **nomination**, but his candidacy was vigorously opposed and eventually blocked by rural, **dry** elements within the party **coalition**. That year, Smith received an enduring characterization as "the **Happy Warrior** of the political battlefield" in a **convention** nominating speech by **Franklin D. Roosevelt**.

In 1928, Smith won an easy first-**ballot** nomination from the **Democratic National Convention**, the first Roman Catholic to do so. In the fall **election**, he went down to an overwhelming defeat at the hands of **Republican Party** nominee **Herbert C. Hoover**. Smith's controversial candidacy met with resistance in many traditional Democratic bastions in the South and West, but he attracted large numbers of new voters in the urban Northeast to the party.

In 1932, Smith belatedly and futilely sought the Democratic presidential nomination, which went to his perceived protégé, Franklin D. Roosevelt. Smith later vocally opposed much of Roosevelt's **New Deal**.

SMITH, MARY LOUISE. Republican National Committee chair, 1974–1977. (b. 6 October 1914; d. 22 August 1997). Smith rose through the ranks of the state **party organization** in her native Iowa to become the only woman to date to **chair** the **Republican National Committee** (RNC). Serving on the RNC in 1973, she was elected vice chair. When the chair, **George H. W. Bush**, resigned to join the administration of President **Gerald R. Ford**, both Bush and Ford recommended the elevation of Smith to the position of chair. She worked to revive a party demoralized by the **Watergate** scandals and to unify the party for the 1976 presidential **election** after a divisive challenge by **Ronald W. Reagan** to the nomination of President Ford. She resigned her party post in the wake of the election defeat and was replaced by **William Brock**. In 1982, she accepted an invitation from President Reagan to serve on the U.S. Civil Rights Commission. Her brief tenure was marked by controversy because she resisted the right wing of the **Republican Party**, which was energized and empowered by Reagan's election. She was not reappointed in 1983.

SMITH, SAMUEL. Democratic-Republican president pro tempore of the Senate, 1805–1808, 1828–1831. (b. 27 July 1752; d. 22 April 1839). Smith was elected to the **House of Representatives** from Maryland in 1792, and he served five terms before moving over to the **Senate** in 1803. He was a strong supporter of President **Thomas Jefferson** and often an opponent of President **James Madison**. From 1805 to 1808, Smith was chosen **president pro tempore** on one occasion each year, when the **vice president** was absent. Smith left the Senate in 1815 and returned to the House in 1816 for three more terms. He went back to the Senate in 1822 and served until 1833. During this tenure, his colleagues named him president pro tempore four times, from 1828 to 1831.

SMOKE-FILLED ROOM. A site of deliberations by party leaders, where key nominating decisions are made. The term apparently originated in 1920 with reference to the **Republican National Convention** that nominated **Warren G. Harding** for **president**, but it became widely applicable to **convention** decision making of that era. It evoked pejorative images of party bosses puffing on cigars.

SNELL, BERTRAND H. Republican House minority leader, 1933–1939. (b. 9 December 1870; d. 2 February 1958). Snell entered the **House of Representatives** from New York after winning a **special election** in 1915. He went on to win 11 full terms. From 1933 until his retirement in 1939, when the **New Deal** of Democratic President **Franklin D. Roosevelt** was winning congressional approval and the **Republican Party** was in the **minority**, Snell was the Republican **floor leader**.

SOCIALIST LABOR PARTY. The first nationally based socialist party in the United States, which has demonstrated a remarkable longevity that belies its persistent lack of electoral support. Formed in 1874 as the Social Democratic Workingmen's Party, it adopted its current name in 1877 and contested is first presidential **election** in 1892. Never receiving as much as 1 percent of the popular vote, its best showing was in 1896 (0.3 percent). Its most influential leader was Daniel De Leon (1852–1914), a militant revolutionary socialist and antagonist of the organized labor movement. De Leon's uncompromising style kept the party ideologically pure but undermined its efforts to attract popular support. His legacy endures in party circles to this day.

SOCIALIST PARTY. A **minor party** of long-standing duration in the 20th century. The Socialist Party came into being in 1901. It combined the Social-Democratic Party of **Eugene V. Debs** with a moderate faction of the **Socialist Labor Party**. The party identified itself with the working class and the goal of collective ownership of the means of production and distribution in society. Under Debs's effective leadership, the Socialists soon emerged as a significant minor party. Debs received 6 percent of the popular vote in the 1912 presidential election. That same year, more than 1,000 Socialist candidates won elections to local offices across the land.

During World War I, the Socialists maintained a pacifist stance. Debs was convicted of sedition after making an antiwar speech and served a sentence in a federal penitentiary. From prison, he conducted his 1920 presidential **campaign**, receiving more popular votes than he had in 1912, but his percentage dropped to 3.4 percent.

In 1924, the Socialists joined forces with the **Progressive Party** led by **Robert M. La Follette**, unsuccessfully seeking to develop a formidable farmer–labor alliance. Four years later, and following the death of Debs, they nominated their new leader, Norman Thomas. Thomas headed the quadrennial party ticket from 1928 through 1948. He reached the peak of his public support in 1932, garnering 2.2 percent of the popular vote.

With the success of the **New Deal**, Socialist support declined dramatically, consistently falling below 0.5 percent. The Cold War following World War II exacerbated this problem, and after 1956, the party ceased to contest the presidential election for two decades. The party experienced a revival of sorts in 1976, but its electoral appeal has remained negligible. The end of the Cold War signaled its demise.

SOCIALIST WORKERS PARTY. Initially a **faction** of the **Communist Party** and later a **minor party**. The Socialist Workers began as a faction within the U.S. Communist Party sympathetic to the ideas and person of Russian revolutionary leader Leon Trotsky. After Trotsky lost his battle with Joseph Stalin for leadership of the Soviet Communist Party, Stalin ordered his followers expelled from the U.S. Communist Party in 1936. The American Trotskyites briefly allied with the **Socialist Party** but decided in 1938 to form their own party, which they named the Socialist Workers Party.

The Socialist Workers contested its first presidential **election** in 1948. Its popular support has been negligible, never surpassing 0.1 percent of the vote. In the 1960s, the Socialist Workers emerged as vocal activists on behalf of **civil rights** and against the Vietnam War.

SOFT MONEY. A term with two distinct usages in party politics. Over a century ago, when currency issues dominated political discourse, soft money, also known as easy money, referred to currency that was not fully backed by gold. When the pace of industrialization accelerated in the United States in the decades following the **Civil War**, class-based political divisions began to pit the rising industrial capitalists against the farmers and the laborers. Placed in broader historical context, conflict persisted between creditors and debtors. The latter groups perceived benefits to be derived from a soft money policy, whereas the former steadfastly advocated the **hard money** alternative.

Generally, the **Republican Party** embraced the hard money position, though its coalition included a small **faction** known as the **Silver Republicans**. In turn, the **Democratic Party** developed substantial hard money and soft money factions. **Grover Cleveland** and Alton B. Parker represented the hard money position; **William Jennings Bryan** championed soft money. A number of minor parties developed in support of the soft money position. Notable among them were the **Greenback Party** and the **People's Party**, better known as the Populists. The **critical election** of 1896 resulted in the triumph of the hard money position, and the currency debate receded in salience.

In current usage, soft money is money contributed to political parties ostensibly for use in party-building activities and in nonfederal elections. In contrast, hard money pertains to funds contributed directly to candidates, subject to regulation by the **Federal Election Commission (FEC)**. In 2002, the enactment of the **Bipartisan**

Campaign Reform Act prohibited soft-money contributions to the national political parties, placing them under the restrictive purview of the FEC.

SOLID SOUTH. Traditional reference to the Southern states as a **Democratic Party** stronghold. The inclination of Southern voters to support the Democratic Party had clear roots in the party's founding under **Andrew Jackson**, but it emerged full-blown in the wake of the **Civil War** and the negative reaction in that region to the policies and practices of the **Republican Party**. In the decades that followed, the white South persisted as a key component in the national Democratic **coalition**, whose support enabled the Democrats to remain nominally competitive in an era of national Republican Party dominance.

In presidential politics, the Solid South began to erode in 1928, when **Herbert C. Hoover** made inroads at the Democrats' expense. In 1948, the **Dixiecrats** abandoned the Democrats amid growing concerns about the national party's commitment to **civil rights**. In the 1950s and 1960s, white Southerners proved increasingly willing to vote Republican in presidential elections. A "trickle-down" phenomenon gradually made the Republicans more competitive in statewide and local races as well. In a remarkable inversion, by the mid-1990s the South was clearly tilted toward the Republican camp. *See also* REALIGNMENT; SOUTHERN STRATEGY; YELLOW DOG DEMOCRAT.

SOLIDARY INCENTIVES. Motivations for **partisan** activity grounded in the social rewards such activity provides. They embrace the sense of belonging associated with party involvement. Party fund-raisers can attract financial support by appealing to solidary incentives by, for example, scheduling gala occasions at which contributors can mingle with celebrities. *See also* MATERIAL INCENTIVES; PURPOSIVE INCENTIVES.

SONS OF THE WILD JACKASS. A turn-of-the-20th-century term characterizing a **faction** within the **Republican Party**, based in the Western states, that frustrated the party's **old guard** with its unwillingness to hew to the **party line**, instead embracing **progressive** ideals.

SORE-LOSER LAW. A law that prohibits a candidate who loses in a party **primary** contest from appearing on the **ballot** in the ensuing **general election** as the nominee of another party. The purpose of a sore-loser law is to protect the integrity of the party **nomination** process. Such a law precludes **fusion** nominees. Sore-loser laws are on the books in several states.

SOUTHARD, SAMUEL L. Whig president pro tempore of the Senate, 1841. (b. 9 June 1787; d. 26 June 1842). Southard followed his father and older brother into party politics and government service. He began his political career as a **Democratic-Republican Party** loyalist from New Jersey. He went to the **Senate** in 1821 and left two years later to become secretary of the navy under President **James Monroe.** President **John Quincy Adams** retained him in that position throughout his term. Southard later was elected governor of New Jersey (1832–1833). The split of the Democratic-Republican Party placed him within the camp of the **Whig Party.** Southard went back to the Senate as a Whig in 1833 and remained there for the rest of his life. Late in his Senate service, he became **president pro tempore** on one occasion. His brief tenure took on historic significance because it occurred when the vice presidency was vacant following the death of President **William Henry Harrison** and the accession of Vice President **John Tyler.**

SOUTHERN DEMOCRATIC PARTY. Regional party **faction** that bolted in 1860 and constituted itself as a **minor party.** In 1860, Southern Democrats, insisting on protection for slavery and unwilling to support the presidential nominee of the **Democratic Party, Stephen A. Douglas,** formed their own party and nominated Vice President **John C. Breckinridge** of Kentucky for president. Breckinridge ran on a **party platform** that recognized the right to have slavery in the territories. He carried nine Southern and border states and won 18.1 percent of the overall popular vote. The split in the Democratic ranks allowed the **Republican Party** nominee, **Abraham Lincoln,** to win a popular **plurality** and a **majority** in the **electoral college.** Southern Democrats played leading roles in the government of the Confederacy during the **Civil War.** After the war and the subsequent Reconstruction, they reentered the ranks of the national Democrats.

SOUTHERN STRATEGY. A successful effort by the **Republican Party** beginning in the 1950s to attract the electoral support of white Southern voters who were becoming increasingly disenchanted with the **Democratic Party**, which had traditionally claimed their loyalties. A catalyst for this transformation was the national Democratic Party's commitment to **civil rights**. In addition, post–World War II economic development in the region brought the class system more into line with national patterns, in that more affluent voters were disposed to vote Republican. President **Dwight D. Eisenhower** was an early beneficiary of this strategy, without doing much to promote it. **Barry M. Goldwater, Richard M. Nixon, Ronald W. Reagan**, and both **George H. W. Bush** and **George W. Bush** were much more assertive in their appeals. By the 1980s, the South had clearly shifted toward the Republican camp in presidential elections. Democratic presidential nominees **Jimmy Carter** (1976, 1980) and **Bill Clinton** (1992, 1996), native Southerners, had some limited success in offsetting this trend, but Tennessean **Al Gore** (2000) had none. *See also* REALIGNMENT; SOLID SOUTH.

SPANGLER, HARRISON E. Republican National Committee chair, 1942–1944. (b. 10 June 1879; d. 28 July 1965). An Iowa lawyer, Spangler worked his way up through the ranks of the state **Republican Party** to the position of state party **chair** and a place on the **Republican National Committee**. In the 1930s, he was prominent in the party's efforts to rebuild its **grassroots** support in the wake of the **Great Depression**. In 1942, **Joseph W. Martin Jr.**, the **floor leader** of the Republican **minority** in the **House of Representatives**, resigned his coterminous position as national party chair. Division developed within the national **committee** regarding his successor, and Spangler emerged as a compromise choice, one without a strong identity in either the internationalist or isolationist **factions** of the party. He served until 1944, when the new presidential nominee, **Thomas E. Dewey**, named his **campaign** manager, **Herbert Brownell Jr.**, to the post. Brownell retained Spangler as the general counsel of the national committee.

SPARKMAN, JOHN J. Democratic vice presidential nominee, 1952. (b. 20 December 1899; d. 16 November 1985). Initially elected to the

House of Representatives from Alabama in 1936, Sparkman moved over to the **Senate** in 1946 and remained there until his retirement in 1979. In 1952, Sparkman was the choice of presidential nominee **Adlai E. Stevenson II** to receive the vice presidential bid from the **Democratic National Convention**. The ensuing electoral defeat did not mar Sparkman's standing at home or in the Senate, where he rose through the **seniority system** to become a major presence, chairing the Banking Committee and later the Foreign Relations Committee.

SPEAKER OF THE HOUSE OF REPRESENTATIVES. The constitutionally designated presiding officer of the **House of Representatives**. With the advent of political parties in **Congress**, the office of Speaker became identified with the **majority party**. For over two decades following the ratification of the Constitution, the Speaker was largely a figurehead. However, in 1792 Congress demonstrated the potential significance of the office by establishing the Speaker as third in the line of presidential succession, after the **vice president** and the **president pro tempore** of the Senate.

The election of **Henry Clay** in 1811 signified the emergence of the office as one of preeminent party leadership in the chamber. The power and influence of the Speaker as party leader has ebbed and flowed over the decades. It reached a high-water mark toward the end of the 19th century, carrying over through the first decade of the 20th century under **Thomas B. Reed** and **Joseph G. Cannon**. In 1910, the disenchanted House moved decisively to reduce the power of the Speaker's office. More recently, **Jim Wright**, **Newt Gingrich**, and **Nancy Pelosi** have been extraordinarily assertive in their exercise of the party leadership prerogatives accruing to the Speaker. The presence of **divided party government** tends to enhance the party leadership role of the Speaker.

With regard to presidential succession, legislation in 1886 displaced the congressional officials in favor of **cabinet** officers, beginning with the secretary of state. In 1947, however, the Speaker was elevated to second in line, after the vice president. The 25th Amendment to the **Constitution**, ratified in 1967, provides a procedure for filling a vacancy in the vice presidency, substantially reducing the prospects that a Speaker would be elevated to the presidency via vacancy.

SPECIAL ELECTION. An **election** held outside the normal schedule for an office, owing to a vacancy in that office. The **Constitution** mandates that vacancies in the **House of Representatives** be filled by election rather than appointment, so such vacancies will normally necessitate a special election. *See also* GENERAL ELECTION.

SPEECHWRITER. Someone employed to prepare public remarks, formal and informal, for another person. In the realm of party politics, speechwriters serve candidates for public office and party leaders in both the **party-in-office** and the **party organization**. Speechwriters have become integral figures on campaign staffs, and they often move into governmental offices when their candidates emerge victorious. At the presidential level, the establishment and expansion of the White House staff during the **New Deal** era has afforded modern presidents with the capacity to locate speechwriters close by within the executive office. Lesser governmental executives do likewise, as well as members of **Congress.**

SPIN. A term coined in the late 1980s to refer to a favorable interpretation placed on an event or circumstance, from the perspective of the interpreter. Candidates and officeholders, along with their opponents, provide spin to the media and the public. *See also* SPIN DOCTOR.

SPIN DOCTOR. One who provides **spin**, or an interpretation of an event or situation that favors the political perspective of the interpreter. Contemporary campaigns use spin doctors to put forward interpretations to the media and the public. Spin doctors are especially visible in the aftermath of noteworthy events such as presidential debates and addresses.

SPLINTER GROUP. A component of a larger **coalition** that is dissatisfied with the direction of the coalition. In party politics, a splinter group threatens **party unity**. *See also* FACTION.

SPLIT PARTY GOVERNMENT. *See* DIVIDED PARTY GOVERNMENT.

SPLIT TICKET. *See* TICKET-SPLITTER.

SPOILS SYSTEM. Principle for staffing government positions. The spoils system suggests that electoral victory authorizes the winning party to staff the appointive offices of government with party loyalists. The term itself comes from the old Roman saying, "To the victor belong the spoils," with spoils in this case referring to **patronage** positions in the government.

The roots of the spoils system in American politics can be found at the outset of the presidency of **George Washington**, when his stated criterion for holding federal office, "fitness of character," resulted in appointments for supporters of Treasury Secretary **Alexander Hamilton**. President **Andrew Jackson** openly and enthusiastically embraced the spoils system. It flourished over the next half century, but it began to decline under assault from reformers promoting the ideal of a civil service staffed according to the merit principle. In the wake of the assassination of President **James A. Garfield** by a disappointed office-seeker, the Civil Service Reform Act of 1882, popularly known as the Pendleton Act, instituted such a **merit system**. Over the next century, the merit principle came to cover the great **majority** of federal government jobs. At the state and local levels, the merit principle has made substantial incursions on the spoils system, but pockets of tradition endure. Proponents of the spoils system argue that it ensures loyalty, accountability, and responsiveness in the bureaucracy. Opponents emphasize the likelihood of incompetents being appointed.

SQUARE DEAL. A campaign slogan President **Theodore Roosevelt** offered voters in 1904 to characterize his agenda. It evoked honesty and fairness in explicitly attacking the trusts that dominated the business community.

STALKING HORSE. A **candidate** put forward to advance the political interests of another candidate, perhaps by drawing support away from yet another candidate.

STALWARTS. A **faction** of the **Republican Party** during the **Gilded Age**. Stalwarts were the loyal party regulars who resisted calls for reform. Their leader was New York Senator Roscoe Conkling. They were opposed by a rival party faction, the **Half-Breeds**.

STANDARD-BEARER. A party nominee, typically a top-level one, representing the party and the party **ticket** to the electorate.

STATES' RIGHTS DEMOCRATIC PARTY. A **minor party** representing a regional **faction** of the **Democratic Party** after World War II that bolted from the party in 1948. Many Southern Democrats had become increasingly disenchanted with the national party's embrace of **civil rights** and its willingness to advocate the use of national authority to implement that commitment. This faction became known as the **Dixiecrats**.

Prior to the 1948 **Democratic National Convention**, Dixiecrat spokesmen called on Southern delegates to withdraw from the **convention** if it supported the pro-civil-rights program advocated by President **Harry S. Truman**. When the convention adopted a strong civil rights platform plank, the Mississippi delegation, along with half of their Alabama counterparts, walked out. This group reconvened in Birmingham and nominated South Carolina governor **J. Strom Thurmond** for **president**. The new party's organizers were mainly from the ranks of state-level officials. Members of **Congress** were generally unwilling to identify with it.

In the presidential **election**, the party won only 2.4 percent of the national popular vote. However, it carried four Southern states and thus won their 39 electoral votes. Although President Truman's popular vote only constituted a **plurality** (43 percent), he received a comfortable **majority** in the **electoral college** balloting. After the election, the Dixiecrats reentered the Democratic Party fold. There, they continued to exist as an identifiable faction for about two decades, until the Democratic Party in the South began routinely nominating candidates committed to the cause of civil rights.

STEAMROLLER. An overwhelming show of force by a party or **faction** to defeat opposition.

STEELE, MICHAEL S. Republican National Committee chair, 2009– . (b. 19 October 1958). Steele grew up in the District of Columbia metropolitan area. Educated at Johns Hopkins, Villanova, and George Washington Universities, he prepared for the priesthood, but ultimately received a law degree. Working in the private sector in investments, he became active in the Maryland **Republican Party**, rising to the position of state **chair** in 2000. He was the first African American to serve as a state party chair for the **GOP**. In 2002, he resigned to pursue elective office as the party nominee for lieutenant governor, and the party **ticket** prevailed in the **general election**. Four years later, he became the party nominee for an open seat in the U.S. **Senate**, a race he lost. Following his defeat, he figured in speculation for the position of national party chair, but that position went, at the behest of President **George W. Bush**, to the tandem of Senator **Mel Martinez** as general chair and **Mike Duncan**. Steele went on to head GOPAC, a **political action committee** that funds Republican campaigns. In 2009 Steele, along with others, challenged Duncan's bid for reelection as party chair. Without an **incumbent** president, the members of the **Republican National Committee** had discretion in choosing their leader. Steele emerged as the choice of a **majority** on the sixth **ballot**. He became the first African American to serve as Republican national chair, and the second to do so for a **major party**, the first having been **Ron Brown** for the **Democratic Party**.

STENNIS, JOHN C. Democratic president pro tempore of the Senate, 1987–1989. (b. 3 August 1901; d. 23 April 1995). Stennis entered the **Senate** in 1947 as a Mississippi gubernatorial appointee to fill a vacancy. He subsequently won six terms on his own before his retirement in 1989 after 41 years in office. The **seniority system** elevated him to the position of **chair** of two powerful committees: Armed Services and Appropriations. Very late in his tenure, as the senior Democrat in the chamber, he was named **president pro tempore** for his last two years in office (1987–1989).

STEVENS, THEODORE. Republican president pro tempore of the Senate, 2003–2007. (b. 18 November 1923). Born in Indiana, Ted Stevens practiced law in Alaska before joining the Department of the Interior in the Eisenhower **administration**, where he worked on behalf of statehood for Alaska. Returning to his new home, Stevens won a seat in the state legislature in 1964. Four years later, he was a gubernatorial appointee to fill a vacancy in the U.S. **Senate**. He won a **special election** in 1970 and six subsequent terms. When the Republicans won control of the chamber in 1995, Stevens's seniority made him **chair** of the Governmental Affairs Committee. Two years later, he became chair of the powerful Appropriations Committee. In 2003, with the Republicans again in the **majority**, his status as the longest currently serving Republican senator accorded him the title of **president pro tempore**. The outcome of the 2006 congressional elections placed the Senate under **Democratic Party** control, so Stevens relinquished that title to **Robert C. Byrd**. In 2007, Stevens supplanted **J. Strom Thurmond** as the longest serving Republican senator in history. His 2008 bid for a seventh term was derailed by his indictment and conviction on ethics-related charges, leading to a narrow loss in November. In 2009, following Stevens's appeal of his conviction, the Justice Department dropped the charges, effectively overturning the conviction.

STEVENSON, ADLAI E. Democratic vice president, 1893–1897; Democratic vice presidential nominee, 1900. (b. 25 October 1835; d. 14 June 1914). Born in Kentucky, Stevenson moved with his family to Bloomington, Illinois, during his teenage years. He practiced law and became a supporter of **Stephen A. Douglas**. Stevenson won election to the **House of Representatives** in 1874. He lost his re-election bid in 1876, but he regained his seat in 1878, retiring after a single additional term. When the **Democratic Party** won the White House in 1884, for the first time in a generation, Stevenson received a **patronage** appointment from President **Grover Cleveland** as first assistant postmaster, whence he led the Democrats' effort to reap the benefits of the **spoils system**. In 1889, **lame duck** President Cleveland nominated Stevenson to the Supreme Court, but the Republican **Senate** refused to confirm him, in part in revenge for Stevenson's role in displacing loyal Republicans from their patronage posts.

In 1892, Stevenson won the vice presidential **nomination** of the **Democratic National Convention**, which had earlier renominated Cleveland for **president**. Stevenson's presence on the presidential **ticket** was attractive to the **soft money** proponents of bimetallism, and his **favorite son** candidacy brought Illinois into the Democratic camp for the first time since 1856, two key factors in the Democrats' success in November. Stevenson's vice presidency was uneventful.

In 1900, the **Democratic National Convention** again turned to Stevenson as the vice presidential nominee, this time to accompany

William Jennings Bryan in his second presidential bid. The ticket lost convincingly in November. Eight years later, Stevenson made an unsuccessful bid for governor and then retired from public life.

STEVENSON, ADLAI E., II. Democratic presidential nominee, 1952, 1956. (b. 5 February 1900; d. 14 July 1965). The grandson and namesake of the **vice president** in the second term of President **Grover Cleveland**, Adlai Stevenson was a Chicago lawyer who joined the **administration** of **Franklin D. Roosevelt** as assistant to the secretary of the navy (1941–1944). In 1945, he occupied a parallel position in the State Department. After the war, he entered elective politics, winning the Illinois governorship in 1948. As his term neared its end, he was drawn reluctantly into the contest for the 1952 Democratic presidential **nomination**. He prevailed at the **Democratic National Convention** on the third **ballot** but went down to defeat in November against his popular **Republican Party** opponent, **Dwight D. Eisenhower**.

Stevenson returned to Illinois, but he continued to pursue presidential politics, positioning himself for a rematch with Eisenhower. He actively sought the 1956 nomination and won an easy first-ballot **convention** victory. In the fall **election**, he again fell before an Eisenhower **landslide**.

Despite the pleas of his loyal supporters, he refused to be drawn into the struggle for the 1960 Democratic presidential nomination, which went to **John F. Kennedy**. Stevenson aspired to be secretary of state under Kennedy but settled for the lesser position of United Nations ambassador. Retained in that position by President **Lyndon B. Johnson**, he died in 1965.

STEVENSON, ANDREW. Democratic Speaker of the House of Representatives, 1827–1834. (b. 21 January 1784; d. 25 January 1857). Stevenson won a seat in the **House of Representatives** in 1820. Taking office the following year, he served until 1834, the last seven years as **Speaker**. He was a strong supporter of President **Andrew Jackson** and participated in the formation of the **Democratic Party** in the wake of the split in the **Democratic-Republican Party** into two distinct factions.

STRAIGHT TICKET. A vote that supports all of a party's nominees on the **ballot**. Some states facilitate a straight-ticket vote by allowing the voter to make a single mark that has the effect of a vote for the entire party **ticket**. *See also* PARTY-COLUMN BALLOT.

STRATARCHY. A term coined by political scientist Samuel Eldersveld. It refers to the relative autonomy enjoyed by distinct levels of **party organization** in the decentralized American **party system**, a product of federalism in the governmental order. It contrasts with the more familiar term *hierarchy*, suggesting a clear top-down authority relationship among the various levels.

STRAUSS, ROBERT. Democratic National Committee chair, 1972–1977. (b. 9 October 1918). A Texas lawyer and businessman, Strauss became a leader in the state **Democratic Party** organization before relocating to Washington, D.C., where he played a prominent role in national party politics and government and in the legal community. In 1968, Strauss became a member of the **Democratic National Committee** at the behest of Governor John Connally. He quickly emerged as a major force in that body, joining the executive committee in 1969, being elected treasurer in 1970, and finally being named **chair** in 1972, following the party's disastrous showing in the presidential **election**. As party chair, Strauss guided the party's rising fortunes during the **Watergate** scandals that proved so devastating to the **Republican Party**, culminating in the election of the Democratic presidential nominee, **Jimmy Carter**, in 1976. Carter brought Strauss into the **administration** as his special trade representative, a **cabinet** position. After leaving government, Strauss established himself as a top-level lawyer-lobbyist in the nation's capital. In 1991, fellow Texan **George H. W. Bush** named Strauss ambassador to the Soviet Union. Following the dissolution of the Soviet Union, Strauss remained in Moscow as ambassador to Russia until his resignation in November 1992. Afterward, he resumed his practice of law.

STUART, CHARLES E. Democratic president pro tempore of the Senate, 1856. (b. 25 November 1810; d. 19 May 1887). Stuart served in the state legislature of Michigan before going to the **House of**

Representatives in a **special election** in 1847. He failed in his re-election bid but took back the seat in 1850. In 1852, he was elected to the **Senate**, where he served a single term. In 1856, he briefly served as **president pro tempore** during a vacancy in the vice presidency. Stuart did not seek reelection in 1858. He returned home to Michigan and practiced law.

SUFFRAGE. The right or privilege of voting. Under the original Constitution, states determined voter qualifications. Several constitutional amendments have restricted state discretion in this area. The 15th (race), the 19th (gender), the 24th (poll tax), and the 26th (age) Amendments all establish a single national standard for a specific criterion. Current suffrage requirements pertain to citizenship, residence, and registration.

SUMMERFIELD, ARTHUR E. Republican National Committee chair, 1952–1953. (b. 17 March 1899; d. 26 April 1972). Summerfield was a Michigan automobile executive who became a leader in the state **Republican Party.** He joined the **Republican National Committee** in 1944. There, he played a key role in coordinating the midterm congressional campaigns in the Midwestern states in 1950.

At the 1952 **Republican National Convention,** Summerfield delivered the support of the Michigan delegation to **Dwight D. Eisenhower** at a pivotal moment in the balloting, contributing to Eisenhower's presidential **nomination.** In return, Eisenhower named Summerfield national party **chair.** His role in the presidential **campaign** was initially peripheral. It increased in importance in the context of the controversy over campaign funds received over the years by vice presidential nominee **Richard M. Nixon,** who called on the Republican National Committee to judge whether he should remain on the **ticket.** Following Eisenhower's lead, Summerfield stood by Nixon, and the campaign ended in a convincing victory. After the **election,** Eisenhower brought Summerfield into his **cabinet** as **postmaster general.** Summerfield held that position throughout Eisenhower's presidency and then retired from public life.

SUPERDELEGATES. Democratic **national party convention** delegates who represent the **party-in-office** and the **party organiza-**

tion. Officially labeled unpledged delegates, they are typically designated ex officio. In the mid-1980s, the **Democratic Party** developed delegate selection procedures specifically authorizing superdelegates in an effort primarily to reintegrate the party-in-office and party organization constituencies, which had been substantially displaced by the reforms of the late 1960s and early 1970s. Secondarily, superdelegates were positioned to **broker** a tightly contested **convention** and provide a measure of peer review of delegate selection decisions made in fragmentary fashion over the course of the nominating season. To date, superdelegates have affected convention decision making most decisively in 1984 and 2008. In the former instance, they provided the margin of victory for **Walter F. Mondale** over Gary Hart. In the latter, they did so for **Barack H. Obama** over Hillary Clinton. Approximately one-fifth of the delegates to the 2008 **Democratic National Convention** were superdelegates.

SUPER TUESDAY. The name given to a series of 1988 presidential primaries deliberately held by several Southern states on the same date relatively early in the **presidential primary** schedule. The coordinated decisions to do so represented an attempt by the state Democratic parties in the South, and the state legislatures they controlled, to restore a significant role for the South in the selection of **Democratic Party** presidential nominees. That role had been in decline since the abandonment of the **two-thirds rule** in 1936. More recently, the decline had been exacerbated by the breakup of the **Solid South**, as Southern voters demonstrated an increasing propensity to support **Republican Party** nominees in presidential contests. Since 1988, many Southern states have continued the practice of setting a common presidential primary date. Some states outside the South have joined them, and media commentators continue to use the phrase Super Tuesday to refer to that event.

SWING VOTER. An **independent**, one who declines to establish a **partisan** identity, who relies on election-specific **candidate** and issue factors in making a voting decision. Swing voters typically play a significant role in determining election outcomes. *See also* SWITCHER.

SWITCHER. A member of one party who crosses party lines and, in casting a **ballot** for the **candidate** of another party, at least tentatively identifies with the latter. A switcher differs from a swing voter in claiming a nominal party affiliation and from a **crossover voter** in loosely embracing a new party affiliation. *See also* TICKET-SPLITTER.

– T –

TAFT, ROBERT A. Republican majority leader of the Senate, 1953. (b. 8 September 1889; d. 31 July 1953). The son of President **William H. Taft**, Robert A. Taft was elected to the **Senate** from Ohio in 1938. Two years later, he contended for the presidential **nomination** of the **Republican National Convention** as the **candidate** of the **old guard**, finishing second in the balloting behind **Wendell L. Willkie**. On two subsequent occasions, he was the **convention** runner-up, to **Thomas E. Dewey** in 1948 and **Dwight D. Eisenhower** in 1952. Eisenhower's presidential coattails that year carried the **Republican Party** back into control of the **Senate**, and Taft assumed the position of **majority leader**. However, he was in failing health and died a few months later.

TAFT, WILLIAM H. Republican president, 1909–1912. (b. 15 September 1857; d. 8 March 1930). Taft was an Ohio state judge when President **Benjamin Harrison** named him solicitor general in 1890. Two years later, Harrison placed him on the federal bench as a judge in a circuit court of appeals. In 1900, President **William McKinley** prevailed on him to leave the judicial slot to head the newly established Philippine Commission and subsequently to become civil governor of the Philippines (1901–1904). President **Theodore Roosevelt** brought Taft back to Washington as secretary of war in 1904 and then designated him as his **heir apparent** in 1908, when Roosevelt retired from office. Taft won easy **nomination** and **election** victories.

However, Taft's performance as president disappointed Roosevelt, who viewed Taft's policies as a betrayal of his own **progressive** vision. In 1912, Roosevelt came out of retirement to challenge Taft for the Republican presidential **nomination**. Taft easily prevailed at the **Republican National Convention**, but he could not prevent Roosevelt from continuing his candidacy as the **standard-bearer** of the **Progressive Party**. Roosevelt's **minor party** candidacy divided the traditional Republican constituency and ensured the election of **Democratic Party** nominee **Woodrow Wilson**. Taft ran a poor third in both the popular and electoral votes.

Once out of office, Taft taught constitutional law at his alma mater, Yale. In 1918, President Wilson named him cochair of the National War Labor Board. When a vacancy in the position of chief justice of the Supreme Court occurred in 1921, President **Warren G. Harding** satisfied Taft's long-standing ambition for the seat and made him the only person to date to hold the top executive and judicial offices in the federal government. He served with distinction until his death almost nine years later.

TAGGART, THOMAS. Democratic National Committee chair, 1904–1908. (b. 17 November 1856; d. 6 March 1929). Taggart, an Indiana newspaper publisher, worked his way up through the organizational ranks of the local and state **Democratic Party**. He became **chair** of the **Democratic National Committee** during a time when the party's national fortunes were in decline. In 1904, he led the **party organization** during the ill-fated challenge by Judge Alton B. Parker to the bid by President **Theodore Roosevelt** for a term in his own right, and the **Republican Party** maintained solid majorities in both houses of **Congress** that year and again in 1906. Taggart departed the office as the 1908 **campaign** got under way. Some years later, in 1916, he held a **Senate** seat from Indiana by appointment for a few months.

TAMMANY HALL. The **Democratic Party** organization in New York City. Founded in 1789, Tammany was originally a fraternal organization, named after a 17th-century Indian chief. Tammany Hall was the building where the organization met. With the emergence of political parties, Tammany gradually became identified first with the **Democratic-Republican Party**, where its statewide supporters were known as Bucktails, and subsequently with the Democratic Party. This identification was clearly established prior to the **Civil War**. The **machine** provided material services for city residents, targeting the teeming immigrant populations, in return for their electoral support. The city became a Democratic stronghold, providing votes that made the party competitive on both the state and national levels.

After the war, Tammany Hall developed a notorious reputation for graft and corruption under its leader, or grand **sachem**, William M. Tweed. Tweed served simultaneously as county **chair** of the Democratic Party, personifying and solidifying the connection between the two institutions. The Tweed Ring was overthrown in the early 1870s, but the stench of corruption endured. Tammany Hall remained a target of waves of **progressive** reformers in both major political parties. Ultimately, in the 1930s, a **coalition** of reformers that included governor and then president **Franklin D. Roosevelt** and **fusion** mayor Fiorello La Guardia brought the Tammany organization to its knees, ending its lengthy influence over state and national Democratic Party politics.

TARIFF. A tax on imports, intended to generate revenue and perhaps to protect domestic industries against foreign competition. The tariff issue has generated interparty and intraparty divisions since the emergence of U.S. political parties. In his controversial *Report of Manufactures* (1791), treasury secretary and **Federalist Party** leader **Alexander Hamilton** advocated a protective tariff. Secretary of state and **Democratic-Republican Party** leader **Thomas Jefferson** led the opposition to this policy proposal. Hamilton's ideas were subsequently embraced by **Henry Clay**, who made them central to his nationalistic "**American System**." Reflecting regional economic interests, tariff supporters were more prevalent in the industrial North than the agricultural South. The **Democratic Party** was perennially divided on the issue, and its traditionally strong Southern base tilted the party against high tariffs. The Federalists, **Whigs**, and **Republicans** were all generally more favorably disposed. After World War II, a **bipartisan** consensus favoring lowering and even eliminating tariffs emerged on behalf of free trade. More recently, amid globalization, the old division within the Democratic Party has reemerged. Now, however, its labor union constituencies, centered in the North, are advocating fair trade, as opposed to free trade, embracing tariffs in efforts to protect the wages of American workers against foreign counterparts working for multinational corporations.

TAX-CUT PARTY. *See* AMERICA FIRST PARTY; AMERICAN PARTY.

TAYLOR, JOHN W. Democratic-Republican Speaker of the House, 1820–1821, 1825–1827. (b. 26 March 1784; d. 8 September 1854). Taylor was elected to the **House of Representatives** from New York in 1812, and he served 10 terms. On two occasions, he was elected **Speaker**. In 1820, after **Henry Clay** resigned, the speakership became involved in sectional controversy associated with the passage of the Missouri Compromise. Taylor was the candidate of the antislavery **faction** within his party. On the 22nd **ballot**, he attained **majority** support. When the House convened after the fall elections, Taylor sought reelection as Speaker, but he lost in a multicandidate battle within the dominant party, to **Philip P. Barbour** of Virginia.

Two years later, Clay returned to the House and supplanted Barbour as leader. After the controversial 1824 presidential **election,** Clay joined the **administration** of **John Quincy Adams**, leaving the House increasingly faction-ridden. In 1825, Taylor won a second-ballot victory in his bid to return to the Speaker's office. Two years later, as the faction within the party led by **Andrew Jackson** gained ascendancy, **Andrew Stevenson** of Virginia replaced Taylor as Speaker. Taylor served three more terms as representative before leaving office.

TAYLOR, ZACHARY. Whig president, 1849–1850. (b. 24 November 1784; d. 9 July 1850). Taylor was a career army officer who distinguished himself as a major general commanding troops in the Mexican War. In 1848, the **Whig Party**, seeking to capitalize on Taylor's popularity, chose him as its presidential nominee over rivals **Henry Clay** and **Winfield Scott**. Taylor won a comfortable popular vote and **electoral college** victory over Democrat **Lewis Cass** in a race that also included former president **Martin Van Buren**, running under the **Free Soil Party** banner. Some 16 uneventful months after his inauguration, Taylor died, and the vice president, **Millard Fillmore**, became president.

TAZEWELL, HENRY. President pro tempore of the Senate, 1795. (b. 15 November 1753; d. 24 January 1799). Tazewell entered the

Senate from Virginia in 1795. His death in 1799 cut short his term. Once during the 3rd **Congress**, and once more during the 4th, he was designated **president pro tempore**. His son, **Littleton Waller Tazewell**, subsequently became president pro tempore of the body, making them the only father and son to both hold that office to date.

TAZEWELL, LITTLETON WALLER. Democratic president pro tempore of the Senate, 1832. (b. 17 December 1774; d. 6 May 1860). The son of Henry Tazewell, Littleton Waller Tazewell won a **special election** to the **House of Representatives** in 1800 to finish an unexpired term. Over two decades later, in 1824, he went to the **Senate** to finish another unexpired term. In 1832, the first session of the 22nd **Congress** designated him **president pro tempore** on one occasion. Leaving the Senate later that year, he went on to serve a single term as governor of Virginia (1834–1836). In 1840, the **Democratic National Convention** declined to renominate the sitting **vice president, Richard M. Johnson**. Instead, it encouraged each state party to designate a **running mate** for President **Martin Van Buren** who would be attractive to its electors. Most states opted for Johnson, but Tazewell was the choice of the Democrats in South Carolina, and he received their 11 votes in the **electoral college** balloting.

TELFAIR, EDWARD. Electoral vote recipient, 1789 (Democratic-Republican). (b. 1735; d. 17 September 1807). Telfair represented Georgia on three occasions in the Continental Congress (1778–1782, 1784–1785, and 1788–1789). He also served as his state's governor on two occasions (1786 and 1790–1793). In the first **electoral college** balloting in 1789, he got one **favorite son** vote.

THIRD PARTY. *See* MINOR PARTY.

THIRD PARTY SYSTEM. Pattern of party competition in effect from 1860 to 1896. Following the demise of the **Second Party System**, the 1860 presidential **election** of **Republican Party** nominee **Abraham Lincoln** inaugurated the **Third Party System**, a distinct era in the evolution of party competition in the United States. The Third Party System pitted the new Republican Party against the well-established **Democratic Party**, which was in disarray during the **Civil War** but revitalized in its wake. Each party had a distinct regional base. The Republicans prevailed in the North, although they were stronger in the rural areas than in the cities. In the South, as well as in the urban North, the Democrats were dominant. This pattern typically produced highly competitive presidential elections, although the Republicans generally came out on top, and frequent shifts in party control of Congress. The **critical election** of 1896 catapulted the Republicans into a position of greater dominance and ushered in the **Fourth Party System**. *See also* PARTY SYSTEM.

THURMAN, ALLEN G. Democratic president pro tempore of the Senate, 1879–1881. (b. 13 November 1813; d. 12 December 1895). Thurman served a single term in the **House of Representatives** from Ohio (1845–1847). After leaving the House, he served for five years on the Ohio Supreme Court (1851–1856). Much later, he won two terms in the **Senate** (1869–1881). Throughout the 46th **Congress**, he was **president pro tempore**.

In 1888, President **Grover Cleveland** was seeking renomination. His **vice president, Thomas A. Hendricks**, had died in 1885, so the **Democratic National Convention** had to name a new **running mate**. Thurmond was the clear choice of the delegates, winning a comfortable first-**ballot** victory for the vice presidential nomination. The Cleveland-Thurmond ticket won a narrow **plurality** of popular votes, but lost in the **electoral college** balloting to their **Republican Party** challengers, **Benjamin Harrison** and Levi Martin.

THURMOND, J. STROM. Republican president pro tempore of the Senate, 1981–1987, 1995–2001, 2001. (b. 5 December 1902; d. 26 June 2003). As the Democratic governor of South Carolina (1947–1951), Thurmond bolted from the party in 1948 to lead the challenge of the **States' Rights Democratic Party**, also known as the **Dixiecrats**, against the **nomination** and **election** of President **Harry S. Truman**. In 1954, back in the **Democratic Party** fold, Thurmond was elected to the **Senate**. He vacated the office for a few months in 1956, but after returning, he held the seat into the 21st century. However, in 1964, four years after his initial reelection, he again abandoned the Democrats, this time joining the **Republican Party**, whose senatorial leadership generously granted him full seniority in their ranks. Thus, in 1981, when the Republicans gained control of the Senate, Thurmond, their senior member, became **president pro tempore** for the six years they were in the **majority**. In addition, he chaired the powerful Judiciary Committee. In 1995, the Republicans regained control, and Thurmond resumed the office of president pro tempore. He lost it twice in 2001, in the wake of the 2000 elections, which resulted in an evenly divided Senate. In the interim between the convening of **Congress** and the presidential inauguration, **lame duck** Vice President **Al Gore** cast the decisive vote giving the Democrats temporary control. After January 20, incoming Vice President **Richard B. Cheney** shifted party control back to the Republicans, restoring Thurmond's status. However, a party **switcher** in June 2001 placed the Democrats back in control of the chamber. The **Republican Conference** conferred on Thurmond the title of president pro tempore emeritus, which he held for the remainder of his senatorial service. He did not seek reelection in 2002, retiring at age 100 as the longest serving senator in history. In 2006, **Robert C. Byrd** supplanted him in seniority.

TICKET. A **slate** of party nominees, presented for **election** as a unit. More precisely, it refers to paired nominees for linked elective offices, such as president and vice president, or governor and lieutenant governor. *See also* BALANCED TICKET.

TICKET-SPLITTER. A voter who casts a **ballot** for nominees of more than one party. The opposite of a ticket-splitter is a **straight ticket** voter. Ticket-splitting became more common around the turn of the 20th century, in the wake of the introduction of the **Australian ballot**, and it is a prime cause of **divided party government**. An **office-bloc ballot** form encourages ticket-splitting more than a **party-column ballot** does.

TILDEN, SAMUEL. Democratic presidential nominee, 1876. (b. 9 February 1814; d. 4 August 1886). A New York lawyer, Samuel Tilden served in municipal government and as state party **chair** before his election as governor in 1874. His reform **administration** brought him national attention, as well as the opposition of the urban **machine**, **Tammany Hall**. In 1876, he was the second-**ballot**

presidential nominee of the **Democratic National Convention**. In November, he led in the popular vote balloting but fell one vote short of a required **majority** in the **electoral college**, with 20 electoral votes in dispute. An election commission established by **Congress** decided to authorize electors pledged to Tilden's **Republican Party** opponent, **Rutherford B. Hayes**, who thus became president. Tilden died a decade later, leaving a considerable bequest that provided for the creation of the New York Public Library.

TILSON, JOHN Q. Republican majority leader of the House of Representatives, 1925–1931. (b. 5 April 1866; d. 14 August 1958). Tilson was elected to the **House of Representatives** from Connecticut in 1908. He served two terms before losing in 1912. He regained his seat in 1914 and held it until 1932. From the 69th through the 71st Congresses, Tilson was the **floor leader** for the Republican **majority**. When the **Republican Party** lost control of the House in the 1930 elections, he stepped down as floor leader, and he retired before the end of the next term.

TITULAR LEADER. One who has leadership status by virtue of a title. In the United States the term typically refers to a defeated presidential nominee, who retains that identity until the next national party **convention** designates a new nominee.

TOMPKINS, DANIEL D. Democratic-Republican vice president, 1817–1825. (b. 21 June 1774; d. 11 June 1825). Tompkins was a prominent figure in New York party politics. Elected to the **House of Representatives** in 1804, he resigned to accept an appointment to the state supreme court. In 1807, he was elected governor. Only 33 years old when elected, he held that office for a decade, spurning an offer by President **James Madison** to become secretary of state in 1814.

Tompkins contended unsuccessfully for the presidential **nomination** of the **Democratic-Republican Party** in 1816, which went to **James Monroe**. He accepted the nomination for **vice president**, continuing the tradition within the party whereby the **balanced ticket** would be headed by a Virginian backed up by a New Yorker. Following the **electoral college** victory, scandalous allegations surfaced regarding his financial management as New York's chief executive.

In a quest for public vindication, he ran for governor in 1820 but lost to the **incumbent**, DeWitt Clinton.

Nevertheless, Tompkins was renominated and reelected as vice president. He continued to neglect his national responsibilities in his effort to rebuild his reputation as a **favorite son**. He did not participate in the inaugural ceremonies for the second term, taking his oath of office privately in New York. In 1823, he made clear to the **Senate** that he would not be available to preside, encouraging them to designate a **president pro tempore** in his continuing absence. He died shortly after his term ended in 1825.

TOSS ONE'S HAT IN THE RING. To announce one's candidacy for public office. **Theodore Roosevelt** applied this well-known phrase associated with boxing competitions to the political arena.

TRACY, URIAH. Federalist president pro tempore of the Senate, 1800. (b. 2 February 1755; d. 19 July 1807). Tracy was elected to the **House of Representatives** from Connecticut in 1792. While serving his second term, he was chosen for a **Senate** seat, which he occupied for over a decade. On May 14, 1800, the Senate named him **president pro tempore**.

TRUMAN, HARRY S. Democratic vice president, 1945; Democratic president, 1945–1953. (b. 8 May 1884; d. 26 December 1972). Truman was an obscure county judge in western Missouri when he was chosen by the Pendergast **machine** as the nominee of the **Democratic Party** for the U.S. **Senate** in 1934. He won the **general election** and was reelected in 1940. He received national attention for his leadership of a special Senate committee organized to investigate the national defense program. In 1944, with the support of the **chair** of the **Democratic National Committee**, **Robert Hannegan**, an old political ally from St. Louis, Truman emerged as the choice of President **Franklin D. Roosevelt** to join him on the party **ticket** as the nominee for **vice president**. They won easily that fall, and Truman became first in line for the presidency. When Roosevelt died in April 1945, Truman finished his term, presiding over the end of the war and the critical foreign and domestic policy adjustments that followed.

In 1948, Truman sought a term in his own right. The **Democratic National Convention** gave him an overwhelming **nomination** victory, but significant party factions broke away, with some liberals embracing Henry Wallace in his **Progressive Party** candidacy and some Southerners following **Dixiecrat** nominee **J. Strom Thurmond** to the **States' Rights Democratic Party** banner. Truman's electoral prospects appeared bleak, but he persisted with an energetic **campaign,** which brought him an upset **plurality** victory over **Republican Party** nominee **Thomas E. Dewey** and his **minor party** rivals that translated into a healthy **majority** in the **electoral college.**

During his subsequent term, foreign policy concerns remained high, with the onset of the Cold War and the outbreak of the Korean War. At home, post–World War II demobilization continued to promote unrest, and minor scandals plagued the **administration.** Truman declined to seek a second full term in 1952. He returned home to Missouri, where, during a lengthy retirement, he presided over the construction of his presidential library and became a colorful party **elder statesman.**

TRUMBULL, JONATHAN. Federalist Speaker of the House of Representatives, 1791–1793. (b. 26 March 1740; d. 7 August 1809). Trumbull was chosen by his Connecticut district as a member of the **House of Representatives** for the 1st **Congress.** He served three terms, the second as **Speaker.** His tenure coincided with the emergence of clear **partisan** divisions within the House, and he used his leadership position to support the policies and programs of the Washington **administration** against an increasingly cohesive opposition. He left the House in 1795 to join the **Senate,** where he served only a year. In 1797, he became governor of Connecticut, and served for 12 years.

TUESDAY GROUP. A **caucus** of moderate Republicans in the House of Representatives in the early years of the 21st century. They can be differentiated from the **Republican Main Street Partnership** in that they exist exclusively in the House, whereas the latter operates in both chambers. The Tuesday Group organized out of a concern that the **Republican Party** was drifting too far toward the **right wing** and was in danger of losing touch with centrist voters.

TURNOUT. Reference to how many voters cast ballots in an **election.** Calculating turnout requires more than simply counting voters. The number of voters must be compared with the total of eligible voters—those who have actually met **suffrage** requirements—or potential voters, those who appear to satisfy the requirements but may not have taken the necessary steps to become eligible voters. In the post–World War II era, voter turnout of eligibles in presidential elections rose above 60 percent and stayed at that level until 1972, when it dropped into the 50 percent range. It exceeded the 60 percent level once again in 2004 and 2008. *Turnout* can also refer to the crowd that assembles at a political event.

TWEEDLEDUM AND TWEEDLEDEE. A pejorative reference to the two major parties in the U.S. political system, from the perspective of outsiders who bemoan their centrist similarities. Tweedledum and Tweedledee were characters in Lewis Carroll's 19th-century children's story *Through the Looking-Glass. See also* TWO-PARTY SYSTEM.

TWO-PARTY SYSTEM. A system in which two major political parties dominate the political landscape. A two-party system does not preclude the existence and occasional success of other parties, but a **minor party** faces formidable obstacles in seeking to become competitive. The United States is a classic example of a national two-party system. This is attributable to social, cultural, and institutional features. In particular, American society has embodied a persistent dualism that manifests itself in two broad political groupings. In turn, cultural consensus facilitates the broad cooperation and accommodation necessary to sustain partisan coalitions of diverse interests. Finally, such institutional features as a unified executive, separated from the legislature, and **single-member district, winner-take-all** electoral arrangements effectively discourage challenges by minor parties. Once established, a two-party system can use its governmental power to stifle competition from potential challengers through such devices as restrictive **ballot** access rules. Critics complain that a two-party system stifles diversity. Its supporters counter that it promotes stability. *See also* MULTIPARTY SYSTEM; SINGLE-PARTY SYSTEM.

TWO-THIRDS RULE. The requirement of a two-thirds convention **majority** for nominating a **Democratic Party** presidential **ticket**, which prevailed from 1832 until 1936. The inaugural **Democratic National Convention** in 1832 established the rule to promote broad consensus in its presidential nominations. The 1936 Democratic National Convention voted to abolish the rule.

During the years of its application, at two national conventions a presidential aspirant received a majority of votes cast in a **ballot**, but ultimately failed to meet the two-thirds requirement. They were **Martin Van Buren** in 1844 and **James B. "Champ" Clark** in 1912. On several other occasions, the rule played a significant role in convention strategies, tactics, and decision making. In particular, the rule effectively granted the **Solid South** a veto over unsatisfactory nominees. Its 1936 abrogation came with the encouragement of President **Franklin D. Roosevelt**.

TYLER, JOHN. Democratic president pro tempore of the Senate, 1834–1835; Whig vice presidential nominee, 1836; Whig vice president, 1841; Whig president, 1841–1845. (b. 29 March 1790; d. 18 January 1862). John Tyler served several terms in the Virginia House of Delegates, before and after going to Washington in 1817 as a member of the **House of Representatives**. He was elected governor in 1825 and **senator** in 1827. As the **Second Party System** took shape, Tyler initially identified with the emerging **Democratic Party**. On March 3, 1835, he was elected **president pro tempore** for the last day of the 23rd **Congress**.

In 1836, at odds with his party leader, **Andrew Jackson**, Tyler embraced the newly formed **Whig Party**, resigning his Senate seat and running unsuccessfully for vice president on two of the Whigs' regional tickets. Back in the Virginia state legislature, he sought to return to the Senate in 1839 but was rebuffed by his erstwhile Whig allies. Nevertheless, the Whigs again turned to him in 1840 to run for **vice president** on the **ticket** headed by **William Henry Harrison**. Following the Whig victory, Harrison became ill immediately after his inauguration and died a month later. Tyler took decisive action in an ambiguous constitutional situation, taking the oath of office and assuming the presidency, thus becoming the first **accidental president**.

Tyler lacked the political base to be effective as chief executive. He clashed repeatedly with the Whig congressional leadership, most notably **Henry Clay**, who harbored abiding presidential ambitions. As the 1844 presidential season approached, Tyler attracted some support from a conservative Democratic **faction**, but mainstream Democrats and Whigs alike rejected him. He toyed with a **minor party** candidacy but ultimately endorsed the Democratic nominee, **James K. Polk**, who went on to win the **election**.

In retirement back home in Virginia, Tyler remained politically visible, continuing to present himself as a conciliator who could bring together competing parties and factions. When Virginia seceded in 1861, Tyler followed his state, accepting election to the Confederacy's Provisional Congress and then its House of Representatives. His health failed, and he died soon after.

– U –

UNDERWOOD, OSCAR W. Democratic majority leader of the House of Representatives, 1911–1915; Democratic minority leader of the Senate, 1920–1923. (b. 6 May 1862; d. 25 January 1929). Underwood won his initial election to the **House of Representatives** from Alabama in 1894. He vacated the office in 1896 but won reelection later that year and served nine more terms. In 1910, the **Democratic Party** gained control of the House, and the previous **minority leader**, **James B. "Champ" Clark**, became **Speaker**. The party **caucus** chose Underwood to be the **floor leader**. He also chaired the powerful Ways and Means Committee. The office of Speaker was in decline after the revolt against Speaker **Joseph G. Cannon** in 1910, and Underwood, not Clark, typically spoke for the Democratic **majority**. He was in place two years later when Democrat **Woodrow Wilson** won the presidential **election** and proposed an ambitious legislative agenda, the **New Freedom**, which Underwood successfully guided through the House.

In 1914, Underwood was elected to a **Senate** seat. Shortly before his reelection bid in 1920, he became minority leader, following the death of **Thomas S. Martin** of Virginia. He served for the remainder of the 66th **Congress** and throughout the 67th. When the 68th Congress convened, the Democrats replaced Underwood with **Joseph T. Robinson** of Arkansas. Underwood retired when his second term ended.

UNIFIED PARTY GOVERNMENT. The condition that pertains in a separation of powers political system when the same **political party** controls both the legislature and the executive. Unified party government is a precondition for responsible party government. From the outset of party competition in the United States until the **Gilded Age**, unified party government was the norm, and **divided party government** the exception. The **critical election** of 1896 reinstated the norm that generally prevailed over the next five decades. Around mid-20th century, a clear reversal took place, fueled in large measure by an increase in **ticket-splitters** that in turn reflected weakening partisan attachments in the electorate associated with **dealignment**. Since World War II, unified party government has occurred under the leadership of the **Democratic Party** (1949–1953, 1961–1969, 1977–1981, 1993–1995, and 2009) and **Republican Party** (1953–1955, 2001, 2003–2007).

UNION PARTY. Party label employed by the **Republican Party** in the 1864 presidential **election**, and a **minor party** in the 1930s. With the **Civil War** raging, the **incumbent** Republicans sought **bipartisan** support by nominating a border-state Democrat who had remained loyal to the Union, **Andrew Johnson** of Tennessee, to run for **vice president** on the **ticket** with President **Abraham Lincoln**. They styled this effort the Union Party; it was also known as the National Union Party. With the end of the war and Lincoln's assassination, this bipartisan **coalition** disintegrated in intense conflict between President Johnson and the congressional Republicans.

More than 70 years later, another short-lived Union Party appeared on the scene. It brought together a coalition opposed to the 1936 reelection of President **Franklin D. Roosevelt**. Its figurehead presidential nominee was William Lemke, a Republican member of **Congress** from North Dakota. The impetus for organizing the party came from Reverend Charles E. Coughlin and his National Center for Social Justice. Joining forces with Father Coughlin were two other vocal Roosevelt critics: Dr. Francis E. Townsend, promoter of a visionary pension plan, and Gerald L. K. Smith, who had taken up the "share the wealth" banner of the assassinated Louisiana senator Huey P. Long, adding to it a virulent anti-Semitism. Lemke's campaign found support among only 2 percent of the voters. The party disbanded before the next presidential election.

UNIT RULE. A provision whereby a delegation casts its vote unanimously, on behalf of the **candidate** or issue position with the most support within that delegation. In American party politics, the unit rule has had three significant applications. The first, and most enduring, has been in the **electoral college**, where it was instituted almost unanimously among the states in the early decades of the 19th century and continues to be utilized today. The clear intent of states in adopting this requirement has been to maximize a state's influence in presidential selection.

Second, in the **Democratic Party**, the rules of the **Democratic National Convention** traditionally authorized state parties to require that their delegates vote as a unit in casting ballots. The similar purpose of this application of the unit rule was to maximize a state's influence over **convention** decision making. After the abolition of the **two-thirds rule**, the Southern states remained stalwart in their defense of the unit rule. However, it was clearly falling into disuse before the 1968 Democratic National Convention voted to abandon it. In the **Republican Party**, the unit rule was occasionally and informally practiced in national convention proceedings, but it never attained institutional status.

The rarest utilization of the unit rule is the only one with constitutional sanction. In the contingency procedure for electing the **president** by the **House of Representatives**, in the event that the electoral college fails to arrive at a **majority** choice, each state delegation in the House casts a single vote, thereby operating under a form of the unit rule. This contingency procedure was required in 1801 and 1825.

U.S. LABOR PARTY. A recent **minor party**. The U.S. Labor Party appeared on the presidential **election** scene in 1976, as an alliance of fringe labor groups promoting a Marxist vision. Its nominee, Lyndon LaRouche, appeared on the **ballot** in almost half the states, but received less than 0.1 percent of the popular vote. LaRouche became something of a fixture in the next several presidential elections, but he abandoned the banner of the U.S. Labor Party in these later efforts.

– V –

VAN BUREN, MARTIN. Democratic vice president, 1837–1841; Democratic president, 1841–1845. (b. 5 December 1782; d. 24 July 1862). Van Buren represented New York in the **Senate** (1821–1828). Elected governor in 1828, he served only two months before joining the incoming administration of President **Andrew Jackson** as secretary of state. He proved himself to be a loyal Jackson ally over the next two years, and he played a key role in the reconstitution of the Jackson **faction** of the **Democratic-Republican Party** into the **Democratic Party**. Van Buren resigned in 1831 and was nominated shortly afterward as minister to Great Britain. However, the Senate rejected the **nomination.**

When Jackson successfully sought reelection in 1832, Van Buren joined him on the party **ticket** as the nominee for **vice president.** In 1836, the Democrats named Van Buren their presidential **standard-bearer**, and he defeated several **Whig Party** opponents. However, his own reelection bid failed in 1840. He was a strong contender for the 1844 presidential nomination of his party, but he fell short owing to the **two-thirds rule**, which required an extraordinary **majority.** In 1848, with the slavery controversy heightening in intensity, he bolted from his party to accept the presidential nomination of the **Free Soil Party**. He received over 10 percent of the popular vote but carried no states. He then retired from public life.

VANDENBERG, ARTHUR H. Republican president pro tempore of the Senate, 1947–1949. (b. 22 March 1884; d. 18 April 1951). Vandenberg began his lengthy **Senate** service on behalf of Michigan in 1928, finishing an unexpired term, and he held his seat until his death. He became highly respected on Capitol Hill for his **bipartisan**

approach to foreign policy. In 1946, the **Republican Party** won control of the Senate. Vandenberg, as senior member of the **Republican Conference**, became **president pro tempore** for the 80th **Congress**, with the vice presidency vacant. In a time of **divided party government**, he supported the Cold War initiatives of President **Harry S. Truman**, including the Marshall Plan, which promoted economic recovery in war-ravaged Western Europe. Vandenberg lost his leadership position when the **Democratic Party** recaptured control in 1948.

VARNUM, JOSEPH. Speaker of the House of Representatives, 1807–1811; president pro tempore of the Senate, 1813. (b. 29 January 1750; d. 21 September 1821). Varnum won election to the **House of Representatives** from Massachusetts in 1794. He resisted the temptation to identify openly with one of the emerging political parties of that decade. Varnum remained in the House for 16 years. He was chosen **Speaker** in 1807, when the 10th **Congress** convened. He was reelected two years later. In 1811, he was chosen for the **Senate**, where he served for six years. On December 6, 1813, when the second session of the 13th Congress began, Varnum was named **president pro tempore**.

VEEP. A nickname for the **vice president**. It derives from the initials, VP. **Alben W. Barkley**, vice president under **Harry S. Truman**, was the first to be so called.

VICE PRESIDENT. A federal office established by the **Constitution**. The qualifications for vice president are identical to those for **president**: natural-born citizen, at least 35 years of age, and at least 14 years a resident of the United States. Like the president, the vice president is elected by the **electoral college**. Initially, the Constitution required each elector to cast a presidential **ballot** with two names. The candidate receiving **majority** support from the electors would become president, and the runner-up would become the vice president.

This procedure had to be modified when political parties began nominating presidential tickets and seeking the selection of presidential electors pledged to a **ticket**. In 1800, this practice produced a tie in the electoral college, when a majority of electors voted for both **Thomas Jefferson** and **Aaron Burr**, the nominees of the **Democratic-Republican Party**. This outcome necessitated a resort to the contingency procedure established in the Constitution, and the **House of Representatives** elected Jefferson president and Burr vice president.

The 12th Amendment to the Constitution altered the balloting arrangement, whereby electors now cast two ballots, clearly differentiating their choices. If no vice presidential nominee receives majority support in the electoral college, the amendment provides that the **Senate** shall choose between the two top contenders in the electoral college vote. To date, this contingency has been invoked only once. In the 1836 electoral college balloting, no nominee received the required majority, and the Senate then elected the **Democratic Party** nominee, **Richard M. Johnson,** to join his running mate, **Martin Van Buren**.

The main constitutional purpose of the office of vice president is to provide a successor in the event of a presidential vacancy. Vacancies have occurred on nine occasions, beginning in 1841, when President **William Henry Harrison** died, and Vice President **John Tyler** succeeded him. The other nonelectoral presidential transitions were in 1849 (**Zachary Taylor–Millard Fillmore**); 1865 (**Abraham Lincoln–Andrew Johnson**); 1881 (**James A. Garfield–Chester A. Arthur**); 1901 (**William McKinley–Theodore Roosevelt**); 1923 (**Warren G. Harding–Calvin Coolidge**); 1945 (**Franklin D. Roosevelt–Harry S. Truman**); 1963 (**John F. Kennedy–Lyndon B. Johnson**); 1974 (**Richard M. Nixon–Gerald R. Ford**). Unlike the others, the last resulted from a presidential resignation rather than the death of the **incumbent**.

In 1967, the 25th Amendment to the Constitution established a procedure for filling a vacancy in the vice presidency. Such a vacancy had existed in the instances above, as well as on six occasions when incumbent vice presidents had died (**George Clinton**, 1812; **Elbridge Gerry**, 1814; **William R. King**, 1853; **Henry Wilson**, 1875; **Thomas A. Hendricks**, 1885; and **James S. Sherman**, 1912), and once when **John C. Calhoun** resigned in 1832. The procedure calls for **nomination** by the president and confirmation by both houses of Congress.

Since ratification, one vice president has resigned, **Spiro T. Agnew** in 1973. President Nixon named Ford as his successor. In turn, when Ford became president following Nixon's resignation, his choice as vice president was **Nelson A. Rockefeller**.

Otherwise, the Constitution establishes the vice president as the president, or presiding officer, of the Senate. The Constitution also authorizes a **president pro tempore**, to preside in the absence of the vice president. Early on, the vice presidents were generally attentive to their presiding responsibilities. Twentieth-century vice presidents were less so.

The emergence of political parties, along with the ensuing 12th Amendment, subtly altered the constitutional standing of the vice president. The constitutional framers envisioned the vice president as the electors' second choice as president. With the evolution of **partisan** nominating institutions, the vice president emerged as the choice first of the legislative **caucus** and then of the national **convention** to contribute most effectively to the election of its presidential nominee. Subsequently, the presidential nominee has come to exercise overriding influence on the convention's choice. In any event, the notion of the vice president as the next-best president has receded.

In the 19th century, presidents and vice presidents were frequently factional rivals, paired on the party ticket by state party bosses. As such, vice presidents were rarely close associates and advisers of the chief executive. More recently, with presidential nominees exercising their prerogative of recommending the vice presidential nominee for ratification by the convention, vice presidents have become more visible in their respective administrations.

One particular chore many recent vice presidents have taken on relates to party leadership. There is an inherent conflict between the roles of president as national leader and president as party leader. Presidents can deal with this issue by delegating certain party-leadership chores to the vice president as deputy party leader, enabling the vice president to develop and maintain support with the party faithful.

In part because of this trend, modern vice presidents have become much more likely than their traditional predecessors to become presidential nominees themselves. No 19th-century **accidental president** went on to win the presidential nomination of the ensuing national party convention. All of the 20th-century counterparts have done so. In 1960, Richard Nixon was the first incumbent vice president to win his party's presidential nomination since Martin Van Buren in 1836. Since then, the ranks of the major party presidential nominees have included three incumbent vice presidents, **Hubert H. Humphrey** (1968), **George H. W. Bush** (1988), and **Al Gore** (2000), along with former vice presidents Nixon (1968) and **Walter F. Mondale** (1984). Bush was the first incumbent vice president since Van Buren to be elected president.

VOLUNTEER. Unpaid worker in a political campaign. A volunteer can be differentiated from an amateur in that the former typically occupies a menial position in the campaign organization.

– W –

WADE, BENJAMIN F. Republican president pro tempore of the Senate, 1867–1869. (b. 22 November 1800; d. 2 March 1878). Wade went to the **Senate** from Ohio in 1851 as a representative of the **Whig Party**. In 1857, with the Whigs disintegrating, he shifted his allegiance to the newly formed **Republican Party** and quickly emerged as a prominent leader. In the immediate aftermath of the **Civil War**, he led the **Radical Republicans** in **Congress** in their opposition to the Reconstruction policy of President **Andrew Johnson**. As the 39th Congress prepared to adjourn in March 1867, Wade was named **president pro tempore**. He continued to hold that office throughout the 40th Congress. As such, he was next in line in the existing order of presidential succession when the Senate tried President Johnson on the impeachment charges voted by the **House of Representatives**. Wade supported the removal of Johnson, which would have made him **president**, but the Senate vote fell one short of the required two-thirds majority. Wade retired from public life shortly afterward, at the end of his third term in 1869.

WALKER, FRANK C. Democratic National Committee chair, 1943–1944. (b. 30 May 1886; d. 13 September 1959). Walker was a Pennsylvania native who relocated to Montana, where he practiced law and pursued his interest in **Democratic Party** politics, serving as a prosecuting attorney and state legislator. He moved to New York City in 1924. There, he became associated with **Franklin D. Roosevelt**, whose political interests he served henceforth. In 1932, Roosevelt installed him as treasurer of the **Democratic National Committee**. After the **election**, Walker received a presidential appointment as an executive branch coordinator of the expansive governmental institutions generated by the **New Deal**. Walker left his government and party posts before the end of Roosevelt's first term, but he continued to advise the **president**. In 1940, when **James A. Farley** resigned his dual positions as **postmaster general** and national party **chair**, Roosevelt called on Walker to head the Post Office, while naming Edward J. Flynn to head the national party. Flynn's 1943 resignation led Roosevelt to combine the two positions again, this time under Walker's leadership. Walker resigned both posts in 1944. In his private practice of law, he continued to serve as one of the president's key advisers until Roosevelt's death in 1945.

WALKING-AROUND MONEY. Cash payments a **campaign** organization provides for its **precinct** workers responsible for getting out the vote. The funds can be employed at the discretion of those in the field, who can either retain the money for themselves as a payment for services or expense reimbursement or pass it along to supporters in the electorate.

WALLACE, GEORGE C. American Independent Party presidential nominee, 1968. (b. 25 August 1919; d. 13 September 1998). Wallace was elected governor of Alabama in 1962 as the nominee of the **Democratic Party**. He came to power as the **civil rights** movement was accelerating its agitation for eliminating the system of racial segregation that remained substantially intact in Alabama and throughout the South. Wallace positioned himself in opposition to this movement, maintaining his popularity with the white **majority** in his state, but bringing him into conflict with a federal government increasingly committed to civil rights. Prohibited by the state constitution from seeking reelection in 1966, he surrendered the statehouse to his wife, Lurleen.

More and more disenchanted with the direction of the national Democratic Party, he mounted a minor party presidential **campaign** in 1968, establishing the **American Independent Party** as his campaign vehicle. He broadened his anti–civil rights agenda to include opposition to the widening welfare state of the **Great Society** promoted by President **Lyndon B. Johnson**. In turn, he generally supported an aggressive prosecution of the Vietnam War. In November, Wallace received over 9 million popular votes, and he carried five Southern states, gaining 46 votes in the **electoral college**, making his one of the more powerful challenges to **major party** dominance.

Reelected as Democratic governor in 1970, in 1972 Wallace returned to the national Democratic Party fold and sought its presidential **nomination**. Campaigning in Maryland, he was the target of an assassination attempt that left him paralyzed for life. He made another brief run at the Democratic presidential nomination in 1976. He did not run for reelection in 1978, but he returned yet again to the governor's office in 1983 for another four-year term.

WALLACE, HENRY A. Democratic vice president, 1941–1945; Progressive presidential nominee, 1948. (b. 17 October 1888; d. 18 November 1965). Wallace's father edited an agricultural magazine and was active in the **Republican Party**, serving as secretary of agriculture under both **Warren G. Harding** and **Calvin Coolidge**. The son shared his father's agricultural interests, but he embraced the Democratic Party in the late 1920s, taking over his father's old portfolio as secretary of agriculture in the **cabinet** of **Franklin D. Roosevelt** in 1933. Roosevelt's **New Deal** included agricultural assistance programs that elevated Wallace's public visibility and popular appeal.

In 1940, Roosevelt accepted the presidential **nomination** of the **Democratic National Convention** for an unprecedented third term, over the objections of his **vice president, John Nance Garner**. Wallace replaced Garner as the vice presidential nominee on the **ticket** that prevailed in the fall **election**. As vice president, Wallace emerged as a strong advocate of foreign policy internationalism and wartime and postwar cooperation with the Soviet Union. His **liberal** views brought him into conflict with rivals within the Democratic

Party, who encouraged Roosevelt to drop him from the ticket for the 1944 presidential election. Replaced as vice presidential nominee by **Harry S. Truman**, Wallace nevertheless campaigned energetically for the party **slate**. In reward for his loyalty, Roosevelt brought him back into the cabinet as secretary of commerce after the inauguration.

After Truman's accession to the presidency following Roosevelt's death, Wallace opposed Truman's developing hard-line postwar stance toward the Soviet Union. Truman removed him from the cabinet in 1946, but Wallace continued his public advocacy of cooperation as Cold War tensions began to mount.

In 1948, Wallace accepted the presidential nomination of the **Progressive Party**, which received the endorsement of the American **Communist Party**. His **campaign** failed to generate popular support. He won only 2 percent of the vote and carried no states in the **electoral college**, and Truman won an upset victory in his quest for a term in his own right. Wallace then retired from public life and resumed his agricultural vocation.

WAR CHEST. A store of **campaign** funds. Candidates and parties assemble war chests in anticipation of a campaign, sometimes in hopes of discouraging opposition.

WARD. A municipal political subdivision.

WARD, MARCUS L. Republican National Committee chair, 1866–1868. (b. 9 November 1812; d. 25 April 1884). Ward was a prominent candle manufacturer in New Jersey who became involved in **Republican Party** politics when that party came on the scene. He quickly rose in its statewide ranks, serving as state party **chair** when the **Civil War** began. He ran for governor in 1863 but lost. He ran again two years later and won.

While serving as governor, Ward, generally considered a party moderate, allied himself with the **Radical Republicans** on the **Republican National Committee** (**RNC**) who were seeking to replace **Henry J. Raymond** as national party chair. Raymond had antagonized the radicals with his ostensible endorsement of the attempt by President **Andrew Johnson** to develop political support for himself through the organizational apparatus of the **Union Party**, the **bipartisan** vehicle that had elected **Abraham Lincoln**, with Johnson as his **running mate**, in 1864. In a specially called meeting of the RNC, a **minority** of members voted to expel Raymond and elected Ward in his place. Although Raymond disputed the legitimacy of the action, Ward served as chair until the **Republican National Convention** met in 1868, when **William Claflin** was chosen as chair by the national committee. Ward then returned to manufacturing. In 1872, he was elected to a single term in the **House of Representatives**.

WARD HEELER. A derogative term for a low-level political worker. *See also* HACK.

WARHORSE. An experienced politician, one who has weathered many a tough **campaign**. The term was borrowed from military usage.

WARREN, EARL. Republican vice presidential nominee, 1948. (b. 19 March 1891; d. 9 July 1974). Warren rose quickly in California politics, where his lifelong affiliation with the **Republican Party** accommodated strong **bipartisan** appeal. Elected governor in 1942, he held that office for a decade. In 1948, he mounted a **favorite son** candidacy for the presidential **nomination** of the **Republican National Convention**. Although he did not generate broader **convention** support, he was the vice presidential choice of presidential nominee **Thomas E. Dewey**. When the **ticket** lost unexpectedly in November, Warren remained governor of California. In 1952, he made another favorite-son bid for the Republican presidential nomination but again fell well short. He backed the eventual winner, **Dwight D. Eisenhower**, who subsequently named him chief justice of the Supreme Court. Warren's lengthy tenure (1953–1969) featured strong leadership and controversial rulings on civil rights and rights of criminal defendants.

WASHINGTON, GEORGE. President, 1789–1797. (b. 22 February 1732; d. 14 December 1799). Washington was a prominent member of both the First and Second Continental Congresses (1774, 1775). The latter Congress named him commander in chief of the colonial army, and he held this position until the Revolutionary War ended in 1783. Virginia sent him to the 1787 Constitutional Convention, where the other delegates named him their presiding officer. As the delegates discussed the creation of the office of **president**, Washington was regarded as the obvious occupant. When the presidential electors first met in 1789, every elector named Washington on his **ballot**, making him their unanimous choice. In 1792, they did so again. Four years later, he declined to seek a third term, proclaiming his retirement. Still, one North Carolina and one Virginia elector put forward his name in the presidential balloting. Washington retired from public life to his plantation at Mount Vernon.

During his presidency, Washington discouraged and remained aloof from the emerging **partisan** division and strife. Nevertheless, he typically supported the policy initiatives put forward by Treasury Secretary **Alexander Hamilton**. Thus, the **Federalist Party** tended to view Washington's presidency more sympathetically than did the followers of Secretary of State **Thomas Jefferson**, who made up the **Democratic-Republican Party**.

WATERGATE. A related series of scandals associated with the presidency of **Richard M. Nixon** that resulted in his unprecedented resignation. The scandals began to come to light on June 17, 1972, when burglars were apprehended in the offices of the **Democratic National Committee**, located in the Watergate office building in Washington, D.C. It turned out that the burglars were agents of the **Committee to Reelect the President (CREEP)**, President Nixon's **campaign** organization.

Early on, the Watergate burglary appeared to be more of a minor embarrassment than a major threat to the Nixon presidency. Indeed, the president won a **landslide** reelection victory in November 1972. However, investigations by the media, the Justice Department, a special prosecutor, and **Congress** gradually revealed a wide array of criminal and otherwise inappropriate activity undertaken by the **president** and his top aides in connection with his reelection efforts and his broader political interests. Central among them was obstruction of justice in seeking to cover up their involvement in the Watergate break-in. In March 1974, several of his top assistants were indicted, and the president was named an unindicted coconspirator. Facing imminent impeachment by the **House of Representatives** and likely conviction and removal by the Senate, Nixon resigned on August 9, 1974.

WATERSHED ELECTION. *See* CRITICAL ELECTION.

WATSON, JAMES E. Republican majority leader of the Senate, 1929–1933. (b. 2 November 1863; d. 29 July 1948). Watson won election to the **House of Representatives** from Indiana in 1894. He failed to win reelection in 1896, but he returned to that office in 1898 for five more terms. He went to the **Senate** in 1916 to finish a term and won two more of his own. In 1929, he replaced the new **vice president, Charles Curtis,** as **floor leader** of the **Republican Party,** which constituted the **majority** of the chamber. He held the position for four years, departing after a reelection defeat in 1932 that contributed to the Republicans' loss of control of the chamber.

"WAVE THE BLOODY SHIRT." A **Civil War**–era phrase employed by the **Republican Party** that identified the **Democratic Party** with the rebellious South. Subsequently, proponents of sectional reconciliation denounced those who continued to wave the bloody shirt.

WEAVER, JAMES B. Greenback Party presidential nominee, 1880; People's Party presidential nominee, 1892. (b. 12 June 1833; d. 6 February 1912). Weaver was elected to the **House of Representatives** from Iowa in 1878 for a single term. In 1880, he was the presidential nominee of the **Greenback Party** when the electoral fortunes of this noteworthy **minor party** opposed to the reestablishment of the gold standard were declining. In a disappointing showing, Weaver received only 3.3 percent of the popular vote and no statewide majorities. Four years later, Iowa voters returned Weaver to the House for two terms.

In 1892, the agrarian electoral constituency that had earlier undergirded the Greenback Party had transferred its loyalties to the **People's Party,** and Weaver emerged as the **Populist** standard-bearer. This time, his issues resonated better with the electorate. Weaver received over a million popular votes, carrying four states and receiving 22 votes in the **electoral college.** His abiding efforts to secure **major party** support for his policy objectives met with success four years later, when the **Democratic Party** co-opted the Populists by nominating **William Jennings Bryan**. Weaver embraced the Democratic label and disappeared from national attention, though he remained active in local politics in Iowa.

WEBLOG. An Internet website featuring entries providing commentary. Often referred to as a blog, weblogs have emerged in the early 21st century as a major medium of communication between party elites and **grassroots** activists, with the activist bloggers often exercising initiative. As such, weblogs are a significant democratizing force in party politics.

WEBSTER, DANIEL. Whig presidential nominee, 1836. (b. 18 January 1782; d. 24 October 1852). Webster, of Massachusetts, was a major figure in national politics for four decades. Initially elected to the **House of Representatives** in 1812, he served two consecutive terms (1813–1817), returned in 1823 for two more, and was chosen for the **Senate** in 1827. His formidable oratorical skills made him a significant force within the upper chamber, joining colleagues **Henry Clay** and **John C. Calhoun** as a virtual triumvirate. With factional divisions developing in the dominant **Democratic-Republican Party**, Webster, along with Clay, cast his lot with the **National Republicans** and then the **Whig Party** as the **Second Party System** developed.

In 1836, Webster was the choice of Whig strategists to run as one of three regionally based presidential nominees. They hoped he could secure the electoral votes of the New England states, thereby preventing the achievement of a **majority** in the **electoral college** for the dominant **Democratic Party** and sending the election to the House. There, the Whigs saw their prospects in a brighter light. Webster carried his native Massachusetts and won its 14 electoral votes, but the overall strategy failed to derail the Democratic **ticket** headed by Vice President **Martin Van Buren**.

In 1841, Webster joined the inaugural Whig **administration** of President **William Henry Harrison** as secretary of state. Shortly afterward, the accession of the **vice president**, **John Tyler**, following Harrison's death diminished Webster's influence, and he left the cabinet in 1843. He returned to the Senate in 1845 and resumed his informal leadership role. In 1850, President **Millard Fillmore** recalled Webster to the cabinet as secretary of state. He died in office.

WESTWOOD, JEAN. Democratic National Committee chair, 1972. (b. 22 November 1923; d. 18 August 1997). Westwood was active in state party politics in Utah, where she headed the presidential campaigns for the **Democratic Party** in 1964 and 1968. As the 1972 presidential **campaign** season began, she signed on in support of the **dark horse** candidacy of **George S. McGovern,** cochairing his national organization. At the **Democratic National Convention** that summer, she played a key role in the developments that ensured McGovern's controversial **nomination.** As a result, McGovern named her national party **chair,** the first woman to occupy that post. Her first weeks as chair were consumed by the crisis that developed when the vice presidential nominee, **Thomas F. Eagleton,** was found to have undergone psychiatric treatment. She was instrumental in Eagleton's withdrawal from the **ticket** and the convening of a special meeting of the **Democratic National Committee** to choose his replacement, **R. Sargent Shriver.**

When McGovern suffered a **landslide** defeat in November, Westwood became the scapegoat in the eyes of the **party organization.** The national **committee** met in December and elected **Robert Strauss** as her replacement. Westwood remained active in national party affairs, playing a leading role in the advancement of the reform agenda initiated by the **McGovern–Fraser Commission** and working on behalf of contenders for presidential nominations. She made an abortive bid for a **Senate** seat in Utah in 1974, then moved to Arizona later that year.

WET. An antiprohibition position, also used to describe a person who opposes efforts to prohibit the manufacture and sale of intoxicating beverages. "Wets" comprised a significant **faction** in the **Democratic Party** in the early decades of the 20th century, opposing the rising **Prohibition** tide that culminated in the ratification of the 18th Amendment to the **Constitution** in 1919. The wets persisted and eventually secured the repeal of Prohibition through the 21st Amendment in 1933. *See also* DRY.

WHEELER, WILLIAM A. Republican vice president, 1877–1881. (b. 30 June 1819; d. 4 June 1887). An upstate New York lawyer, Wheeler was elected to the state legislature as the **Whig Party** nominee in 1850. He transferred his loyalty to the new **Republican Party** in the mid-1850s and won **election** to a single term in the **House of Representatives** (1861–1863). He resumed his congressional career in 1869 and served there until his election as **vice president**.

At the 1876 **Republican National Convention**, the obscure Wheeler drew support from the delegates because of his reputation for honesty and his residence in New York, a key state in the **electoral college** and one that balanced the Ohio roots of the presidential nominee, **Rutherford B. Hayes**. The **general election** resulted in a narrow popular vote victory for the **Democratic Party** team of New York governor **Samuel Tilden**, who carried his state, and **Thomas A. Hendricks**. However, it also featured a controversy over the credentials of electors in several states that left Tilden one vote short of the required **majority** in the electoral college. Eventually, a commission authorized by **Congress** legitimized the disputed Republican electors in these states, and Hayes and Wheeler prevailed. Following his unremarkable term as vice president, Wheeler retired to his home in upstate New York.

WHEELHORSE. A party regular, one whose **party loyalty** is reliable and who will perform necessary party chores willingly.

WHERRY, KENNETH S. Republican minority leader of the Senate, 1949–1951. (b. 28 February 1892; d. 29 November 1951). Wherry was elected to the **Senate** from Nebraska in 1942 and reelected in 1948. In 1949, the **minority** Republicans named him their **floor leader** to replace **Wallace H. White Jr.** of Maine, who had been **majority leader** in the previous **Congress**. Wherry served until his death almost two years later.

WHIG PARTY. Major **political party** for three decades preceding the **Civil War**, during the **Second Party System**. In the wake of the split of the dominant **Democratic-Republican Party** after the **Era of Good Feelings**, the Whig Party appeared in the 1830s as the primary alternative to the now-entrenched **Democratic Party**, led by **An-**

drew **Jackson**. The label "Whig" had a strong historical and cultural resonance rooted in experiences in England and colonial America. Seventeenth-century British Whigs had opposed the Stuart kings' efforts to expand monarchical prerogatives against those of the Parliament. Similarly, 18th-century American colonists challenging George III styled themselves Whigs. Thus, those opposed to Jackson's expansion of executive power found the Whig label appropriate.

The Whig **coalition** brought together a diverse and unstable array of interests antagonistic to Jackson. It uneasily embraced states'-rights Southerners, business and commercial forces alarmed by Jackson's anti–national bank stance, and nationalists, particularly those supportive of an aggressive program of public works. This alliance lacked coherence, especially following Jackson's retirement, when the personal passions he ignited dimmed.

The Whigs achieved noteworthy successes in presidential politics in 1840 and 1848, when their nominees, **William Henry Harrison** and **Zachary Taylor**, respectively, emerged victorious. They controlled both houses of the 27th **Congress** (1841–1843), the **Senate** alone in the 28th (1843–1845), and the **House of Representatives** alone in the 30th (1847–1849).

Both Harrison and Taylor were military heroes. In turning twice to a **man on horseback**, the Whigs sought to take advantage of **nonpartisan**, personal appeals to counter the stronger **partisan** base of the Democrats. Unfortunately for them and their party, both Harrison and Taylor died shortly after taking office, and their control of the presidency did not enable the Whigs to expand their electoral coalition.

In the 1850s, the increasingly inflammatory slavery issue first divided and then destroyed the Whig Party. In 1852, the Whigs nominated another military leader for **president**. General **Winfield Scott** went down to defeat at the hands of Democrat **Franklin Pierce**. Four years later, a few old-line Whigs, known as the **Silver Grays**, met in convention to endorse former president **Millard Fillmore**, who had already accepted the presidential **nomination** of the **American Party** (Know-Nothings). Fillmore won only 2.7 percent of the popular vote, carrying one state, Maryland. The bulk of the Whigs' Northern constituency apparently shifted to the new **Republican Party**, whereas the Southern Whigs joined forces with the Democrats.

WHIP. A second-level legislative party leader, whose assignment is to communicate information between the top leaders and the **backbenchers**. Whips notify legislators of the schedule of upcoming votes and the **party line** on the votes. They also provide the leaders with assessments of the voting intentions of the **rank and file**. Each party **caucus** in the bicameral national legislature designates a whip.

WHIRLWIND CAMPAIGN. A campaign that is conducted feverishly. It entails much movement and excitement.

WHISTLESTOP CAMPAIGN. A campaign that is conducted on a railroad train, pausing at each stop along the route for a brief speech to the assembled **grassroots** onlookers. Whistlestop campaigns became popular in the early years of the twentieth century, owing to two developments: more active personal campaigning by candidates, and railroads that connected communities throughout the country. *See also* FRONT-PORCH CAMPAIGN.

WHITE, GEORGE H. Democratic National Committee chair, 1920–1921. (b. 21 August 1872; d. 15 December 1953). White was elected to the **House of Representatives** from Ohio in 1910. He served two terms before losing a reelection bid in 1914. He was reelected in 1916 for a single term. Leaving the House in 1919, he became **chair** of the **Democratic National Committee** the next year, following the presidential **nomination** of fellow Ohioan **James M. Cox**. White oversaw the fall **campaign** and resigned several months after its unsuccessful conclusion. A decade later, he was elected governor of Ohio, serving four years.

WHITE, HUGH LAWSON. President pro tempore of the Senate, 1832–1834; Whig presidential nominee, 1836. (b. 30 October 1773; d. 10 April 1840). White went to the **Senate** in 1825 and served almost a decade without clearly identifying with any of the national political parties in the time of turmoil and instability that followed the **Era of Good Feelings**. In December 1832, when the 22nd **Congress** convened for its second session, White was chosen **president pro tempore**. Later that month, Vice President **John C. Calhoun**

resigned, making White constitutionally responsible for presiding. He continued to hold that office until midway into the first session of the 23rd Congress, when the Senate named **George Poindexter** of Mississippi.

By 1836, White had cast his lot with the **Whig Party**, running for **president** on one of its regionally based tickets. The Whig strategists hoped that White and his running mate, **John Tyler**, could win sufficient support in their native South to keep the dominant **Democratic Party** from winning a **majority** in the **electoral college**, sending the election to the **House of Representatives**. There, the Whigs hoped to unite behind their leading **candidate** and gain the presidency. White won two states, with 26 electoral votes, but the Democratic nominee, Vice President **Martin Van Buren**, won a comfortable electoral victory.

WHITE, JOHN. Whig Speaker of the House of Representatives, 1841–1843. (b. 14 February 1802; d. 22 September 1845). White was elected to the **House of Representatives** from Kentucky as a member of the recently established **Whig Party** in 1835, and he served five terms. In 1841, the 27th **Congress**, the first with a Whig **majority**, named him **Speaker**. The **Democratic Party** recaptured control of the House in 1842, ending White's tenure as Speaker.

WHITE, JOHN C. Democratic National Committee chair, 1978–1981. (b. 26 November 1924; d. 20 January 1995). White was a longtime activist in Texas politics, serving 14 terms as agricultural commissioner. In 1977, he joined the **administration** of President **Jimmy Carter** as assistant secretary of agriculture. When **Kenneth Curtis**, the **chair** of the **Democratic National Committee**, resigned amid tensions between national party headquarters and the Carter White House, White, appreciated for his party loyalty, was Carter's noncontroversial choice as replacement. White steadfastly supported Carter's declining political fortunes, quietly but effectively backing the president against the intraparty **nomination** challenge of Senator Edward Kennedy, which featured an attempt to supplant White. After Carter lost in the fall **election** to **Ronald W. Reagan**, White resigned when it became clear that he would face a challenge to his reelection. He became a Washington lobbyist.

WHITE, WALLACE H., JR. Republican minority leader of the Senate, 1945–1947; Republican majority leader of the Senate, 1947–1949. (b. 6 August 1877; d. 31 March 1952). White followed his grandfather, William P. Frye, into Maine **Republican Party** politics and to the U.S. **Congress**. White was initially elected to the **House of Representatives** in 1916, and he served seven terms. In 1930, he was elected to the **Senate**, where he held his seat for three terms. In 1945, at the outset of the 79th Congress, he was named **floor leader** for the **minority** Republicans. When the **GOP** captured control of Congress in 1946, he became **majority leader** for the 80th Congress. Afterward, he retired from public office.

WILHELM, DAVID. Democratic National Committee chair, 1993–1995. (b. 2 October 1956). A Chicago political consultant who developed his reputation managing local and statewide campaigns, Wilhelm made his entry on the national scene when he assisted Senator **Joseph R. Biden Jr.** of Delaware in his unsuccessful 1988 run for the presidential **nomination** of the **Democratic Party**. Four years later, Wilhelm played a key managerial role in the presidential nomination and **election** of **Bill Clinton**. His reward was the position of **chair** of the **Democratic National Committee**. He was the youngest ever to attain this position. From party headquarters, Wilhelm sought to mobilize **grassroots** support for the president's controversial health care policy initiative. He presided over the party's disastrous showing in the 1994 **midterm elections**, in which it lost control of both houses of **Congress**. He resigned shortly afterward and became an investment banker and venture capitalist. He continues to work on behalf of Democratic presidential aspirants.

WILLCOX, WILLIAM R. Republican National Committee chair, 1916–1918. (b. 11 April 1863; d. 9 April 1940). Born in upstate New York, Willcox practiced law in New York City and became identified with the progressive **wing** of the **Republican Party**, led by **Theodore Roosevelt**. In 1905, President Roosevelt named Willcox postmaster of New York City. The next year, he supported **Charles Evans Hughes** in a gubernatorial bid that prevailed over the opposition of the regular Republican organization. In 1916, Willcox was practicing law in New York City when presidential nominee Hughes tapped him to head the **Republican National Committee**. The campaign suffered a narrow defeat in its effort to displace President **Woodrow Wilson**, and Willcox found himself discredited among the **old guard** elements of the **party organization**. He resigned in 1918 and returned to his law practice.

WILLIAMS, JOHN SHARP. Democratic minority leader of the House of Representatives, 1903–1908. (b. 30 July 1854; d. 27 September 1932). Williams was elected to the **House of Representatives** from Mississippi in 1892. He served eight terms. In 1903, he became **floor leader** for the **Democratic Party**, a **minority** in the chamber. He succeeded in garnering from autocratic Speaker **Joseph G. Cannon** the power to designate minority members of committees. He held his office until 1908, when **James B. "Champ" Clark** replaced him. Leaving the House in 1909, he entered the Senate in 1911, where he served two terms.

WILLKIE, WENDELL L. Republican presidential nominee, 1940. (b. 18 February 1892; d. 8 October 1944). Wendell Willkie was an Indiana native who became a successful New York utility executive. As the **New Deal** took shape in the 1930s, Willkie decried the encroachment of the federal government on private enterprise. In 1940, only weeks before the **Republican National Convention**, he came out of nowhere, a **dark horse** riding the wave of a media blitz and support from the party's **Eastern establishment**, to contend for the presidential **nomination**. He emerged victorious on the sixth **ballot**, defeating **Robert A. Taft**, the **candidate** of the party's **old guard**. In the fall **election**, Willkie went down to defeat as **Franklin D. Roosevelt** won an unprecedented third term. Afterward, as the international situation worsened, in **bipartisan** fashion Willkie generally supported Roosevelt's foreign policy initiatives and responses.

WILSON, HENRY. Republican vice president, 1873–1875. (b. 16 February 1812; d. 22 November 1875). Born in poverty in New Hampshire, Wilson moved to Massachusetts, where he became a prosperous shoe manufacturer. He began his career in public service in 1840, when he was elected to the state legislature as a representative of the **Whig Party**. His antislavery position led him to abandon the Whigs in 1848, in support of the **Free Soil Party**, and he later identified briefly with the Know-Nothings, who constituted the **American Party**.

In 1855, the Massachusetts legislature selected Wilson to finish an unexpired term in the U.S. Senate. There, he switched to the new **Republican Party**. He remained in the **Senate** until 1873. He was a strident opponent of slavery in the years leading up to the **Civil War**. After the war, he participated in the **Radical Republicans'** attack on the Reconstruction policy of President **Andrew Johnson**, and he supported the move to impeach and remove Johnson.

In 1872, the **Republican National Convention** unanimously renominated President **Ulysses S. Grant**. However, opposition developed to retaining Vice President **Schuyler Colfax** on the **ticket**, and Wilson emerged as the preferred alternative. Like Colfax, Wilson was tainted by his alleged involvement in the Credit Mobilier scandal. Nevertheless, the ticket coasted to victory that fall. Shortly after his **election**, Wilson suffered a stroke that limited his capacity to preside over the Senate. A second stroke in 1875 killed him, leaving a vacancy in the vice presidential office.

WILSON, WOODROW. Democratic president, 1913–1921. (b. 28 December 1856; d. 3 February 1924). Woodrow Wilson attained prominence in academia before entering the political arena. A highly regarded political scientist, he became president of his alma mater, Princeton University, in 1902. In 1910, he ran for governor of New Jersey, and his **election** made him a contender for the 1912 Democratic presidential **nomination**. The **Democratic National Convention** took 46 ballots to settle on Wilson as its nominee.

In the fall elections, he faced a divided **Republican Party**. The **president, William H. Taft**, had been opposed for renomination by a former Republican president, **Theodore Roosevelt**. After Taft's **convention** victory, Roosevelt bolted and mounted a **minor party** effort as the leader of the **Progressive Party**. With the Republicans badly split, Wilson's popular vote **plurality** translated into a comfortable **majority** in the **electoral college**.

In office, Wilson pursued a **progressive** domestic policy agenda, the **New Freedom**, while seeking to keep the United States aloof from the developing conflict in Europe that erupted in 1914. He ran for reelection in 1916 on the popular slogan, "He kept us out of war." He narrowly prevailed in his reelection bid against a reunified Republican Party led by **Charles Evans Hughes**.

In his second term, sentiment shifted, and Wilson brought the United States into World War I on the side of the Allies. His war aims were laid down in the Fourteen Points. Given the American role in winning the war, Wilson was active in the peace negotiations, which only partly embodied his goals in the Treaty of Versailles. His actions won him the Nobel Peace Prize in 1919. Nevertheless, his sponsorship of the League of Nations generated formidable opposition in the U.S. **Senate**, which had the constitutional responsibility of ratification. Wilson's health broke in 1919 under the strain of his futile attempt to generate popular support for his diplomacy. He left office an invalid and died in 1924.

WINNER TAKE ALL. A feature of **single-member district** electoral arrangements, which generally prevail in the United States. The candidate with the most votes wins the office being sought, regardless of the margin of victory. *See also* MULTIMEMBER DISTRICT; PROPORTIONAL REPRESENTATION.

WINTHROP, ROBERT C. Whig Speaker of the House of Representatives, 1847–1849. (b. 12 May 1809; d. 16 November 1894). Winthrop was a Massachusetts representative of the **Whig Party** who began a fragmented decade in the **House of Representatives** in 1840. In 1847, he was the choice of the Whig **majority** to be **Speaker** for the 30th **Congress**. Two years later, the Whigs lost their majority, but the **faction**-ridden **Democratic Party** was initially divided on its candidate to replace him. After extensive balloting, Democrat **Howell Cobb** narrowly won the contest for the speakership. The next year, Winthrop was elected to the **Senate** to finish an unexpired term.

WIRT, WILLIAM. Anti-Masonic presidential nominee, 1832. (b. 8 November 1772; d. 18 February 1834). Wirt was a prominent figure in Maryland party politics, identified with the dominant **Democratic-Republican Party**. He entered the national political arena in 1817, when President **James Monroe** named him attorney general, following the early departure of Monroe's initial choice, **Richard Rush**, a holdover from the **administration** of President **James Madison**. Wirt occupied the office of attorney general throughout the remainder of Monroe's two terms, and he was retained in that office by Monroe's successor, **John Quincy Adams**. He holds the record for longevity in that **cabinet** position. Wirt left public office following Adams's loss in 1828 to **Andrew Jackson**, in a time of turmoil and instability. The **faction**-ridden **single-party system** of the disintegrating **Era of Good Feelings** was giving way to the **Second Party System**.

In 1831, the newly formed **Anti-Masonic Party** innovatively assembled a national convention to choose a presidential **ticket**. As their name clearly indicates, the Anti-Masons united around their opposition to the institution of freemasonry and its alleged secret political influence. Wirt, a former Mason, was their eventual choice, after **Henry Clay**, among others, had resisted the overtures of party organizers. Wirt was an unenthusiastic nominee. Nevertheless, the new party attracted considerable support. It won 8 percent of the popular vote and carried the state of Vermont, thus winning seven votes in the **electoral college**, an impressive showing for a **minor party**. After the **election**, the party disbanded, and its adherents tended to drift toward the anti-Jackson faction that soon formed the **Whig Party**.

WORK, HUBERT. Republican National Committee chair, 1928–1929. (b. 3 July 1860; d. 14 December 1942). Work was a prominent Colorado physician who became active in state **Republican Party** politics. In 1912, he was chosen state party **chair**, and the next year he went on the **Republican National Committee (RNC)**. After the 1920 presidential **election** of **Warren G. Harding**, Work received a key appointment in the Post Office. A year later, when his superior, **Will Hays**, departed, Work replaced him as **postmaster general**. In 1923, President Harding moved Work over to the scandal-ridden Interior Department as secretary. President **Calvin Coolidge** retained him in that capacity. In 1928, Work early and openly backed the presidential candidacy of his **cabinet** colleague, **Herbert C. Hoover**. In a reversal of practice, the RNC recommended to nominee Hoover that Work be named its **chair** for the upcoming presidential **campaign**.

Work's campaign role was peripheral, and he declined to accept President Hoover's offer to name him ambassador to Japan. Instead, he resumed his medical practice.

WORKERS' PARTY. *See* COMMUNIST PARTY.

WORKERS WORLD PARTY. Post–World War II **minor party**. The Workers World Party began as a splinter group within the ranks of the **Socialist Workers Party** in the late 1950s. Its avowed purpose was to support worker uprisings throughout the world. In practice, however, it supported the efforts of communist governments to suppress such uprisings. The party entered the presidential fray in 1980 and has consistently contested presidential elections in a handful of states since then. Its voter support is minimal.

WRIGHT, JAMES C., JR. Democratic majority leader of the House of Representatives, 1977–1987; Democratic Speaker of the House of Representatives, 1987–1989. (b. 22 December 1922). Jim Wright returned from World War II to begin a career in politics. He won election to a seat in the Texas legislature in 1946, but he lost his bid for reelection. After serving two terms as mayor of Weatherford, Texas, he undertook a successful **primary** challenge against a Democratic Party **incumbent** for a **House of Representatives** seat in 1954. Over the next three decades, he moderated his ideological liberalism and ascended in the ranks of the party leadership. In 1977, he was the choice of the party **caucus** as **majority leader**, and he held that office for a decade under Speaker **Thomas P. (Tip) O'Neill.** A decade later, when O'Neill retired, Wright became **Speaker.**

In the setting of **divided party government** that prevailed with Republican **Ronald W. Reagan** in the White House and Democrats holding majorities in both houses of **Congress**, Wright was very assertive and controversial in exercising the prerogatives of office. He emerged as a major Democratic voice in the capital, forcefully challenging the foreign policy initiatives of the Reagan **administration** in Central America. Wright came under severe partisan attack for alleged ethics violations, and he resigned the speakership and his House seat in 1989. In retirement, he began teaching at Texas Christian University in Forth Worth.

WRITE-IN VOTE. A vote cast on behalf of a **candidate**, whose name does not appear on the **ballot** but is written in by the voter.

– Y –

YELLOW DOG DEMOCRATS. Passionate **Democratic Party** loyalists who would allegedly vote for a yellow dog if it ran on the party **slate**. The term originated in the **Solid South**, and its declining usage remains largely identified with that region. *See also* BLUE DOG DEMOCRATS.

YEUTTER, CLAYTON. Republican National Committee chair, 1991–1992. (b. 20 December 1930). Yeutter was a Nebraska native with a background in agriculture. He earned a law degree as well as a doctorate in agricultural economics. Yeutter taught briefly and then entered government service at the state level. In 1970, he emerged on the national scene when he accepted a position in the **administration** of President **Richard M. Nixon**, in the department of agriculture. He stayed on when **Gerald R. Ford** became president, and in 1975, Ford named him deputy trade representative. After Ford's defeat in 1976, Yeutter practiced law and then became head of the Chicago Mercantile Exchange. President **Ronald W. Reagan** brought him back into government as his trade representative. When **George H. W. Bush** became **president**, Yeutter was his choice as secretary of agriculture.

In January 1991, with **Lee Atwater**, the **chair** of the **Republican National Committee**, incapacitated by illness, Bush moved Yeutter out of the agriculture department and over to the national party headquarters as Atwater's replacement. Atwater received the nominal title of general chair for the remaining two months of his life. Yeutter operated in a low-key fashion during his brief tenure as national party chair. In February 1992, with the presidential **campaign** heating up, Bush brought Yeutter into the White House in an advisory capacity and replaced him as party chair with **Richard Bond**. Following Bush's defeat in November, Yeutter returned to private life as a lawyer-lobbyist in Washington.

Appendix A: Presidents of the United States, 1789–2009

President	Party	Term
George Washington	none	1789–1797
John Adams	Federalist	1797–1801
Thomas Jefferson	Democratic-Republican	1801–1809
James Madison	Democratic-Republican	1809–1817
James Monroe	Democratic-Republican	1817–1825
John Quincy Adams	Democratic-Republican	1825–1829
Andrew Jackson	Democratic	1829–1837
Martin Van Buren	Democratic	1837–1841
William Henry Harrison	Whig	1841
John Tyler	Whig	1841–1845
James K. Polk	Democratic	1845–1849
Zachary Taylor	Whig	1849–1850
Millard Fillmore	Whig	1850–1853
Franklin Pierce	Democratic	1853–1857
James Buchanan	Democratic	1857–1861
Abraham Lincoln	Republican	1861–1865
Andrew Johnson	Republican	1865–1869
Ulysses S. Grant	Republican	1869–1877
Rutherford B. Hayes	Republican	1877–1881
James A. Garfield	Republican	1881
Chester A. Arthur	Republican	1881–1885
Grover Cleveland	Democratic	1885–1889
Benjamin Harrison	Republican	1889–1893
Grover Cleveland	Democratic	1893–1897
William McKinley	Republican	1897–1901
Theodore Roosevelt	Republican	1901–1909
William H. Taft	Republican	1909–1913
Woodrow Wilson	Democratic	1913–1921
Warren G. Harding	Republican	1921–1923
Calvin Coolidge	Republican	1923–1929
Herbert Hoover	Republican	1929–1933
Franklin D. Roosevelt	Democratic	1933–1945

(continued)

President	Party	Term
Harry S. Truman	Democratic	1945–1953
Dwight D. Eisenhower	Republican	1953–1961
John F. Kennedy	Democratic	1961–1963
Lyndon B. Johnson	Democratic	1963–1969
Richard M. Nixon	Republican	1969–1974
Gerald R. Ford	Republican	1974–1977
Jimmy Carter	Democratic	1977–1981
Ronald Reagan	Republican	1981–1989
George H. W. Bush	Republican	1989–1993
Bill Clinton	Democratic	1993–2001
George W. Bush	Republican	2001–2009
Barack H. Obama	Democratic	2009–

Appendix B: Vice Presidents of the United States, 1789–2009

Vice President	Party	Term
John Adams	Federalist	1789–1797
Thomas Jefferson	Democratic-Republican	1797–1801
Aaron Burr	Democratic-Republican	1801–1805
George Clinton	Democratic-Republican	1805–1812
Elbridge Gerry	Democratic-Republican	1813–1814
Daniel D. Tompkins	Democratic-Republican	1817–1825
John C. Calhoun	Democratic-Republican	1825–1832
Martin Van Buren	Democratic	1833–1837
Richard M. Johnson	Democratic	1837–1841
John Tyler	Whig	1841
George M. Dallas	Democratic	1845–1849
Millard Fillmore	Whig	1849–1850
William R. King	Democratic	1853
John C. Breckinridge	Democratic	1857–1861
Hannibal Hamlin	Republican	1861–1865
Andrew Johnson	Republican	1865
Schuyler Colfax	Republican	1869–1873
Henry Wilson	Republican	1873–1875
William A. Wheeler	Republican	1877–1881
Chester A. Arthur	Republican	1881
Thomas A. Hendricks	Democratic	1885
Levi P. Morton	Republican	1889–1893
Aldai E. Stevenson	Democratic	1893–1897
Garret A. Hobart	Republican	1897–1899
Theodore Roosevelt	Republican	1901
Charles W. Fairbanks	Republican	1905–1909
James S. Sherman	Republican	1909–1912
Thomas R. Marshall	Democratic	1913–1921
Calvin Coolidge	Republican	1921–1923
Charles G. Dawes	Republican	1925–1929
Charles Curtis	Republican	1929–1933
John N. Garner	Democratic	1933–1941

(continued)

Vice President	Party	Term
Henry A. Wallace	Democratic	1941–1945
Harry S. Truman	Democratic	1945
Alben W. Barkley	Democratic	1949–1953
Richard M. Nixon	Republican	1953–1961
Lyndon B. Johnson	Democratic	1961–1963
Hubert H. Humphrey	Democratic	1965–1969
Spiro T. Agnew	Republican	1969–1973
Gerald R. Ford	Republican	1973–1974
Nelson A. Rockefeller	Republican	1974–1977
Walter F. Mondale	Democratic	1977–1981
George Bush	Republican	1981–1989
Dan Quayle	Republican	1989–1993
Al Gore	Democratic	1993–2001
Richard Cheney	Republican	2001–2009
Joseph R. Biden	Democratic	2009–

Appendix C: Speakers of the House of Representatives, 1789–2009

Congress	Name and State	Party
1st (1789–1791)	Frederick A. C. Muhlenberg/Pennsylvania	none
2nd (1791–1793)	Jonathan Trumbull/Connecticut	none
3rd (1793–1795)	Frederick A. C. Muhlenberg/Pennsylvania	none
4th (1795–1797)	Jonathan Dayton/New Jersey	Federalist
5th (1787–1799)	Jonathan Dayton/New Jersey	Federalist
6th (1799–1801)	Theodore Sedgwick/Massachusetts	Federalist
7th (1801–1803)	Nathaniel Macon/North Carolina	Democratic-Republican
8th (1803–1805)	Nathaniel Macon/North Carolina	Democratic-Republican
9th (1805–1807)	Nathaniel Macon/North Carolina	Democratic-Republican
10th (1807–1809)	Joseph B. Varnum/Massachusetts	Democratic-Republican
11th (1809–1811)	Joseph B. Varnum/Massachusetts	Democratic-Republican
12th (1811–1813)	Henry Clay/Kentucky	Democratic-Republican
13th (1813–1815)	Henry Clay/Kentucky	Democratic-Republican
	Landon Cheves/South Carolina (1814)	Democratic-Republican
14th (1815–1817)	Henry Clay/Kentucky	Democratic-Republican
15th (1817–1819)	Henry Clay/Kentucky	Democratic-Republican
16th (1819–1821)	Henry Clay/Kentucky	Democratic-Republican
	John W. Taylor/New York (1820)	Democratic-Republican
17th (1821–1823)	Philip P. Barbour/Virginia	Democratic-Republican

(continued)

Congress	Name and State	Party
18th (1823–1825)	Henry Clay/Kentucky	Democratic-Republican
19th (1825–1827)	John W. Taylor/New York	Democratic-Republican
20th (1827–1829)	Andrew Stevenson/Virginia	Democratic-Republican
21st (1829–1831)	Andrew Stevenson/Virginia	Democratic
22nd (1831–1833)	Andrew Stevenson/Virginia	Democratic
23rd (1833–1835)	Andrew Stevenson/Virginia	Democratic
	John Bell/Tennessee (1834)	Whig
24th (1835–1837)	James K. Polk/Tennessee	Democratic
25th (1837–1839)	James K. Polk/Tennessee	Democratic
26th (1839–1841)	Robert M. T. Hunter/Virginia	Democratic
27th (1841–1843)	John White/Kentucky	Whig
28th (1843–1845)	John W. Jones/Virginia	Democratic
29th (1845–1847)	John W. Davis/Indiana	Democratic
30th (1847–1849)	Robert C. Winthrop/Massachusetts	Whig
31st (1849–1851)	Howell Cobb/Georgia	Democratic
32nd (1851–1853)	Linn Boyd/Kentucky	Democratic
33rd (1853–1855)	Linn Boyd/Kentucky	Democratic
34th (1855–1857)	Nathaniel P. Banks/Massachusetts	American
35th (1857–1859)	James L. Orr/South Carolina	Democratic
36th (1859–1861)	William Pennington/New Jersey	Whig
37th (1861–1863)	Galusha Grow/Pennsylvania	Republican
38th (1863–1865)	Schuyler Colfax/Indiana	Republican
39th (1865–1867)	Schuyler Colfax/Indiana	Republican
40th (1867–1869)	Schuyler Colfax/Indiana	Republican
	Theodore M. Pomeroy/New York (1869)	Republican
41st (1869–1871)	James G. Blaine/Maine	Republican
42nd (1871–1873)	James G. Blaine/Maine	Republican
43rd (1873–1875)	James G. Blaine/Maine	Republican
44th (1875–1877)	Michael C. Kerr/Indiana	Democratic
	Samuel Randall/Pennsylvania (1876)	Democratic
45th (1877–1879)	Samuel Randall/Pennsylvania	Democratic
46th (1879–1881)	Samuel Randall/Pennsylvania	Democratic
47th (1881–1883)	J. Warren Keifer/Ohio	Republican
48th (1883–1885)	John G. Carlisle/Kentucky	Democratic
49th (1885–1887)	John G. Carlisle/Kentucky	Democratic
50th (1887–1889)	John G. Carlisle/Kentucky	Democratic
51st (1889–1891)	Thomas B. Reed/Maine	Republican
52nd (1891–1893)	Charles F. Crisp/Georgia	Democratic
53rd (1893–1895)	Charles F. Crisp/Georgia	Democratic
54th (1895–1897)	Thomas B. Reed/Maine	Republican
55th (1897–1899)	Thomas B. Reed/Maine	Republican

Congress	Name and State	Party
56th (1899–1901)	David B. Henderson/Iowa	Republican
57th (1901–1903)	David B. Henderson/Iowa	Republican
58th (1903–1905)	Joseph G. Cannon/Illinois	Republican
59th (1905–1907)	Joseph G. Cannon/Illinois	Republican
60th (1907–1909)	Joseph G. Cannon/Illinois	Republican
61st (1909–1911)	Joseph G. Cannon/Illinois	Republican
62nd (1911–1913)	James B. "Champ" Clark/Missouri	Democratic
63rd (1913–1915)	James B. "Champ" Clark/Missouri	Democratic
64th (1915–1917)	James B. "Champ" Clark/Missouri	Democratic
65th (1917–1919)	James B. "Champ" Clark/Missouri	Democratic
66th (1919–1921)	Frederick H. Gillett/Massachusetts	Republican
67th (1921–1923)	Frederick H. Gillett/Massachusetts	Republican
68th (1923–1925)	Frederick H. Gillett/Massachusetts	Republican
69th (1925–1927)	Nicholas Longworth/Ohio	Republican
70th (1927–1929)	Nicholas Longworth/Ohio	Republican
71st (1929–1931)	Nicholas Longworth/Ohio	Republican
72nd (1931–1933)	John Nance Garner/Texas	Democratic
73rd (1933–1935)	Henry T. Rainey/Illinois	Democratic
74th (1935–1937)	Joseph W. Byrns/Tennessee	Democratic
	William M. Bankhead/Alabama (1936)	Democratic
75th (1937–1939)	William M. Bankhead/Alabama	Democratic
76th (1939–1941)	William M. Bankhead/Alabama	Democratic
	Samuel T. Rayburn/Texas (1940)	Democratic
77th (1941–1943)	Samuel T. Rayburn/Texas	Democratic
78th (1943–1945)	Samuel T. Rayburn/Texas	Democratic
79th (1945–1947)	Samuel T. Rayburn/Texas	Democratic
80th (1947–1949)	Joseph W. Martin Jr./Massachusetts	Republican
81st (1949–1951)	Samuel T. Rayburn/Texas	Democratic
82nd (1951–1953)	Samuel T. Rayburn/Texas	Democratic
83rd (1953–1955)	Joseph W. Martin Jr./Massachusetts	Republican
84th (1955–1957)	Samuel T. Rayburn/Texas	Democratic
85th (1957–1959)	Samuel T. Rayburn/Texas	Democratic
86th (1959–1961)	Samuel T. Rayburn/Texas	Democratic
87th (1961–1963)	Samuel T. Rayburn/Texas	Democratic
	John W. McCormack/Massachusetts (1962)	Democratic
88th (1963–1965)	John W. McCormack/Massachusetts	Democratic
89th (1965–1967)	John W. McCormack/Massachusetts	Democratic
90th (1967–1969)	John W. McCormack/Massachusetts	Democratic
91st (1969–1971)	John W. McCormack/Massachusetts	Democratic
92nd (1971–1973)	Carl Albert/Oklahoma	Democratic
93rd (1973–1975)	Carl Albert/Oklahoma	Democratic
94th (1975–1977)	Carl Albert/Oklahoma	Democratic

(*continued*)

Congress	Name and State	Party
95th (1977–1979)	Thomas P. "Tip" O'Neill Jr./Massachusetts	Democratic
96th (1979–1981)	Thomas P. "Tip" O'Neill Jr./Massachusetts	Democratic
97th (1981–1983)	Thomas P. "Tip" O'Neill Jr./Massachusetts	Democratic
98th (1983–1985)	Thomas P. "Tip" O'Neill Jr./Massachusetts	Democratic
99th (1985–1987)	Thomas P. "Tip" O'Neill Jr./Massachusetts	Democratic
100th (1987–1989)	James C. Wright Jr./Texas	Democratic
	Thomas Foley/Washington (1989)	Democratic
101st (1989–1991)	Thomas Foley/Washington	Democratic
102nd (1991–1993)	Thomas Foley/Washington	Democratic
103rd (1993–1995)	Thomas Foley/Washington	Democratic
104th (1995–1997)	Newton L. Gingrich/Georgia	Republican
105th (1997–1999)	Newton L. Gingrich/Georgia	Republican
106th (1999–2001)	Dennis Hastert/Illinois	Republican
107th (2001–2003)	Dennis Hastert/Illinois	Republican
108th (2003–2005)	Dennis Hastert/Illinois	Republican
109th (2005–2007)	Dennis Hastert/Illinois	Republican
110th (2007–2009)	Nancy Pelosi/California	Democratic
111th (2009–2111)	Nancy Pelosi/California	Democratic

Appendix D: Presidents Pro Tempore of the Senate, 1789–2009

Congress	Name and State	Party
1st (1789–1791)	John A. Langdon/New Hampshire	Democratic-Republican
2nd (1791–1793)	Richard Henry Lee/Virginia (1792)	none
	John A. Langdon/New Hampshire (1793)	Democratic-Republican
3rd (1793–1795)	Ralph Izard/South Carolina (1794)	none
	Henry Tazewell/Virginia (1795)	none
4th (1795–1797)	Henry Tazewell/Virginia	none
	Samuel Livermore/New Hampshire (1796)	none
	William Bingham/Pennsylvania (1797)	Federalist
5th (1787–1799)	William Bradford/Rhode Island	none
	Jacob Read/South Carolina (1797)	Federalist
	Theodore Sedgwick/Massachusetts (1798)	Federalist
	John Laurance/New York (1798)	none
	James Ross/Pennsylvania (1799)	Federalist
6th (1799–1801)	Samuel Livermore/New Hampshire	none
	Uriah Tracy/Connecticut (1800)	Federalist
	John E. Howard/Maryland (1800)	Federalist
	James Hillhouse/Connecticut (1801)	Federalist
7th (1801–1803)	Abraham Baldwin/Georgia	Federalist
	Stephen R. Bradley/Vermont (1802)	Democratic-Republican
8th (1803–1805)	John Brown/Kentucky	none
	Jesse Franklin/North Carolina (1804)	Democratic-Republican
	Joseph Anderson/Tennessee (1805)	none
9th (1805–1807)	Samuel Smith/Maryland	Democratic-Republican
10th (1807–1809)	Samuel Smith/Maryland (1808)	Democratic-Republican
	Stephen R. Bradley/Vermont (1808)	Democratic-Republican

(continued)

355

Congress	Name and State	Party
11th (1809–1811)	John Milledge/Georgia (1809)	none
	Andrew Gregg/Pennsylvania	none
	John Gaillard/South Carolina (1810)	Democratic-Republican
	John Pope/Kentucky (1811)	Democratic-Republican
12th (1811–1813)	William H. Crawford/Georgia (1812)	Democratic-Republican
13th (1813–1815)	Joseph B. Varnum/Massachusetts (1813)	none
	John Gaillard/South Carolina (1814)	Democratic-Republican
14th (1815–1817)	John Gaillard/South Carolina	Democratic-Republican
15th (1817–1819)	John Gaillard/South Carolina	Democratic-Republican
	James Barbour/Virginia (1819)	Democratic-Republican
16th (1819–1821)	James Barbour/Virginia	Democratic-Republican
	John Gaillard/South Carolina (1820)	Democratic-Republican
17th (1821–1823)	John Gaillard/South Carolina (1822)	Democratic-Republican
18th (1823–1825)	John Gaillard/South Carolina (1824)	Democratic-Republican
19th (1825–1827)	John Gaillard/South Carolina	Democratic-Republican
	Nathaniel Macon/North Carolina (1826)	Democratic-Republican
20th (1827–1829)	Samuel Smith/Maryland (1828)	Democratic-Republican
21st (1829–1831)	Samuel Smith/Maryland	Democratic-Republican
22nd (1831–1833)	Littleton W. Tazewell/Virginia (1832)	Democratic
	Hugh Lawson White/Tennessee (1832)	Whig
23rd (1833–1835)	George Poindexter/Mississippi (1834)	none
	John Tyler/Virginia (1835)	Democratic
24th (1835–1837)	William R. King/Alabama (1836)	Democratic
25th (1837–1839)	William R. King/Alabama	Democratic
26th (1839–1841)	William R. King/Alabama	Democratic
27th (1841–1843)	William R. King/Alabama	Democratic
	Samuel L. Southard/New Jersey (1841)	Whig
	Willie P. Mangum/North Carolina (1842)	Whig
28th (1843–1845)	Willie P. Mangum/North Carolina	Whig

Congress	Name and State	Party
29th (1845–1847)	Ambrose H. Sevier*/Arkansas	Democratic
	David R. Atchison/Missouri (1846)	Whig
30th (1847–1849)	David R. Atchison/Missouri (1848)	Whig
31st (1849–1851)	William R. King/Alabama (1850)	Democratic
32nd (1851–1853)	William R. King/Alabama	Democratic
	David R. Atchison/Missouri (1852)	Whig
33rd (1853–1855)	David R. Atchison/Missouri	Whig
	Lewis Cass/Michigan (1854)	Democratic
	Jesse D. Bright/Indiana (1854)	Democratic
34th (1855–1857)	Jesse D. Bright/Indiana	Democratic
	Charles E. Stuart/Michigan (1856)	Democratic
	James M. Mason/Virginia (1856)	Democratic
35th (1857–1859)	James M. Mason/Virginia	Democratic
	Thomas J. Rusk/Texas (1857)	Democratic
	Benjamin Fitzpatrick/Alabama (1857)	Democratic
36th (1859–1861)	Benjamin Fitzpatrick/Alabama	Democratic
	Jesse D. Bright/Indiana (1860)	Democratic
	Solomon Foot/Vermont (1861)	Republican
37th (1861–1863)	Solomon Foot/Vermont	Republican
38th (1863–1865)	Solomon Foot/Vermont	Republican
	Daniel Clark/New Hampshire (1864)	Republican
39th (1865–1867)	Lafayette S. Foster/Connecticut (1865)	Republican
	Benjamin F. Wade/Ohio (1867)	Republican
40th (1867–1869)	Benjamin F. Wade/Ohio	Republican
41st (1869–1871)	Henry B. Anthony/Rhode Island	Republican
42nd (1871–1873)	Henry B. Anthony/Rhode Island	Republican
43rd (1873–1875)	Matthew H. Carpenter/Wisconsin	Republican
	Henry B. Anthony/Rhode Island (1875)	Republican
44th (1875–1877)	Thomas W. Ferry/Michigan	Republican
45th (1877–1879)	Thomas W. Ferry/Michigan	Republican
46th (1879–1881)	Allen G. Thurman/Ohio	Democratic
47th (1881–1883)	Thomas F. Bayard/Delaware	Republican
	David Davis/Illinois (1881)	Republican
	George F. Edmunds/Vermont (1883)	Republican
48th (1883–1885)	George F. Edmunds/Vermont	Republican
49th (1885–1887)	John Sherman/Ohio	Republican
	John J. Ingalls/Kansas (1887)	Republican
50th (1887–1889)	John J. Ingalls/Kansas	Republican
51st (1889–1891)	John J. Ingalls/Kansas	Republican
	Charles F. Manderson/Nebraska (1891)	Republican
52nd (1891–1893)	Charles F. Manderson/Nebraska	Republican
53rd (1893–1895)	Isham G. Harris/Tennessee	Democratic

(continued)

Congress	Name and State	Party
	Matt W. Ransom/North Carolina (1895)	Democratic
	Isham G. Harris/Tennessee (1895)	Democratic
54th (1895–1897)	William P. Frye/Maine (1896)	Republican
55th (1897–1899)	William P. Frye/Maine	Republican
56th (1899–1901)	William P. Frye/Maine	Republican
57th (1901–1903)	William P. Frye/Maine	Republican
58th (1903–1905)	William P. Frye/Maine	Republican
59th (1905–1907)	William P. Frye/Maine	Republican
60th (1907–1909)	William P. Frye/Maine	Republican
61st (1909–1911)	William P. Frye/Maine	Republican
62nd (1911–1913)	William P. Frye/Maine	Republican
	Charles Curtis/Kansas (1911)	Republican
	Augustus O. Bacon/Georgia (1912)	Democratic
	Frank B. Brandegee/Connecticut (1912)	Republican
	Jacob H. Gallinger/New Hampshire (1912)	Republican
	Henry Cabot Lodge/Massachusetts (1912)	Republican
	Jacob H. Gallinger/New Hampshire (1913)	Republican
63rd (1913–1915)	James P. Clarke/Arkansas	Democratic
64th (1915–1917)	James P. Clarke/Arkansas	Democratic
	Willard Saulsbury/Delaware (1916)	Democratic
65th (1917–1919)	Willard Saulsbury/Delaware	Democratic
66th (1919–1921)	Albert B. Cummins/Iowa	Republican
67th (1921–1923)	Albert B. Cummins/Iowa	Republican
68th (1923–1925)	Albert B. Cummins/Iowa	Republican
69th (1925–1927)	George H. Moses/New Hampshire	Republican
70th (1927–1929)	George H. Moses/New Hampshire	Republican
71st (1929–1931)	George H. Moses/New Hampshire	Republican
72nd (1931–1933)	George H. Moses/New Hampshire	Republican
73rd (1933–1935)	Key Pittman/Nevada	Democratic
74th (1935–1937)	Key Pittman/Nevada	Democratic
75th (1937–1939)	Key Pittman/Nevada	Democratic
76th (1939–1941)	Key Pittman/Nevada	Democratic
	William H. King/Utah (1940)	Democratic
77th (1941–1943)	Pat Harrison/Mississippi	Democratic
	Carter Glass/Virginia (1941)	Democratic
78th (1943–1945)	Carter Glass/Virginia	Democratic
79th (1945–1947)	Kenneth McKellar/Tennessee	Democratic
80th (1947–1949)	Arthur H. Vandenberg/Michigan	Republican
81st (1949–1951)	Kenneth McKellar/Tennessee	Democratic
82nd (1951–1953)	Kenneth McKellar/Tennessee	Democratic
83rd (1953–1955)	Styles Bridges/New Hampshire	Republican
84th (1955–1957)	Walter George/Georgia	Democratic
85th (1957–1959)	Carl Hayden/Arizona	Democratic
86th (1959–1961)	Carl Hayden/Arizona	Democratic

Congress	Name and State	Party
87th (1961–1963)	Carl Hayden/Arizona	Democratic
88th (1963–1965)	Carl Hayden/Arizona	Democratic
89th (1965–1967)	Carl Hayden/Arizona	Democratic
90th (1967–1969)	Carl Hayden/Arizona	Democratic
91st (1969–1971)	Richard B. Russell/Georgia	Democratic
92nd (1971–1973)	Richard B. Russell/Georgia	Democratic
	Allen J. Ellender/Louisiana (1971)	Democratic
	James O. Eastland/Mississippi (1972)	Democratic
93rd (1973–1975)	James O. Eastland/Mississippi	Democratic
94th (1975–1977)	James O. Eastland/Mississippi	Democratic
95th (1977–1979)	James O. Eastland/Mississippi	Democratic
96th (1979–1981)	Warren G. Magnuson/Washington	Democratic
97th (1981–1983)	J. Strom Thurmond/South Carolina	Republican
98th (1983–1985)	J. Strom Thurmond/South Carolina	Republican
99th (1985–1987)	J. Strom Thurmond/South Carolina	Republican
100th (1987–1989)	John C. Stennis/Mississippi	Democratic
101st (1989–1991)	Robert C. Byrd/West Virginia	Democratic
102nd (1991–1993)	Robert C. Byrd/West Virginia	Democratic
103rd (1993–1995)	Robert C. Byrd/West Virginia	Democratic
104th (1995–1997)	J. Strom Thurmond/South Carolina	Republican
105th (1997–1999)	J. Strom Thurmond/South Carolina	Republican
106th (1999–2001)	J. Strom Thurmond/South Carolina	Republican
107th (2001–2003)	Robert C. Byrd/West Virginia	Democratic
	J. Strom Thurmond/South Carolina	Republican
	Robert C. Byrd/West Virginia	Democratic
108th (2003–2005)	Theodore F. Stevens/Alaska	Republican
109th (2005–2007)	Theodore F. Stevens/Alaska	Republican
110th (2007–2009)	Robert C. Byrd/West Virginia	Democratic
111th (2009–2111)	Robert C. Byrd/West Virginia	Democratic

*Ambrose H. Sevier served under designation of the vice president.

Appendix E: Floor Leaders, House of Representatives, 1899–2009

Congress	Majority	Minority
56th (1899–1901)	Sereno E. Payne (R), New York	James D. Richardson (D), Tennessee
57th (1901–1903)	Sereno E. Payne (R), New York	James D. Richardson (D), Tennessee
58th (1903–1905)	Sereno E. Payne (R), New York	John Sharp Williams (D), Mississippi
59th (1905–1907)	Sereno E. Payne (R), New York	John Sharp Williams (D), Mississippi
60th (1907–1909)	Sereno E. Payne (R), New York	John Sharp Williams (D), Mississippi; J.B. "Champ" Clark (D), Missouri (1908)
61st (1909–1911)	Sereno E. Payne (R), New York	J. B. "Champ" Clark (D), Missouri
62nd (1911–1913)	Oscar W. Underwood (D), Alabama	James R. Mann (R), Illinois
63rd (1913–1915)	Oscar W. Underwood (D), Alabama	James R. Mann (R), Illinois
64th (1915–1917)	Claude Kitchin (D), Alabama	James R. Mann (R), Illinois
65th (1917–1919)	Claude Kitchin (D), Alabama	James R. Mann (R), Illinois
66th (1919–1921)	Franklin W. Mondell (R), Wyoming	J. B. "Champ" Clark (D), Missouri
67th (1921–1923)	Franklin W. Mondell (R), Wyoming	Claude Kitchin (D), Alabama
68th (1923–1925)	Nicholas Longworth (R), Ohio	Finis J. Garrett (D), Tennessee
69th (1925–1927)	John Q. Tilson (R), Connecticut	Finis J. Garrett (D), Tennessee
70th (1927–1929)	John Q. Tilson (R), Connecticut	Finis J. Garrett (D), Tennessee
71st (1929–1931)	John Q. Tilson (R), Connecticut	John N. Garner (D), Texas
72nd (1931–1933)	Henry T. Rainey (D), Illinois	Bertrand H. Snell (R), New York
73rd (1933–1935)	Joseph W. Byrns (D), Tennessee	Bertrand H. Snell (R), New York
74th (1935–1937)	William B. Bankhead (D), Alabama	Bertrand H. Snell (R), New York
75th (1937–1939)	Samuel T. Rayburn (D), Texas	Bertrand H. Snell (R), New York
76th (1939–1941)	Samuel T. Rayburn (D), Texas; John W. McCormack (D), Massachusetts (1940)	Joseph W. Martin (R), Massachusetts
77th (1941–1943)	John W. McCormack (D), Massachusetts	Joseph W. Martin (R), Massachusetts
78th (1943–1945)	John W. McCormack (D), Massachusetts	Joseph W. Martin (R), Massachusetts
79th (1945–1947)	John W. McCormack (D), Massachusetts	Joseph W. Martin (R), Massachusetts
80th (1947–1949)	Charles A. Halleck (R), Indiana	Samuel T. Rayburn (D), Texas

81st (1949–1951)	John W. McCormack (D), Massachusetts	Joseph W. Martin (R), Massachusetts
82nd (1951–1953)	John W. McCormack (D), Massachusetts	Joseph W. Martin (R), Massachusetts
83rd (1953–1955)	Charles A. Halleck (R), Indiana	Samuel T. Rayburn (D), Texas
84th (1955–1957)	John W. McCormack (D), Massachusetts	Joseph W. Martin (R), Massachusetts
85th (1957–1959)	John W. McCormack (D), Massachusetts	Joseph W. Martin (R), Massachusetts
86th (1959–1961)	John W. McCormack (D), Massachusetts	Charles A. Halleck (R), Indiana
87th (1961–1963)	John W. McCormack (D), Massachusetts	Charles A. Halleck (R), Indiana
88th (1963–1965)	Carl Albert (D), Oklahoma (1962)	Charles A. Halleck (R), Indiana
89th (1965–1967)	Carl Albert (D), Oklahoma	Gerald R. Ford (R), Michigan
90th (1967–1969)	Carl Albert (D), Oklahoma	Gerald R. Ford (R), Michigan
91st (1969–1971)	Carl Albert (D), Oklahoma	Gerald R. Ford (R), Michigan
92nd (1971–1973)	Carl Albert (D), Oklahoma	Gerald R. Ford (R), Michigan
93rd (1973–1975)	Hale Boggs (D), Louisiana	Gerald R. Ford (R), Michigan
	Thomas P. O'Neill (D), Massachusetts	John J. Rhodes (R), Arizona (1973)
94th (1975–1977)	Thomas P. O'Neill (D), Massachusetts	John J. Rhodes (R), Arizona
95th (1977–1979)	James C. Wright (D), Texas	John J. Rhodes (R), Arizona
96th (1979–1981)	James C. Wright (D), Texas	John J. Rhodes (R), Arizona
97th (1981–1983)	James C. Wright (D), Texas	Robert H. Michel (R), Illinois
98th (1983–1985)	James C. Wright (D), Texas	Robert H. Michel (R), Illinois
99th (1985–1987)	James C. Wright (D), Texas	Robert H. Michel (R), Illinois
100th (1987–1989)	Thomas Foley (D), Washington	Robert H. Michel (R), Illinois
	Richard Gephardt (D), Missouri (1989)	
101st (1989–1991)	Richard Gephardt (D), Missouri	Robert H. Michel (R), Illinois
102nd (1991–1993)	Richard Gephardt (D), Missouri	Robert H. Michel (R), Illinois
103rd (1993–1995)	Richard Gephardt (D), Missouri	Robert H. Michel (R), Illinois
104th (1995–1997)	Richard Armey (R), Texas	Richard Gephardt (D), Missouri

(continued)

Congress	Majority	Minority
105th (1997–1999)	Richard Armey (R), Texas	Richard Gephardt (D), Missouri
106th (1999–2001)	Richard Armey (R), Texas	Richard Gephardt (D), Missouri
107th (2001–2003)	Richard Armey (R), Texas	Richard Gephardt (D), Missouri
108th (2003–2005)	Thomas Delay (R), Texas	Richard Gephardt (D), Missouri
109th (2005–2007)	Thomas Delay (R), Texas	
	John Boehner (R), Ohio (2006)	Nancy Pelosi (D), California
110th (2007–2009)	Steny H. Hoyer (D), Maryland	John Boehner(R), Ohio
111th (2009–2011)	Steny H. Hoyer (D), Maryland	John Boehner(R), Ohio

Appendix F: Floor Leaders, Senate 1911–2009

Congress	Majority	Minority
62nd (1911–1913)	Shelby M. Cullom (R), Illinois	Thomas S. Martin (D), Virginia
63rd (1913–1915)	John W. Kern (D), Indiana	Jacob H. Gallinger (R), New Hampshire
64th (1915–1917)	John W. Kern (D), Indiana	Jacob H. Gallinger(R), New Hampshire
65th (1917–1919)	Thomas S. Martin (D), Virginia	Jacob H. Gallinger(R), New Hampshire
		Henry Cabot Lodge (R), Massachusetts (1918)
66th (1919–1921)	Henry Cabot Lodge (R), Massachusetts	Thomas S. Martin (D), Virginia
		Oscar W. Underwood (D), Alabama (1920)
67th (1921–1923)	Henry Cabot Lodge (R), Massachusetts	Oscar W. Underwood (D), Alabama
68th (1923–1925)	Henry Cabot Lodge (R), Massachusetts	Joseph T. Robinson (D), Arkansas
	Charles Curtis (R), Kansas (1924)	
69th (1925–1927)	Charles Curtis (R), Kansas	Joseph T. Robinson (D), Arkansas
70th (1927–1929)	Charles Curtis (R), Kansas	Joseph T. Robinson (D), Arkansas
71st (1929–1931)	James E. Watson (R), Indiana	Joseph T. Robinson (D), Arkansas
72nd (1931–1933)	James E. Watson (R), Indiana	Joseph T. Robinson (D), Arkansas
73rd (1933–1935)	Joseph T. Robinson (D), Arkansas	Charles L. McNary (R), Oregon
74th (1935–1937)	Joseph T. Robinson (D), Arkansas	Charles L. McNary (R), Oregon
75th (1937–1939)	Joseph T. Robinson (D), Arkansas	Charles L. McNary (R), Oregon
	Alben W. Barkley (D), Kentucky	
76th (1939–1941)	Alben W. Barkley (D), Kentucky	Charles L. McNary (R), Oregon
77th (1941–1943)	Alben W. Barkley (D), Kentucky	Charles L. McNary (R), Oregon
78th (1943–1945)	Alben W. Barkley (D), Kentucky	Charles L. McNary (R), Oregon
79th (1945–1947)	Alben W. Barkley (D), Kentucky	Wallace H. White (R), Maine
80th (1947–1949)	Wallace H. White (R), Maine	Alben W. Barkley (D), Kentucky
81st (1949–1951)	Scott W. Lucas (D), Illinois	Kenneth S. Wherry (R), Nebraska
82nd (1951–1953)	Ernest W. McFarland (D), Arizona	Kenneth S. Wherry (R), Nebraska
		Styles Bridges (R), New Hampshire (1952)
83rd (1953–1955)	Robert A. Taft (R), Ohio	Lyndon B. Johnson (D), Texas

Congress		
84th (1955–1957)	William F. Knowland (R), California (1953)	William F. Knowland (R), California
85th (1957–1959)	Lyndon B. Johnson (D), Texas	William F. Knowland (R), California
86th (1959–1961)	Lyndon B. Johnson (D), Texas	William F. Knowland (R), California
87th (1961–1963)	Lyndon B. Johnson (D), Texas	Everett M. Dirksen (R), Illinois
88th (1963–1965)	Michael Mansfield (D), Montana	Everett M. Dirksen (R), Illinois
89th (1965–1967)	Michael Mansfield (D), Montana	Everett M. Dirksen (R), Illinois
90th (1967–1969)	Michael Mansfield (D), Montana	Everett M. Dirksen (R), Illinois
91st (1969–1971)	Michael Mansfield (D), Montana	Everett M. Dirksen (R), Illinois
		Hugh D. Scott (R), Pennsylvania (1969)
92nd (1971–1973)	Michael Mansfield (D), Montana	Hugh D. Scott (R), Pennsylvania
93rd (1973–1975)	Michael Mansfield (D), Montana	Hugh D. Scott (R), Pennsylvania
94th (1975–1977)	Michael Mansfield (D), Montana	Hugh D. Scott (R), Pennsylvania
95th (1977–1979)	Robert C. Byrd (D), West Virginia	Howard H. Baker (R), Tennessee
96th (1979–1981)	Robert C. Byrd (D), West Virginia	Howard H. Baker (R), Tennessee
97th (1981–1983)	Howard H. Baker (R), Tennessee	Robert C. Byrd (D), West Virginia
98th (1983–1985)	Howard H. Baker (R), Tennessee	Robert C. Byrd (D), West Virginia
99th (1985–1987)	Robert J. Dole (R), Kansas	Robert C. Byrd (D), West Virginia
100th (1987–1989)	Robert C. Byrd (D), West Virginia	Robert J. Dole (R), Kansas
101st (1989–1991)	George C. Mitchell (D), Maine	Robert J. Dole (R), Kansas
102nd (1991–1993)	George C. Mitchell (D), Maine	Robert J. Dole (R), Kansas
103rd (1993–1995)	George C. Mitchell (D), Maine	Robert J. Dole (R), Kansas
104th (1995–1997)	Robert J. Dole (R), Kansas	Thomas Daschle (D), South Dakota
	Trent Lott (R), Mississippi	
105th (1997–1999)	Trent Lott (R), Mississippi	Thomas Daschle (D), South Dakota
106th (1999–2001)	Trent Lott (R), Mississippi	Thomas Daschle (D), South Dakota

(continued)

Congress	Majority	Minority
107th (2001–2003)	Thomas Daschle (D), South Dakota	Trent Lott (R), Mississippi
	Trent Lott (R), Mississippi (2001)	Thomas Daschle (D), South Dakota (2001)
	Thomas Daschle (2001)	Trent Lott (R), Mississippi (2001)
108th (2003–2005)	William Frist (R), Tennessee	Thomas Daschle (D), South Dakota
109th (2005–2007)	William Frist (R), Tennessee	Harry Reid (D), Nevada
110th (2007–2009)	Harry Reid (D), Nevada	Mitchell McConnell (R), Kentucky
111th (2009–2011)	Harry Reid (D), Nevada	Mitchell McConnell (R), Kentucky

Appendix G: Democratic National Conventions 1832–2008

Year	City	Dates	Nominees	Ballot
1832	Baltimore	21–23 May	Andrew Jackson/Martin Van Buren	1/1
1836	Baltimore	20–23 May 1835	Martin Van Buren/Richard M. Johnson	1/1
1840	Baltimore	5–6 May	Martin Van Buren/No VP nominee	A[a]/
1844	Baltimore	27–29 May	James K. Polk/George M. Dallas	9/3
1848	Baltimore	22–26 May	Lewis Cass/William O. Butler	4/2
1852	Baltimore	1–6 June	Franklin Pierce/William R. King	49/2
1856	Cincinnati	2–5 June	James Buchanan/John C. Breckinridge	17/2
1860	Charleston	23 April–3 May	Stephen A Douglas/Benjamin Fitzpatrick[b]	57
	Baltimore	18–23 June		2/1
1864	Chicago	29–31 August	George B. McClellan/George H. Pendleton	1/1
1868	New York	4–9 July	Horatio Seymour/Francis P. Blair	22/1
1872	Baltimore	9–10 July	Horace Greeley/Benjamin G. Brown	1/1
1876	St. Louis	27–29 June	Samuel J. Tilden/Thomas A. Hendricks	2/1
1880	Cincinnati	22–24 June	Winfield S. Hancock/William H. English	2/A
1884	Chicago	8–11 July	Grover Cleveland/Thomas A. Hendricks	2/1
1888	St. Louis	5–7 June	Grover Cleveland/Allen G. Thurman	A/1
1892	Chicago	21–23 June	Grover Cleveland/Adlai E. Stevenson	1/1
1896	Chicago	7–11 July	William J. Bryan/Arthur Sewall	5/5
1900	Kansas City	4–6 July	William J. Bryan/Adlai E. Stevenson	1/1
1904	St. Louis	6–9 July	Alton B. Parker/Henry G. Davis	1/1
1908	Denver	7–10 July	William J. Bryan/John W. Kern	1/A
1912	Baltimore	25 June–2 July	Woodrow Wilson/Thomas R. Marshall	46/2
1916	St. Louis	14–16 June	Woodrow Wilson/Thomas R. Marshall	1/A
1920	San Francisco	28 June–5 July	James M. Cox/Franklin D. Roosevelt	44/A

Year	City	Dates	Nominees (President/Vice President)	Ballots
1924	New York	24 June–9 July	John W. Davis/Charles W. Bryan	103/1
1928	Houston	26–29 June	Alfred E. Smith/Joseph T. Robinson	1/1
1932	Chicago	27 June–2 July	Franklin D. Roosevelt/John Nance Garner	4/A
1936	Philadelphia	23–27 June	Franklin D. Roosevelt/John Nance Garner	A/A
1940	Chicago	15—19 June	Franklin D. Roosevelt/Henry A. Wallace	1/1
1944	Chicago	19–21 July	Franklin D. Roosevelt/Harry S. Truman	1/2
1948	Philadelphia	12–15 July	Harry S. Truman/Alben W. Barkley	1/A
1952	Chicago	21–26 July	Adlai E. Stevenson/John J. Sparkman	3/A
1956	Chicago	13–17 August	Adlai E. Stevenson/Estes Kefauver	1/2
1960	Los Angeles	11–15 July	John F. Kennedy/Lyndon B. Johnson	1/A
1964	Atlantic City	24–27 August	Lyndon B. Johnson/Hubert H. Humphrey	A/A
1968	Chicago	26–29 August	Hubert H. Humphrey/Edmund S. Muskie	1/A
1972	Miami Beach	10–13 July	George S. McGovern/Thomas Eagleton[c]	1/A
1976	New York	12–15 July	Jimmy Carter/Walter F. Mondale	1/1
1980	New York	11–14 August	Jimmy Carter/Walter F. Mondale	1/A
1984	San Francisco	16–19 July	Walter F. Mondale/Geraldine Ferraro	1/A
1988	Atlanta	18–21 July	Michael S. Dukakis/Lloyd M. Bentsen	1/A
1992	New York	13–16 July	Bill Clinton/Al Gore	1/1
1996	Chicago	26–29 August	Bill Clinton/Al Gore	1/1
2000	Los Angeles	14–17 August	Al Gore/Joseph Lieberman	1/1
2004	Boston	26–29 July	John Kerry/John Edwards	1/1
2008	Denver	25–28 August	Barack Obama/Joseph Biden	1/1

[a]A = by acclamation

[b]Fitzpatrick declined the vice presidential nomination. The Democratic National Committee convened a week later and designated Hershel V. Johnson as the vice presidential nominee.

[c]Eagleton withdrew his nomination more than two weeks later. The Democratic National Committee met on 8 August and named R. Sargent Shriver the vice presidential nominee.

Appendix H: Republican National Conventions 1856–2008

Year	City	Dates	Nominees	Ballot
1856	Philadelphia	17–19 June	John C. Fremont/William L. Dayton	2/1
1860	Chicago	16–18 May	Abraham Lincoln/Hannibal Hamlin	3/2
1864	Baltimore	7–8 June	Abraham Lincoln/Andrew Johnson	1/1
1868	Chicago	20–21 May	Ulysses S. Grant/Schuyler Colfax	1/5
1872	Philadelphia	5–6 June	Ulysses S. Grant/Henry Wilson	1/1
1876	Cincinnati	14–16 June	Rutherford B. Hayes/William A. Wheeler	7/A[a]
1880	Chicago	2–8 June	James A. Garfield/Chester A. Arthur	36/1
1884	Chicago	3–6 June	James G. Blaine/John A. Logan	4/1
1888	Chicago	19–25 June	Benjamin Harrison/Levi P. Morton	8/1
1892	Minneapolis	7–11 June	Benjamin Harrison/Whitelaw Reid	1/A
1896	St. Louis	16–18 June	William McKinley/Garret A. Hobart	1/1
1900	Philadelphia	19–21 June	William McKinley/Theodore Roosevelt	1/1
1904	Chicago	21–23 June	Theodore Roosevelt/Charles W. Fairbanks	1/A
1908	Chicago	16–20 June	William H. Taft/James S. Sherman	1/1
1912	Chicago	18–22 June	William H. Taft/James S. Sherman[b]	1/1
1916	Chicago	7–10 June	Charles Evans Hughes/Charles W. Fairbanks	3/1
1920	Chicago	8–12 June	Warren G. Harding/Calvin Coolidge	10/1
1924	Cleveland	10–12 June	Calvin Coolidge/Charles G. Dawes	1/3
1928	Kansas City	12–15 June	Herbert Hoover/Charles Curtis	1/1
1932	Chicago	14–16 June	Herbert Hoover/Charles Curtis	1/1
1936	Cleveland	9–12 June	Alfred M. Landon/Frank Knox	1/1

Year	City	Dates	Ticket	
1940	Philadelphia	24–28 June	Wendell Willkie/Charles L. McNary	6/1
1944	Chicago	26–28 June	Thomas E. Dewey/John W. Bricker	1/1
1948	Philadelphia	21–25 June	Thomas E. Dewey/Earl Warren	3/A
1952	Chicago	7–11 July	Dwight D. Eisenhower/Richard M. Nixon	1/1
1956	San Francisco	20–24 August	Dwight D. Eisenhower/Richard M. Nixon	1/1
1960	Chicago	25–28 July	Richard M. Nixon/Henry Cabot Lodge	1/1
1964	San Francisco	13–16 July	Barry M. Goldwater/William E. Miller	1/1
1968	Miami Beach	5–9 August	Richard M. Nixon/Spiro T. Agnew	1/1
1972	Miami Beach	21–23 August	Richard M. Nixon/Spiro T. Agnew	1/1
1976	Kansas City	16–19 August	Gerald R. Ford/Robert J. Dole	1/1
1980	Detroit	14–17 July	Ronald Reagan/George H. W. Bush	1/1
1984	Dallas	20–23 August	Ronald Reagan/George H. W. Bush	1/(same ballot)
1988	New Orleans	15–18 August	George H. W. Bush/Dan Quayle	1/A
1992	Houston	17–20 August	George H. W. Bush/Dan Quayle	1/1
1996	San Diego	12–15August	Robert J. Dole/Jack Kemp	1/A
2000	Philadelphia	31 July–3 August 3	George W. Bush/Richard Cheney	1/1
2004	New York	30 August–2 September	George W. Bush/Richard Cheney	1/A
2008	Minneapolis/St. Paul	1–4 September	John S. McCain/Sarah Palin	1/1

a A = by acclamation

b Vice President Sherman died on 30 October 1908, less than a week before the general election. After that election, the Republican National Committee designated Nicholas Murray Butler to receive the vice presidential votes of Republican electors.

Appendix I: Democratic National Committee Chairs, 1848–2009

Name	State	Years of Service
Benjamin F. Hallet	Massachusetts	1848–1852
Robert M. McLane	Maryland	1852–1856
David A. Smalley	Vermont	1856–1860
August Belmont	New York	1860–1872
Augustus Schell	New York	1872–1876
Abram S. Hewitt	New York	1876–1877
William H. Barnum	Connecticut	1877–1889
Calvin S. Brice	Ohio	1889–1892
William F. Harrity	Pennsylvania	1892–1896
James K. Jones	Arkansas	1896–1904
Thomas Taggart	Indiana	1904–1908
Norman E. Mack	New York	1908–1912
William F. McCombs	New York	1912–1916
Vance C. McCormick	Pennsylvania	1916–1919
Homer S. Cummings	Connecticut	1919–1920
George H. White	Ohio	1920–1921
Cordell Hull	Tennessee	1921–1924
Clement L. Shaver	West Virginia	1924–1928
John J. Raskob	New York	1928–1932
James A. Farley	New York	1932–1940
Edward J. Flynn	New York	1940–1943
Frank C. Walker	New York	1943–1944
Robert E. Hannegan	Missouri	1944–1947
J. Howard McGrath	Rhode Island	1947–1949
William M. Boyle Jr.	Missouri	1949–1951
Frank E. McKinney	Indiana	1951–1952
Stephen A. Mitchell	Illinois	1952–1954
Paul M. Butler	Indiana	1955–1960
Henry M. Jackson	Washington	1960–1961
John M. Bailey	Connecticut	1961–1968
Lawrence F. O'Brien	Massachusetts	1968–1969
Fred R. Harris	Oklahoma	1969–1970

(*continued*)

Name	State	Years of Service
Lawrence F. O'Brien	Massachusetts	1970–1972
Jean Westwood	Utah	1972
Robert Strauss	Texas	1972–1977
Kenneth Curtis	Maine	1977–1978
John C. White	Texas	1978–1981
Charles A. Manatt	California	1981–1985
Paul G. Kirk Jr.	Massachusetts	1985–1989
Ronald H. Brown	Washington, D.C.	1989–1993
David Wilhelm	Illinois	1993–1995
Christopher Dodd	Connecticut	1995–1997 (general chair)
Donald Fowler	South Carolina	1995–1997
Roy Romer	Colorado	1997–1999 (general chair)
Steven Grossman	Massachusetts	1997–1999
Joe Andrew	Indiana	1999–2001
Edward Rendell	Pennsylvania	1999–2001 (general chair)
Terrence McAuliffe	Virginia	2001–2005
Howard Dean	Vermont	2005–2009
Tim Kaine	Virginia	2009–

Appendix J: Republican National Committee Chairs, 1856–2009

Name	State	Years of Service
Edwin D. Morgan	New York	1856–1864
Henry J. Raymond	New York	1864–1866
Marcus L. Ward	New Jersey	1866–1868
William Claflin	Massachusetts	1868–1872
Edwin D. Morgan	New York	1872–1876
Zachariah Chandler	Michigan	1876–1879
J. Donald Cameron	Pennsylvania	1879–1880
Marshall Jewell	Connecticut	1880–1883
Dwight M. Sabin	Minnesota	1883–1884
Benjamin F. Jones	Pennsylvania	1884–1888
Matthew S. Quay	Pennsylvania	1888–1891
James S. Clarkson	Iowa	1891–1892
Thomas H. Carter	Montana	1892–1896
Marcus A. Hanna	Ohio	1896–1904
Henry C. Payne	Wisconsin	1904
George B. Cortelyou	New York	1904–1907
Harry S. New	Indiana	1907–1908
Frank H. Hitchcock	Massachusetts	1908–1909
John F. Hill	Maine	1909–1912
Victor Rosewater	Nebraska	1912
Charles D. Hilles	New York	1912–1916
William R. Willcox	New York	1916–1918
Will Hays	Indiana	1918–1921
John T. Adams	Iowa	1921–1924
William M. Butler	Massachusetts	1924–1928
Hubert Work	Colorado	1928–1929
Claudius H. Huston	Tennessee	1929–1930
Simeon D. Fess	Ohio	1930–1932
Everett Sanders	Indiana	1932–1934
Henry P. Fletcher	Pennsylvania	1934–1936
John D. M. Hamilton	Kansas	1936–1940
Joseph W. Martin Jr.	Massachusetts	1940–1942

(continued)

Name	State	Years of Service
Harrison E. Spangler	Iowa	1942–1944
Herbert Brownell Jr.	New York	1944–1946
B. Carroll Reece	Tennessee	1946–1948
Hugh D. Scott Jr.	Pennsylvania	1948–1949
Guy George Gabrielson	New Jersey	1949–1952
Arthur E. Summerfield	Michigan	1952–1953
C. Wesley Roberts	Kansas	1953
Leonard W. Hall	New York	1953–1957
H. Meade Alcorn Jr.	Connecticut	1957–1959
Thruston B. Morton	Kentucky	1959–1961
William E. Miller	New York	1961–1964
Dean Burch	Arizona	1964–1965
Ray C. Bliss	Ohio	1965–1969
Rogers C. B. Morton	Maryland	1969–1971
Robert J. Dole	Kansas	1971–1973
George Bush	Texas	1973–1974
Mary Louise Smith	Iowa	1974–1977
William Brock	Tennessee	1977–1981
Richard Richards	Utah	1981–1983
Paul Laxalt	Nevada	1983–1986 (general chair)
Frank Fahrenkopf	Nevada	1983–1989
H. Lee Atwater	South Carolina	1989–1991/1991 (general chair)
Clayton Yeutter	Nebraska	1991–1992
Richard Bond	New York	1992–1993
Haley Barbour	Mississippi	1993–1997
Jim Nicholson	Colorado	1997–2001
James Gilmore	Virginia	2001–2002
Marc Racicot	Montana	2002–2003
Ed Gillespie	District of Columbia	2003–2005
Ken Mehlman	Maryland	2005–2007
Mel Martinez	Florida	2006–2007 (general chair)
Mike Duncan	Kentucky	2007–2009
Michael Steele	Maryland	2009–

Appendix K: Electoral College Votes for President, 1789–2008

Election	Nominee	Party	Votes
1789	George Washington		69
	John Adams		34
	John Jay		9
	Robert Harrison		6
	John Rutledge		6
	John Hancock		4
	George Clinton		3
	Samuel Huntington		2
	John Milton		2
	James Armstrong		1
	Benjamin Lincoln		1
	Edward Telfair		1
			138/182
1792	George Washington		132
	John Adams		77
	George Clinton		50
	Thomas Jefferson		4
	Aaron Burr		1
			264/270
1796	John Adams	Federalist	71
	Thomas Jefferson	Democratic-Republican	68
	Thomas Pinckney	Federalist	59
	Aaron Burr	Democratic-Republican	30
	Samuel Adams	Federalist	15
	Oliver Ellsworth	Federalist	11
	George Clinton	Democratic-Republican	7
	John Jay	Federalist	5
	James Iredell	Federalist	3
	John Henry	Democratic-Republican	2
	Samuel Johnston	Federalist	2

(continued)

Election	Nominee	Party	Votes
	George Washington		2
	Charles Pinckney	Federalist	1
			276
1800	Thomas Jefferson	Democratic-Republican	73
	Aaron Burr	Democratic-Republican	73
	John Adams	Federalist	65
	Charles Pinckney	Federalist	64
	John Jay	Federalist	1
			276
1804	Thomas Jefferson	Democratic-Republican	162
	Charles Pinckney	Federalist	14
			176
1808	James Madison	Democratic-Republican	122
	Charles Pinckney	Federalist	47
	George Clinton	Democratic-Republican	6
			175/176
1812	James Madison	Democratic-Republican	128
	DeWitt Clinton	Federalist/Democratic-Republican	89
			217/218
1816	James Monroe	Democratic-Republican	183
	Rufus King	Federalist	34
			217/221
1820	James Monroe	Democratic-Republican	231
	John Quincy Adams	Democratic-Republican	1
			232/235
1824	Andrew Jackson	Democratic-Republican	99
	John Quincy Adams	Democratic-Republican	84
	William Crawford	Democratic-Republican	41
	Henry Clay	Democratic-Republican	37
			261
1828	Andrew Jackson	Democratic	178
	John Quincy Adams	National Republican	83
			261
1832	Andrew Jackson	Democratic	219
	Henry Clay	National Republican	49

Election	Nominee	Party	Votes
	John Floyd	Independent (Democratic)	11
	William Wirt	Anti-Masonic	7
			286/288
1836	Martin Van Buren	Democratic	170
	William H. Harrison	Whig	73
	Hugh White	Whig	26
	Daniel Webster	Whig	14
	Willie Mangum	Independent (Whig)	11
			294
1840	William H. Harrison	Whig	234
	Martin Van Buren	Democratic	60
			294
1844	James K. Polk	Democratic	170
	Henry Clay	Whig	105
			275
1848	Zachary Taylor	Whig	163
	Lewis Cass	Democratic	127
			290
1852	Franklin Pierce	Democratic	254
	Winfield Scott	Whig	42
			296
1856	James Buchanan	Democratic	174
	John C. Fremont	Republican	114
	Millard Fillmore	American	8
			296
1860	Abraham Lincoln	Republican	180
	John Breckinridge	Southern Democratic	72
	John Bell	Constitutional Union	39
	Stephen Douglas	Democratic	12
			303
1864	Abraham Lincoln	Republican	212
	George McClellan	Democratic	21
			233/234
1868	Ulysses S. Grant	Republican	214
	Horatio Seymour	Democratic	80
			294

(*continued*)

Election	Nominee	Party	Votes
1872	Ulysses S. Grant	Republican	286
	Thomas Hendricks	Democratic	42
	Benjamin G. Brown	Liberal Republican/Democratic	18
	Charles Jenkins	Democratic	2
	David Davis	Democratic	1
			349/366
1876	Rutherford Hayes	Republican	185
	Samuel Tilden	Democratic	184
			369
1880	James Garfield	Republican	214
	Winfield S. Hancock	Democratic	155
			369
1884	Grover Cleveland	Democratic	219
	James G. Blaine	Republican	182
			401
1888	Benjamin Harrison	Republican	233
	Grover Cleveland	Democratic	168
			401
1892	Grover Cleveland	Democratic	277
	Benjamin Harrison	Republican	145
	James Weaver	People's	22
			444
1896	William McKinley	Republican	271
	William J. Bryan	Democratic/People's	176
			447
1900	William McKinley	Republican	292
	William J. Bryan	Democratic	155
			447
1904	Theodore Roosevelt	Republican	336
	Alton Parker	Democratic	140
			476
1908	William H. Taft	Republican	321
	William J. Bryan	Democratic	162
			483

Election	Nominee	Party	Votes
1912	Woodrow Wilson	Democratic	435
	Theodore Roosevelt	Progressive	88
	William H. Taft	Republican	8
			531
1916	Woodrow Wilson	Democratic	277
	Charles E. Hughes	Republican	254
			531
1920	Warren Harding	Republican	404
	James Cox	Democratic	127
			531
1924	Calvin Coolidge	Republican	382
	John Davis	Democratic	136
	Robert LaFollette	Progressive	13
			531
1928	Herbert Hoover	Republican	444
	Alfred Smith	Democratic	87
			531
1932	Franklin Roosevelt	Democratic	472
	Herbert Hoover	Republican	59
			531
1936	Franklin Roosevelt	Democrat	523
	Alfred Landon	Republican	8
			531
1940	Franklin Roosevelt	Democrat	449
	Wendell Willkie	Republican	82
			531
1944	Franklin Roosevelt	Democrat	432
	Thomas Dewey	Republican	99
			531
1948	Harry Truman	Democrat	303
	Thomas Dewey	Republican	189
	Strom Thurmond	States' Rights Democratic	39
			531

(*continued*)

Election	Nominee	Party	Votes
1952	Dwight Eisenhower	Republican	442
	Adlai Stevenson	Democratic	89
			531
1956	Dwight Eisenhower	Republican	457
	Adlai Stevenson	Democratic	73
	Walter Jones	Independent (Democratic)	1
			531
1960	John Kennedy	Democratic	303
	Richard Nixon	Republican	219
	Harry Byrd	Independent (Democratic)	15
			537
1964	Lyndon Johnson	Democratic	486
	Barry Goldwater	Republican	52
			538
1968	Richard Nixon	Republican	301
	Hubert Humphrey	Democratic	191
	George Wallace	American Independent	46
			538
1972	Richard Nixon	Republican	520
	George McGovern	Democratic	17
	John Hospers	Libertarian	1
			538
1976	Jimmy Carter	Democratic	297
	Gerald Ford	Republican	240
	Ronald Reagan	Republican	1
			538
1980	Ronald Reagan	Republican	489
	Jimmy Carter	Democratic	49
			538
1984	Ronald Reagan	Republican	525
	Walter Mondale	Democratic	13
			538
1988	George H. W. Bush	Republican	426
	Michael Dukakis	Democratic	111
	Lloyd Bentsen	Democratic	1
			538

Election	Nominee	Party	Votes
1992	Bill Clinton	Democratic	370
	George H. W. Bush	Republican	168
			538
1996	Bill Clinton	Democratic	379
	Robert Dole	Republican	159
			538
2000	George W. Bush	Republican	271
	Al Gore	Democrat	266
			537/538
2004	George W. Bush	Republican	286
	John Kerry	Democrat	251
	John Edwards	Democrat	1
			538
2008	Barack Obama	Democrat	365
	John McCain	Republican	173
			538

Note: On 10 occasions in presidential balloting, the number of votes cast by electors has not matched the number of electoral votes authorized by the Constitution. In 1789, New York failed to designate electors, North Carolina had yet to ratify the Constitution, and two electors each from Maryland and Virginia did not vote. In 1792, two Maryland electors and one from Vermont did not vote. In 1808, one Kentucky elector did not vote. In 1812, one Ohio elector did not vote. In 1816, one Delaware and three Maryland electors did not vote. In 1820, one elector each from Mississippi, Pennsylvania, and Tennessee did not vote. In 1832, two Maryland electors did not vote. In 1864, one Nevada elector did not vote. In 1872, Congress refused to accept the electoral votes cast by Arkansas (six) and Louisiana (eight), owing to Reconstruction-related unrest. In addition, three electoral votes from Georgia, cast for Greeley, were not counted. In 2000, one District of Columbia delegate did not cast her presidential ballot.

Appendix L: Popular Votes for President, 1824–2008

Election	Nominee	Party	Percent of Votes	Total Votes
1824	Andrew Jackson	Dem-Rep[a]	41.3	
	John Quincy Adams	Dem-Rep	30.9	
	Henry Clay	Dem-Rep	13.0	
	William Crawford	Dem-Rep	11.2	
	Other		3.6	
				365,833
1828	Andrew Jackson	Dem[b]	56.0	
	John Quincy Adams	Nat Rep[c]	43.6	
	Other		0.4	
				1,148,018
1832	Andrew Jackson	Dem	54.2	
	Henry Clay	Nat Rep	37.4	
	William Wirt	Anti-Masonic	7.8	
	Other		0.6	
				1,293,973
1836	Martin Van Buren	Dem	50.8	
	William H. Harrison	Whig	36.6	
	Hugh White	Whig	9.7	
	Daniel Webster	Whig	2.7	
	Other		0.1	
				1,503,534
1840	William H. Harrison	Whig	52.9	
	Martin Van Buren	Dem	46.8	
	Other		0.3	
				2,411,808
1844	James K. Polk	Dem	49.5	
	Henry Clay	Whig	48.1	
	Other		2.4	
				002,703,659

(continued)

Election	Nominee	Party	Percent of Votes	Total Votes
1848	Zachary Taylor	Whig	47.3	
	Lewis Cass	Dem	42.5	
	Martin Van Buren	Free Soil	10.1	
	Other		0.1	
				2,879,184
1852	Franklin Pierce	Dem	50.8	
	Winfield Scott	Whig	43.9	
	Other		5.3	
				3,161,830
1856	James Buchanan	Dem	45.3	
	John C. Fremont	Rep[d]	33.1	
	Millard Fillmore	American	21.5	
	Other		0.1	
				4,054,647
1860	Abraham Lincoln	Rep	39.8	
	Stephen Douglas	Dem	29.5	
	John Breckinridge	So Dem[e]	18.1	
	John Bell	Const Union[f]	12.6	
				4,685,561
1864	Abraham Lincoln	Rep	55.0	
	George McClellan	Dem	45.0	
				4,031,887
1868	Ulysses S. Grant	Rep	52.7	
	Horatio Seymour	Dem	47.3	
				5,722,440
1872	Ulysses S. Grant	Rep	55.6	
	Horace Greeley	Dem/Lib Rep[g]	43.8	
	Other		0.6	
				6,467,679
1876	Rutherford Hayes	Rep	47.9	
	Samuel Tilden	Dem	51.0	
	Other		1.1	
				8,413,101
1880	James Garfield	Rep	48.3	
	Winfield S. Hancock	Dem	48.2	
	Other		3.5	
				9,210,420
1884	Grover Cleveland	Dem	48.5	
	James G. Blaine	Rep	48.2	
	Other		3.2	
				10,049,754

Election	Nominee	Party	Percent of Votes	Total Votes
1888	Benjamin Harrison	Rep	47.8	
	Grover Cleveland	Dem	48.6	
	Other		3.6	
				11,383,320
1892	Grover Cleveland	Dem	46.1	
	Benjamin Harrison	Rep	43.0	
	James B. Weaver	People's	8.5	
	Other		2.4	
				12,056,097
1896	William McKinley	Rep	51.0	
	William J. Bryan	Dem/People's	46.7	
	Other		2.3	
				13,935,738
1900	William McKinley	Rep	51.7	
	William J. Bryan	Dem	45.5	
	Other		2.8	
				13,970,470
1904	Theodore Roosevelt	Rep	56.4	
	Alton Parker	Dem	37.6	
	Other		6.0	
				13,518,964
1908	William H. Taft	Rep	51.6	
	William J. Bryan	Dem	43.0	
	Other		5.3	
				14,882,734
1912	Woodrow Wilson	Dem	41.8	
	Theodore Roosevelt	Progressive	27.4	
	William H. Taft	Rep	23.2	
	Eugene V. Debs	Socialist	6.0	
	Other		1.6	
				15,040,963
1916	Woodrow Wilson	Dem	49.2	
	Charles E. Hughes	Rep	46.1	
	Other		4.7	
				18,535,022
1920	Warren Harding	Rep	60.3	
	James Cox	Dem	34.2	
	Other		5.5	
				26,762,613

(*continued*)

Election	Nominee	Party	Percent of Votes	Total Votes
1924	Calvin Coolidge	Rep	54.1	
	John Davis	Dem	28.8	
	Robert LaFollette	Progressive	16.6	
	Other		0.5	
				29,095,023
1928	Herbert Hoover	Rep	58.2	
	Alfred Smith	Dem	40.8	
	Other		0.9	
				36,805,951
1932	Franklin Roosevelt	Dem	57.4	
	Herbert Hoover	Rep	39.6	
	Other		3.0	
				39,758,759
1936	Franklin Roosevelt	Dem	60.8	
	Alfred Landon	Rep	36.5	
	Other		2.7	
				45,654,763
1940	Franklin Roosevelt	Dem	54.7	
	Wendell Willkie	Rep	44.8	
	Other		0.4	
				49,900,418
1944	Franklin Roosevelt	Dem	53.4	
	Thomas Dewey	Rep	45.9	
	Other		0.8	
				47,976,670
1948	Harry Truman	Dem	49.5	
	Thomas Dewey	Rep	45.1	
	Other		5.4	
				48,793,826
1952	Dwight Eisenhower	Rep	55.1	
	Adlai Stevenson	Dem	44.4	
	Other		0.4	
				61,550,918
1956	Dwight Eisenhower	Rep	57.4	
	Adlai Stevenson	Dem	42.0	
	Other		0.7	
				62,026,908
1960	John Kennedy	Dem	49.7	
	Richard Nixon	Rep	49.5	
	Other		0.8	
				68,838,219

Election	Nominee	Party	Percent of Votes	Total Votes
1964	Lyndon Johnson	Dem	61.1	
	Barry Goldwater	Rep	38.5	
	Other		0.5	
				70,645,592
1968	Richard Nixon	Rep	43.4	
	Hubert Humphrey	Dem	42.7	
	George Wallace	Am Ind[h]	13.5	
	Other		0.4	
				73,211,875
1972	Richard Nixon	Rep	60.7	
	George McGovern	Dem	37.5	
	Other		1.8	
				77,718,554
1976	Jimmy Carter	Dem	50.1	
	Gerald Ford	Rep	48.0	
	Other		1.9	
				81,555,889
1980	Ronald Reagan	Rep	50.7	
	Jimmy Carter	Dem	41.0	
	John Anderson	Ind	6.6	
	Other		1.7	
				86,515,221
1984	Ronald Reagan	Rep	58.8	
	Walter Mondale	Dem	40.6	
	Other		0.6	
				92,652,700
1988	George H.W. Bush	Rep	53.4	
	Michael Dukakis	Dem	45.6	
	Other		1.0	
				91,594,805
1992	Bill Clinton	Dem	43.0	
	George H.W. Bush	Rep	37.4	
	Ross Perot	Ind[i]	18.9	
	Other		0.7	
				104,428,377
1996	Bill Clinton	Dem	49.2	
	Robert Dole	Rep	40.7	
	Ross Perot	Reform	8.4	
	Other		1.6	
				96,277,872

(*continued*)

Election	Nominee	Party	Percent of Votes	Total Votes
2000	George W. Bush	Rep	47.9	
	Al Gore	Dem	48.4	
	Other		3.7	
				105,399,313
2004	George W. Bush	Rep	50.7	
	John Kerry	Dem	48.3	
	Other		1.0	
				122,265,430
2008	Barack Obama	Dem	52.9	
	John McCain	Rep	45.7	
	Other		1.4	
				131,257,542

[a]Dem-Rep = Democratic Republican
[b]Dem = Democratic
[c]Nat Rep = National Republican
[d]Rep = Republican
[e]So Dem = Southern Democratic
[f]Const Union = Constitutional Union
[g]Lib Rep = Liberal Republican
[h]Am Ind = American Independent
[i]Ind = Independent

Appendix M: Minor Party Nominees and Independent Candidates Receiving Electoral College Votes, 1808–2008

Year	Nominee/Candidate	Party	Votes
1808	George Clinton	Independent (Democratic-Republican)	6
1832	John Floyd	Independent (Democratic)	11
1832	William Wirt	Anti-Masonic	7
1836	Willie P. Mangum	Independent (Whig)	11
1856	Millard Fillmore	American (Know-Nothing)	8
1860	John Breckinridge	Southern Democratic	72
1860	John Bell	Constitutional Union	39
1892	James B. Weaver	People's (Populist)	22
1912	Theodore Roosevelt	Progressive (Bull Moose)	88
1924	Robert M. LaFollette	Progressive	13
1948	J. Strom Thurmond	States' Rights Democratic	39
1956	Walter B. Jones	Independent (Democratic)	1
1960	Harry F. Byrd	Independent (Democratic)	15
1968	George C. Wallace	American Independent	46
1972	John Hospers	Libertarian	1

Appendix N: Minor Parties and Independent Candidates with 5% of Popular Vote for President, 1848–2008

Year	Party	Nominee	Popular Vote (%)	Electoral Votes
1848	Free Soil	Martin Van Buren	10.1	0
1856	American (Know Nothing)	Millard Fillmore	21.5	8
1860	Southern Democrats	John Breckinridge	18.1	72
1860	Constitutional Union	John Bell	12.6	39
1892	People's (Populist)	James B. Weaver	8.5	22
1912	Progressive (Bull Moose)	Theodore Roosevelt	27.4	88
1912	Socialist	Eugene Debs	6.0	0
1924	Progressive	Robert LaFollette	16.6	13
1968	American Independent	George Wallace	13.5	46
1980	Independent	John Anderson	6.6	0
1992	Independent	Ross Perot	19.0	0
1996	Reform	Ross Perot	8.4	

Appendix O: Presidential Fund-raising and Spending, 1976–2008

Year	Total Contributions to Presidential Candidates (in Millions of Dollars)	Total Spending by Presidential Candidates (in Millions of Dollars)
1976	171.0	66.9
1980	161.9	92.3
1984	202.0	103.6
1988	324.4	210.7
1992	331.1	192.2
1996	425.7	239.9
2000	528.9	343.1
2004	880.5	717.9
2008 (as of October 20, 2008)	1,633.8	1,324.7

Note: Receipts include primary receipts, general election public funding, general election private funding, and convention public funding. Totals are not adjusted for inflation.
Source: The Center for Responsive Politics, www.opensecrets.org.

Bibliography

CONTENTS

INTRODUCTION

An attempt to develop a systematic, thorough bibliography on the history of U.S. political parties is a daunting task. By their very nature, political parties are integrating institutions. As such, they extend themselves throughout a political system. Thus, most writings on American politics relate, directly or indirectly, to the role and status of political parties. What follows is my idiosyncratic effort to identify some of the more noteworthy works on the topic.

A substantial challenge is to develop a categorization scheme for the works to be included. A well-designed schema should be exhaustive, mutually exclusive, and illuminating. Here again, the integrative character of political parties complicates the assignment of works to one particular category, so that the current effort falls short of the ideal. Many, if not most, of the works included could conceivably be assigned to one or more categories. But although my classification is not perfect, I trust that it is serviceable and will lead the reader to helpful information.

In each category, I emphasize book-length treatments, complemented on occasion by journal articles and chapters in edited collections. At the outset of each category, I recommend a handful of key works to acquaint the interested reader with the topic.

The first category is reference volumes, followed by noteworthy texts and general works on political parties. A plurality of volumes included address the historical evolution of two-party competition in the United States, addressing partisan alignments, realignments, and dealignments. The developments are subdivided into general treatments, followed by works on specific eras of major party competition, also known as party systems. Because of the historical character of the current volume, when works can appropriately be classified within the context of a particular party system, that option is generally taken. The next section considers minor parties that have unsuccessfully challenged their major counterparts in these party systems, as well as ideological factions.

Following this historically organized section, other works are categorized more analytically, as they address the structural components of a political party: party-in-office, party organization, and party in the electorate. The first of these is divided into sections on the president and Congress. Party organization incorporates not only institutions but also the activists who maintain them. The section on electoral behavior points toward the ensuing units on campaigns and elections and campaign finance.

Next, I identify key works in the literature on responsible party government and its counterpart, divided party government. A final category addresses party politics subnationally, in particular regions, the states, and localities. In this category, note the considerable extent to which the South has generated scholarly attention.

In my effort to keep this bibliography to a manageable length, I have not included the many bibliographies on party leaders that are available.

I. REFERENCE WORKS

Recommendation: Congressional Quarterly's *Guides* are exceptionally valuable reference sources.

Bain, Richard C., and Judith H. Parris. *Convention Decisions and Voting Records*. 2d ed. Washington, D.C.: Brookings Institution, 1973.

Biographical Directory of the U.S. Congress, 1774–2005. Washington, D.C.: U.S. Government Printing Office, 2005.

Carruth, Gorton. *The Encyclopedia of American Facts and Dates*. 10th ed. New York: HarperCollins, 1997.

Cohen, Norman S. *The American Presidents: An Annotated Bibliography*. Pasadena, Calif.: Salem Press, 1989.

Congressional Quarterly. *Congressional Quarterly's Guide to Congress*. 6th ed. 2 vols. Washington, D.C.: Congressional Quarterly, 2007.

———. *Congressional Quarterly's Guide to U.S. Elections*. 5th ed. 2 vols. Washington, D.C.: Congressional Quarterly, 2005.

———. *National Party Conventions, 1831–2004*. Washington, D.C.: Congressional Quarterly, 2005.

———. *Presidential Elections, 1789–2004*. Washington, D.C.: Congressional Quarterly, 2005.

Johnson, Allen, ed. *Dictionary of American Biography*. New York: Charles Scribner's Sons, 1928.

Kurian, George Thomas, ed. *The Encyclopedia of the Republican Party*; *The Encyclopedia of the Democratic Party*. 4 vols. Armonk, N.Y.: M. E. Sharpe, 1997.

Maisel, L. Sandy, ed. *Political Parties and Elections in the United States: An Encyclopedia*. 2 vols. New York: Garland, 1991.

Morris, Jeffrey B., and Richard B. Morris, eds. *Encyclopedia of American History*. 7th ed., rev. and updated. New York: HarperCollins, 1996.

Nelson, Michael, ed. *Congressional Quarterly's Guide to the Presidency*. 4th ed. 2 vols. Washington, D.C.: Congressional Quarterly, 2008.

Plano, Jack C., and Milton Greenberg. *The American Political Dictionary*. 10th ed. New York: Harcourt Brace, 1996.

Porter, Kirk H., and Donald Bruce Johnson, comps. *National Party Platforms, 1840–1968*. Urbana: University of Illinois Press, 1972.

Safire, William. *Safire's Political Dictionary*. New York: Oxford University Press, 2008.

Schlesinger, Arthur M., ed. *History of U.S. Political Parties*. 4 vols. New York: Chelsea House, 1973.

II. TEXTS AND GENERAL CONSIDERATIONS

Recommendations: Hershey's *Party Politics in America* is the 13th edition of a textbook originally authored by Frank Sorauf, who later added Paul Allen Beck as a coauthor. Beck in turn enlisted Hershey, who now carries the project forward. It has withstood the test of time for more than four decades and merits the label "classic." Rosenbaum's *On the Side of Angels* looks appreciatively at political parties in the face of a culture that views them more negatively.

Almond, Gabriel. *Political Development*. Boston: Little, Brown, 1970.

Beller, Dennis C., and Frank C. Belloni, eds. *Faction Politics: Political Parties and Factionalism in Comparative Perspective*. Santa Barbara, Calif.: ABC-Clio, 1978.

Cohen, Jeffrey E., Richard Fleisher, and Paul Kantor. *American Political Parties: Decline or Resurgence?* Washington, D.C.: CQ Press, 2001.

Commager, Henry S. "The American Political Party." *American Scholar* 29 (Summer 1950): 309–16.

Crotty, William J. "A Perspective for the Comparative Analysis of Political Parties." *Comparative Political Studies* 3 (October 1970): 267–96.

———. *Political Reform and the American Experiment*. New York: Thomas Y. Crowell, 1977.

———, ed. *The Party Symbol: Readings on Political Parties*. San Francisco: Freeman, 1980.

Crotty, William J., Donald M. Freeman, and Douglas S. Gatlin, eds. *Political Parties and Political Behavior*. Boston: Allyn & Bacon, 1966.

Crotty, William J., and Gary C. Jacobson. *American Parties in Decline*. Boston: Little, Brown, 1980.

Downs, Anthony. *An Economic Theory of Democracy*. New York: Harper & Row, 1957.

Duverger, Maurice. *Political Parties: Their Organization and Activity in the Modern State*. New York: John Wiley & Sons, 1963.

Eldersveld, Samuel J. *Political Parties: A Behavioral Analysis*. Chicago: Rand McNally, 1964.

———. *Political Parties in American Society*. New York: Basic Books, 1985.

Epstein, Leon. *Political Parties in the American Mold*. Madison: University of Wisconsin Press, 1986.

———. *Political Parties in Western Democracies*. New York: Praeger, 1967.

Fishel, Jeff, ed. *Parties and Elections in an Anti-Party Age: American Politics and the Crisis of Confidence*. Bloomington: Indiana University Press, 1978.

Fleishman, Joel L., ed. The *Future of American Political Parties*. Englewood Cliffs, N.J.: Prentice-Hall, 1982.

Green, John C., and Daniel J. Coffey. *The State of the Parties: The Changing Role of Contemporary American Parties*. 5th ed. Lanham, Md.: Rowman & Littlefield, 2006.

Greenstein, Fred. *The American Party System and the American People*. 2d ed. Englewood Cliffs, N.J.: Prentice-Hall, 1970.

Grodzins, Martin. "Political Parties and the American System." *Western Political Quarterly* 8 (December 1960): 974–98.

Harmel, Robert, and Kenneth Janda. *Parties and Their Environments: Limits to Reform*. New York: Longman, 1982.

Hershey, Marjorie Randon. *Party Politics in America*. 13th ed. New York: Longman, 2009.

Hetheringon, Marc J., and William J. Keefe. *Politics, Parties, and Public Policy in America*. 10th ed. Washington, D.C.: CQ Press, 2006.

Janda, Kenneth. *Political Parties: A Cross-National Survey*. New York: Free Press, 1980.

Kayden, Xandra, and Eddie Mahe Jr. *The Party Goes On*. New York: Basic Books, 1985.

Key, V. O., Jr. *Politics, Parties, and Pressure Groups.* 5th ed. New York: Thomas Y. Crowell, 1964.

Knoke, David. *Change and Continuity in American Politics: The Social Bases of Political Parties.* Baltimore, Md.: Johns Hopkins University Press, 1976.

Ladd, Everett Carll. *American Political Parties: Social Change and Political Response.* New York: W. W. Norton, 1970.

————. *Where Have All the Voters Gone? The Fracturing of America's Political Parties.* 2d ed. New York: W. W. Norton, 1982.

Leiserson, Avery. "The Place of Parties in the Study of Politics." *American Political Science Review* 51 (December 1957): 943–54.

————. *Political Parties: An Institutional and Behavioral Approach.* New York: Alfred A. Knopf, 1958.

Lijpart, Arend. *Electoral Systems and Party Systems: A Study of Twenty-Seven Democracies, 1945–1990.* New York: Oxford University Press, 1994.

Lipset, Seymour Martin, and Stein Rokkan, eds. *Party Systems and Voter Alignments.* New York: Free Press, 1967.

Lubell, Samuel. *The Future of American Politics.* 3d ed. New York: Harper, 1965.

————. *The Hidden Crisis in American Politics.* New York: W. W. Norton, 1971.

Maisel, L. Sandy, ed. *The Parties Respond: Changes in American Parties and Campaigns.* 4th ed. Boulder, Colo.: Westview Press, 2002.

Maisel, L. Sandy, and Mark D. Brewer. *Parties and Elections in America: The Electoral Process.* 5th ed. Lanham, Md.: Rowman & Littlefield, 2008.

Maisel, L. Sandy, and Joseph Cooper, eds. *Political Parties: Development and Decay.* Beverly Hills, Calif.: Sage, 1978.

Maisel, L. Sandy, and Paul M. Sacks, eds. *The Future of Political Parties.* Beverly Hills, Calif.: Sage, 1975.

Mayhew, David R. *Placing Parties in American Politics: Organization, Electoral Settings, and Government Activity in the Twentieth Century.* Princeton, N.J.: Princeton University Press, 1986.

McDonald, Neil A. *The Study of Political Parties.* New York: Random House, 1955.

McSweeney, Dean, and John Zvesper. *American Political Parties: The Formation, Decline, and Reform of the American Political System.* London: Routledge, 1991.

Merriam, Charles E. *The American Political Party System: An Introduction to the Study of Political Parties.* 4th ed. New York: Macmillan, 1949.

Michels, Robert. *Political Parties: A Sociological Study of the Oligarchical Tendencies of Modern Democracy.* Glencoe, Ill.: Free Press, 1958.

Ostrogorski, Moisei. *Democracy and the Organization of Political Parties: The United States.* Brooklyn, N.Y.: Haskell Booksellers, 1970.

Pomper, Gerald M. *Passions and Interests: Political Party Concepts of American Democracy.* Lawrence: University Press of Kansas, 1992.

———, ed. *Party Renewal in America: Theory and Practice.* New York: Praeger, 1980.

Price, David E. *Bringing Back the Parties.* Washington, D.C.: CQ Press, 1984.

Rae, Douglas W., and Michael J. Taylor. *The Analysis of Political Cleavages.* New Haven, Conn.: Yale University Press, 1970.

Ranney, Austin, and Willmore Kendall. *Democracy and the American Party System.* New York: Harcourt, Brace & World, 1956.

Riker, William. *The Theory of Political Coalitions.* New Haven, Conn.: Yale University Press, 1962.

Rosenbaum, Nancy L. *On the Side of Angels: An Appreciation of Parties and Partisanship.* Princeton, N.J.: Princeton University Press, 2008.

Saloma, John S., III, and Frederick H. Sontag. *Parties: The Real Opportunity for Effective Citizen Politics.* New York: Alfred A. Knopf, 1972.

Sartori, Giovanni. *Parties and Party Systems: A Framework for Analysis.* Vol. 1. Cambridge: Cambridge University Press, 1976; reprint, 2005.

Schlesinger, Joseph A. "The New American Political Party." *American Political Science Review* 79 (December 1985): 1152–69.

———. *Political Parties and the Winning of Office.* Ann Arbor: University of Michigan Press, 1991.

———. "The Primary Goals of Political Parties: A Clarification of Positive Theory." *American Political Science Review* 69 (September 1975): 840–49.

Sindler, Allen P. *Political Parties in the United States.* New York: St. Martin's Press, 1966.

III. TWO-PARTY COMPETITION: HISTORICAL ALIGNMENTS, REALIGNMENTS, AND DEALIGNMENTS

A. General Works

Recommendation: Key's seminal articles on critical elections and secular realignment have provided the foundation for generations of scholarly discussion and debate. Mayhew's critique of the realignment concept is most useful.

Advisory Committee on Intergovernmental Relations. *The Transformation of American Politics: Implications for Federalism*. Washington, D.C.: Advisory Committee on Intergovernmental Relations, 1986.

Aldrich, John H. *Why Parties? The Origin and Transformation of Political Parties in America*. Chicago: University of Chicago Press, 1995.

Beck, Paul Allen. "The Electoral Cycle and Patterns of American Politics." *British Journal of Political Science* 9 (April 1979): 129–56.

Beck, Paul Allen, and M. Kent Jennings. "Political Periods and Political Participation." *American Political Science Review* 73 (September 1979): 737–50.

Binkley, Wilfred E. *American Political Parties: Their Natural History*. 4th ed. New York: Alfred A. Knopf, 1963.

Borden, Morton, ed. *Political Parties in American History*. 3 vols. New York: Capricorn, 1974.

Brady, David W. *Critical Elections and Congressional Policy Making*. Stanford, Calif.: Stanford University Press, 1988.

———. "A Reevaluation of Realignments in American Politics: Evidence from the House of Representatives." *American Political Science Review* 79 (March 1985): 28–49.

Brady, David W., and Joseph Stewart Jr. "Congressional Party Realignment and the Transformation of Public Policy in Three Realignment Eras." *American Journal of Political Science* 26 (May 1982): 333–60.

Broder, David S. *The Party's Over: The Failure of Politics in America*. New York: Harper Colophon Books, 1972.

Burnham, Walter Dean. *Critical Elections and the Mainsprings of American Politics*. New York: W. W. Norton, 1970.

———. *The Current Crisis in American Politics*. New York: Oxford University Press, 1982.

Burns, James MacGregor. *The Deadlock of Democracy: Four-Party Politics in America*. Englewood Cliffs, N.J.: Prentice-Hall, 1967.

Campbell, Bruce A., and Richard Trilling. *Realignment in American Politics: Toward a Theory*. Austin: University of Texas Press, 1980.

Chambers, William Nisbet, and Walter Dean Burnham, eds. *The American Party Systems: Stages of Political Development*. 2d ed. New York: Oxford University Press, 1975.

Clubb, Jerome M., and Howard W. Allen, eds. *Electoral Change and Stability in American History*. New York: Free Press, 1971.

Clubb, Jerome M., William H. Flanigan, and Nancy H. Zingale. *Partisan Realignment: Voters, Parties, and Government in American History*. Beverly Hills, Calif.: Sage, 1980.

Cummings, Milton C., ed. *V. O. Key and the Study of American Politics*. Washington, D.C.: American Political Science Association, 1983.

David, Paul T. *Party Strength in the United States*. Charlottesville: University Press of Virginia, 1972.

Fairlie, Henry. *The Parties: Republicans and Democrats in This Century*. New York: St. Martin's Press, 1978.

Ferguson, Thomas. *Golden Rule: The Investment Theory of Party Competition and the Logic of Money-Driven Political Systems*. Chicago: University of Chicago Press, 1995.

Formisano, Ronald P. *The Transformation of Political Culture: Massachusetts Parties, 1790s–1840s*. New York: Oxford University Press, 1983.

Gerring, John. *Party Ideologies in America, 1828–1996*. New York: Cambridge University Press, 1998.

Goldman, Ralph M. *The Democratic Party in American Politics*. New York: Macmillan, 1966.

Hofstadter, Richard. *The Idea of a Party System: The Rise of Legitimate Opposition in the United States, 1780–1840*. Berkeley and Los Angeles: University of California Press, 1969.

Jones, Charles O. *The Republican Party in American Politics*. New York: Macmillan, 1965.

Kelley, Robert. *The Cultural Pattern in American Politics: The First Century*. New York: Alfred A. Knopf, 1979.

Key, V. O., Jr. "Secular Realignment and the Party System." *Journal of Politics* 21 (May 1959): 198–210.

——. "A Theory of Critical Elections." *Journal of Politics* 17 (February 1955): 3–18.

Kleppner, Paul, Walter Dean Burnham, Ronald P. Formisano, Samuel P. Hays, Richard Jensen, and William G. Shade. *The Evolution of American Electoral Systems*. Westport, Conn.: Greenwood Press, 1981.

Ladd, Everett Carll, with Charles D. Hadley. *Transformations of the American Party System*. 2d ed. New York: W. W. Norton, 1978.

Lowi, Theodore. "Toward Functionalism in Political Science: The Case of Innovation in Party Systems." *American Political Science Review* 57 (1963): 570–83.

Mayer, George H. *The Republican Party, 1854–1964*. New York: Oxford University Press, 1964.

Mayhew, David R. *Electoral Realignments: A Critique of an American Genre*. New Haven, Conn.: Yale University Press, 2004.

——. "Party Systems in American History." *Polity* 1 (Fall 1968): 134–43.

McCormick, Richard P. "The Party Period and Public Policy: An Exploratory Hypothesis." *Journal of American History* 66 (September 1979): 279–98.

——. *The Party Period and Public Policy: American Politics from the Age of Jackson to the Progressive Era*. New York: Oxford University Press, 1986.

McGerr, Michael E. *The Decline of Popular Politics: The American North, 1865–1928*. New York: Oxford University Press, 1986.

Moos, Malcolm. *The Republicans: A History of Their Party*. New York: Random House, 1956.

Nichols, Roy F. *The Invention of American Political Parties: A Study of Political Improvisation*. New York: Free Press, 1967.

———. *The Stakes of Power, 1845–1877*. New York: Hill & Wang, 1961.

Reichley, A. James. *The Life of the Parties: A History of American Political Parties*. New York: Free Press, 1992.

Rossiter, Clinton. *Parties and Politics in America*. Ithaca, N.Y.: Cornell University Press, 1964.

Sabato, Larry. *The Party's Just Begun*. Glenview, Ill.: Scott Foresman/Little, Brown, 1988.

Schlesinger, Arthur M., Jr. *The Cycles of American History*. Boston: Houghton Mifflin, 1986.

———, ed. *The Coming to Power: Critical Presidential Elections in American History*. New York: Chelsea House, 1981.

Shafer, Byron E., ed. *The End of Realignment: Interpreting American Electoral Eras*. Madison: University of Wisconsin Press, 1991.

Sibley, Joel H. *The American Political Nation, 1838–1893*. Stanford, Calif.: Stanford University Press, 1991.

———. *The Partisan Imperative: The Dynamics of American Politics before the Civil War*. New York: Oxford University Press, 1985.

Sundquist, James L. *Dynamics of the American Party System: Alignment and Realignment of Political Parties in the United States*. Rev. ed. Washington, D.C.: Brookings Institution, 1983.

Van Buren, Martin. *Inquiry into the Origin and Course of Political Parties in the United States*. New York: A. M. Kelley, 1867.

B. First Party System (1790s–1820s)

Recommendation: Chambers's volume is an excellent general introduction to the topic, and Cunningham's work on the Jeffersonians astutely assesses the victors in the first era of party competition.

Aldrich, John H., and Ruth W. Grant. "The Antifederalists, the First Congress, and the First Parties." *Journal of Politics* 55 (May 1993): 295–26.

Ammon, Harry. "The Genet Mission and the Development of American Political Parties." *Journal of American History* 52 (March 1966): 725–41.

Bailyn, Bernard. *The Origins of American Politics*. New York: Random House, 1968.

Beard, Charles. *Economic Origins of Jeffersonian Democracy*. New York: Macmillan, 1965.

Becker, Carl Lotus. *The History of Political Parties in the Province of New York, 1760–1776*. With a foreword by Arthur M. Schlesinger. Madison: University of Wisconsin Press, 1968.

Borden, Morton. *Parties and Politics in the Early Republic, 1789–1815*. New York: Thomas Y. Crowell, 1967.

Brown, Stuart Gerry. *The First Republicans: Political Philosophy and Public Policy in the Party of Jefferson and Madison*. Syracuse, N.Y.: Syracuse University Press, 1954.

Chambers, William Nisbet. *Political Parties in a New Nation: The American Experience, 1776–1809*. London: Oxford University Press, 1963.

Charles, Joseph. *The Origins of the American Party System*. Williamsburg, Va.: Institute of Early American History and Culture, 1956.

Cunningham, Noble, Jr. *The Jeffersonian Republicans: The Formation of Party Organization, 1789–1801*. Chapel Hill: University of North Carolina Press, 1957.

——. *The Jeffersonian Republicans in Power: Party Operations, 1801–1809*. Chapel Hill: University of North Carolina Press, 1963.

——, ed. *The Making of the American Party System*. Englewood Cliffs, N.J.: Prentice-Hall, 1965.

Dangerfield, George. *The Era of Good Feelings*. New York: Harcourt, Brace & World, 1952.

Dauer, Manning J. *The Adams Federalists*. Baltimore, Md.: Johns Hopkins University Press, 1953.

Fischer, David H. *The Revolution of American Conservatism: The Federalist Party in the Era of Jeffersonian Democracy*. New York: Harper & Row, 1969.

Hoadley, John F. *Origins of American Political Parties, 1789–1803*. Lexington: University Press of Kentucky, 1986.

Ketchum, Ralph. *Presidents above Party: The First American Presidency, 1789–1829*. Chapel Hill: University of North Carolina Press, 1984.

Main, Jackson. *Political Parties before the Constitution*. Chapel Hill: University of North Carolina Press, 1973.

Miller, John. *The Federalist Era, 1789–1801*. New York: Harper & Row, 1960.

Patterson, Stephen E. *Political Parties in Revolutionary Massachusetts*. Madison: University of Wisconsin Press, 1973.

Risjord, Norman K. *The Old Republicans: Southern Conservatism in the Age of Jefferson.* New York: Columbia University Press, 1965.

Robinson, William A. *Jeffersonian Democracy in New England.* New Haven, Conn.: Yale University Press, 1916.

Ryan, Mary P. "Party Formation in the United States Congress, 1789–1796." *William and Mary Quarterly* 28 (October 1971): 523–42.

Smelser, Marshall. "The Federalist Period as an Age of Passion." *American Quarterly* 10 (Winter 1958): 391–419.

Sydnor, Charles S. "The One-Party Period in American History." *American Historical Review* 51 (April 1946): 439–51.

White, Leonard. *The Federalists: A Study in Administrative History.* New York: Macmillan, 1956.

———. *The Jeffersonians: A Study in Administrative History, 1801–1829.* New York: Macmillan, 1959.

Young, James Sterling. *The Washington Community, 1800–1828.* New York: Columbia University Press, 1966.

C. Second Party System (1820s–1850s)

Recommendation: McCormick's *The Second American Party System* and Remini's consideration of Van Buren's party-building efforts are most informative.

Benson, Lee. *The Concept of Jacksonian Democracy: New York as a Test Case.* Princeton, N.J.: Princeton University Press, 1961.

Carroll, E. Malcolm. *Origins of the Whig Party.* New York: Da Capo Press, 1970.

Formisano, Ronald P. *The Birth of Mass Political Parties: Michigan, 1827–1861.* Princeton, N.J.: Princeton University Press, 1971.

———. "Political Character, Antipartyism, and the Second Party System." *American Quarterly* 21 (Winter 1969): 683–709.

Marshall, Lynn. "The Strange Stillbirth of the Whig Party." *American Historical Review* 72 (January 1967): 445–68.

McCormick, Richard P. "New Perspectives on Jacksonian Politics." *American Historical Review* 65 (January 1960): 288–301.

———. *The Second American Party System: Party Formation in the Jacksonian Era.* New York: W. W. Norton, 1966.

Myers, Marvin. *The Jacksonian Persuasion.* New York: Random House, 1957.

Nichols, Roy F. *The Democratic Machine, 1850–1854.* New York: AMS Press, 1923.

——. *The Disruption of American Democracy*. New York: Macmillan, 1948.

Remini, Robert V. *The Election of Andrew Jackson*. Philadelphia, Pa.: J. B. Lippincott, 1964.

——. *Martin Van Buren and the Making of the Democratic Party*. New York: Columbia University Press, 1959.

Schlesinger, Arthur M., Jr. *The Age of Jackson*. Boston: Little, Brown, 1945.

Sibley, Joel H. *The Shrine of Party*. Pittsburgh, Pa.: University of Pittsburgh Press, 1966.

——. *The Transformation of American Politics, 1840–1860*. Englewood Cliffs, N.J.: Prentice-Hall, 1967.

Smith, T. C. *Parties and Slavery, 1850–1859*. New York: Harper, 1906.

Van Deusen, Glyndon. *The Jacksonian Era, 1828–1841*. New York: Harper & Row, 1959.

White, Leonard. *The Jacksonians: A Study in Administrative History, 1828–1848*. New York: Macmillan, 1954.

D. Third Party System (1850s–1890s)

Recommendation: Kleppner's *The Third Electoral System* provides an excellent overview of the era.

Beale, Howard K. *The Critical Year: A Study of Andrew Johnson and Reconstruction*. New York: Frederick Ungar, 1958.

Cox, John, and Lawanda Cox. *Politics, Principle, and Prejudice, 1865–1866: Dilemma of Reconstruction*. New York: Free Press, 1966.

Donald, David. *The Politics of Reconstruction, 1863–1867*. Baton Rouge: Louisiana State University Press, 1965.

Foner, Eric. *Free Soil, Free Labor, Free Men: The Ideology of the Republican Party before the Civil War*. Oxford: Oxford University Press, 1970.

Gienapp, William E. *The Origins of the Republican Party, 1852–1856*. New York: Oxford University Press, 1987.

Hirshon, Stanley. *Farewell to the Bloody Shirt: Northern Republicans and the Southern Negro, 1872–1873*. Bloomington: University of Indiana Press, 1962.

Hollingsworth, J. Rogers. *The Whirligig of Politics: The Democracy of Cleveland and Bryan*. Chicago: University of Chicago Press, 1963.

Jensen, Richard. *The Winning of the Midwest: Social and Political Conflict, 1888–1896*. Chicago: University of Chicago Press, 1971.

Josephson, Matthew. *The Politicos, 1856–1896*. New York: Harcourt, Brace & World, 1966.

Kleppner, Paul. *The Cross of Culture: A Social Analysis of Midwestern Politics, 1850–1900*. New York: Free Press, 1970.

——. *The Third Electoral System, 1853–1892: Parties, Voters, and Political Culture.* Chapel Hill: University of North Carolina Press, 1979.

Marcus, Robert D. *Grand Old Party: Political Structure in the Gilded Age.* New York: Oxford University Press, 1971.

McSeveney, Samuel T. *The Politics of Depression: Voting Behavior in the Northeast, 1893–1896.* New York: Oxford University Press, 1972.

Merrill, Horace S. *Bourbon Democracy of the Middle West, 1865–1896.* Seattle: University of Washington Press, 1953.

——. *Bourbon Leader: Grover Cleveland and the Democratic Party.* Boston: Little, Brown, 1957.

Morgan, H. Wayne. *From Hayes to McKinley: National Party Politics, 1877–1896.* Syracuse, N.Y.: Syracuse University Press, 1969.

——. *The Gilded Age.* Syracuse, N.Y.: Syracuse University Press, 1970.

Sharkey, Robert F. *Money, Class, and Party: An Economic Study of the Civil War and Reconstruction.* Baltimore, Md.: Johns Hopkins University Press, 1959.

Sibley, Joel H. *A Respectable Minority: The Democratic Party during the Civil War Era, 1860–1868.* New York: W. W. Norton, 1977.

Sproat, John. *The Best Men: Liberal Reformers in the Gilded Age.* Oxford: Oxford University Press, 1968.

E. Fourth Party System (1890s–1930s)

Recommendation: Once again, Kleppner offers a first-rate overview.

Burner, David. *The Politics of Provincialism: The Democratic Party in Transition, 1918–1932.* New York: Alfred A. Knopf, 1968.

Hofstadter, Richard. *The Age of Reform: From Bryan to FDR.* New York: Random House, 1955.

Holt, James. *Congressional Insurgents and the Party System, 1909–1916.* Cambridge, Mass.: Harvard University Press, 1967.

Kleppner, Paul. *Continuity and Change in Electoral Politics, 1893–1928.* Westport, Conn.: Greenwood Press, 1981.

McCormick, Richard L. *From Realignment to Reform: Political Change in New York State, 1893–1910.* Ithaca, N.Y.: Cornell University Press, 1981.

F. Fifth Party System (1930s–)

Recommendation: Anderson presents a solid account of the foundations on which the New Deal era rested. The volume edited by Fraser and Gerstle provides a useful overview of subsequent developments.

Allswang, John M. *The New Deal and American Politics: A Study in Political Change*. New York: John Wiley & Sons, 1978.

Anderson, Kristi. *Creation of a Democratic Majority, 1928–1936*. Chicago: University of Chicago Press, 1979.

Campbell, James E. "Sources of the New Deal Alignment: The Contributions of Conversion and Mobilization to Partisan Change." *Western Political Quarterly* 38 (September 1985): 357–76.

Erikson, Robert S., and Kent L. Tedin. "The 1928–1936 Partisan Realignment: The Case for the Conversion Hypothesis." *American Political Science Review* 75 (December 1981): 951–63.

Feinman, Ronald A. *The Twilight of Progressivism: The Western Republican Senators and the New Deal*. Baltimore, Md.: Johns Hopkins University Press, 1981.

Fraser, Steve, and Gary Gerstle, eds. *The Rise and Fall of the New Deal Order, 1930–1980*. Princeton, N.J.: Princeton University Press, 1989.

Greeley, Andrew M. *Building Coalitions: American Politics in the 1970s*. New York: Franklin Watts, 1974.

Hess, Stephen, and David S. Broder. *The Republican Establishment: The Present and Future of the GOP*. New York: Harper & Row, 1967.

Johnson, Donald B. *The Republican Party and Wendell Willkie*. Urbana: University of Illinois Press, 1960.

Ladd, Everett Carll, and Charles D. Hadley. *Political Parties and Political Issues: Patterns of Political Differentiation since the New Deal*. Beverly Hills, Calif.: Sage, 1973.

Marra, Robin F., and Charles W. Ostrom Jr. "Explaining Seat Change in the U.S. House of Representatives, 1950–86." *American Journal of Political Science* 33 (August 1989): 541–69.

Parmet, Herbert. *The Democrats: The Years after FDR*. New York: Oxford University Press, 1976.

Patterson, James T. *Congressional Conservatism and the New Deal*. Lexington: University of Kentucky Press, 1967.

Petrocik, John R. *Party Coalitions: Realignments and the Decline of the New Deal Party System*. Chicago: University of Chicago Press, 1981.

Phillips, Kevin P. *The Emerging Republican Majority*. New Rochelle, N.Y.: Arlington House, 1969.

———. *Mediacracy: American Parties and Politics in the Communications Age*. Garden City, N.Y.: Doubleday, 1975.

Rae, Nicol C. *The Decline and Fall of the Liberal Republicans: From 1952 to the Present*. New York: Oxford University Press, 1989.

———. *Southern Democrats*. New York: Oxford University Press, 1994.

Reichard, Gary W. *The Reaffirmation of Republicanism: Eisenhower and the Eighty-Third Congress*. Knoxville: University of Tennessee Press, 1975.

Reinhard, David W. *The Republican Right since 1945*. Lexington: University of Kentucky Press, 1983.

Savage, Sean. *Roosevelt: The Party Leader, 1932–1945*. Lexington: University of Kentucky Press, 1991.

———. *Truman and the Democratic Party*. Lexington: University of Kentucky Press, 1997.

Shafer, Byron E., ed. *Partisan Approaches to Postwar American Politics*. Chatham, N.J.: Chatham House, 1998.

Sinclair, Barbara. *Congressional Realignment: 1925–1978*. Austin: University of Texas Press, 1982.

Sternsher, Bernard. "The Emergence of the New Deal Party System: A Problem in Historical Analysis of Political Behavior." *Journal of Interdisciplinary History* 6 (Summer 1975): 127–49.

———. "The Emergence of the New Deal Party System: A Reappraisal." *Journal of Interdisciplinary History* 15 (Summer 1984): 53–81.

Sundquist, James L. *Politics and Policy: The Eisenhower, Kennedy, and Johnson Years*. Washington, D.C.: Brookings Institution, 1968.

Ware, Alan. *The Breakdown of Democratic Party Organization, 1940–1980*. Oxford: Oxford University Press, 1985.

Wattenberg, Martin P. *The Decline of American Political Parties, 1952–1996*. Cambridge, Mass.: Harvard University Press, 1998.

Weiss, Nancy. *Farewell to the Party of Lincoln: Black Politics in the Age of FDR*. Princeton, N.J.: Princeton University Press, 1983.

G. Contemporary Party Competition

Recommendation: The volume edited by Nivola and Brady contains several excellent analyses. Shafer and Claggett are also helpful in understanding the current situation.

Brownstein, Ronald. *The Second Civil War: How Extreme Partisanship Has Paralyzed Washington and Polarized America*. New York: Penguin Press, 2007.

Carmines, Edward G., and James A. Stimson. *Issue Evolution: Race and the Transformation of American Politics*. Princeton, N.J.: Princeton University Press, 1989.

Edsall, Thomas Byrne. *Building Red America: The New Conservative Coalition and the Drive for Permanent Power*. New York: Basic Books, 2006.

Ferguson, Thomas, and Joel Rogers. *Right Turn: The Decline of the Democrats and the Future of American Politics*. New York: Hill & Wang, 1986.

Galston, William, and Elaine Ciulla Kamarck. *The Politics of Evasion: Democrats and the Presidency.* Washington, D.C.: Progressive Policy Institute, 1989.

Gillon, Steven M. *The Democrats' Dilemma: Walter F. Mondale and the Liberal Legacy.* New York: Columbia University Press, 1992.

Lipset, Seymour Martin, ed. *Emerging Coalitions in American Politics.* San Francisco: Institute for Contemporary Studies, 1978.

——. *Party Coalitions in the 1980s.* San Francisco: Institute for Contemporary Studies, 1981.

Mayer, William G. *The Divided Democrats: Ideological Unity, Party Reform, and Presidential Elections.* Boulder, Colo.: Westview Press, 1996.

Nivola, Pietro S., and David W. Brady, eds. *Red and Blue Nation: Characteristics and Causes of America's Polarized Politics.* Washington, D.C.: Brookings, 2006.

Paulson, Arthur. *Realignment and Party Revival: Understanding American Electoral Politics at the Turn of the Twenty-First Century.* Westport, Conn.: Praeger, 2000.

Pierson, Paul, and Theda Skocpol, eds. *The Transformation of American Politics: Activist Government and the Rise of Conservatism.* Princeton, N.J.: Princeton University Press, 2007.

Shafer, Byron E., and William J. M. Claggett. *The Two Majorities: The Issue Context of Modern American Politics.* Baltimore, Md.: Johns Hopkins University Press, 1995.

——, ed. *Present Discontents: American Politics in the Very Late Twentieth Century.* Chatham, N.J.: Chatham House, 1997.

Ward, James F. "Toward a Sixth Party System? Partisanship and Political Development." *Western Political Quarterly* 26 (September 1973): 385–413.

IV. MINOR PARTIES AND IDEOLOGICAL FACTIONS

Recommendation: Nash ably accounts for developments up to the middle of the 20th century. Both Mazmanian and Smallwood focus on presidential elections. Rapoport and Stone provide a late-20th-century assessment.

Bell, Daniel, ed. *The Radical Right.* Garden City, N.Y.: Doubleday, 1962.

Bennett, David H. *Demagogues in the Depression: American Radicals and the Union Party, 1932–1936.* New Brunswick, N.J.: Rutgers University Press, 1969.

Blue, Frederick J. *The Free Soilers: Third Party Politics, 1848–54*. Urbana: University of Illinois Press, 1973.

Donovan, Herbert D. A. *The Barnburners*. New York: New York University Press, 1925.

Gillespie, J. David. *Politics at the Periphery*. Columbia: University of South Carolina Press, 1993.

Goodwin, Lawrence. *Democratic Promise: The Populist Movement in America*. New York: Oxford University Press, 1976.

Hazlett, Joseph M., II. *The Libertarian Party*. Jefferson, N.C.: McFarland, 1992.

Hicks, John D. *The Populist Revolt: A History of the Farmers' Alliance and the People's Party*. Minneapolis: University of Minnesota Press, 1931.

Howe, Irving, and Lewis Coser. *The American Communist Party: A Critical History*. New York: Praeger, 1967.

MacKay, Kenneth C. *The Progressive Movement of 1924*. New York: Columbia University Press, 1947.

Mazmanian, Daniel A. *Third Parties in Presidential Elections*. Washington, D.C.: Brookings Institution, 1974.

Miles, Michael W. *The Odyssey of the American Right*. New York: Oxford University Press, 1980.

Nash, Howard P., Jr. *Third Parties in American Politics*. Washington, D.C.: Public Affairs Press, 1958.

Pinchot, Amos R. E. *History of the Progressive Party, 1912–1916*. Edited by Helene Maxwell Hooker. New York: New York University Press, 1958.

Rapoport, Ronald B., and Walter J. Stone. *Three's a Crowd: The Dynamic of Third Parties, Ross Perot, and the Republican Resurgence*. Ann Arbor: University of Michigan Press, 2005.

Rosenstone, Steven, Roy L. Behr, and Edward H. Lazarus. *Third Parties in America: Citizen Response to Major Party Failure*. Princeton, N.J.: Princeton University Press, 1984.

Saloutous, Theodore. *Farmers Movements in the South, 1865–1937*. Berkeley and Los Angeles: University of California Press, 1960.

Shannon, David A. *The Socialist Party of America: A History*. 2d ed. Chicago: Quadrangle, 1967.

Smallwood, Frank. *The Other Candidates: Third Parties in Presidential Elections*. Hanover, N.H.: University Press of New England, 1983.

Starobin, Joseph. *American Communism in Crisis, 1943–1957*. Cambridge, Mass.: Harvard University Press, 1972.

Stedman, Murray S., and Susan W. Stedman. *Discontent at the Polls: A Study of Farmer and Labor Parties, 1827–1948*. New York: Columbia University Press, 1950.

Weinstein, James. *The Decline of American Socialism, 1912–1925*. New York: Monthly Review Press, 1967.

Wilcox, Clyde. *Onward Christian Soldiers: The Religious Right in American Politics*. Boulder, Colo.: Westview Press, 1996.

V. PARTY-IN-OFFICE

A. Presidential Parties

1. Presidential Selection

Recommendation: Cohen et al. offer a fine contemporary analysis of the nomination process. Shafer, in *Bifurcated Politics*, ably treats the emergence of the modern national convention; David, Goldman, and Bain provide the classic treatment of conventions through the mid-20th century. Wayne's textbook treatment of presidential elections is most useful.

Aldrich, John H. *Before the Convention*. Chicago: University of Chicago Press, 1980.

Barber, James David. *The Pulse of Politics: Electing Presidents in the Media Age*. New York: W. W. Norton, 1980.

Bartels, Larry. *Presidential Primaries and the Dynamics of Public Choice*. Princeton, N.J.: Princeton University Press, 1988.

Bibby, John F., and Herbert E. Alexander. *The Politics of National Convention Finances and Arrangements*. Studies in Money and Politics, Monograph 14. Princeton, N.J.: Citizens Research Foundation, n.d.

Ceaser, James. *Reforming the Reforms: A Critical Analysis of the Presidential Selection Process*. Cambridge, Mass.: Ballinger, 1982.

Chase, James S. *Emergence of the Presidential Nominating System, 1789–1832*. Urbana: University of Illinois Press, 1973.

———. "Jacksonian Democracy and the Rise of the Nominating Convention." *Mid-America* 21 (Winter 1966): 3350.

Cohen, Marty, David Karol, Hans Noel, and John Zaller. *The Party Decides: Presidential Nominations Before and After Reform*. Chicago: University of Chicago Press, 2008.

Crotty, William J. *Decision for the Democrats*. Baltimore, Md.: Johns Hopkins University Press, 1978.

Crotty, William J., and John S. Jackson III. *Presidential Primaries and Nominations*. Washington, D.C.: CQ Press, 1985.

David, Paul T., Ralph M. Goldman, and Richard C. Bain. *The Politics of National Party Conventions*. Washington, D.C.: Brookings Institution, 1960.

Davis, James W. *Presidential Primaries: The Road to the White House*. New York: Thomas Y. Crowell, 1967.

Geer, John G. *Nominating Presidents: An Evaluation of Voters and Primaries*. New York: Greenwood, 1989.

Heale, M. J. *The Presidential Quest: Candidates and Images in American Political Culture, 1787–1852*. New York: Longman, 1982.

Longley, Lawrence D., and Neil R. Pierce. *The Electoral College Primer*. New Haven, Conn.: Yale University Press, 1996.

Mayer, William G., ed. *In Pursuit of the White House: How We Choose Our Presidential Nominees*. Chatham, N.J.: Chatham House, 1996.

Miller, Warren E., and Teresa Levitin. *Leadership and Change: Presidential Elections from 1952 to 1976*. Cambridge, Mass.: Winthrop, 1986.

Norrander, Barbara. *Super Tuesday: Regional Politics and Presidential Primaries*. Lexington: University of Kentucky Press, 1993.

Ogden, Daniel M., Jr., and Arthur L. Peterson. *Electing the President*. Rev. ed. San Francisco: Chandler, 1968.

Page, Benjamin I. *Choices and Echoes in Presidential Elections: Rational Man and Electoral Democracy*. Chicago: University of Chicago Press, 1978.

Polsby, Nelson W. *Consequences of Party Reform*. New York: Oxford University Press, 1983.

Polsby, Nelson W., and Aaron Wildavsky. *Presidential Elections: Strategies and Structures of American Politics*. 10th ed. New York: Chatham House Publishers, 2000.

Pomper, Gerald M. "Classification of Presidential Elections." *Journal of Politics* 29 (August 1967): 535–66.

Ranney, Austin. *Curing the Mischiefs of Faction: Party Reform in America*. Berkeley and Los Angeles: University of California Press, 1975.

Reiter, Howard. *Selecting the President*. Philadelphia: University of Pennsylvania Press, 1985.

Sayre, Wallace S., and Judith H. Parris. *The Electoral College and the American Political System*. Washington, D.C.: Brookings Institution, 1970.

Schantz, Harvey L. *American Presidential Elections: Process, Policy, and Political Change*. Albany: State University of New York Press, 1996.

Schlesinger, Arthur M., and Fred L. Israel, eds. *History of American Presidential Elections*. 10 vols. New York: Chelsea House, 1986.

Shafer, Byron E. *Bifurcated Politics: Evolution and Reform in the National Party Convention*. Cambridge, Mass.: Harvard University Press, 1988.

———. *Quiet Revolution: The Struggle for the Democratic Party and the Shaping of Post-Reform Politics*. New York: Russell Sage Foundation, 1983.

Thompson, Charles. *The Rise and Fall of the Nominating Caucus.* New Haven, Conn.: Yale University Press, 1902.

Tillet, Paul. *Inside Politics: The National Conventions, 1960.* Dobbs Ferry, N.Y.: Oceana, 1962.

Wattenberg, Martin P. *The Rise of Candidate-Centered Politics: Presidential Elections in the 1980s.* Cambridge, Mass.: Harvard University Press, 1991.

Wayne, Stephen J. *The Road to the White House, 2008: The Politics of Presidential Elections.* 8th ed. New York: Wadsworth, 2008.

2. President as Party Leader

Recommendation: Davis offers the most comprehensive assessment. Milkis's *The President and the Parties* is a first-rate consideration of the transformation of that relationship in the New Deal era.

Bond, John R., and Richard Fleisher. *The President in the Legislative Arena.* Chicago: University of Chicago Press, 1990.

Born, Richard. "Reassessing the Decline of Presidential Coattails: U.S. House Elections from 1952–80." *Journal of Politics* 46 (February 1984): 60–79.

Calvert, Randall L., and John A. Ferejohn. "Coattail Voting in Recent Presidential Elections." *American Political Science Review* 77 (June 1983): 407–19.

Campbell, James E. "Explaining Presidential Losses in Midterm Congressional Elections." *Journal of Politics* 47 (November 1985): 1140–57.

———. "Predicting Seat Gains from Presidential Coattails." *American Journal of Political Science* 30 (February 1986): 164–83.

Campbell, James E., and Joe A. Sumners. "Presidential Coattails in Senate Elections." *American Political Science Review* 84 (June 1990): 512–24.

Cooper, Joseph, and Gary Bombadier. "Presidential Leadership and Party Success." *Journal of Politics* 30 (December 1968): 1012–27.

Cotter, Cornelius P. "Eisenhower as Party Leader." *Political Science Quarterly* 98 (Summer 1983): 255–83.

Davis, James W. *The President as Party Leader.* New York: Praeger, 1992.

Ferejohn, John A., and Randall L. Calvert. "Presidential Coattails in Historical Perspective." *American Journal of Political Science* 28 (February 1984): 127–46.

Goldman, Ralph M. "Titular Leadership of Presidential Parties." In *The Presidency*, edited by Aaron Wildavsky, 384–410. Boston: Little, Brown, 1969.

Harmel, Robert, ed. *Presidents and Their Parties: Leadership or Neglect?* New York: Praeger, 1983.

James, Scott. *Presidents, Parties, and the State: A Party System Perspective on Democratic Regulatory Choice: 1884-1936.* New York: Cambridge University Press, 2000.

Kessel, John H. *Presidential Parties.* Homewood, Ill.: Dorsey, 1984.

Milkis, Sidney M. *The President and the Parties: The Transformation of the American Party System since the New Deal.* New York: Oxford University Press, 1993.

Milkis, Sidney M., and Michael Nelson. *The American Presidency: Origins and Development, 1776–2007.* 5th ed. Washington, D.C.: CQ Press, 2007.

Miller, Warren E. "Presidential Coattails: A Study in Political Myth and Methodology." *Public Opinion Quarterly* 19 (Winter 1955–56): 353–68.

Moos, Malcolm. *Politics, Presidents, and Coattails.* Baltimore, Md.: Johns Hopkins University Press, 1952.

Odegard, Peter. "Presidential Leadership and Party Responsibility." *Annals of the American Academy of Political and Social Science* 307 (September 1956): 66–81.

Press, Charles. "Presidential Coattails and Party Cohesion." *Midwest Journal of Political Science* 7 (November 1963): 320–25.

———. "Voting Studies and Presidential Coattails." *American Political Science Review* 52 (December 1958): 1041–50.

Remini, Robert V. "The Emergence of Political Parties and Their Effect on the Presidency." In *Power and the Presidency,* edited by Philip C. Dolce and George H. Skau, 24–34. New York: Scribner's, 1976.

3. Party in the Executive

Recommendation: Mansfield's article is a good introduction to the topic.

Brown, Roger G. "Party and Bureaucracy: From Kennedy to Reagan." *Political Science Quarterly* 97 (Summer 1982): 279–94.

Cullinan, Gerald. *The Post Office Department.* New York: Praeger, 1968.

David, Paul T. "The Vice Presidency: Its Institutional Evolution and Contemporary Status." *Journal of Politics* 29 (November 1967): 721–48.

Fenno, Richard. *The President's Cabinet: An Analysis of the Period from Wilson to Eisenhower.* Cambridge, Mass.: Harvard University Press, 1959.

Fowler, Dorothy G. *The Cabinet Politician: The Postmaster General, 1829–1909.* New York: Columbia University Press, 1943.

Freedman, Anne. *Patronage: An American Tradition.* Chicago: Nelson-Hall, 1994.

Heclo, Hugh. *A Government of Strangers*. Washington, D.C.: Brookings Institution, 1977.

Hoogenboom, Ari. *Outlawing the Spoils: A History of the Civil Service Reform Movement, 1865–1893*. Urbana: University of Illinois Press, 1961.

Kelley, Stanley. "Patronage and Presidential Legislative Leadership." In *The Presidency*, edited by Aaron Wildavsky, 268–80. Boston: Little, Brown, 1969.

Mansfield, Harvey C. "Political Parties, Patronage, and the Federal Government Service." In *The Federal Government Service*, edited by Wallace S. Sayre, 114–62. Englewood Cliffs, N.J.: Prentice Hall, 1965.

B. Congressional Parties

Recommendation: Smith's *Party Influence in Congress* is an excellent place to start considering this topic.

Alexander, Thomas B. *Sectional Stress and Party Strength: A Study of Roll-Call Voting Patterns in the United States House of Representatives, 1836–1860*. Nashville, Tenn.: Vanderbilt University Press, 1967.

Brady, David W., and Philip Althoff. "Party Voting in the U.S. House of Representatives, 1890–1910." *Journal of Politics* 36 (August 1974): 753–75.

Brady, David W., Joseph Cooper, and Patricia A. Hurley. "The Decline of Party in the U.S. House of Representatives, 1887–1968." *Legislative Studies Quarterly* 4 (August 1979): 381–407.

Cheney, Richard B., and Lynne V. Cheney. *Kings of the Hill: Power and Personality in the House of Representatives*. New York: Continuum, 1983.

Clubb, Jerome M., and Santa A. Traugott. "Partisan Cleavage and Cohesion in the House of Representatives." *Journal of Interdisciplinary History* 7 (Winter 1977): 374–401.

Cooper, Joseph, and David W. Brady. "Institutional Context and Leadership Style: The House from Cannon to Rayburn." *American Political Science Review* 75 (June 1981): 411–25.

Cox, Gary W., and Matthew D. McCubbins. *Legislative Leviathan: Party Government in the House*. Berkeley and Los Angeles: University of California Press, 1993.

Follet, Mary P. *The Speaker of the House of Representatives*. New York: Longmans, Green, 1896.

Gimpel, James G. *Legislating the Revolution: The Contract with America in Its First 100 Days*. Boston: Allyn & Bacon, 1996.

Huitt, Ralph K. "Democratic Party Leadership in the Senate." *American Political Science Review* 55 (June 1961): 333–44.

Jones, Charles O. *The Minority Party in Congress.* Boston: Little, Brown, 1970.

———. *Party and Policy-Making: The House Republican Policy Committee.* New Brunswick, N.J.: Rutgers University Press, 1974.

McCubbins, Matthew D., and David Brady, eds. *Party, Process, and Political Change in Congress: New Perspectives on the History of Congress.* Palo Alto, Calif.: Stanford University Press, 2002.

Monroe, Nathan W., Jason M. Roberts, and David W. Rohde. *Why Not Parties? Party Effects in the United States Senate.* Chicago: University of Chicago Press, 2008.

Peabody, Robert L. *Leadership in Congress: Stability, Succession, and Change.* Boston: Little, Brown, 1969.

Peters, Ronald M. *The American Speakership: The Office in Historical Perspective.* Baltimore, Md.: Johns Hopkins University Press, 1990.

———, ed. *The Speaker: Leadership in the House of Representatives.* Washington, D.C.: Congressional Quarterly, 1994.

Polsby, Nelson W. "The Institutionalization of the United States House of Representatives." *American Political Science Review* 62 (March 1968): 144–68.

Polsby, Nelson W., Miriam A. Gallaher, and Barry Spencer Rundquist. "The Growth of the Seniority System in the U.S. House of Representatives." *American Political Science Review* 63 (September 1969): 787–807.

Ripley, Randall B. *Majority Party Leadership in Congress.* Boston: Little, Brown, 1969.

———. *Party Leaders in the House of Representatives.* Washington, D.C.: Brookings Institution, 1967.

Rohde, David W. *Parties and Leaders in the Postreform House.* Chicago: University of Chicago Press, 1991.

Schneider, Jerrold. *Ideological Coalitions in Congress.* Westport, Conn.: Greenwood Press, 1979.

Sinclair, Barbara. *Legislators, Leaders, and Lawmaking: The House of Representatives in the Postreform Era.* Baltimore, Md.: Johns Hopkins University Press, 1995.

Smith, Steven S. *Majority Party Leadership in the U.S. House.* Baltimore, Md.: Johns Hopkins University Press, 1983.

———. *Party Influence in Congress.* New York: Cambridge University Press, 2007.

Stevens, Arthur G., Arthur H. Miller, and Thomas E. Mann. "Mobilization of Liberal Strength in the House, 1955–1970: The Democratic Study Group." *American Political Science Review* 68 (June 1974): 667–81.

Truman, David B. *The Congressional Party: A Case Study.* New York: John Wiley & Sons, 1959.

VI. PARTY ORGANIZATION AND ACTIVISTS

Recommendation: Wilson's *Political Organizations* is quite useful. Cotter and Hennessy provide the classic consideration of the national party committees. Klinkner offers a more recent treatment of the out-party national committees.

Baer, Denise L., and David A. Bositis. *Elite Cadres and Party Coalitions: Representing the Public in Party Politics.* Westport, Conn.: Greenwood Press, 1988.

Bone, Hugh A. *Party Committees and National Politics.* Seattle: University of Washington Press, 1958.

Bruce, John M., John A. Clark, and John H. Kessel. "Advocacy Politics in Presidential Parties." *American Political Science Review* 85 (December 1991): 1089–1105.

Cotter, Cornelius P., and John F. Bibby. "Institutional Development and the Thesis of Party Decline." *Political Science Quarterly* 95 (Spring 1980): 1–27.

Cotter, Cornelius P., James L. Gibson, John F. Bibby, and Robert J. Huckshorn. *Party Organizations in American Politics.* New York: Praeger, 1984.

Cotter, Cornelius P., and Bernard C. Hennessy. *Politics without Power: The National Party Committees.* New York: Atherton Press, 1964.

Crotty, William J., ed. *Approaches to the Study of Party Organization.* Boston: Allyn & Bacon, 1968.

Goldman, Ralph M. *The National Party Chairman and Committees: Factionalism at the Top.* Armonk, N.Y.: M. E. Sharpe, 1990.

Green, John C., ed. *Politics, Professionalism, and Power: Modern Party Organization and the Legacy of Ray C. Bliss.* Lanham, Md.: University Press of America, 1994.

Jackson, John S., III, Barbara L. Brown, and David Bositis. "Herbert McClosky and Friends Revisited: 1980 Democratic and Republican Party Elites Compared to the Mass Public." *American Politics Quarterly* 10 (April 1982): 158–80.

Kirkpatrick, Jeane J. *The New Presidential Elite: Men and Women in National Politics.* New York: Russell Sage Foundation, 1976.

Klinkner, Philip A. *The Losing Parties: Out-Party National Committees, 1956–1993.* New Haven, Conn.: Yale University Press, 1994.

Margolis, Michael, and John Green, eds. *Machine Politics, Sound Bites, and Nostalgia.* Lanham, Md.: University Press of America, 1993.

McClosky, Herbert, Paul Hoffman, and Rosemary O'Hara. "Issue Conflict and Consensus among Party Leaders and Followers." *American Political Science Review* 54 (June 1960): 406–27.

Miller, Warren E. *Without Consent: Mass-Elite Linkages in Presidential Politics*. Lexington: University of Kentucky Press, 1988.

Miller, Warren E., and M. Kent Jennings. *Parties in Transition: A Longitudinal Study of Party Elites and Party Supporters*. New York: Russell Sage Foundation, 1986.

Nexon, David. "Asymmetry in the Political System: Occasional Activists in the Republican and Democratic Parties, 1956–1964." *American Political Science Review* 65 (September 1971): 716–30.

Rapoport, Ronald B., Alan I. Abramowitz, and John McGlennon, eds. *The Life of the Parties: Activists in Presidential Politics*. Lexington: University of Kentucky Press, 1986.

Redding, Jack. *Inside the Democratic Party*. Indianapolis, Ind.: Bobbs-Merrill, 1958.

Schlesinger, Joseph A. "On the Theory of Party Organization." *Journal of Politics* 46 (May 1984): 369–400.

———. "Political Party Organization." In *Handbook of Organizations*, edited by James G. March, 764–801. Chicago: Rand McNally, 1965.

Scott, James C. "Corruption, Machine Politics, and Machine Change." *American Political Science Review* 63 (December 1969): 1142–58.

Soule, John W., and James W. Clarke. "Amateurs and Professionals: A Study of Delegates to the 1968 Democratic National Convention." *American Political Science Review* 64 (September 1970): 888–98.

———. "Issue Conflict and Consensus: A Comparative Study of Democratic and Republican Delegates to the 1968 National Convention." *Journal of Politics* 33 (February 1971): 72–91.

Soule, John W., and Wilma E. McGrath. "A Comparative Study of Presidential Nomination Conventions: The Democrats, 1968 and 1972." *American Journal of Political Science* 19 (August 1975): 501–17.

Sullivan, Denis G., Jeffrey L. Pressman, Benjamin I. Page, and John J. Lyons. *The Politics of Representation: The Democratic Convention, 1972*. New York: St. Martin's Press, 1974.

Wekkin, Gary W. "National-State Party Relations: The Democrats' New Federal Structure." *Political Science Quarterly* 99 (Spring 1984): 45–72.

Wilson, James Q. *Political Organizations*. New York: Basic Books, 1973.

VII. ELECTORAL BEHAVIOR

Recommendation: *The American Voter*, by Campbell *et al.* is the essential starting point. Lewis-Beck et al. revisit and update this classic study for the current era.

Beck, Paul Allen, Lawrence Baum, Aage Clausen, and Charles E. Smith Jr. "Patterns and Sources of Split-Ticket Voting." *American Political Science Review* 86 (December 1992): 916–28.

Burdick, Eugene, and Arthur J. Brodbeck, eds. *American Voting Behavior.* Glencoe, Ill: Free Press, 1959.

Burnham, Walter Dean. "The Changing Shape of the American Political Universe." *American Political Science Review* 59 (March 1965): 7–28.

Campbell, Angus, Philip E. Converse, Warren E. Miller, and Donald E. Stokes. *The American Voter.* New York: John Wiley & Sons, 1960.

Campbell, Angus, Gerald Gurin, and Warren E. Miller. *The Voter Decides.* Evanston, Ill.: Row, Peterson, 1954.

Clubb, Jerome M., William H. Flanigan, and Nancy H. Zingale. *Analyzing Electoral History: A Guide to the Study of American Voting Behavior.* Beverly Hills, Calif.: Sage, 1980.

Converse, Philip E. *The Dynamics of Party Support: Cohort-Analyzing Party Identification.* Beverly Hills, Calif: Sage: 1976.

DeVries, Walter, and V. Lance Tarrance. *The Ticket Splitter: A New Force in American Politics.* Grand Rapids, Mich.: Eerdmans, 1972.

Fiorina, Morris P. *Retrospective Voting in American National Elections.* New Haven, Conn.: Yale University Press, 1981.

Keith, Bruce E., David G. Magleby, Candice J. Nelson, Elizabeth Orr, Mark C. Westlye, and Raymond E. Wolfinger. *The Myth of the Independent Voter.* Berkeley and Los Angeles: University of California Press, 1992.

Key, V. O., Jr., with Milton C. Cummings Jr. *The Responsible Electorate: Rationality and Presidential Voting, 1936–1960.* Cambridge, Mass.: Harvard University Press, 1966.

Kirkpatrick, Samuel A., ed. *American Electoral Behavior: Change and Stability.* Beverly Hills, Calif.: Sage, 1976.

Kleppner, Paul. *Who Voted? The Dynamics of Electoral Turnout, 1870–1980.* New York: Praeger, 1982.

Lewis-Beck, Michael, William G. Jacoby, Helmut Norpoth, and Herbert F. Weisberg. *The American Voter Revisited.* Ann Arbor: University of Michigan Press, 2008.

McCormick, Richard P. "Suffrage Classes and Voter Alignments: A Study in Voter Behavior." *Mississippi Valley Historical Review* 46 (December 1959): 397–410.

Miller, Warren E., and J. Merrill Shanks. *The New American Voter.* Cambridge, Mass.: Harvard University Press, 1996.

Nie, Norman H., Sidney Verba, and John R. Petrocik. *The Changing American Voter.* Enlarged ed. Cambridge, Mass.: Harvard University Press, 1979.

Niemi, Richard G., and Herbert Weisberg, eds. *Classics in Voting Behavior.* Washington, D.C.: CQ Press, 1993.

———. *Controversies in Voting Behavior.* 2d ed. Washington, D.C.: CQ Press, 1984.

Pomper, Gerald M. *Voters' Choice: Varieties of American Electoral Behavior.* New York: Harper & Row, 1975.

Rusk, Jerrold G. "The Effect of the Australian Ballot Reform on Split-Ticket Voting: 1876–1908." *American Political Science Review* 64 (December 1970): 1220–38.

Scammon, Richard J., and Ben J. Wattenberg. *The Real Majority: An Extraordinary Examination of the American Electorate.* New York: Coward-McCann, 1970.

Sibley, Joel H., Allen G. Bogue, and William H. Flanigan, eds. *The History of American Electoral Behavior.* Princeton, N.J.: Princeton University Press, 1978.

Sibley, Joel H., and Samuel T. McSeveney, eds. *Voters, Parties, and Elections: Quantitative Essays in the History of American Popular Voting.* Lexington, Mass.: Xerox, 1972.

Stonecash, Jeffrey. *Political Parties Matter: Realignment and the Return of Partisan Voting.* Boulder, Colo.: Lynne Rienner, 2006.

Strong, Donald S. *Issue Voting and Party Realignment.* Tuscaloosa: University of Alabama Press, 1977.

Trilling, Richard J. *Party Image and Electoral Behavior.* New York: John Wiley & Sons, 1976.

VIII. CAMPAIGNS AND ELECTIONS

A. General Considerations

Recommendation: Campbell et al., in *Elections in the Political Order*, lay the analytical foundation for inquiry. Kelley is useful from this perspective as well. Modern campaigns rely heavily on political consultants, a topic addressed well in the volume edited by Thurber and Nelson.

Agranoff, Robert, ed. *The New Style of Election Campaigns.* Boston: Holbrook, 1976.

Armstrong, Jerome, and Markos Moulitsas Zuniga. *Netroots, Grassroots, and the Rise of People-Powered Politics.* White River Jct., Vt.: Chelsea Green Publishing, 2006.

Bullock, Charles S., III, and Loch K. Johnson. *Runoff Elections in the United States.* Knoxville: University of Tennessee Press, 1991.

Campbell, Angus, Philip E. Converse, Warren E. Miller, and Donald M. Stokes. *Elections in the Political Order.* New York: John Wiley & Sons, 1966.

Ginsberg, Benjamin, and Martin Shefter. *Politics by Other Means: The Declining Importance of Elections in America*. New York: Basic Books, 1990.

Ginsberg, Benjamin, and Alan Stone. *Do Elections Matter?* Armonk, N.Y.: M. E. Sharpe, 1986.

Harris, Joseph P. *Election Administration in the United States*. Washington, D.C.: Brookings Institution, 1934.

Hawley, Willis D. *Nonpartisan Elections and the Case for Party Politics*. New York: John Wiley & Sons, 1973.

Herrnson, Paul S. *Congressional Elections: Campaigning at Home and in Washington*. Washington, D.C.: CQ Press, 1995.

———. *Party Campaigning in the 1980s*. Cambridge, Mass.: Harvard University Press, 1988.

Kelley, Stanley. *Interpreting Elections*. Princeton, N.J.: Princeton University Press, 1983.

McWilliams, Wilson Carey. *The Politics of Disappointment: American Elections, 1976–1994*. Chatham, N.J.: Chatham House, 1995.

Merriam, Charles E., and Louise Overacker. *Primary Elections*. Chicago: University of Chicago Press, 1928.

Pomper, Gerald M. "The Decline of the Party in American Elections." *Political Science Quarterly* 92 (Spring 1977): 21–41.

Pomper, Gerald M., with Susan S. Lederman. *Elections in America*. 2d ed. New York: Longman, 1980.

Rae, Douglas W. *The Political Consequences of Electoral Law*. New Haven, Conn.: Yale University Press, 1967.

Sabato, Larry. *The Rise of Political Consultants: New Ways of Winning Elections*. New York: Basic Books, 1981.

Shea, Daniel M. *Transforming Democracy: Legislative Campaign Committees and Political Parties*. Albany: State University of New York Press, 1995.

Taebel, Delbert A. "The Effect of Ballot Position on Electoral Success." *American Journal of Political Science* 19 (August 1975): 519–26.

Thurber, James A., and Candace Nelson, eds. *Campaign Warriors: The Role of Political Consultants in Elections*. Washington, D.C.: Brookings, 2000.

Tufte, Edward R. "Determinants of the Outcomes of Midterm Congressional Elections." *American Political Science Review* 69 (September 1975): 812–26.

B. Specific Elections

Recommendation: The White volumes established the standard in this realm. Abramson et al., Ceaser et al., Nelson, and Pomper all have provided valuable series of studies of sequential elections.

Abramson, Paul, John J. Aldrich, and David W. Rohde. *Change and Continuity in the 1980 Elections.* Washington, D.C.: CQ Press, 1982.

——. *Change and Continuity in the 1984 Elections.* Washington, D.C.: CQ Press, 1986.

——. *Change and Continuity in the 1988 Elections.* Washington, D.C.: CQ Press, 1990.

——. *Change and Continuity in the 1992 Elections.* Washington, D.C.: CQ Press, 1994.

——. *Change and Continuity in the 1996 and 1998 Elections.* Washington, D.C.: CQ Press, 1999.

——. *Change and Continuity in the 2000 and 2002 Elections.* Washington, D.C.: CQ Press, 2003.

——. *Change and Continuity in the 2004 and 2006 Elections.* Washington, D.C.: CQ Press, 2007.

Boylon, James R. *The New Deal Coalition and the Election of 1946.* New York: Garland Press, 1981.

Brown, Everett S. "The Presidential Election of 1824–25." *Political Science Quarterly* 40 (September 1925): 384–403.

Calhoun, Charles W. *Minority Victory: Gilded Age Politics and the Front Porch Campaign of 1888.* Lawrence: University Press of Kansas, 2008.

Ceaser, James W., and Andrew E. Busch. *The Perfect Tie: The True Story of the 2000 Presidential Election.* Lanham, Md.: Rowman & Littlefield, 2001.

——. *Red Over Blue: The 2004 Elections and American Politics.* Lanham, Md.: Rowman & Littlefield, 2005.

Ceaser, James W., Andrew E. Busch, and John J. Pitney Jr. *Epic Journey: The 2008 Elections and American Politics.* Lanham, Md.: Rowman & Littlefield, 2009.

Cummings, Milton C., Jr., ed. *The National Election of 1964.* Washington, D.C.: Brookings Institution, 1966.

Dionne, E. J., Jr., and William Kristol, eds. *Bush v. Gore: The Court Cases and the Commentary.* Washington, D.C.: Brookings, 2001.

Ferling, John E. *Adams vs. Jefferson: The Tumultuous Election of 1800.* New York: Oxford University Press, 2004.

Germond, Jack W., and Jules Witcover. *Blue Smoke and Mirrors: How Reagan Won and Why Carter Lost the Election of 1980.* New York: Viking, 1981.

——. *Mad as Hell: Revolt at the Ballot Box, 1992.* New York: Warner Books, 1993.

——. *Whose Broad Stripes and Bright Stars: The Trivial Pursuit of the Presidency, 1988.* New York: Warner Books, 1989.

Goldman, Peter, Thomas M. DeFrank, Mark Miller, Andrew Murr, and Tom Matthews. *Quest for the Presidency: 1992*. College Station: Texas A&M University Press, 1993.

Goldman, Peter, and Tom Matthews, with Lucille Beachy, Thomas M. DeFrank, Shawn Doherty, Vern E. Smith, Bill Turque, Anne Underwood, and Lauren Picker. *The Quest for the Presidency: The 1988 Campaign*. New York: Simon & Schuster, 1989.

Holt, Michael F. *By One Vote: The Disputed Election of 1876*. Lawrence: University Press of Kansas, 2008.

Jamieson, Kathleen Hall, ed.. *Electing the President, 2004: The Insiders' View*. Philadelphia: University of Pennsylvania Press, 2006.

Kessel, John H. *The Goldwater Coalition: Republican Strategies in 1964*. Indianapolis, Ind.: Bobbs-Merrill, 1968.

Lichtman, Allan J. *Prejudice and Old Politics: The Presidential Election of 1928*. Chapel Hill: University of North Carolina Press, 1979.

Mann, Thomas E., and Norman J. Ornstein. *The American Elections of 1982*. Washington, D.C.: American Enterprise Institute, 1983.

Nelson, Michael, ed. *The Elections of 1984*. Washington, D.C.: CQ Press, 1985.

——. *The Elections of 1988*. Washington, D.C.: CQ Press, 1989.

——. *The Elections of 1992*. Washington, D.C.: CQ Press, 1993.

——. *The Elections of 1996*. Washington, D.C.: CQ Press, 1997.

——. *The Elections of 2000*. Washington, D.C.: CQ Press, 2001

——. *The Elections of 2004*. Washington, D.C.: CQ Press, 2005.

——. *The Elections of 2008*. Washington, D.C.: CQ Press, 2009.

Pomper, Gerald M., ed. *The Election of 1976: Reports and Interpretations*. New York: David McKay, 1977.

——. *The Election of 1980: Reports and Interpretations*. Chatham, N.J.: Chatham House, 1981.

——. *The Election of 1984: Reports and Interpretations*. Chatham, N.J.: Chatham House, 1985.

——. *The Election of 1988: Reports and Interpretations*. Chatham, N.J.: Chatham House, 1989.

——. *The Election of 1992: Reports and Interpretations*. Chatham, N.J.: Chatham House, 1993.

——. *The Election of 1996: Reports and Interpretations*. Chatham, N.J.: Chatham House, 1997.

——. *The Election of 2000: Reports and Interpretations*. Chatham, N.J.: Chatham House, 2001.

Ranney, Austin, ed. *The American Elections of 1980*. Washington, D.C.: American Enterprise Institute, 1981.

———. *The American Elections of 1984.* Washington, D.C.: American Enterprise Institute/Duke University, 1985.

Ray, Joseph, ed. *The Coattailless Landslide: El Paso Papers on the 1972 Presidential Campaign.* El Paso: Texas Western Press, 1974.

Ripon Society and Clifford W. Brown Jr. *Jaws of Victory: The Game Plan Politics of 1972, the Crisis of the Republican Party, and the Future of the Constitution.* Boston: Little, Brown, 1973.

Ross, Irwin. *The Loneliest Campaign: The Truman Victory of 1948.* New York: New American Library, 1968.

Sandoz, Ellis, and Cecil V. Crabb Jr., eds. *The 1980 Elections and Their Meaning.* Washington, D.C.: CQ Press, 1981.

———. *Election 84: Landslide Without a Mandate?* New York: New American Library, 1985.

Silva, Ruth V. *Rum, Religion, and Votes: 1928 Reconsidered.* University Park: University of Pennsylvania Press, 1962.

Thompson, Charles A. H., and Frances M. Shattuck. *The 1956 Presidential Campaign.* Washington, D.C.: Brookings Institution, 1960.

Turner, Lynn W. "The Electoral Vote against Monroe in 1820: An American Legend." *Mississippi Valley Historical Review* 42 (September 1955): 250–73.

Weisberger, Bernard A. *America Afire: Jefferson, Adams and the Revolutionary Election of 1800.* New York: HarperCollins, 2000.

White, Theodore H. *The Making of the President, 1960.* New York: Atheneum, 1961.

———. *The Making of the President, 1964.* New York: Atheneum, 1965.

———. *The Making of the President, 1968.* New York: Atheneum, 1969.

———. *The Making of the President, 1972.* New York: Atheneum, 1973.

Witcover, Jules. *Marathon: The Pursuit of the Presidency, 1972–1976.* New York: Viking, 1977.

IX. CAMPAIGN FINANCE

Recommendation: Alexander and Heard are the standard-setters in this field.

Alexander, Herbert E. *Financing the 1960 Election.* Princeton, N.J.: Citizens' Research Foundation, 1962.

———. *Financing the 1964 Election.* Princeton, N.J.: Citizens' Research Foundation, 1966.

———. *Financing the 1968 Election.* Lexington, Mass.: Heath, 1971.

———. *Financing the 1972 Election.* Lexington, Mass.: Heath, 1976.

———. *Financing the 1976 Election*. Washington, D.C.: Congressional Quarterly, 1979.

———. *Financing the 1980 Election*. Lexington, Mass.: Heath, 1983.

———. *Money in Politics*. Washington, D.C.: Public Affairs Press, 1972.

Alexander, Herbert E., with Monica Bauer. *Financing the 1988 Election*. Boulder, Colo.: Westview Press, 1991.

Alexander, Herbert E., with Anthony Corrado. *Financing the 1992 Election*. Armonk, N.Y.: M. E. Sharpe, 1995.

Alexander, Herbert E., with Brian A. Haggerty. *Financing the 1984 Election*. Lexington, Mass.: Heath, 1987.

Brown, Clifford W., Lynda W. Powell, and Clyde Wilcox. *Serious Money: Fundraising and Contributing in Presidential Nomination Campaigns*. New York: Cambridge University Press, 1995.

Corrado, Anthony, Trevor Potter, and Thomas Mann, eds. *Inside the Campaign Finance Battle: Court Testimony on the New Reforms*. Washington, D.C.: Brookings, 2003.

Heard, Alexander. *The Costs of Democracy*. Chapel Hill: University of North Carolina Press, 1960.

Malbin, Michael J., ed. *Money and Politics in the United States: Financing Elections in the 1980s*. Chatham, N.J.: Chatham House, 1984.

Overacker, Louise. *Money in Elections*. New York: Macmillan, 1932.

———. *Presidential Campaign Funds*. Boston: Boston University Press, 1944.

Sorauf, Frank J. *Inside Campaign Finance: Myths and Realities*. New Haven, Conn.: Yale University Press, 1992.

———. *Money in American Elections*. Glenview, Ill.: Scott, Foresman, 1988.

Thayer, George. *Who Shakes the Money Tree?* New York: Simon & Schuster, 1973.

X. RESPONSIBLE PARTY GOVERNMENT

Recommendation: The APSA committee report is the essential mid-20th-century advocacy statement. Green and Herrnson bring the debate into the 21st century in their edited volume.

Committee on Political Parties of the American Political Science Association. "Toward a More Responsible Two-Party System." *American Political Science Review* 44 (September 1950): Supplement.

Green, John, and Paul Herrnson, eds. *Responsible Partisanship? The Evolution of American Political Parties Since 1950*. Lawrence: University Press of Kansas, 2002.

Kirkpatrick, Evron. "Toward a More Responsible Two-Party System: Political Science, Policy Science, or Pseudo Science." *American Political Science Review* 65 (September 1971): 965–90.

Ranney, Austin. *The Doctrine of Responsible Party Government: Its Origins and Present State.* Urbana: University of Illinois Press, 1954.

Schattschneider, Elmer E. *Party Government.* New York: Holt, Rinehart & Winston, 1942.

Sullivan, Denis G. "Party Unity: Appearance and Reality." *Political Science Quarterly* 92 (Winter 1977–1978): 635–45.

Turner, Julius. "Responsible Parties: A Dissent from the Floor." *American Political Science Review* 45 (March 1951): 143–52.

White, John Kenneth, and Jerome M. Mileur, eds. *Challenges to Party Government.* Carbondale: Southern Illinois University Press, 1992.

XI. DIVIDED PARTY GOVERNMENT

Recommendation: Sundquist addresses the issue from both historical and analytical perspectives. Mayhew's work set the agenda for subsequent empirical debate.

Burden, Barry C., and David C. Kimball. *Why Americans Split Their Tickets: Campaigns, Competition, and Divided Government.* Ann Arbor: University of Michigan Press, 2002.

Conley, Richard. *The Presidency, Congress, and Divided Government: A Postwar Assessment.* College Station: Texas A&M University Press, 2003.

Cox, Gary W., and Samuel Kernell, eds. *The Politics of Divided Government.* Boulder, Colo.: Westview Press, 1990.

Fiorina, Morris P. *Divided Government.* New York: Macmillan, 1992.

Jacobson, Gary. *The Electoral Origins of Divided Government: Competition in U.S. House Elections, 1946–1988.* Boulder, Colo.: Westview Press, 1988.

Jones, Charles O. *The Presidency in a Separated System.* Washington, D.C.: Brookings Institution, 1994.

Mayhew, David R. *Divided We Govern: Party Control, Lawmaking, and Investigations, 1946–1990.* New Haven, Conn.: Yale University Press, 1991.

Sundquist, James L. "Needed: A Political Theory for the New Era of Coalition Government in the United States." *Political Science Quarterly* 103 (Winter 1988–1989): 613–35.

XII. SUBNATIONAL PARTY POLITICS

Recommendation: The South has been the regional focus of the most noteworthy scholarship. Key made the classic statement. The Blacks' trilogy is essential reading. Shafer and Johnston offer the most compelling contemporary consideration.

Bass, Jack, and Walter DeVries. *The Transformation of Southern Politics: Social Change and Political Consequences since 1945.* New York: Basic Books, 1976.

Bibby, John F. *Republicans and the Metropolis: The Role of National Party Leadership.* Chicago: Center for Research in Urban Government, Loyola University, 1967.

Black, Earl, and Merle Black. *Politics and Society in the South.* Cambridge, Mass.: Harvard University Press, 1987.

———. *The Rise of Southern Republicans.* Cambridge, Mass.: Harvard University Press, 2002.

———. *The Vital South: How Presidents Are Elected.* Cambridge, Mass.: Harvard University Press, 1992.

Brown, M. Craig, and Charles N. Halaby. "Machine Politics in America." *Journal of Interdisciplinary History* 17 (Winter 1987): 587–612.

Bullock, Charles S., and Mark J. Rozell, eds. *The New Politics of the Old South.* Lanham, Md.: Rowman & Littlefield, 1998.

Callow, Alexander, Jr. *The Tweed Ring.* New York: Oxford University Press, 1965.

Clark, John A., and Charles L. Prysby, eds. *Southern Political Party Activists: Patterns of Conflict and Change: 1991–2001.* Lexington: University Press of Kentucky, 2004.

Crotty, William J., ed. *Political Parties in Local Areas.* Knoxville: University of Tennessee Press, 1986.

Degler, Carl. "American Political Parties and the Rise of the City." *Journal of American History* 51 (June 1964): 41–59.

Fenton, John H. *Midwest Politics.* New York: Holt, Rinehart & Winston, 1966.

Finegold, Kenneth. *Experts and Politicians: Reform Challenges to Machine Politics in New York, Cleveland, and Chicago.* Princeton, N.J.: Princeton University Press, 1995.

Galderisi, Peter F., Michael S. Lyons, Randy T. Simmons, and John G. Francis, eds. *The Politics of Realignment: Party Change in the Mountain West.* Boulder, Colo.: Westview Press, 1987.

Gimpel, James G., and Jason E. Schuknecht. *Patchwork Nation: Sectionalism and Political Change in American Politics.* Ann Arbor: University of Michigan Press, 2003.

Glaser, James. *The Hand of the Past in Contemporary Southern Politics.* New Haven, Conn.: Yale University Press, 2005.

Hadley, Charles D., and Lewis Bowman, eds. *Southern State Party Organizations and Activists.* Westport, Conn.: Praeger, 1995.

Havard, William C., ed. *The Changing Politics of the South.* Baton Rouge: Louisiana State University Press, 1972.

Heard, Alexander. *A Two-Party South?* Chapel Hill: University of North Carolina Press, 1952.

Huckshorn, Robert J. *Party Leadership in the States.* Amherst: University of Massachusetts Press, 1976.

Jewell, Malcolm E., and David M. Olson. *Political Parties and Elections in the American States.* Chicago: Dorsey, 1988.

Key, V. O., Jr. *Southern Politics in State and Nation.* New York: Alfred A. Knopf, 1949.

Lamis, Alexander. *The Two-Party South.* Exp. ed. New York: Oxford University Press, 1988.

——, ed. *Southern Politics in the 1990s.* Baton Rouge: Louisiana State University Press, 1999.

Lublin, David. *The Republican South: Democratization and Partisan Change.* Princeton, N.J.: Princeton University Press, 2004.

Mushkat, Jerome. *Tammany: The Evolution of a Political Machine, 1789–1865.* Syracuse, N.Y.: Syracuse University Press, 1971.

Riordan, William L. *Plunkitt of Tammany Hall.* New York: Dutton, 1963.

Seagull, Lewis M. *Southern Republicanism.* New York: John Wiley & Sons, 1975.

Shafer, Byron E., and Richard Johnston. *The End of Southern Exceptionalism: Race, Class, and the Partisan Change in the Postwar South.* Cambridge, Mass.: Harvard University Press, 2006.

Stanley, Harold V. "Southern Partisan Changes: Realignment, Dealignment, or Both?" *Journal of Politics* 50 (February 1988): 64–88.

Steed, Robert P., Lawrence W. Moreland, and Tod A. Baker, eds. *The 1984 Presidential Elections in the South: Patterns of Southern Party Politics.* New York: Praeger, 1986.

——. *Party Politics in the South.* New York: Praeger, 1980.

Wilson, James Q. *The Amateur Democrat: Club Politics in Three Cities.* Chicago: University of Chicago Press, 1962.

Wolfinger, Raymond. "Why Political Machines Have Not Withered Away and Other Revisionist Thoughts." *Journal of Politics* 34 (May 1972): 365–98.

Internet Resources

White House: http://www.whitehouse.gov/
House of Representatives: http://www.house.gov/
    House Republican Conference: http://www.gop.gov/
    House Democratic Leadership: www.Speaker.gov
                    www.democraticleader.house.gov
                    www.democraticwhip.house.gov
Senate: http://www.senate.gov/
    Senate Republican Policy Committee: http://www.senate.gov/~rpc/
    Senate Democratic Leadership: http://democrats.senate.gov/
Judiciary: http://www.uscourts.gov/
    Supreme Court: http://www.supremecourtus.gov/
    Federal District and Appeals Courts: http://www.uscourts.gov/courtlinks/
Democratic National Committee: http://www.democrats.org/
    Democratic Congressional Campaign Committee: http://www.dccc.org/
    Democratic Senatorial Campaign Committee: http://www.dscc.org/
    Democratic Leadership Council: http://www.ndol.org/
Republican National Committee: http://www.rnc.org/
    National Republican Congressional Committee: http://www.nrcc.org/
    National Republican Senatorial Committee: http://www.nrsc.org/
Campaign Finance: http://www.opensecrets.org/
Communist Party U.S.A.: http://www.cpusa.org/
Constitution Party: http://www.constitutionparty.com/
Democratic Socialists of America: http://www.dsausa.org/dsa.html
Green Party: http://www.gp.org/
Libertarian Party: http://www.lp.org/
Natural Law Party: http://www.natural-law.org/
Socialist Party U.S.A.: http://www.sp-usa.org/

About the Author

Harold F. Bass Jr. is professor of political science and dean of the Sutton School of Social Sciences at Ouachita Baptist University, where he has been teaching since 1976. He received his undergraduate degree in economics and political science from Baylor University in 1971 and his M.A. and Ph.D. in political science from Vanderbilt University in 1974 and 1978, respectively. Bass specializes in studies of the American presidency and political parties, with a focus on presidential party leadership. He has authored numerous journal articles, book chapters, and book reviews on these topics. Active in the political science profession at the state, regional, and national levels, he is a former president of both the Arkansas Political Science Association and the Southwestern Social Science Association.